The Day Gone By

RICHARD ADAMS

The Day Gone By

AN AUTOBIOGRAPHY

ALFRED A. KNOPF   NEW YORK   1991

THIS IS A BORZOI BOOK PUBLISHED BY ALFRED A. KNOPF, INC.

Library of Congress Cataloging-in-Publication Data
Adams, Richard, [date]
The day gone by : an autobiography / Richard Adams. — 1st American ed.
p. cm.
"Originally published in Great Britain by Century Hutchinson. London, in 1990"
—T.p. verso.
Includes index.
ISBN 0-679—40117-2
1. Adams, Richard, 1920- —Biography—Youth. 2. Novelists, English—20th century—Biography—Youth. 3. World War, 1939-1945—Personal narratives, British. 4. Newbury (England)—Social life and customs. I. Title.
PR6051.D345Z465 1991 823'.914—dc20[B] 90-53394 CIP

Manufactured in the United States of America
First American Edition

To my grand-daughters,
Lucy Johnson and Sarah Mahony
with love and best wishes
for the years to come.

Illustrations

Acknowledgements

I am grateful to Miss A. Page, of the Oxford City Surveyor's department, who kindly supplied me with the map of old St Ebbe's which appears on page 219.

I am much indebted to Geoffrey Powell, formerly of Airborne Forces and author of *The Devil's Birthday: The Bridges to Arnhem*, for checking the accuracy of the chapters about Operation 'Market Garden' and making valuable comments: and also for kindly giving consent for the reproduction of the map of the plan for Operation 'Market Garden' on page 338.

I am most grateful to Richard and Hailz-Emily Osborne, of Bradfield, who gave invaluable help over the Bradfield photographs, and to Jimmy Stow, who was equally helpful over Horris Hill.

I thank warmly my secretary, Mrs Elizabeth Aydon, who not only typed the book most accurately and conscientiously, but also picked up for me those slips and inconsistencies to which most, if not all, authors are prone.

All That's Past

Very old are the woods;
  And the buds that break
Out of the brier's boughs,
  When March winds wake,
So old with their beauty are—
  Oh, no man knows
Through what wild centuries
  Roves back the rose.

Very old are the brooks;
  And the rills that rise
Where snow sleeps cold beneath
  The azure skies
Sing such a history
  Of come and gone,
Their every drop is as wise
  As Solomon.

Very old are we men;
  Our dreams are tales
Told in dim Eden
  By Eve's nightingales;
We wake and whisper awhile,
  But, the day gone by,
Silence and sleep like fields
  Of amaranth lie.

Walter de la Mare

The Day Gone By

I

My paternal grandfather, Joseph Dixon Adams, was born in 1837 – the year of Queen Victoria's accession. There is a story in the family that one night in 1854 he was awakened by the stir in the village caused by a horseman bringing news of the great British victory of the Alma, in the Crimea. The village was Martock, in Somerset, lying between Taunton and Yeovil.

People were poor enough in those days: the labourers lived largely on beans, and there was a saying that if you could shake a Martock man you could hear the beans rattle: if you *could* shake him. A few Martock men, poor devils, were caught up in Monmouth's rebellion of 1685 and duly appeared before Judge Jeffreys in the Bloody Assize. Martock has a beautiful church, with a magnificent interior roof. On the south wall, going on towards the east end, is a brass plaque in memory of my grandfather, extolling *inter alia* his running of the local fire brigade. They must all have been part-time volunteers, for my grandfather was not a fire officer but a doctor – a Victorian country doctor who paid visits on horseback and made up his own prescriptions. I have two of his pharmaceutical white-earthenware, lidded jars, each about ten inches high, handsomely decorated in blue and gold. One is lettered 'Tamarinds' and the other 'Honey'. (Tamarind pods were used as a laxative and also for 'allaying fever'; honey was for coughs.) There would have been a third jar for leeches, but this I have never seen.

In his maturity Joseph was well-to-do, with social standing in the locality and a fine house and garden (it's still there) called 'The Lawn'. A lot must have been due to his wealthy marriage. At some time during the eighteen-sixties – and this is another family story – he rode alone to the county ball at Taunton, where he met and danced with Arabella, the daughter of Sir Cecil Beadon. Sir Cecil had recently retired as Lieutenant-Governor of Bengal. He was a grandson of Richard Beadon, Bishop of Bath and Wells (in reply to whom Hannah More wrote her famous letter defending Sunday schools. The latitudinarian bishop, who didn't like the notion of educating the poor, had told her to lay off, but she was up to him). Cecil, who was born in 1816, joined the Bengal civil service (through nepotism, of course) in 1836. He came to the notice of Lord Dalhousie and had an eminently successful career until about the last five years of his service, when – largely due to ill health – as lieutenant-governor he came bàdly unstuck over his handling of – or failure to handle – the terrible Orissa famine. A commission of inquiry reported unfavourably on him; the Governor-General, Sir John Lawrence, saw no reason to take a different view and Cecil, albeit with a knighthood of the Star of India, retired in 1866, with plenty of money but his brilliant reputation overshadowed. He was twice married. His first wife, Arabella's mother, was born Harriet Sneyd, daughter of a major in the Bengal cavalry.

Joseph Adams married Arabella Beadon, and George, their eldest son and my father, was born in 1870. He, too, became a doctor (he ultimately became an F.R.C.S.), and was a student at Bart's during the 'nineties. Then he returned to Martock and went into partnership with his own father. To distinguish between the two, the villagers used to refer to my grandfather as 'Dr Adams' and my father as 'Dr Jarge'. It must have been about 1962 when I last visited Martock, and in the church came upon a lady tidying and polishing. We chatted, and when I told her who my father had been she called her husband from the vestry, saying 'Ben, this is Doctor Jarge's son.' 'Well, I never!' said he. 'Doctor Jarge! I 'member 'im well – 'im and 'is motor-cars!' (Long before the First World War, during the reign of Edward VII, my father had been one of the first 'Toad of Toad Hall' motorists, with a De Dion Bouton. My mother used to tell me how one day, when he was driving along a country lane, he saw, to his gratification, two farm-hands in a field throw down their hoes and run to the hedge to watch him go by. As he passed, one said to the other 'Reckon that bloody fool won't live long.')

Joseph had three other children: Katharine (to whom my father was deeply attached), Ernest and Lilian. Ernest deserves a little notice here, both on account of his impulsive, extravagant, flamboyant character (which I believe to have been passed on to some extent to myself) and also because of his affinity with birds and animals, which amounted to a gift. As a medical student he was up to all manner of larks and used to play the banjo, with a black face, a straw hat, white trousers and scarlet blazer. He had a pet tawny owl which my father said used to blunder about, knocking ornaments off the mantelpiece and 'shitting all over everything'. He had a marvellous dog, Esau, which he had trained himself. When Ernest took the 'bus from his digs to Bart's in the mornings, Esau would keep pace along the pavement and rejoin him when he got off. People used to say that Esau could do everything but talk (though he would bark when told to).

Ernest, with his pranks, his animals and birds, his unpredictable capers and his extravagance, must, I think, have been something of a worry, if not an actual embarrassment, to my grandfather, who took his social position in the county very seriously. In later life he was a formidable man. Once, Katharine and Lilian were persuaded by their partners to stay out late after a dance. 'That's all right. We'll see you home: we'll explain to your father.' When they got home all was dark, locked, bolted and barred. They had to ring and knock. At length, through the hall window, a candle was seen approaching, bolt after bolt was drawn and the heavy door slowly opened. There stood my grandfather in his nightshirt. Such was the sight that the two young men turned tail and fled into the night. Katharine and Lilian had to do their own explaining.

When Ernest reached his early thirties he went out to East Africa as a doctor. I suspect that he may have been given a bit of impulsion in that direction, though both his temperament and his love of nature would have made him nothing loath. He duly arrived in Nairobi and, as Shakespeare's Beatrice puts it, set up his bills. Before long, however, reports began to reach home of wild expenditure. Ernest was giving elaborate parties. He had designed a gaudy uniform and clothed all his black servants in it. My grandfather became alarmed. Ernest was quite capable of landing the family with his debts. Besides, what were people going to say? My grandfather told my father that he would have to go out to Nairobi, read Ernest the Riot Act and straighten things out.

But before my father could sail, worse news came. Ernest was dead of black-water fever. I have always felt so sorry. I wish I had known him: I'm sure we would have got on well. I have often felt in myself his instability, his impetuosity, his irresponsible hilarity and his feeling for the country and for birds and animals.

When sorrows come, they come not single spies, but in battalions. Within a few months of the death of Ernest, his sister Katharine also died. A pet dog which she was fondling bit her in the face and blood-poisoning developed.

I don't think my father ever really recovered from these bereavements. He was by nature a sensitive, reticent man, 'not a good mixer', as he himself used to say, and though he had a dry sense of humour, I never knew him actually to laugh or to show the least turn for glee or jollity. Anyway, cancelling the booking for Mombasa, he continued in practice with my grandfather. He was now nearly forty and still unmarried.

It was one day in 1909 that he decided that an old lady, a patient of his, would be the better for a resident nurse, and asked for one from the hospital at Bath. The girl they sent – who was aged about twenty-five – was a Miss Lilian Rosa Button, the second daughter of a not very well-off violinist in Bath. She had been brought up a Methodist. Socially, of course (and it must be remembered that this was 1909), she was entirely beneath my grandfather's notice – the next thing to a housemaid and a good cut below a governess. But she was a pretty girl, vivacious and amusing, with plenty of common sense. My father, for the first time in his life, found himself in love. Her social inferiority was a great help, for it dissolved his natural shyness and diffidence. He could let her make the running and simply be what he was. They took to meeting secretly in the lanes, down the garden – anywhere they could.

When my father said he was going to marry Lilian Button there was a hell of a row. The Adamses and the Beadons didn't half create. One fragment only my mother passed on to me. They said to her 'We've got a Lilian already in the family, so we're going to call you Rosie.' If this doesn't strike you as humiliating, reader, try it on yourself.

There were worse humiliations, I am fairly sure. However, there must have been a degree of acceptance, for I have two amusing recollections of my mother's from about those times. Martock lies only a mile or so from Montacute, and the Adamses were, of course, on friendly terms with the Powys family, which included those three egregious authors, the brothers John Cowper, Llewelyn and T.F. Powys. There used to be visits to Montacute. My mother once told me how, while she was sitting on the terrace with one of the brothers – she didn't say which one – he suddenly asked her 'Doesn't the intense beauty of that cloud give you a pain?'

'Whatever did you say, Mummy?'

'I said "No".' (She uttered it in a tone of perplexity mingled with the faintest touch of exasperation.) That apparently concluded the conversation.

At some other time during my childhood my mother remarked, apropos of nothing in particular, 'That Mr Hardy wasn't a very nice old man.' I have often wondered since whether she might have met Florence (she could not have met Emma) and if so, what she thought of *her*.

Anyway, what happened was that my father married his Lilian (who abjured her Methodism and became C. of E.), told my grandfather that he had no wish to continue in practice with him and bought a practice at Newbury in Berkshire.

At first they lived in a distinctly modest, rather ugly house in a Pooteresque, unfashionable street. At Newbury Hospital my sister Katharine was born in 1911 and my brother John in 1913. In 1914 my father tried to enlist in the R.A.M.C., but they wouldn't have him: by then he was forty-four. My brother Robert was born in 1916 and in 1919 died in the terrible influenza epidemic which swept Europe in the wake of the war. Thereafter my parents, sister and brother never spoke of Robert, and as a little boy I never even knew of his existence.

I was born in May 1920. I have sometimes wondered whether, if poor Robert had lived, I would have been born at all, for my father – who was usually up-to-date – knew all about Marie Stopes and possessed a copy of her book *Married Love* (which he kept locked up). This wasn't the sort of question about which you could ever have asked my parents: but my conception must have been intended, I think.

In spite of his humble start my father had got on well in Newbury, both in the hospital and in the country round. One of his patients was the famous John Porter of Kingsclere, who had been racehorse trainer to Edward VII and trained Minoru and goodness knows how many more great winners. (My father once told me that at Christmas 1916, when virtually no luxuries whatever were to be obtained, John Porter sent him not a bottle, but a case of cherry brandy.) If my father was going to build up a good practice among wealthy people (which he did), he needed a better house in a more distinguished neighbourhood.

Apart from the death of Robert, a year or two before my birth, two things happened. My grandfather died, aged about eighty, and my father bought the beautiful house out at Wash Common (then outside Newbury) where I was born. My mother told me an odd story about this: apparently my father came home one day and said to her 'I don't know what you'll say, but I've gone and bought Miss Bruxner's house.' She told me this with pleasure and with no air of resentment whatever – it was, after all, a marvellous change for the better – yet it seems strange that apparently she herself didn't get a look at the house or even hear of his intention before he bought it.

It certainly was a splendid place to grow up in. The house, 'Oakdene', had been built about 1895, in a style that was then rather popular with upper middle-class people in the south of England. It was L-shaped, with the long arm facing due south and the short, east. It was of brick, with a tile-floored, pilastered verandah running the whole south length. The upper storey (there were only two) was half-timbered against cream-coloured plastering. The tiled roofs were pitched. Downstairs was a parquet-floored hall, also running the length of the house, and off this opened at one end the dining-room (where we mostly lived), at the other the drawing-room (which was not sacrosanct, like some, but was also used a good deal, especially since it contained my brother's piano); my father's consulting-room and study; and the pantry, which led to the kitchen, scullery, larder and mangle-room. There were no fewer than seven bedrooms, two of them for servants. One of these became my nursery.

There were three acres of land altogether and a gardener's cottage, which had its own small garden. The superb view to the south was across the open country of ploughland, meadows and copses typical of the Berkshire-Hampshire border, stretching away four or five miles to the distant line of the Hampshire Downs – the steep escarpment formed by Cottington's Hill, Cannon Heath

Down, Watership Down and Ladle Hill.

Only part of the garden was cultivated. The lawn was big enough for a tennis court, a clock golf green and a small croquet-ground. Beyond it lay the long herbaceous border, and beyond that, the meadow we called the Paddock. To the west, behind the hundred-yard-long hornbeam hedge, was the kitchen garden, with its pear, plum and apple trees.

But this was only half the substance of that garden. To the east lay a little copse, known as the Wild Wood; and beyond that the drying-ground with its clothes-lines and rough grass, among which lay the netted raspberry bed and a broken-down, disused pig-sty.

Just to the north of these lay Bull Banks. (Beatrix Potter: 'The Tale of Mr Tod'.) Bull Banks was an actual bank of considerable size, perhaps twenty-five yards long, five feet high and ten broad, planted with laurel, forsythia, cydonia, lilac and other shrubs and crowned along the top with three silver birches. In front of it, outside the dining-room windows, lay the rose garden and behind it the potting-shed, a vegetable patch and the sizeable stables (part of which had become the garage). Here was a place and a half! In Bull Banks you could go to ground and no one could tell where you might be. ('If you're called you're to *answer*, Richard!' 'Shan't!') It could represent anything – a fortress, the council-rooms of a kingdom, a series of caves or dwellings, a dangerous jungle. But reality was often more delightful than pretending. Thrushes, blackbirds and chaffinches nested in Bull Banks. A small child, lying still among the bushes, was better placed to watch them than an adult. In due course the fledglings, all brown feathers and glum beaks turned down at the corners, would come out to fly. I would catch caterpillars off the leaves, put them down in the open and see how close a blackbird was ready to come to take them. (They never came to the hand, though.) Once, I fabricated a nest and brought my sister to see it, claiming to have found it. It didn't deceive her and I'm glad she didn't pretend it did. I hated being condescended to, and in fact I can't remember that anyone in the family ever did condescend to me, though sometimes they grew evasive. ('When you're older . . . ')

Bull Banks extended almost to the kitchen windows on the east side of the house, ending in a great bush of bay, the kitchen fence, a bed of wallflowers and on the house wall a wistaria. On the other side – the sunset side – of the house stood the conservatory and beyond that, in another wide patch of rough ground, the hazelnut trees, the swing and the rhododendrons. There were two great clumps of rhododendrons, one red and one mauve. When I was small, these affected me more deeply than any other flowers in the garden – more even than the roses or the dwarf begonias. I can remember once, after a shower of rain, standing on tiptoe and thrusting my head and shoulders up through the dripping branches and foliage to come face-to-face with a great cluster of blooms, covered with drops, glowing fresh, their brilliantly coloured trumpet mouths all maculate within, the whole bigger than my own face. In early childhood, I believe, awareness works on two levels at once: there is a paradox. Wonderful things are often apprehended composedly (after all, they're tangibly there), while ordinary things can seem miraculous in a way in which they never do again. I remember feeling soaking wet – including my feet, which I hated – and at the same time recognizing a kind of abasement before the rhododendrons: that is, there was nothing I could do adequately to respond to something so beautiful. They were beautiful beyond comprehension, beyond assimilation. You would never be able to say 'Well, now I've seen them.' You felt you ought to look at them for ever. They were beyond anything one could have expected or imagined. Saying even this much is really cheating – bringing in hindsight and words to try to express a child's incoherent, inarticulate sense of being utterly bowled over.

Nothing else in the garden affected me like the rhododendrons – which also, of course, provided caves, hiding-places and the dwellings of my imaginary friends. (I had plenty of those, as well as real ones.) But the dwarf begonias ran them pretty close. There is still, sixty years later, no garden flower with richer colours. I used to be allowed to gather up the fallen ones and float them in shallow bowls of water, and this gave me enormous pleasure. They were mine – mine! If only they had lasted a bit longer. One day I had an idea. I picked one or two *unfallen* ones on the sly. No one noticed. I believe this was the start of a certain unscrupulous streak in small matters which has remained with me all my life. It never got as far as pinching shirts, like Dylan Thomas; but by and large I believe it's done me more harm than good. I'm sorry I got away with those unfallen begonias.

My earliest memories are, first, of making my way through the paddock, among the long grass of June, with the sorrel and moon-daisies taller than my own head. I was perhaps three. The moon-daisies, if you gripped four or five stalks, would actually support your weight as you leaned backwards. Secondly, I remember lying in bed in the morning – my mother already up and gone – listening to a bird singing in the dew-glittering silver birch on the edge of the lawn. The bird sang 'Bringing it! Bringing it! Bringing it! Marguerite! Marguerite! Knee-deep! Knee-deep! Wait! Wait! Wait! Wait!' It was, of course, a song-thrush, but I didn't know that then. I just felt it was beautiful – so vigorous and clear – and nothing to interrupt or stop it. But those are words, too. Cheating.

Another special flower – a wild flower, this time – was the orange hawkweed ('Grim the Collier' or 'Fox and Cubs'). It's not very common, but, like many wild flowers, where you do come across it, it's usually fairly profuse. It flowered here and there in the long grass by the rhododendrons, between the Spanish chestnut and the swing. It's a dandelion type of flower (*composita*). The clustered blooms, deep orange, are at the top of a stalk about as tall as a milk bottle, and are not large – perhaps each as broad as an adult's little finger nail. This was my own, secret flower. I knew that even my father didn't know it was there; or if he did, he'd never spoken of it. I loved its colour and vaguely knew it to be a shade uncommon, for you never seemed to find it anywhere else. In my imagination I attributed magical properties to it, though these I never put to the test. To this day I love to come upon one.

The insects continually fascinated me. There were huge slugs – yes, I know they're not insects – bigger than my thumb, some of them. They didn't disgust me, though naturally I preferred the snails. If you put them on a sheet of glass you could watch the pulsation along the base of their bodies, a regular alternation of colours as they slid along. I liked the earwigs, too, that fell out of the dahlias; and the woodlice which curled up defensively when you came upon them under bark or in old boxes in the potting-shed. But best of all were the centipedes and millipedes. For these you had to dig with a trowel – usually in the Wild Wood. The centipedes, bright chestnut, dashed away at speed, articulated and wriggling all ways. The millipedes – barely an inch long – shammed death, curling up like woodlice. But if you put them in a jam-jar and waited, after a while they would uncurl and start going round and round, with their wonderful, undulant motion on innumerable, fluent, flexible legs. The motion of these legs was weirdly smooth, as they followed one another down the length of the body. In the jam-jar the millipedes had a peculiar smell, not very pleasant. It occurs to me now that this may be a natural deterrent reaction against enemies.

The only insects we killed were – apart from greenfly – ants and wasps. The tile-floored verandah harboured colonies of black ants. When they flew, it was a sight to see. The air was filled with them. They could bite sharply, but as a rule they didn't hurt you if you didn't provoke them. Sometimes, however, they became so numerous that my mother would decide that they must be reduced. (I don't think total extermination would have been practicable – not in those days.) The job was done with relays of kettles of boiling water, which percolated through the long, thin cracks in the tiles. This never seemed to create any panic among the ants. Those who died, died at once, of course. Those who didn't simply carried on. I don't think these onslaughts really had much effect. They certainly had no long-term effect. Anyway, my father rather condoned the ants, because they kept down the greenfly on the climbing roses growing up the fluted wooden pillars of the verandah. Lovely roses they were: I can smell them now, and remember their names, too: Lady Hillingdon (yellow): Clos Vougeot (dark red); Madame Butterfly (pink); and the little, thornless yellow Banksia rose, which grew right up to the bedroom windows and flowered so profusely that you were allowed to pick a bloom or two if you wanted. At one end of the verandah was a white, scented jasmine and at the other end a ceanothus, whose blunt, smoky-blue cones of bloom I then thought rather dull. In those days I wanted all flowers to be fragrant (that was the only thing wrong with the rhododendrons and begonias) and hadn't much time for Canterbury Bells, gladioli (they were all pink in those days) or forget-me-nots. It was wallflowers for me, night-scented stock, lilac, viburnum, chrysanthemums, blue lupins on a hot afternoon: and above all, the scent of the Siberian crab-apple in bloom. It is the literal truth that I am half-afraid to smell one now, for it turns my heart over and makes me want to weep for Bull Banks. Bull Banks is gone, for ever. After the war, and long after we had sold the house, the house was pulled down.

The whole place was built over. The former garden – even the great oak trees were felled – is now the site of twenty-two small dwellings.

The other insects that got killed were wasps; and this was serious stuff. By August they had nearly always become a nasty nuisance. The lesser part of the campaign consisted of the cook – no, I must say 'Cook', for she was never called anything else and to this day I don't know her name – resorting to the traditional wasp-trap of jam and diluted beer in glass jars hung up outside the back door. Into these the wasps fell, struggled and drowned. I thought it cruel then and I think so now; the wasps swam a long time. Anyway, I believe the traps attracted more wasps than would otherwise have come to the kitchen. 'But what else you goin' to do, Mas' Richard?'

There was a lot. My father was a nailer at tracking down wasps' nests. In the evening he would wander round the garden, or stand quietly about until he had detected the general flight-line of passing, homeward-bound wasps. This he would patiently follow up. Or he would stroll in the lane beyond the paddock, observing the verges and banks, with occasional forays into the great harvest-field opposite. I have known him to find six nests in an evening.

The crunch came later, after sunset and at a time when I was always in bed. My father, accompanied by the gardener, Thorn, would set out again for his quarry. Being a doctor, he had access to poisons, and the poison he used was the deadly potassium cyanide. One sniff kills you in a second, or so I've always understood. The jar was kept locked up. I never even saw it: the idea alone frightened me. Arrived at the nest, Thorn would clear away round the entrance, and then my father would put in the cyanide with a teaspoon lashed to a longish stick. On these raids they quite often got stung, and for this the palliative was bicarbonate of soda. (Milton hadn't yet been invented. It's enormously effective: on the aforementioned trip to Martock in 1962, four-year-old Juliet was stung by a bee in the churchyard. Elizabeth, my wife, applied Milton at once and Juliet didn't even cry.) I recall being taken to see a poisoned nest the morning after. Each wasp, as it flew over the cyanide, dropped dead instantly.

We always had plenty of apples, and stored them through the winter in a special room in the stable, equipped with what I can only describe as big chests of drawers, made of plain, unvarnished wood, each drawer slatted and open to the air. Every few days you inspected them and took out any gone-rotten ones. Stewed apple and custard was pudding every day throughout the winter. It must have saved a lot of money. I never got tired of it: it was delicious with cream.

My father must have spent more than he could afford on the conservatory, which was quite big and opened off the drawing-room by glass double-doors. It was heated by a coke stove and hot-water pipes, and all winter was as warm as in summer. Always, there was a mélange of fragrances in the air. In those days, cyclamen had a characteristic, singular scent which went all up your nose. Its pungency made you jerk back your head. They've lost it now, for some reason. There were brilliant purple cinerarias, pink primulas and mop-headed chrysanthemums taller than I was, crisply viscid and smelling like pine and cedar-oil.

During the winter these splendid pot-plants used to be brought in relays into the drawing-room: all but the arum lilies. Nurses, throughout the profession, are superstitious, and none of their superstitions is stronger than the tabu on lilies in a ward or a house. However, I can't remember my mother observing any other superstitions. I'm sure my father wouldn't have liked it. He might even have uttered his characteristic dismissal, 'Pooh! Silly, I call that!' He was by no means an assertive man – rather the reverse – yet somehow what he said carried authority.

The water-butt in the conservatory was a fine plaything. It was not quite as high as my shoulders – or that's how I remember it – a convenient height for leaning over. You could, of course, sail toy boats on it, but once again reality was more absorbing. In summer it was full of little larvae, which hung suspended, head downward, their tails held by the surface tension. If you startled them by a bang on the tank they went jerking and wriggling away, but soon returned to their motionless suspension. They had tiny hairs on their bodies and a broad thoracic region, a slightly bulbous section (for they were segmented) behind the head. These, of course, were the larvae of the culicine mosquito. I didn't know that then, but I knew well enough that they were bound to turn into something or other, as tadpoles turned into frogs. I hated mosquitoes. They really go for children – I suppose the blood's sweeter than adults' – and I could never let the bites alone, but scratched and scratched them till they bled. However, the larvae in the tank I didn't regard as enemies.

The upper end of the tank lay immediately below a glass pane at one end of the drawing-room, and in sunny weather the water-reflections would spangle and glitter elastically, flashing back and forth across the white ceiling above the piano. My brother played well, and to watch the dancing, glinting ceiling while he played Chopin was another of those unselfconscious delights of childhood whose worth is not realized until years afterwards. I was lucky to have that as a start to the pleasure of music.

It was my father who taught me to recognize and love the birds. That half-wild, wooded and lawned garden was full of them. (Many birds love a lawn; even those, like nuthatches and swallows, who don't alight are attracted by the insects flying over it.) Thrushes, blackbirds, starlings, sparrows, chaffinches, greenfinches and robins came and went continually and tussled over the food my mother put out for them. ('The rats' dinner', my father sardonically called it, but in fact we didn't seem to suffer from rats – or very little.) Bones and half-coconuts were hung up in the verandah, just outside the dining-room window. Anyone spotting a blue tit or a great tit would call out 'Tit on bone!' and others would come to have a look at close quarters. Coal tits we didn't seem to get; I don't know why. (They prefer conifers?) In spring black-and-white house martins built their mud nests under the eaves, and I loved to watch them coming and going. You could see the fledglings looking out of the nests, and hear them squeaking with excitement. The swallows and swifts swooped, hunting, over the lawn. You could get a fair idea of coming weather from observing how high or low they were – which was how high or low the flies were, of course. To this day the screaming of swifts in a clear sky recalls Oakdene – the pointed, back-swept wings of the fleet birds black against the blue. I love swifts.

In wet weather particularly, pied wagtails would quarter the lawn, their long tails bobbing as they ran about in short sprints. I liked their vigour and energy and their dipping, flirting flight all mixed up with the running. Wash Common is high up, a hilly watershed between the Kennet and the Enborne, so during my infancy I never saw a grey wagtail, that riverside dweller. As for yellow wagtails, it wasn't until, in my thirties, I visited Connemara that I saw one at all. They're common enough there.

In spring and summer my father often used to sit on the lawn in a deck-chair, the newspaper a mere pretence folded across his knee. He was not only watching the birds: he was listening to those he couldn't necessarily see. His particular aversion was to the bullfinches which used to pick the buds off the prunus tree. This they commonly did round about March. '*Look* at the blighter!' he would say, pointing at it angrily. Yet he never did anything about it. There wasn't really much you could do, short of shooting it with a catapult, perhaps. But that wouldn't have been what Harry Wharton & Co. used to call 'the proper caper'.

As he sat in the deck-chair in May or June, my father would locate the song-posts of the various summer visitors to the garden, particularly the warblers. As I grew older he taught me to recognize their songs – blackcap, chiff-chaff and willow warbler (which he always called a willow-wren: I don't know why). Since then I have read in certain bird books that the songs of the blackcap and the garden warbler are virtually indistinguishable. I can't agree. They are fairly plainly distinguishable. Both, certainly, are similar and arresting, but the garden warbler's song is more contralto, sustained and unpausing, while the blackcap's is higher and broken up into particular phrases that one can learn to recognize. With the dying fall of the willow warbler I soon became familiar; and I noticed, too, that when a robin is singing he is almost always asserting himself against another robin a little distance off. He will sing a few phrases, then stop and listen, and if you listen too you can generally hear the other robin answering. Robins are aggressive and fight for territory. In autumn, as the summer visitors depart, they lay claim to the wider, less insect-filled territory they are going to need for the winter.

Spotted flycatchers used to build on projecting ledges of the verandah or the stable, and sit conspicuously on the netting round the tennis court, fluttering away and back in their hunting. The few conifers – there were only three or four – on the west side of the garden attracted both nuthatches and tree-creepers. The nuthatches would come for nuts to the bird-table, but I don't recall that tree-creepers ever came. Occasionally a green woodpecker would visit the garden, but never seemed to stay. As a child, I never saw the greater spotted.

One summer afternoon we were having tea on the verandah when suddenly there came the sound of a fairly heavy blow on a pane of the glass at the far end. Though loud enough to be startling, it was a kind of padded thump, as though the glass had been struck by the soft knob at the top of the stick of a gong. We went down to have a look. A lesser spotted woodpecker had flown full tilt against the glass, and now lay, plainly injured, in the flowerbed at its foot. My father picked it up. It was a male, with a red crown to its head, a buff-coloured breast and black-and-white speckled wings. It died a few moments later in his hand. I've never seen one since, though I have heard them drumming. (They drum shorter and faster than the greater spotted.)

.   .   .

Robert Louis Stevenson was right.

> And does it not seem hard to you
> When all the sky is clear and blue,
> And I should like so much to play,
> To have to go to bed by day?

On summer nights it *was* hard to lie down and go to sleep. Mosquitoes or no mosquitoes, the thing was to get out of bed, stand in the twilight and look out of the open window. Immediately below was the wistaria, which covered half the upper storey of the long south wall. Sometimes you could actually lean out, lift up a raceme in your hand and smell it: nothing smells more beautiful. From beyond drifted the smell of night-scented stock or, later in the summer, of the tobacco-plants (nicotianas). There were moths, and bats would be hunting them silently, flitter and gone. Half-way down the paddock, on the left, eastern side, stood a big oak tree, and behind this, in season, the full moon would rise, magnified and brumously honey-coloured in the horizon haze, then turning to clear silver as it climbed above the oak. As often as not, this would reveal a hedgehog grubbing about the lawn or having a go at the left-out remains of the rats' dinner. Beyond the prunus the dark cone of the cypress tree, from grass to pointed peak, rose still as moss. The tawny owls set out, calling to one another as they went – the first call of four notes, a pause and then the second call of six. I don't remember that we were ever visited by a barn owl.

In August the stubbled cornfield would be dotted, in regular symmetry, with the dark humps of the wheat-sheaves piled together in shocks. The oak trees might be rustling, the clouds might be moving, but the sheaves stood completely motionless. Ten years or so later, when I first came across A. E. Housman's lyric 'Tell Me Not Here, It Needs Not Saying', I was at once struck by the lines

> Or marshalled under moons of harvest,
> Stand still all night the sheaves.

I drew it to the attention of my father. 'Pooh!' he said. 'What d'you expect them to do – run about?' It didn't hurt my feelings. He loved poetry. I felt he had a point; but I felt Housman had one, too. I knew exactly what he meant.

'Here, you ought to be in bed, my boy! You'll be no good in the morning.' Or perhaps it would be my mother, a little more plaintive. 'Oh, Dicky, I thought you'd be *asleep*!' And soon I would be.

They were indulgent, of course, because of the child they'd lost. But I wasn't to know that. I was spoilt, really: all on account of poor Robert.

On fine summer mornings, about eight o'clock, there would be 'pyjama walking', a splendid institution invented by my father. Bare-footed in our pyjamas, we would walk about the lawn and grass paths of the garden looking at butterflies, flowers – whatever there was to be seen. Ever since, I've felt that at this time of day a garden is at its best. How the dew shines! Sometimes my father would bring secateurs and we would cut any particularly good roses we fancied. I learned how to cut a rose – just above the point on the stalk where there is an outward-pointing shoot-bud. Or again, he might bring a stubby little broken knife and we would cut stalks of asparagus, if any were ready. But more often we were content simply to walk about, admire the zinnias, the snapdragons or the asters and then hobble back across the gravel to the verandah, wipe our feet and go upstairs to clean them off in the bath. I loved pyjama walking, partly because my elder brother and sister never went in for it. It remained something between my father and myself.

Perhaps my greatest excitement came from climbing trees. Heaven knows there were plenty to climb: but I had my favourites. Pines I learnt to distrust and dislike. They were dirty – gummy – and the dry branches were brittle and unreliable. One day a pine branch from which I was hanging by both arms (no footholds) broke. I fell, suffering nothing worse than a nasty thump on the back. But I knew I'd had a lucky escape and after that avoided pines.

Limes were all right, but again tended to be powdery, sticky and dirty. Not much latitude, either. You just went up – and came down. Dull. The child tree-climber wants to get *about* in a tree; not just up it. We had no beeches, and it was only later that I discovered the joys of climbing this particular tree. But the horse chestnuts were good, and so was the Spanish chestnut. For some reason the Spanish chestnut had been pollarded, but quite high up – maybe twenty feet – so you could climb to the top and then sit on a kind of flat throne, surrounded by upward-slanting boughs – a bower, in fact. I loved the smell of the Spanish chestnut and delighted in its lanceolate, alternate leaves with their saw-edged 'teeth'. The round, green, softly-prickly husks of the fruit were pleasant to handle, too: but you couldn't eat the nuts, whatever people said. They never really filled out and ripened. They don't, much, in England.

What a child wants in a tree is breadth; and pliant boughs near the ground, so that he can readily get up into it. There was one tree – a blossoming tree on the western edge of the Wild Wood – which I now know to have been an amelanchier (probably *lamarckii*, for it was a fair size – not by any means a shrub). The modest spring blossom was near-white and the foliage tinged with red. It had horizontal boughs, springy but entirely reliable. I could be down that tree in seconds, hang-and-drop, hang-and-drop and onto the ground. I used to sit up in it and watch my elders playing tennis, for it almost overhung one end of the court. One summer, using dust-sheets, I made a tree-house in the topmost boughs; but soon dismantled it. It was frowsty: the dust-sheets grew damp and smelly, while on the one hand you couldn't look out properly and on the other, everyone could see it and know you were there. I called this tree The Thinking Tree. You could sit up there, rocking gently on a pliant branch, and think out your problems – such as they ever were.

Ah, but the oaks! For the child tree-climber the oak is the acme, the *ne plus ultra*. The real problem is to get up into it, for a decent oak has a round, branchless trunk going up eight or ten feet. I had to grow older before I could tackle the great oaks along the paddock-hedges. To start with, I had to be big enough to be able to carry a step-ladder down there. (I couldn't ask someone else to do that.) The only alternative was to try a flying leap at the far end of a lateral branch, but they weren't low enough for a small child.

Once up into the fork, what a prospect opened! The tree appeared vast, a world in itself. You could not only climb to the top; you could explore out along each of about five great, lateral branches, as far as they would bear you. That took a whole afternoon. One tree overhung the lane, and you could pelt passers-by with acorns. They took it good-humouredly enough. ''Ullo, young doctor; still up to tricks, then?' 'You wants come down out o' that; I'll give you what-for.'

If I were put up into any common tree today, blindfold, I think I could identify it by touch and smell.

My greatest friend at this time was the little girl across the road, Jean Leggatt, whose father was also a doctor. Jean was just two months younger than I, and as babies we had been pushed out in our prams together; she by her dear nursemaid Minnie, and I by my no less dear nursemaid Constance. Constance was a Cripps. Like the Starkadders at Cold Comfort, there have always been Crippses at Wash Common. There were probably some on the touchline at the first battle of Newbury in 1643, and there are some now. I loved Constance dearly, even though she did address me as 'Baby': I knew it was from affection. (It certainly wasn't American: this was before the days of talking pictures.) I loved Jean dearly, too, and had vague ideas that one day I would marry her. We have remained friends all our lives and she lives not far away now.

One June afternoon Jean and I were playing in the paddock, when she suggested that we should strip buttercup petals and the little red flowers of the sorrel, and mix them together. It became clear that Jean had done this before: she was purposeful; we soon had quite a nice little heap, which she regarded with satisfaction.

'What do you do with it?' I asked.

'You throw it at people,' answered Jean sedately.

We duly showered Minnie and Constance with this beautiful confetti. They thought it was fun – country girls didn't have 'hair-do's' in those days: though Constance did enquire whatever the mistress was going to say, for it was 'regular all over: no gettin' rid of it.' She still had some when she bathed me that evening. I can't speak for Minnie.

Every first of May, the village children used to black their faces, dress up in such gaudy finery as they could get hold of – the general effect was sort of gipsyfied – and come round with a maypole. This they set up in the front drive and danced round it, singing

'First of May,
Sooty-bob day;
Give me a penny I'll go away,
All round the 'ouse.'

As I suppose this must be a genuine folk rhyme, I may as well give the air. (It's not in Cecil Sharp.)

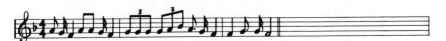

From my mother they used to get perhaps twopence or threepence. They couldn't, however, expect anything from my father. It was begging. His ideas had been formed well before the days of Cecil Sharp, and the preservation of charming old customs hadn't been thought of – or not in Martock, anyway.

The carol singers used to come, too. There was no organized carol-singing. Several groups of three or four village children would come during the season (not more than three or four; that would have made the 'split' too small). Their repertoire was small, too. 'Good King Wenceslas', 'Nowell', 'Once in Royal David's City' and 'O come all ye faithful' were about the size of it. In those days you never heard 'We Three Kings' or the partridge in a pear tree. Music in schools has come on a lot since then, of course. Once, I remember, in an Uncle Ernest-like spasm of excessive liberality, I had to be physically restrained from going to the front door and giving the carol singers half-a-crown which someone (Aunt Lilian, I think) had given me early for Christmas. They were quite right to restrain me. It was, in purchasing power, a very considerable sum. It might have been appropriate, perhaps, from the head of a household – though it would have been devilish generous – but from a little boy it would have been downright embarrassing and could only have led the village children to dislike me for a little beast who had all that money to waste.

I suppose it may have been something to do with my own delight in singing. I loved it. I was brought up to love it. My mother sang to me as a matter of course. She sang to me in the bath or in bed or while I was getting dressed. (Constance and she used to share these jobs, for Constance was also a housemaid, with appropriate duties.) If I happened to be ill in bed, she would sing while I was convalescent. Here's one of her songs.

> Johnny used to grind the coffee mill
> And mix up the sugar with the sand.
> When the shop was shut, at the corner pub,
> Drinks all round he'd stand.
>
> He grinds a different mill just now
> And he's breaking up a lot of stone:
> And all because the poor boy mixed up
> His master's money with his own.

Here's the air:

She told me that when she was a nurse the medical students used to come round outside the wards with banjos and boaters (just like Uncle Ernest) and that that was one of their favourite songs.

'Oh, and Sister used to get so cross! "*Will* you girls come away from that window and get on with your *work*?" and "Johnny used to *grind* the coffee mill" coming up from outside . . . '

I wasn't altogether clear what the song meant, but it was one I loved and used to ask for again and again.

My mother sang traditional songs, too. (Not folk songs. Real folk songs have never been popular songs, of course. I quote from the Introduction to the *Penguin Book of English Folk Songs*: 'An old Suffolk labourer with a fine folk song repertory and a delicate, rather gnat-like voice, once remarked: "I used to be reckoned a good singer before these here *tunes* came in." The *tunes* he spoke of with such scorn had come in with a vengeance, and it seemed that his kind of songs, once so much admired, would be swept away by the flood of commercial popular music.')

I remember, once, being convalescent in bed and my mother coming back from the town in high feather. We had been talking of getting a book of songs, chiefly for the words, for my mother couldn't read music: either she knew a tune or she didn't. 'Dicky, I've *got* a book, and it's got "Clementine" and "John Peel" and "Polly Wolly Doodle" and all those!' I think we started in right away. 'Polly Wolly Doodle', of course, was also a mystery to me. Later, I used to think it must be about a runaway slave. Now, I think it's about a Confederate deserter in the Civil War.

My mother used to tell me, too, about Violet Lorraine in *The Bing Boys*, and sing 'If you were the only girl in the world'. And of course there was 'All the nice girls love a sailor' and 'Tipperary' and many more.

I think that if you want a child to grow up to love music, singing to it is important. The thing was, my mother enjoyed the singing as much as I did, and *I was the only person she could do it with*. Otherwise she would have been self-conscious. I don't know why, but somehow my mother couldn't have sung with my brother on the piano. She had to be unaccompanied and uncriticized.

She read to me, too. Beatrix Potter, of course. And Pooh. This was the heyday of A.A. Milne – 1924 to 1928. Everyone read *When We Were Very Young* and Pooh: everyone quoted them. Everyone knew that Christopher Robin went down with Alice, and that he said his prayers. What do I think of it now? I think a lot of the light verse is pleasant for a child, but needs to be mixed up with better stuff. As for the stories, I think them too trivial, but they are redeemed by the marvellous characters. Characters are the essence of fiction. This is the limitation of folk tales, of course: marvellous stories and no characters. The prince is a prince and the dragon is a dragon like other dragons. 'Pooh' will survive on the characters all right, no danger. But Beatrix Potter will survive on story, style and characters. She reads much better than Pooh once you're grown-up and, as C.S. Lewis said, 'A book that's not worth reading when you're sixty is not worth reading when you're six.' I wouldn't say Pooh is not worth reading, but I do think there's a detectable condescension and self-conscious 'cuteness' about it.

My mother also read me poetry. Robert Louis Stevenson's *Child's Garden of Verses*, and 'Young Lochinvar' and 'John Gilpin' and 'The Pied Piper' and 'Up the Airy Mountain' and pretty well everything else that a child can take in. I used to shiver at 'La Belle Dame Sans Merci', and indeed I'd think twice, myself, before letting it loose on a small child. The great virtue of Stevenson, as I see it now, is that it's poetry for poetry's sake – not poetry telling stories. You can start a child on pure poetry with Stevenson.

As I got older, my father used to read to me, too. He wouldn't have read Beatrix Potter – and certainly not Pooh – but he would read R.M. Ballantyne – *The Coral Island*, *The Gorilla Hunters*, etc. – and *Treasure Island* and *Kidnapped*; and even the 'Dimsie' stories of Dorita Fairlie Bruce. Above all, we read *Dr Dolittle*. The Dr Dolittle books were coming out new at this time, 1922 to 1932. (Hugh Lofting evidently wrote at great speed.) The shortcomings of the Dolittle books are easy enough for an adult to pin down. The animals, in their mentalities, are really just human beings in a way in which the animals in the *Jungle Books* are not (or not quite). For example, the White Mouse knows what grand opera is, and Too-Too the owl can do arithmetic. But Lofting wrote with warmth and humour, and again, the characters are likeable and well-drawn. In the best of the books the narrative grip is powerful. Above all, the author obviously felt real compassion for animals. If I am up to the neck in the animal rights movement today, Dr Dolittle must answer for it.

Here are some lines from a poem I wrote at the age of sixteen, remembering those early days.

> I remember all my road, the tiny lanes
> Running between the honeysuckled hedges;
> The streams, and moorhens twining through the sedges;
> The snails upon the shining hornbeam leaves,

And glow-worms in the evening grass.
I remember how that Childhood used to pass;
The great red moon, the scent of August phlox,
Grasshoppers in the fields, the chiming clocks
Scarce audible from the far town below;
The yellow corn-sheaves and the sky above;
All simple things, Memories that all men know,
The earliest foundations of this love.

II

In those days, Wash Common was still a village a good mile or
more outside Newbury, up Wash Hill on the Andover Road. Its
population would have been a few hundred, I suppose, and there
was open country between it and Newbury. Newbury really began
(conveniently for my father) at the hospital, a mile down the hill
from our gate.

The first battle of Newbury, at which Lord Falkland, a leading
cavalier, was killed (some say suicidally), was fought on 22
September 1643 at Wash Common and on the lower land lying
between Wash Common and Newbury. In my day this was
something which every Wash Commoner knew and could talk
about with at least a smattering of local topographical knowledge.
('Ah, that's where they put the guns, see?')

The Royalist army, under the King and his nephew Prince
Rupert, had been besieging Gloucester. Gloucester was defended for
the Roundheads by the gallant young Colonel Massey, and
Parliament, determined to relieve him, had sent an army from
London, commanded by the Earl of Essex. The siege was raised
and Essex duly set out to march back to London. If he couldn't get
there his army would disintegrate for lack of supplies. Rupert was
eager to outstrip Essex and put the King's army between him and
London. To this end he urged the King to push on hard, by way
of Marlborough and Hungerford, to the town of Newbury on the
river Kennet.

Essex, also hoping to outstrip the enemy, was moving by a more
southerly route, and approached Newbury south of the Kennet, via
Kintbury and Enborne. Near Enborne you can still see 'Essex's
Cottage', where he slept (briefly) the night before the battle.

The Royalist army reached Newbury first, and since any

manoeuvre to the north was blocked by the Kennet, Essex had no alternative but to fight for his disputed course eastward. On the morning of the 22nd, the Royalist army came up Wash Hill and took position on Wash Common. Essex perforce attacked them.

Compared with other battles of the Civil War, relatively little is known about First Newbury; though everyone knows that Falkland (who was very much undecided about the rights and wrongs of the whole business) said to someone that morning that he would 'be out of it all by nightfall'; and later rode, as it seemed deliberately, into a gap covered by a Parliament gun. He died of wounds in a house still called Falkland Lodge. (Everything's 'Falkland' on Wash Common. The cricket team's always been called Falkland, for instance – though no pub bears the name.)

Some maintain that most of the fighting must have taken place north of Wash Common, down below the plateau and south of the Kennet, on ground east of the village of Enborne and west of what is now the Comprehensive School. I don't subscribe to this view for two reasons. First, the vital road which Essex needed, if he was going to by-pass Newbury on the south, was Monks' Lane (Monkey Lane, as everyone calls it), which ran directly eastwards, south of our paddock and the aforementioned oak trees, to Pinchington Lane and Greenham Common. To gain access to this lane he had to fight his way across Wash Common.

Secondly, there are the grave mounds. In the middle of the village (more-or-less), there has always been an open space, something over an acre, known as 'The Battle-Field'. This is still a public recreation ground. On it are two fair-sized tumuli, marked at the summit with rectangular stones saying '1643'. (The stones are later, of course: Victorian, I should think.) These are mass graves, where the locals buried the dead after the battle. Obviously they wouldn't carry them any further than they had to, and certainly not up onto the Wash Common plateau from down below.

Of the fighting little is known, but at the end of the day the Royalists fell back into Newbury and on the following morning did not resume the battle. Essex, so the books say, 'blew a trumpet blast', but got no response. So on he went, down Monkey Lane, across Greenham Common and so on to Aldermaston and the London road. Rupert was so indignant at the failure of the Royalists to renew the battle that he took his cavalry to Aldermaston and fought a harassing action; but this did not avail to stop the Parliamentary army, which reached London in tolerably good shape.

Charles I was always a bungler. Perhaps he failed to appreciate that if he had put all he had into defeating Essex at Newbury, he would probably have won the war.

About two hundred yards south-west from where we lived, and in the village, as it was, stands the Falkland Memorial – quite a large affair – on a little green. Here hounds sometimes used to meet, and I would come with Constance to pat them, to stare up wonderingly at the big men in 'pink' and to smell the exciting smell of horses. Here, too, the village adolescents would congregate of an evening – with or without bikes – to smoke Woodbines, crack jokes, shove around and waste their time. My mother called them 'the Idle-ees' and I was told to have nothing to do with them. Not that I'd have dared to. To me they seemed like men; big, rough and – I must say it – smelly. People *were* smelly in those days. There were no anti-perspirants and they had thick shirts and few, if any, changes of clothes. Smelly was just taken for granted.

The Royalist guns, it is believed, were sited near here, and one of the two pubs hard by is called 'The Gun'. (The other is 'The Bell', of which more anon.)

When I was a very little boy – about three or four – the Andover Road and Monkey Lane, which form an acute angle at the Bell corner and ran either side of our garden, were still white dust roads. In those days roads were still regarded as being primarily for horses, sheep and cattle. Cars were a minor matter. I think perhaps the Great War had retarded progress in this respect. In summer the dust was dry and powdery. You could see approaching flocks of sheep or herds of cattle a long way off, by the clouds of dust. Stirred up, it fell on the hawthorn hedges, making the leaves white until the next shower of rain. It had a pleasant, singular smell – to me the smell of high summer. Later, in adolescence, I was to be struck by King Lear's lines, in the cornfield scene with Gloucester.

> Why, this would make a man, a man of salt,
> To use his eyes for garden water pots,
> Ay, and laying autumn's dust.

A cottage garden beside a road needed a good deal of dust-laying to keep it green and fresh.

One of my earliest memories – as early as the rhododendrons – is of being taken by Constance, in my pushchair, down the little lane leading off the Andover Road into Sandleford Park. Sandleford Park is not a municipal park, but a tract of open country a mile square, with woods, meadows and a brook. (It was from here that Hazel and his rabbits were later to set off on their adventures.) The lane led past some rather rough cottages, in one of which lived Mrs Dolimore, the milk lady. She used to come to our back door with the milk in a great metal drum with a lid, and from this, with a metal dipper, she would dip as much milk as we wanted. The milk and the metal also had their own smells.

The lane ran on between elms and high hedges into the Park meadows themselves. I remember the smell of the dust, the smell of dried cow-dung and of nettles and woundworts in the ditches. In the Park were some old, gnarled hawthorn trees, all bent every which way. One was bent into a regular 'S', and formed a natural seat. This seemed wonderful, and I always used to go and sit on it. Even a light breeze would bring out a whispering from the boughs of these isolated trees.

> Still through the hawthorn blows the cold wind,
> Says suum mun, hey nonny nonny.
> Dolphin my boy, boy! – sessa! . . .

Close by the Falkland Memorial lay the Pond. There were actually two sizeable ponds on Wash Common (for watering passing horses, flocks and herds), but this was the better known and more used. It lay between The Gun and Mr Jessop's house. I remember the herds of cows – huge beasts to me – on their way to Newbury market, wading knee-deep (hence the thrush's song) in the brown water, lowing and splashing, and the dogs holding them there while the drovers went into The Gun for a well-earned pint. (4d.: that is, a bit less than 2p today.) Being shallow, the pond often froze hard in winter. I used to go sliding with the village boys (the ban on Idle-ees was somehow lifted) and had a lot of fun. I don't recall a single person ever skating on the pond, though.

The upper pond, at the west end of the village, was lonelier and different. It was overhung with trees on the further side, and it was bigger, greener and more rural. There were rushes and reeds, including the Great Reed Mace; coots and moorhens and, in summer, reed warblers. Here, too, I sometimes slid and also learned how to throw 'ducks and drakes'. This pond, in winter, I associate now in my mind with T.S. Eliot's lines in 'Little Gidding'.

> When the short day is brightest, with frost and fire,
> The brief sun flames the ice, on pond and ditches,
> In windless cold that is the heart's heat,
> Reflecting in a watery mirror
> A glare that is blindness in the early afternoon.

This pond was all of half a mile from our home. Constance and I didn't go there much, unless we were doing the Cope Hall walk, or else, perhaps, going to Nutworth's (that is not its true name), the village shop and post office. There were exciting things on sale at Nutworth's. One of these was windmills – so-called. A windmill consisted of four vanes of curved, brightly-coloured, mottled celluloid, pierced and held together by a central pin at the top of a stick. You held it up like a sceptre in your right hand and ran along, and the vanes, catching the wind through their curvature, would rotate in a medley of colours – red and blue making purple, blue and yellow making green – and a light clattering and justling of crisp celluloid.

Almost better, however, was the bluebird. He worked on the same principle: a model blue bird, about four inches long, held to a stick by some nine inches of string in the middle of his back. He had a long blue tail of three or four 'feathers' – strips secured by a central nail – and similar wings. You waved the stick round your head and he 'flew'.

These were cheap German toys, which in those days were imported and sold in numbers. All sorts of cheap clockwork toys, too, were stamped 'Made in Germany'. On account of the war, I suppose, and on account of their cheapness and fragility, the phrase 'Made in Germany' was used as a derisory taunt. 'Yah! Mide in Germany!' the village children would shout at some egregious victim: to which there was, really, no effective retort. Best ignored.

There were also, of course, sweets on sale at Nutworth's, but my brother had somehow put it into my head that they were not nice, and I generally went elsewhere. There was no ice-cream – not yet by eight or nine years, which were to see refrigeration introduced.

(My mother never possessed a 'fridge in her life, which ended in 1957.) Ginger beer and fizzy 'lemonade' in bottles, un-iced, were the best to be had in hot weather.

The real reason, as I now understand, for people feeling that there was something wrong with Nutworth's was the Nutworths. They were unsmiling, disobliging and down on life: with good reason; they had an only son who was hideously deformed. Mrs Nutworth was a little, sharp, black-eyed woman whom you always felt was waiting for a pretext to snap at you. Mr N. was a quiet, rather surly man who never bantered, or called you 'young doctor', like the other grown-up villagers.

But Cecil, the son, was the frightening one. Poor Cecil! He was a hunchback – a really bad one, with a great hump, a pigeon chest and his head, with no perceptible neck, sunk between them. He had a good enough face, but he wore his straight, black hair long, which made him appear even more sinister. Small children, of course, feel no pity for deformity – only curiosity if it's slight and fear if it's severe. The very possibility that Cecil might be going to serve you was enough to make you think twice before going into Nutworth's – certainly if you were alone.

However, you couldn't entirely avoid Cecil, because of Mavis. Mavis was a private 'bus – very rattly, and bottom gear up Wash Hill. (I suppose Mavis may have been Mrs Nutworth's name.) It was painted in yellow, in a flowing script, down each side of the 'bus, which was brown and held perhaps twenty-five people when (and if) full. It went down into Newbury and back twice in the morning and twice in the afternoon – 2d. for an adult and 1d. for a child. (Rather less than 1p and rather less than ½p.) Mr N. drove and Cecil was the conductor, with a ping-ping ticket-punch at his belt. There were no official stops. You just held up your hand anywhere along the road and Mavis would stop. Once aboard, it was tensile to be aware, not daring to look behind, of Cecil ping-pinging his way up the 'bus until he was standing over you. He never spoke. Later on, as I grew up, Boris Karloff got few shivers out of me: I'd been inoculated by Cecil.

I feel so sorry for them, now. I never used to see Mrs Nutworth at the Women's Institute gatherings, where I sometimes went with my mother (competitions, amateur dramatics, concerts, whist drives – not half bad fun, actually), and I never saw Mr N. in The

Bell either. (Perhaps he went to The Gun, though.) They were not liked. A damned shame, I reckon.

The other shop was Leader's. This was nearer home – only about half the distance to Nutworth's. Leader's really *was* Ginger and Pickles – or Sally Henny Penny's, perhaps. Mrs Leader, a warm, genial woman with a beautiful voice, certainly sold bootlaces and hairpins, if not mutton chops. Again, sweets and ginger beer were about my range. Mr Leader was moustached and loquacious – sententious, even. Later on, however, as a young adult in The Bell, I came to enjoy his company. They were childless, I rather think. Mrs Leader played golf, which was unusual for a village woman in those days. It rather raised her standing.

Another early memory, going back to when I was perhaps four or five, is of the tarmac being laid in the Andover Road and in Essex Street. Essex Street was the principal street in Wash Common, leading from the pond and the Falkland Memorial about half a mile west, past Nutworth's and the upper pond to Wash Common Farm. (Cotterell's, it was called then, and a Cotterell farms it now.)

The men on the laying – and all workmen in general – my mother used to call 'Jims'. ('There'll be some Jims coming tomorrow, Dicky, to do the front gate. You can help them if you like.' The 'helping', of course, consisted of standing about and chatting – picking their brains, really, for like all children I wanted to learn what it was like to be grown-up. You acquired ideas from things let fall rather than from direct instruction. E.g., 'You wants t'ang on to that there box, 'Arry. See 'im Friday, old Jack'll give you threepence for 'e.') A whole army of Jims, of course, turned up to tarmacadam the Andover Road, equipped with wonderful things – tar-boilers, tar-spreaders, broad rakes and a real steam-roller. Nearer and nearer to the house they came, day by day, up Wash Hill, until they were actually outside, great men with walrus moustaches, thick braces and string round the knees of their trousers, calling out things like 'Couple o' foot, then, Fred' and 'Take 'er steady, Joe.'

One of these Jims I remember clearly. He had come into our garage yard for some reason or other, and had been talking to Thorn, our gardener, about a screwdriver or some such. I was around and he began talking to me. He told me, seriously and earnestly, about soldiering on the western front during the Great War, addressing me as 'Boy'. I liked this. It seemed more grown-up than 'Master Richard' or 'Young doctor'. Jim Hawkins to the life! 'And when we come out o' them there trenches, boy,' he said, 'we was proper *lousy*. Yer, proper lousy we was!' I could sense all right how nasty this must have been.

Then he began explaining to me how a pistol worked. 'That's what they calls the mechanicism, see, boy,' he said, demonstrating with his left fore-finger crooked in the palm of his right hand. 'The mechanicism of the trigger.' I was impressed. No stranger grown-up had ever talked to me like this before – seriously setting out to communicate grown-up matters, without banter. Tobacco, sweat, an old waistcoat all ragged, rough hands ingrained with tar. He was majestic: I'd have done anything for him.

But as a matter of fact it was he who did anything for me. A few days later Constance and I were going up the village to Leader's, when by the pond we came upon a whole squad of Jims gathered round the steam-roller. They had laid the tar and raked it and now it was to be rolled. My friend was among them, and he began chatting up Constance. After a bit he said 'You wants get up in there, boy, 'ave a look. That's steam-powered, that is.' He lifted me up bodily and the man who was driving the roller took me from him. Inside the roller the fire was flaming before my very face, roaring in its iron boiler. The steam blew back at us out of the funnel in front. Then the driver, leaving me to myself, set to and spun the control-wheel by its projecting handle. There was a tremendous, accelerating crescendo of puffs and heavy rumblings as with a crunching and a shaking, we began to go *backwards*! Forward and back we went, forward and back, Constance watching half-afraid. ('Whatever'll the mistress –') I held on tight. When at last they lifted me down I was far too much over-awed to say Thank you. This was something like an experience! I suppose my feelings were more or less equivalent to those of an adult witnessing a volcanic eruption.

The Jims, day by day, moved on until they were far off. No more summer dust on the hawthorn – for ever. But at least they'd compensated me as handsomely as they could.

They built a bridge, too, did those Jims – or some Jims did. The nearest water to our home which you could call a river was the little Enborne brook – still, as then, the county boundary between Berkshire and Hampshire. As a child, I was familiar with two crossings. One, a little over a mile away to the south of and below the Wash Common plateau, was Wash Water, on the Andover Road (the A343, as it now is). This had had a road bridge since before I was born. The other, about a mile to the east, was Newtown Water, where the A34, the main Southampton to Birmingham road, crosses the Enborne. When I was a very small boy, in the early 'twenties, this was just a ford with a footbridge, and I remember being driven through it in the car. As part of the job of tarring and modernizing that road, the bridge which is there today was built. Whenever I join the volume of traffic which almost continuously crosses Newtown Water now, it really brings home to me how greatly times have changed in sixty years.

Our nearest friends on Wash Common – apart from Dr Leggatt, Jean's father, who lived directly opposite – were the Jessops. Mr Jessop was a stockbroker, and they had an only son, Hugh, who was about ten years older than I (grown-up, in fact, to me). Hugh was one of the first pupils at Stowe, the brand-new and rather revolutionary public school which was beginning to make its name under its famous headmaster, Roxburgh. (Hugh later had a distinguished and gallant naval career in the war and then became a silver dealer in London.)

There were two things that fascinated me about 'Uncle' Jessop's house. The first were the lions. As you went through the front door into the porch, you were confronted (head on, if you were only five) by a pair of jet-black lions carved in ebony. (They were oriental, as I now suppose.) They were each about as big as a big dog, and sitting on their haunches, snarling with open mouths and bared white teeth. Each carried in its front paws an ivory tusk. Although to an adult they would appear very much stylized, they were far and away the biggest and most realistic works of visual art that I had yet seen. I was terrified of them, and always had to be led past, with reassurance. Uncle Jessop, though always kind, was an imposing person with a big moustache and a growly voice, and it occurs to me now that subconsciously I may have rather lumped him and the lions together.

The other thing was the fountain. Although, as I have said, our own garden was big and delightful, it had no water. Uncle Jessop had a lily pond with a fountain. The fountain could be controlled by a foot-high, upright iron tap in the gravel, and to me this was a source of great pleasure and excitement. You could turn the jet into a circular fan of water, its thin streams, like rain, falling all around to transform the surface of the pool into winking, plopping coruscation. You could then bring it up higher, into the faint semblance, perhaps, of a standing figure, an ondine made all of ascending water. And then, finally – if they'd let you, for you weren't allowed long; it was too much indulgence of a little boy with mechanism that was not considered a toy – you could turn it into a single, immensely tall spout, which shot up into the air as high as the first-floor windows and fell back onto the surface with a most satisfying smack and splash. I always felt a little guilty about going all the way with the fountain, because you had to plead for it to get a grudging 'Well, all right, but only for a minute, mind.' I was not to know that fountains are among the oldest and favourite toys of mankind, and that kings and emperors have played with and delighted in them. (My brother, good pianist as he was, was not quite up to Ravel's *Jeux d'eau*. I was about nineteen when I first heard that; it evoked an immediate response of recognition.)

Another neighbour, with whom I was to become well acquainted as the years went by, was Captain Cornwallis. (That is not his true name.) He attracted me – as he attracted many – by his generosity, high spirits and enjoyment of life. Captain Cornwallis (I learned all this much later, of course) had originated God knows where, and before the First World War had been a strolling, needy adventurer – a sort of figure from the pages of 'Sapper' – with nothing much for ammunition except a pleasing geniality and a great ability for things like golf and bridge, which he played for money. Wounded in the war, he found himself in hospital, being tended by an ugly little V.A.D. nurse called Sally. From gossip he learned that Sally came from a wealthy family and had a lot of money. As soon as he was convalescent he set about courting her, and was successful. Sally Cornwallis was very small – tiny – with no physical attractions (to say the least) and so little intellect that even a child could perceive the lack. It was hard to tell whether she liked you or not, because her manner and brief speech, unsmiling and flat, were the same to everyone – except servants, to whom she was a tyrant and a bully. (When first married, the Cornwallises had spent some time in India.) Nevertheless, she and the Captain were happy enough on her money (though the Captain went in for brief absences now and then, which earned contemptuous inferences from my father – probably justified, I now think; though I personally can't say I blame him or see that they did any harm).

The Cornwallises arrived on Wash Common during my early childhood. The Captain bought a farm, its fields comprising the stony, unproductive upland of the plateau above the Enborne. It was about half a mile from our home. He employed two men, but the place was not a true farm; not a going, commercial concern. When not playing bridge or golf, though, he could shoot rabbits on the land. They had two sons; the elder, Duncan, was about my age and a cripple, his speech badly defective and his legs in irons. He could barely walk and used to get about the place on a tricycle. The younger, Arthur, was a year or two younger than myself, and as the years went by became my close associate, for I grew up fairly proficient at swimming and at hitting various kinds of ball, and the Captain thought it good for Arthur to have a slightly older friend who could extend him a little. During our 'teens our friendship became more limited, since Arthur grew up a straightforward, practical, outdoor fellow, while I became a swot who went the length of liking poetry and classical music. We remained friends, however, right up till after Hitler's war, when Arthur ('Can't farm here: it's nothing but damn' pioneering on gravel') emigrated to Canada, where he has done well.

The great attraction and benefit to me of the Captain was his easy-going generosity. What was his was yours, in effect. He built a swimming-pool and a squash court, and these our family were free to use whenever we liked. The summer holidays of the 'thirties, when I was in my 'teens, to a considerable degree revolved round the Cornwallises – sauntering up there in the hot mornings, along the verge of the big cornfield, to swim; tennis in the afternoon and perhaps a bridge lesson from the Captain in the evening. The Captain was most articulate and liked to talk gaily and freely, and this always seemed strange to me – almost unnatural – for my own father, of whom I was so fond, spoke little and smiled hardly at all. I have never forgotten that when my sister Katharine was about twenty-two, she and a friend called Dorothea Rowand decided to enter for an amateur tennis tournament at Hunstanton in north Norfolk and have a bit of fun at the seaside into the bargain. Captain Cornwallis, unasked, lent them his own Bugatti – a superb car – to drive up there and back and to use as their own for the holiday.

My father detested the Captain for a jumped-up cad and a bounder, though he never tried to stop us going up there and mostly kept his feelings to himself. Now and then, however, he would come out with brief and contemptuous references to patent lies that the Captain had told, or ill-bred boasts which he had made at the South Berks Club in Newbury, or with a scornful mention of his 'farm', which was no farm at all. I liked the Captain and I liked my father, and sometimes I would try to mediate. 'But, Daddy, even if he is a bounder, you must agree he's very generous.' 'Yes,' replied my father, 'with other people's money.'

Another time, when I was older – perhaps sixteen – and presumably to be relied upon not to repeat things, he and I were talking about the Captain when I asked some question or other about how he had come to be where he was.

'Why, he married that woman for her money, of course,' answered my father. 'You couldn't marry her for anything else, could you?'

I realize now that to my father, who had endured disapprobation and family hostility to marry my mother without a penny, for love, this would seem the ultimate in caddishness. And yet I myself am not so sure. Mrs C. lived as happily as she could well have hoped to. She liked and respected her husband, who was always genial and friendly to her. She had two sons and, under his dispensation, more fun than, with her looks and disposition, she could possibly have had otherwise. Whatever infidelities he went in for he kept well away from his own doorstep, and I never heard the least trace of a cross word between them. Yes, he was a sharp scamp (he could always spot in a moment how any card trick was done), but one of Falstaffian charm. I wonder, might my father's resentment have had in it an ingredient of jealousy? He himself had always been a shy, correct and upright man. 'Lo, these many years have I served thee, neither transgressed I at any time thy commandments. Yet thou never gavest me a kid . . . '

We never had quite enough money for our establishment.

Throughout the eighteen years of my childhood the servants gradually grew fewer and fewer, until at last there was none. My father suffered much financial anxiety, I know. But I think I perceive, now, another factor also. He himself, as he always used to say, was a poor mixer; except for my elder sister's and brother's tennis parties in the summer, we didn't entertain much, and we never went away for holidays. My father, celibate for forty years, had for all I know lived a rather restricted life, working at home with my grandfather. His reward was his sense of his own correctness. But then he had torn up the rule-book and married my mother. Mightn't an uncharitable person possibly have compared *her* to Captain Cornwallis? (Though she played her social part admirably and had adapted very well: I doubt whether anyone round Newbury thought her socially below my father.) The Captain, coming from nowhere, could handle people and had got what he was after by means of cheek and an outgoing temperament. My father's style, on the other hand, was based on reticence and propriety. How aware was he that this was because, when put to it, he had little real force of character? There is nothing in Christian doctrine which forbids marrying for money. It was, rather, the Captain's style which my father disliked. Yet my childhood would have been far less enjoyable without the Captain.

Another neighbour, whom my father did like, was 'Uncle' Urling. Uncle Urling was also a stockbroker. I remember him as a portly, ruddy-faced, genial man, who enjoyed spending money. He had two daughters, Mary and Sheila. Mary was my own age and a friend and playmate – my best friend, I think, next to Jean Leggatt and Ann Lester. (Ann was the daughter of the manager of the Newbury Waterworks.) I would dispute any idea that I preferred the company of girls to that of boys. It was just the way things fell out. Mary played the piano well and my mother wanted me to do the same; but somehow I never could take to it. (More of this anon.) The Urlings had a hard tennis court, the very latest thing, with a loose, green-granulated surface, not an asphalt red one. (The early hard courts were quite smooth and had a surface like maroon asphalt.) Mary was a kind-hearted, slightly nervous little girl, who never said a cross word and made me feel protective. ('Am I doing it right, Richard?') She had a wind-up gramophone, and by its means I became acquainted with 'Coal Black Mammy',

'It Ain't Gonna Rain No More, No More', 'All By Yourself in the Moonlight' and other hits of the 'twenties.

When I was about ten a tremendous thing happened. Uncle Urling was hammered on the Stock Exchange. I didn't in the least know what this meant, and I was carefully not told, but it was plain enough that the Urlings were in trouble. My father was sympathetic and did all he could to help. Uncle Urling arranged with him that we should, by private arrangement, 'borrow' his (Mary's) beautiful grand piano – a Steinway – to save it from being sequestered (or whatever it's called). So our good old upright – the pianola – was put away and the Steinway, which seemed to fill half the drawing-room, was installed. My brother, of course, was delighted, and used to play even more. I felt almost in awe of the instrument, which was mostly kept closed and covered with a thick, heavy, brown cloth embroidered in gold braid with elephants and lions. It stayed with us for about five years, I think, before Uncle Urling was in a position to take it back. When, ten years later, I read *Emma* for the first time, I was able to respond exactly as Jane Austen would have wished to the moment when Jane Fairfax receives the mysterious piano.

It was a bit of a limitation in one way, though. From my earliest days (well, say four or five) I had loved playing the pianola. When I first began to play it I was so small and light that someone had to hold my chair firm; otherwise my feet, pressing the pedals, slid me bodily backwards. The rolls were what you would expect: *Cavalleria Rusticana*, Chopin's *Valse Brillante*, *The Russian Church Parade*, *Pagliacci*, 'Where My Caravan Has Rested', 'Lilac Time' and many more. I realize now how lucky I was to have this sort of introduction to instrumental music.

I *responded* to music all right; almost over-sensitively, as a matter of fact. My brother, too, had a wind-up gramophone, and I recall that one day, when I was about six, he played me the *Unfinished Symphony*. The quality of the reproduction, of course, would today be beneath contempt, but it was more than enough for me. The opening theme, in the 'cellos and basses, at once seemed to me to convey menace and dread. It frightened me. Something terrible was going to happen. I think now that this was perfectly valid. It does. The second movement was no better. The pizzicato opening seemed grim and dire. I felt (although, of course, it hadn't yet been written) like Simon, in William Golding's *Lord of the Flies*, confronted by the pig's head on a stick. It assured him that life was a bad business. But Schubert seemed not to be trying to frighten me as a bully would. 'I *know* this is frightening,' he seemed to be saying. 'I can't help it. It frightens me, too.' I have gone on finding a lot of Schubert frightening from that day to this – the *Octet*, the *A minor Quartet*, the big piano sonatas: so frightening that I prefer not to try to think it out further. Let's drop it.

Surely a good teacher could have made a player out of a child as sensitive as this? I'll always maintain that it was as a result of hidebound, insensitive teaching and regime that I never could make a go of learning to play the piano. I think this is worth mentioning here, not in order to excuse me, but because it may possibly help other parents. My first teacher, at my kindergarten, was a decent but distinctly limited woman, who also turned an honest penny by driving her car for hire. Her teaching was boring and uninspired and as far as I remember she never played any music for my enjoyment or praised me for anything I did. I was with her for about two years or thereabouts. Then I went on to prep school (boarding school), and here I came under the tuition of a lady who was, even at that date (1929), an anachronism. Miss Jarvis (not her name) was the archetypal Victorian governess: a maiden lady in later middle age, grave and admonitory in manner, she taught French and arithmetic to the smaller boys and the piano to all those who were 'put down' for it. She seldom smiled and never made a joke. The two essentials for a teacher are warmth and humour, but Miss Jarvis possessed neither. Her best quality was her sense of duty. Upon her death (which occurred when I was about twelve and still at the school), the headmaster made a moving speech about the long and honourable service she had given, including, during the First World War, extra duty, for which she had refused to take a penny. She was certainly a worthy and, I suppose, rather a sad lady; she made you work, but one thing she could not communicate (I doubt now whether she really possessed it herself) was the joy or magic of music. I see her clearly in memory, her slightly aquiline features fixed severely upon a pupil as she reproved him for his own good, looking out from under the broad-brimmed, dark-blue straw hat which she always wore indoors. She wore it quite straight, of course, and it was fastened by a big hat-pin which was so low that you would have sworn that it must go through her head and not just through her white hair. I have a memory of her at the school concert. Three boys were to play a trio on one piano. They sat down to play, and Miss Jarvis stood behind them throughout, tapping their shoulders and whispering (you could see her lips moving) '*One* two three four, *One* two three four.'

During all the six years that I learned the piano, no one ever told me anything about the great composers, no one played any great piece of music and explained it or invited me to love it as they did, no one ever represented the piano to me as a wonderful, glorious accomplishment which would one day be mine; no one ever took me to a recital. At my prep school, practices and lessons with Miss Jarvis were all conducted in what was, for other boys, play time. The pianos were situated in the different classrooms, and it wasn't always easy for a junior boy to make his way into a relatively senior classroom, where there might be ten or twelve bigger boys none too pleased that he was come to play the piano badly. Nor was it any fun coming in on a fine summer half-holiday afternoon, when others were out of doors, to sit in a queue and wait, perhaps for nearly an hour, while Miss Jarvis took each in turn. No wonder that when I was eleven I persuaded my mother, with tears, to let me give up the piano. It was nothing but drudgery without reward even held out in prospect.

Years later, I saw to it that none of this took place with my elder daughter. Everything was done to encourage her, help her to love music, build up her morale and convince her that she was doing better all the time. She finished school a Grade 8 pianist.

Although I liked 'having a friend to tea' (usually Jean, Ann or Mary) and playing in the garden for the afternoon, big children's parties were another matter. There was no lack of fairly wealthy (and some really wealthy) families round Newbury. Several of these regularly gave children's parties, and naturally the family doctor's children were invited. As I was so much younger than my sister and brother, I used to get asked to different parties, for smaller children – alone. Of course, my father didn't like the invitations to be refused. If it was Ann's or Mary's party this wasn't so bad, but some of the big parties at wealthy houses, among a crowd of rich children who were mostly strangers, were unnerving – quite as bad as a parachute jump was to prove later. I was socially timid, used to solitary play, and nervously uneasy among the rather reserved and self-possessed boys and girls, well equipped to fulfil the roles expected of upper middle-class children in those days. For the most part I got on badly.

One of these parties was for me the occasion of a genuine Freudian trauma, the origin of a behaviour pattern of cracking under stress which has remained with me all my life: I know it well and can spot it whenever it turns up. This was a big party, given by the parents of a boy I hardly knew (he later kept wicket for Eton), and it was fancy-dress. I went as a Red Indian, though you could hardly have guessed it. The costume, such as it was, was old and shabby and had been lying in some cupboard since before I was born. It did fit, but what it amounted to was a crumpled jacket and trousers of thin, brown cloth, edged with strips of red and blue canvas. You couldn't wear it with any swank, which is surely the whole point of fancy dress. I could just about get by in it – and perhaps not even quite that. We hadn't the money for smart fancy dress.

I knew hardly anybody at the party. Most of the children were a little older than I. There were some splendid costumes. I remember a fairy, with wings and starry wand, to take your breath away. There was also another Red Indian, finely attired, with a tomahawk and a head-dress of coloured feathers half-way down his back. He didn't speak to me.

After a while we were assembled to watch the Punch and Judy show. I had never seen this before and had no idea what I was in for – a series of brutal and savage murders. I watched in mounting panic. Surely there must be some way out of this? Eventually Punch took the baby, Judy exited and Punch began banging the baby's head against the side of the box.

That did it. I was quite near the back. I got up and slipped out of the room. I didn't care where I went, as long as it was away from Mr Punch. No one seemed to have noticed me go, and in the hall there was no one about. I went upstairs, into a long, cool, empty corridor with closed doors on either side. It seemed to me that one would be as good as another. By this time I was in such a state of horror that I had the fancy that it was quite likely that Mr Punch would come and get *me*. *Credo quia impossibile est.* I could, of course, have been reasoned out of this, but there was no one to do it. Since then I have seen grown-up people give way to fears as absurd.

I opened a door at random. It was a bedroom, with the bed, head to the wall, aligned just to the left of the hinge side of the door. I got between the bed and the door, and then pulled the door wide, to an obtuse angle, till it touched the bed, thus forming a thin, hollow triangle – door, bed, wall. Here I felt myself in a place of refuge, a place of hiding and protection – a womb, of course, as we have all learned to think since then.

'Aha!' I kept murmuring silently to myself. 'Mr Punch can't get me here! Mr Punch can't get me here!' I had no idea of consequences: I mean, any idea that obviously this couldn't continue indefinitely. I just felt that where I was, I was safe from Mr Punch. That was enough.

After a while – I don't know how long – the search began. I heard footsteps, and voices calling 'Richard!' Some passed by the open door. Then a grown-up – I couldn't see who – actually came into the room, looked round and went out, saying to someone else 'No, he's not in there'.

I stayed put and never made a sound. I don't know why, since the calling voices were kind enough. I suppose my fear had somehow extended to include all the strangers in the house. Also, as I think we all recognize, panics and escapades possess a kind of in-built impetus. It is like being on a roller-coaster. You can't get off. Someone else has to stop it.

Eventually someone – a lady – came into the room again, swung back the door and found me. They were all far too much relieved to be cross, and also, of course, I was their guest. I can't remember the rest of the affair, though I remember trying to explain my fear. I think I just rejoined the party, which by now had got on to 'Nuts in May', 'Hunt the Slipper' and similar harmless activities.

But although I was not to realize it consciously for years, something fundamental and seminal had occurred. A behaviour pattern had formed. It might be described like this. First, I knew and accepted that it was possible for me to be genuinely and in all truth driven beyond the point of endurance by something that evidently didn't bother other people at all (or perhaps something that they *could* endure). Secondly, I could get out of this by taking solitary action, involving some sort of retreat into hiding; possibly an actual, physical refuge or else an infantile state (illness, breakdown, etc.). Thirdly, if only I could keep it up, heedless of its effect on my standing or reputation, it would get me out of the situation, whatever it might be.

This, however, didn't turn into a really bad neurosis. My home was much too supportive for that, my family too kind and understanding and the world too full of exciting, happy things. But it had come to stay; and under any relatively heavy strain, up it has been popping ever since; sometimes controlled and pushed back into its cage, sometimes not. Also, the notion of the enclosed refuge has remained as a permanent fantasy. 'I'm all right: I'm hiding in here.'

Not all the big, rich parties, however, were frightening. One I always looked forward to and enjoyed was Mr Behrend's annual firework party. Mr Behrend was a wealthy man who lived out at Burghclere, a village a few miles away, and he and his family were patients of my father. Mrs Behrend had been a Miss Sandham, and had lost her brother, Harry Sandham, in Mesopotamia in the First World War. It was at this time that the Sandham Memorial Chapel was built by the Behrends at Burghclere – where, under their patronage, Stanley Spencer was executing his big mural paintings and smaller canvases depicting scenes from the First World War in the Near East. We – my brother, sister and I – were sometimes taken to watch him at work on the murals.

I don't remember ever feeling nervous or in deep water at the Behrends' parties. If I recall rightly, Julie Behrend was a little older than I and Georgie about the same age. There always seemed to me to be a great crowd of children – far more than the modest parties for twelve or fourteen which were the form for Jean, Ann, me and our friends. Although, naturally, there were a lot of strangers, the children were not formal or stiff with each other, because of the common bond of excitement and expectation about the fireworks. There would be a few games before tea, the preliminaries being spun out by the adults long enough to ensure that it had grown properly dark. Then we would all crowd into the big bay windows – there were at least three, if not four – and get comfortably settled. We were looking out onto the terrace – a gravel path as broad as twelve feet, with a low stone wall about three or four feet high on its opposite side. Here stout poles had been driven into the ground, rockets set up and all other preparations completed.

The reason why we were kept behind glass and not invited out into the garden – as at many firework parties I have been to since – was that the fireworks themselves were so large, noisy and, in some cases, unpredictable. (I have played Mr Behrend's part myself since then, and if I find myself with a circle of six cardboard cylinders conjoined by light strips of wood and instructions to affix to a stout pole or fence, light the blue touch paper and stand clear, I want to feel sure that there aren't any five-year-olds loose in the vicinity.) Mr Behrend's fireworks were spectacular and he presented them really well, with one thing following another in ascending order (or orders) of effect. The vocal response of his audience was what might be expected. I remember one or two children becoming so much excited that they had to be calmed by being embraced by adults or sitting on their knees. I suppose the whole thing probably didn't take more than half an hour, but it wound the children up to fever-pitch with its sudden outbursts of coloured fire, gushing spouts of sparks interspersed with the 'Pouf!' of red or green or purple globules of light, and the hissing uprush of rockets which seemed to disappear into the sky for seconds before exploding into screaming tadpoles or pendent, incandescent parasols hanging motionless, going out only as they at last began to fall.

At the end Mr Behrend, a shadowy figure in the dark, would take off his hat and bow to us – a convenient signal, I suppose, to the grown-ups, who now had on their hands about fifty children wrought to the highest pitch of excitement. I can remember feeling exhausted, although I'd done nothing but watch.

.   .   .

What has been said so far of my father, that silent, reticent, undemonstrative man, who was fifty when I was born and whose life bore a heavy burden of bereavement (of which I knew nothing) may have left a reader wondering how on earth he and I came to be so close. The first characteristic of our relationship – and of this I was unconsciously aware before I could formulate thoughts at all – was that my father spoke to me and treated me to a large extent as though I were grown up and an equal. He didn't go in for stories of the past or for memories, but he would answer questions truthfully and impassively, even to the point where a lot of people nowadays, I suppose, might hesitate or take refuge in euphemism. For example, I remember once asking him by what means the Philistines 'put out' Samson's eyes. 'I expect they burnt them out with red-hot irons,' replied my father, in the straightforward and emotionless tone in which he answered all questions, whether from the servants, my mother or us children. I cried out in horror and began to weep; but my father let this run its course, until after a little a natural opportunity arose to change the subject. I knew that my father could always be relied upon to tell me the truth.

A second characteristic was that he genuinely enjoyed my company and would seek it out, with the suggestion that we might go for a walk (usually with a specific object – always a sensible idea with a child), play cards, or that he might read to me. Sometimes he would ask me to come with him to look at some particular shrub or group of flowers in the garden which had just come into bloom. In this way I learned by degrees the names of all the trees and flowers we grew, and would speak of them unselfconsciously. Eschscholzia, convallaria and coreopsis presented no difficulty to me, because it had never occurred to me that they might. I learned, too, the names of all the roses – not only the ones along the verandah posts – and, as I grew older, was sometimes able to steal a march on my father by coming and asking him whether he knew that the ipomoea on the kitchen garden pergola had put out its first bloom, or that the collinsia was coming out?

My father would not allow you, without mockery of some kind or another, to talk about a 'bird'. If you did, he would put on the falsetto voice of a silly woman, and say 'Oh, Dr Adams, do look at that *funny* bird!' You had to refer to the bird by name. So the Marguerite bird became a song-thrush, and soon I could identify the wren I couldn't see in the bushes by its characteristic, long, sustained trill.

Although he was so familiar with the inland birds of the south country, my father had never gone out of his way to seek out birds of other terrains. I have often wondered why. For example, on his own admission he knew little or nothing of sea-birds – one of the most rewarding of all branches of ornithology – though he knew a certain amount about birds of bog and moorland from younger days in Somerset, when he used to go shooting; and he had sometimes been to Scotland as a shooting and fishing guest. The snipe and the wheatear he certainly knew, but I wonder whether he would have recognized a greenshank: not, I am virtually certain, a red–throated diver. I suppose he simply observed the birds that came in his way. Well, it was no matter. Through him I learned to admire and respect birds and to want to know more about them. Years after his death I was to find the Isle of Man a maritime bird utopia, watching the fulmars gliding up to the cliff-face and turning away without a single beat of the wing, the guillemots racing out across the sea, and the kittiwakes, marble-white heads and shoulders, feeding their young on the ledges. I wish my father could have sailed with me through the Antarctic, to see the Wilson's petrels, the skuas, sheathbills, king penguins and the great albatrosses. Well, it all started in the garden at Oakdene. 'Look at that splendid chap!' he would say, as the spotted flycatcher darted from its nest to its hunting-post on the tennis netting. And in time I became able, now and then, to anticipate him, pointing out a blackcap or a bullfinch.

My father, although he did not play bridge (or cribbage), enjoyed a light-hearted game of cards and I believe now, in retrospect, that he considered cards a good way of sharpening children's wits. (He taught me draughts, halma and chess, too.) Cards began when I was still quite small, by playing two-handed, five-card German whist with my mother. From this I at least learned what a trick was, what a trump was and about following suit. Soon afterwards my father introduced me to bézique. Two-handed bézique is a dull enough game for adults, but I can still remember its excitement and fascination for me as a child. In the first place, it was all new. I was entering upon a novel form of experience and learning and practising a hitherto unexperienced kind of skill. The game seemed so romantic and colourful, with its strange oddities. Why should the tens be worth more than everything but the aces? Why should you get forty for the queen of spades and the jack of diamonds? What did 'bézique' mean, anyway? I can still recall the excitement of realizing that I held four kings or four aces, and the splendid moment when you won a trick, laid them down on the table and clocked up the score on your marker.

But there was a degree of strain in bézique, too. An adult naturally sees so simple a game as a mere way of passing the time, and also knows how much luck there is in it. A child takes it seriously, for to him it is something not yet rooted in experience. It involves decisions. Bézique was for me the first business in which I had to make decisions – decisions which would affect the outcome of the game. 'I'm holding two kings and three queens. They can't all stay. Shall I discard the queens, four of which score only sixty, and trust to getting four kings (eighty)? Or on the other hand, would it be better to play safe and go for the queens?' And you could be disastrously wrong, as I learned in good time. You could spend the whole hand saving for a sequence, only to find that your opponent had been craftily holding both the queens of trumps all the time. Then there was the agony of having acquired something really good – a sequence or even double bézique – when there were only two or three tricks left to play, none of which you could win. I used to get tense and very much involved with the game, occasionally to the point of tears. I think my father sometimes pulled his punches to avoid upsetting me. In his position, I would have done the same. To a seven-year-old, to hold double bézique and be prevented from declaring it is a mortifying experience. But you had to learn to lose with a good grace. (I was yet to see the Australians, in the test series of 1932–33, going virtually berserk over Larwood and Voce.)

Later on came picquet. Since becoming grown-up it has surprised me that, in a country where bridge is widely played and people take it almost for granted that they will be able to make up at least some sort of a table, very few people, by comparison, play picquet. It is by far the best card game for two – elegant and skilful – and during my life I must have had hours of enjoyment from it. I remember reading somewhere that Richelieu used to play picquet, and it amuses me to think of the game being devised at the sophisticated French court of the seventeenth century at more or less the same time as Sir John Suckling (so Aubrey says) was inventing cribbage. Sir Toby Belch (in old age) might have played the latter. Somehow I can't see him playing picquet (although Prince Rupert might very well have played it, I dare say).

Picquet was pretty fast bowling for an eight-year-old. I remember how I began it with no more experience behind me than that of bézique, with the idea that it consisted of virtually no more than collecting honours in the hand. Two things which took me a long time to learn were the importance of planning and playing to win the majority of (or at least to split) the tricks, and the necessity, for the younger hand, of 'guarding' or 'covering' kings or queens, to stop your opponent running through the suit. My father had given my sister a beautiful picquet set – a gilt-lettered red box with two packs and two pads of score sheets – and she was often ready to play. As she was more than nine years older, unless I got very good cards she could wipe the floor with me. My sister held the view that I was spoiled and over-indulged – which was true – and that it would be good for me to take a few sound hidings. I think it was. Most people who have taken up learning a skill, a game or an accomplishment, know the infuriating frustration of watching someone else perform something which you want to be able to do and cannot. For a long time I simply could not get the hang of prudent discarding and of keeping 'stops'. Tears and temper were not uncommon, for I took the business seriously and wanted to master it.

One day I had an idea – an idea not altogether unconnected, perhaps, with Mr Punch. Without consciously formulating the notion in so many words, I realized that picquet was a self-contained business, having no links with anything outside itself. (Unlike, say, dancing, which had all sorts of tedious tie-ups with things like hostesses, partners and conversation.) If I could really master picquet, it would become indestructibly mine, like an object in my pocket. I set myself to do it and since the game is not bottomless, like chess or bridge, in due course, and after a good deal of rather taxing application, I succeeded. That is to say, I could play anyone – any grown-up – without needing indulgence and without doing anything silly. I had it on board, right down to the pleasure to be derived from making something of a rotten hand. (Many years later I was to teach the game, on board ship at literally the other end of the world, to Mike McDowell, the young cruise director of the *Lindblad Explorer*. Mike became adept at making the best of a bad hand, and many a time would save his score with four tens or a quint to the jack.)

I have come to see that there are two perfectly valid ways of feeling about games in general. My wife doesn't really care for – or about – games. If she consents to play, it is to pass time and she doesn't particularly want to win: an admirable approach. 'Games,' she says, 'are a waste of time. They are parenthetical. They are nothing to do with life, with which it's far more fun to be getting on.' (What she gets on with are English ceramics. She is an F.S.A. and an acknowledged expert.) My own view is that any idea of succeeding at Life is futile (as I think George Orwell remarked). But you *can* hope to become proficient at and sometimes succeed at a game, and this gives a lot of satisfaction. My personal view is that no game should be played professionally, though I've no objection to it being *taught* professionally.

In the course of succeeding years I was to take on board one self-contained thing after another, from wild flowers to Brahms to Parliamentary Questions, but I still remained unable to deal with Mr Punch, in whatever guise he came.

But to return to my father. It was the places he took me to which had the strongest formative influence upon me and gave me, in childhood, the most delight. If we went out through the gate at the bottom of the paddock, across the lane (Monkey Lane) and into the big ploughed field, it was a matter of a few hundred yards to a copse of silver birch, oak, ash and hazel bushes. This was damp most of the year, with a rivulet running through it. We called it the Bluebell Wood: in April the bluebells flowered so thickly that the ground was blue as a field is green. To me the density of colour was not, however, their most poignant quality. The blue was composed of myriads of individual blooms, tall, narrow and moving slightly in the breeze. This gave the receding distance of blue a penetrable quality, so that you looked from the flowers at your feet into a near distance where they blended into a less broken, multifoliate blue: and from these into a further distance of a single, hazy blue – single as a cloud is single, a soft mass full of recesses, shadows and dim, dissolving rifts and cavities. To look into that receding infinity of bluebells was to become more lost to all else, more teased out of thought, than when looking up into a clear blue sky and trying to imagine what lay beyond. There couldn't possibly be so many bluebells; yet there they were. Examine a single one: it was perfect. Each one in that infinity was similarly perfect. To grasp this inspired awe as well as delight. Throughout the wood lay the faint but clear scent of the flowers, and somewhere on the edge, in a birch tree, a blackbird would let fall its pausing, unhurried phrases.

Is a small child really conscious of all this, or is memory coloured with hindsight? There is a paradox, I think. In a way, the child takes such things for granted. While he is in the wood, he may very likely be talking about trivial things, or thinking about his friends or a story that has been read to him. He is not consciously observing as an older person would. And yet, on the other hand, his mind and senses are wide open in a way that they will not be in later life. He has seldom or never seen a wood full of bluebells before. Because he has not been told to regard it as wonderful – because he is not like an adult looking at the Taj Mahal – the wood makes its impression with a kind of inevitability like that of a physical law. It falls into his unheeding mind like a stone falling into water. I thought it splendid to pull an armful of bluebells to take home to my mother. Yet I had unconsciously taken away much more – impalpable feelings which were to prove more abiding and which I now try, as best I can, to express in words. No expression of an experience – whether in painting, words or music – recovers the experience itself, but can only be a separate thing. Yet the experience itself existed and was at once more and less transcendental than this subsequent expression derived from it.

There were other flowers in the Bluebell Wood, too; often, as early as February, dog's mercury, with its little green flowers on stalks, would carpet the bare ground before anything else had begun to shoot. It seems strange to me, now, that my father never warned me that it was most dangerously poisonous. Perhaps he didn't know. (Culpeper, the classic herbalist, says 'There is not a more fatal plant, native to our country, than this.') Anyway, I don't think anyone would want to pick dog's mercury. The white wood anemones, too, I soon gave over picking. The flower, once picked, will droop and wither in ten minutes. My favourite in the Bluebell Wood in summer, when all the bluebells had gone, was the creeping jenny. Creeping jenny is a pimpernel by family. It grows in wet, shady places in woods and copses, in long strands of green leaves and yellow, bell-shaped flowers. It still grows in the Bluebell Wood.

One afternoon in April – I suppose I must have been about eight or nine – I was wandering down by the Bluebell Wood alone. On the east side there is open pasture land – a little valley – between this and the next similar but larger copse. I pottered along the eastern edge of the Bluebell Wood and there, on the bank by the south-east corner, I suddenly came upon what struck me then as an oldish man.

Now when you met men on the Sandleford estate and you weren't on the footpath that crosses it from Wash Common to the Newbury-Southampton road (A34), they weren't as a rule friendly. You were trespassing. My father, being Dr Adams and well-known in the neighbourhood, could carry this off, but an eight-year-old on his own was another matter, as I had already had cause to learn. 'D'you know you're doin' wrong goin' across there?' I knew by sight the few men who worked in these fields and whom you were liable to encounter.

This man wasn't any of them and you could tell at once that he wasn't, by his look and bearing. He would have been old for a farm labourer and besides, he didn't appear to be working on any particular sort of job. He, like me, appeared to be at leisure. He greeted me in a friendly way – I can't remember what he said – and although I didn't really know how to talk to him, except by corroboration and general amiability, he was clearly happy enough with my company and (unlike the farm labourers) wasn't particularly conscious of my being 'a young gentleman'. (Class distinctions were much more marked in those days.)

He was gathering twigs and lighting a fire under the bank – something I'd never seen anyone do before – and when we'd got it nicely going he proceeded to boil water in a somewhat old-looking tin can. When it boiled he made tea by throwing the tea leaves in, chatting all the time in a kindly manner about nothing in particular, quite unlike any of the Jims I had ever met. We drank the tea black, though I seem to remember he had some sugar somewhere about him. When we finally parted – and I intuitively felt no suspicion or fear of him – I left him sitting contentedly on the bank.

He remains a mystery to me. Who – and what – on earth could he have been? He was not a tramp or any sort of vagrant; I am sure of that. Even at that age I knew what a tramp was like. They had a general air of resentment and unhappiness which made you sorry for them and angry on their behalf. If they could, they begged from you. Besides, tramps stuck to the roads or to places such as ricks or sheds, close to the roads they had slunk off. They told you about their bad luck. They called you 'sonny'. This man was happy enough, generous with his tea and enjoyed my company. He addressed me by no vocative at all. (I was sensitive to vocatives and unconsciously derived a lot from them about the speaker. 'Sonny'; 'young feller'; 'young man'; 'boy'; 'youngster'. Each of these implied something vague but valid. The one I always hated was 'old chap'. I still hate it and never use it myself. 'It's time you and I had a little talk, old chap.' 'Well, you know, old chap, that's not the sort of thing we expect.' My father would never use such a term: it was either 'Richard' or 'my boy' – which I was.)

Nor was this man a keeper. I knew about keepers, too. They were – and still are – authoritative in a deferential way (like warrant officers). They were usually dressed with a certain degree of neatness and propriety – I suppose, partly to reinforce their authority and partly as befitting the standing of their employer. As a rule they were crisp and sharp. They certainly didn't make stick fires and brew tea in cans. This man, whatever he was doing, was in no hurry and very much relaxed. He was wearing old, worn clothes, yet not the come-by garments of a tramp. Most striking of all was his manner, which was unusually gentle. He didn't seem to regard our meeting as in any way odd. He made – he initiated – mild, trivial conversation. I never met him again – on the Sandleford land or anywhere else.

I have decided – or the best I can come up with after all these years is – that he was in some way connected with felling in the Sandleford copses. These – especially the Bluebell Wood – contained a lot of hazel, and it was the practice to cut this to the ground every few years – to harvest it, in fact – and then let it grow up again. The business, I rather think, was not carried out by the estate but 'sold' to people who specialized in it. I am inclined to guess that this unhurrying, kindly old fellow, taking his time on a pleasant afternoon, who had half an hour to brew tea and wasn't in the least bothered about who I was or whether I was trespassing, was engaged in some sort of examination or reconnaissance of the copses on behalf of what Americans would call 'his outfit', the hazel cutters, who may have been based well beyond Newbury. That would explain this rather Edward Thomasesque encounter.

III

As I have explained, Wash Common is a plateau south of Newbury, between the Kennet and the little Enborne brook. We lived at the north end of the plateau, at the top of Wash Hill. The Newbury-Andover road runs across the plateau and drops down the other side – known as Sandpit Hill – to the Enborne crossing called Wash Water. This was the first stream I ever knew; and here my father used to take me to paddle. It was – and still is – as pretty a brook as could be imagined, in places roofed over with alder in summer, all the air heavy with the scent of meadowsweet, the shallows full of blue brooklime. I remember big, green dragonflies hovering and darting over the water. (I suppose now that they were *Calopteryx splendens.*) The bed is mostly clean gravel, and to paddle I used to wear slip-on rubber sand-shoes. I felt full of excitement as I rather gingerly stepped into the water, pushing my way through the purple loosestrife and great willow-herb, step by step until I was in the middle of the shady stream, which is about eight feet wide and two or three feet deep (if as much). My father, a little way off, strolled about the bank, pretending inattention. I stood for a while, listening to the noise of the water, and then began slowly paddling downstream. After a few yards I entered the tunnel of alders, so thick that the bank on either side became invisible. I startled a fish – a dace, I expect – and watched it shoot away, disappearing into brown gloom. As I went on, until the mouth of the alder tunnel seemed a long way behind, the water became deeper, until it was over my waist. I called out to my father, who answered quietly and reassuringly from somewhere outside the screen of trees.

At length I emerged into the open and stopped for a minute or two to recover myself, hanging on to a plant of ragwort growing on the further bank. (I already knew that my full weight wasn't going to pull that up.) Then I waded on in bright sunshine, following the stream round a bend to the left. And here I came to an unforeseeable marvel. Suddenly I found bricks under my feet and passed under a big, square, rusty iron-bound beam. On either side rose walls of old, crumbling brick. I was among the ruins of a long-abandoned mill, from which the brook, with a little, splashing fall, dropped into a wide, deep pool. My father's composed voice called 'Shouldn't go any further, my boy, I think.' I felt I had gone further alone than ever in my life, and experienced a venture I could never have imagined.

It's all there still, for the time being unchanged. The distance I paddled is about sixty yards.

About a mile to the east of our house lay the public open space of Greenham Common, and here, too, my father would take me to wander and explore. In those days, believe it or not, Greenham was a big, lonely place, a gravelly, heathery waste three miles long and a mile wide. We would leave the car and stray off into this wilderness. Our ostensible purpose was to pick heather – not ling, but purple bell heather (*Erica cinerea*). However, anything was liable to happen. I might become fascinated by an anthill, and lie prone for ten minutes or more, watching the ants dragging their burdens – twigs, leaves, dead insects. I remember the first time I came, in a marshy place, upon sundews (*Drosera rotundifolia*), each with its tall stem of little, white flowers rising from the centre of the ring of orange, crinite, droplet-covered leaves. My father showed me how these plants attracted and closed upon tiny flies and insects. I felt sorry for the flies and wanted to try to release them, but this he deprecated. 'It's nature, my boy. If you don't like it, come on.'

I saw my first stoat on Greenham Common; and it saw me. My father was some little way off and I was lying on my stomach, watching a spider spinning a web in the bracken. The stoat appeared suddenly out of the heather, about fourteen or fifteen feet away. From pictures in books I knew what it must be, but I was startled by the richness of its colouring – the chestnut back and cream-yellow breast and belly. The stoat was also startled. It remained quite still, its back slightly arched, staring at me for several seconds. Then, apparently less alarmed than with an air of deciding to let well alone, it turned and trotted away.

In those days, grass snakes and slow worms were by no means

rare on Greenham Common. They were however, very shy. If you came upon one basking, it would be off in a flash into the heather. No doubt there were adders, too, although I can't remember to have seen one. My father certainly wasn't worried about them. What I did see, one day – and it's the only time – was a smooth snake. It was not in the open, but among the heather. I think it must have been injured in some way – although I don't recall seeing any injury – because its attempts to be off were not very effectual. I could tell that it wasn't a grass snake: it was lighter in colour, with dark spots along the top of its back. (A grass snake's spots – or bars – are along the sides.) As I'd never seen an adder I thought it must be one, and ran back to tell my father, but when we both returned to the place, the snake had, of course, gone. It may, I suppose, have been an adder after all, but all I can say is that I got a very good look at it and I'm satisfied in my own mind that it was a smooth snake. The reason why I am writing thus carefully is that smooth snakes, whatever their habitat and numerosity sixty years ago, are now very rare. (See, e.g., *The Reader's Digest Field Guide to the Animals of Britain*.) The reason, as for most declining creatures all over the world, is destruction of natural habitat. Smooth snakes frequent – or used to frequent – lowland heath in the south country. During the past half-century, more and more of this unproductive heath has been 'taken in' by agriculture. As for Greenham Common, when one reflects what's happened to that, my child-hood encounter with the smooth snake might be taken almost as a morality tale. Why can't Greenham Common now be restored as a public open space?

For several childhood summers my principal motive for going there was to catch grasshoppers. I wanted to colonize the paddock at home, which had none, although there was a fine colony of crickets wood rickets, I rather think: *Nemobius sylvestris*) occupy-ing a dense, round, yellow-leaved holly bush growing between the paddock and the Wild Wood. Grasshoppers abounded on Greenham Common. On a hot summer's day the sound of their zipping was everywhere, and as you walked through the heather they would leap away, gliding for yards in curving flight. I used to like to get up close to one and watch it stridulating, but you had to be stealthy, for they were easily alarmed. Since no less a work than Michael Chinery's *Field Guide to the Insects of Britain and*

Northern Europe speaks of the stridulation as 'song', perhaps I may be acquitted of sentimentality when I say that I still love to listen to them. As a little boy, I sometimes wondered whether it mightn't be possible to put together a sort of grasshopper band, for I had noticed that the songs differed in pitch, while seeming to remain in harmony. I can't do better here than to quote Michael Chinery:

'The "song" of these insects is undoubtedly the most fascinating thing about them. It is produced by a process called stridulation, which involves the rubbing of one part of the body (the "file") over another part (the "scraper"). The file is provided with a series of pegs or ridges that strike the scraper in turn and set up vibrations. You can imitate the action by drawing a comb over the edge of a card. The scraper is always on the wing but the file may be on the leg (grasshoppers) or on the opposite wing (crickets).

'The complete passage of the file over the scraper is usually very rapid and produces a short pulse of sound. Strictly speaking there are several pulses, one for each peg as it strikes the scraper, but these small pulses follow each other so rapidly that we can regard each passage of the file as producing a single pulse. This is the basic "song-producing" mechanism in all the stridulators, but the pattern of the song varies enormously. The pulses come in bursts, or chirps, of varying duration, caused by repeated passage of the file over the scraper. The Common Green Grasshopper, *Omocestus viridulus*, produces a continuous chirp for twenty seconds or more and the whole body quivers as the legs move up and down as much as twenty times a second. Very different is the song of the Common Field Grasshopper, *Chorthippus brunneus*, which produces a series of 6–10 half-second chirps, spread evenly over about twelve seconds. All of our grasshoppers have a fairly fixed song length at a given temperature and the song is repeated at irregular intervals. The crickets, however, have no such fixed song length and in warm weather they chirp indefinitely. Most of our stridulators are quiet in cool weather.

'Volume and pitch also vary from species to species and one can liken the various songs, when amplified, to the sounds of motor mowers, sewing machines, motor cycles and so on. In fact, it is usually easier to identify grasshoppers, in which there is a great colour variation, by their songs than by their appearances.'

There were several kinds of grasshopper on Greenham Common, and at least I distinguished between the brown ones and the green ones. The brown ones would have been *Chorthippus brunneus*, while the green ones were, I suppose, *Omocestus viridulus*, as well, perhaps, as the stripe-winged grasshopper (*Stenobothrus lineatus*) and the mottled grasshopper (*Myrmeleotettix maculatus*).

I now feel constrained to mention something that I know to be a fact, whatever any entomologist may say. Some of the brown grasshoppers I caught had rosy hind wings. I couldn't have invented this and I'm sure I'm not mistaken. Yet the only rosy-winged grasshopper given by Michael Chinery is *Oedipoda germanica*, which he says is a species not normally found in the British Isles. Also, in his illustration, it looks very large – an absolute whopper – and I don't recall that these were. I must just remain puzzled.

I used to catch the grasshoppers with a butterfly net and then transfer them to a shoe-box with ventilation holes and a small trap-door cut in the lid. I became careful not to hold them at all tightly, for if I did so they would exude a drop of orange-coloured fluid from their mouths, and this, I felt sure, must be a reaction to distress. When I got the box home I simply put it in the middle of the paddock, took the lid off and left it.

Yet the paddock never became colonized. No grasshoppers ever appeared the following year. No doubt they pined for their heather and peaty wasteland. They must just have been the wrong sort of grasshoppers, I suppose, for the paddock was a typical enough meadow. I never asked advice, so I remain ignorant of the reason to this day.

My vivid memory of Greenham Common as a great, wide waste of heather, in parts lonely, is reinforced by another incident of quite a different kind – one obviously related to Mr Punch. One summer afternoon I fell out with my sister. This wasn't unusual, of course. Children in families are continually falling out. In fact, it's only when you're grown up and observe other families that you realize how often this occurs – virtually daily. My sister was amiable as a rule and I loved her all through my childhood because she, like my father, could be relied upon to tell you the truth; also, she was apt to produce things from an exciting bag of tricks, like Percy's *Reliques* or the poetry of T. S. Eliot. But she had a sharp tongue, which at times could be really hurtful, and both she and my brother regarded me as – and made me feel that I was – a spoilt little beast. There wasn't, really, any way in which I, at eight, could expect to keep my end up with a highly intelligent seventeen-year-old who was head girl of her school and shortly going up to Girton. If you hit her – which I more than once did, in frenzy – you were automatically in the wrong and in for a wigging. If you tried to answer back you hadn't a hope. The reply would be even more blistering than what you had tried to answer.

I can't recall, after all these years, what this particular row was about: but my sister was so scathing that I felt driven to desperation. (At least Mr Punch, at the party, had not addressed me.) It was her final remark that marshalled me the way that I was going. It was something along the lines of 'And everyone would be only too glad if you *went* away and *stayed* away.'

I didn't have any clear intention of doing that, but I did feel, vaguely, that I wanted to go away and be alone, in solitude, for a good, long time; somewhere where I wouldn't be found. I went down through the paddock and out of the gate into Monkey Lane. Along the lane I walked – it was an empty country lane in those days – and along the next lane (Pinchington Lane) to the west side of Greenham Common. Then I set off across the Common itself.

I remember it was hot but overcast. There was distant thunder about. The meadow browns and cinnabars were perched on the heather and the grasshoppers were zipping. I went on with a feeling of abandonment – of having taken a step further than I knew what to do with. I had no idea what the outcome of this escapade was going to be. I had never done anything like this before; but I was in such a state that I didn't care. I had let go. I simply wanted to go on walking across the expanse of the Common, where you could actually *see* that there was nobody you were going to meet; where you really were alone. Walking was comforting, too: better than hiding would have been, or even smashing a window (a deed I sometimes used to have recourse to when in a temper). The walking soothed my frustration and feeling of grievance. I wasn't hiding: I was doing something.

All that afternoon I walked on across the Common. In the middle there was a lonely cottage, known as 'Noah's Ark'. I came to Noah's Ark and passed it. I felt safe enough in the sense that I didn't feel myself in any danger, but I also felt a little scared, like a child who has ventured into the deep end for the first time. Yet the surroundings were empty and peaceful as could be, and the solitude went on suiting me. Anyway, there was nothing much to do but go on, unless I sat down, to which I didn't feel disposed.

At last I came to the further, eastern edge of the Common. I can't recall, now, exactly how far I got, but I suppose it must have been somewhere on the outskirts of Brimpton. This surprises me now, for I have the map in front of me and from my home the whole distance is certainly over five miles. It was as the Common came to an end that my strange fit – to which it had, of course, formed the setting – came to an end also. Here were houses and people again – the normal world, even though far from home. What should I do now? It was borne in upon me that there was no course – no course at all – open to me but simply to go back. This, as I have since learned over and over, is the only termination to any loss of self-control.

I turned and began tramping back, but I was tired out. My pace across the Common became slower and slower. I had a strong notion, now, that I wouldn't be up to walking the whole way.

And then an odd and lucky chance occurred. I had been vaguely aware, for some little time, of two boys on bicycles passing me, coming back and re-passing, but apart from noticing that they were a little older than myself, I had been too tired and preoccupied to give them any close attention. Finally, however, with a grating of boots on the road, they stopped beside me and asked me where I was going. When I told them that I was walking the length of the Common and further, they were, of course, surprised. 'Cor, that's a bit of a way,' said one of them; but they didn't ask any more questions. Then, friendlily enough, the older one suggested that he should give me a lift on the bar of his bicycle.

I was only too ready. The bar was hard and uncomfortable, and with me perched in front of him the boy was horribly slow and wobbly. But we got along – perhaps as much as a mile and a half. I can't remember what we talked about, except that I asked them whether they were brothers and they said no. They weren't in the least inquisitive about what I was doing or why I was walking so far alone. They maintained a kind of detached sociability, as though they felt they might as well give me a lift as pass the time in any other way.

They took me as far as Noah's Ark. In spite of the wobbliness and the bar pressing into my not-very-well-covered buttocks, I would have liked to ask them to go further, but felt I couldn't decently do so. They dropped me. I thanked them and they set off back, in the summer twilight, towards Brimpton.

I plodded on and eventually got back home dead beat. Well, like the business at Mr Punch's party, it had worked all right. Everyone was in a fine old taking, my mother and my sister close to tears and my father half-minded to alert the police. I had been away four or five hours, if not more. They were too much relieved to scold me. I gave my mother my version of my quarrel with my sister, said I felt better now and not cross any more; had a bath and went to bed. But for several years afterwards my sister and I were never easy together on Greenham Common. She must have suffered a great deal of worry and apprehension that afternoon, and I don't really know that she deserved it. I have often felt, since, that it was a pity that this exploit did work. It would have been better if I had been blamed and punished, for as things turned out they only served to confirm the fancy-dress party behaviour pattern. The best I can plead is that my sister had been exceptionally contemptuous and cutting. My over-reaction, however, had been a general surprise, and not least to me.

The Enborne brook, two miles or so east of the ruined Falkland mill, winds along the southern edge of what used to be Greenham Common – or below it. There were woods and copses all along the left bank, and one of these was known in our family as 'Miss Tull's Wood'. I don't really know who Miss Tull was, but one of my father's patients – and later, a good friend to me – was Mr Bertie Tull, a wealthy landowner with a big house on the northern side of the Common; so I suppose there was some connection. Miss Tull's Wood was the place for primroses. We used to go there with my father in the car – bringing a picnic if the day was warm enough – down the rather steep and narrow lane leading off the Common to the ford. (There were several fords along the length of the Enborne then, and fewer bridges.) The wood was full of primroses. A hundred people could have picked them for an hour and there would still have been masses. We would pick a flat basketful, so that the top was a cushion of primroses packed tight, and then dip the bottom in the shallow river to keep them fresh. I can remember pressing my face into them. Today, their cool softness and scent always recall Miss Tull's Wood. When we were tired of picking primroses we would sit on the bank and watch the stream go by.

One April afternoon my sister and I had been sitting silent and more or less motionless for some time, when from the field beyond a rabbit came loping up to the opposite bank of the river and without hesitation, as though it were in the habit of it, plunged in and swam across, shook itself and disappeared along our bank downstream. I know that all wild animals can swim if they're put to it, but I have never since seen a rabbit swimming.

One day in June, when I was about five or six, my father took me out in the car, through Newbury and westward along the Bath Road – Jane Austen's Bath Road (the A4). There wasn't a great deal of traffic in those days of the 'twenties. It must be borne in mind, too, how much slower cars went and how relatively limited their range was. My father seldom drove much over thirty m.p.h., and when, later, my sister drove at forty, it seemed frighteningly fast. From our Newbury home, Winchester, Pangbourne or Reading were virtually our limit: never London.

Along the Bath Road we went, a matter of a good five miles. Here there is a pub called The Halfway (halfway between Newbury and Hungerford), and opposite the pub a little lane. This lane runs for perhaps three or four hundred yards between hedges covered with honeysuckle and dog rose, and at its foot lies the broad Kennet, spanned by a plank footbridge. We had come to what is still known as The Wilderness.

The reaction of a simple creature – or a child – on first seeing a true river has already been unforgettably expressed by Kenneth Grahame at the opening of *The Wind in the Willows*. I certainly felt everything that the Mole felt and was carried away with delight as I held my father's hand across the plank bridge. What Kenneth Grahame's description doesn't include, however, is any birds or animals (except, of course, the Water Rat). As we stepped off the plank bridge and began strolling up the right bank, almost the first thing I saw was a kingfisher flying past us fast and low on the other side of the river.

This certainly was – and still is – a true wilderness, of a kind almost as different from Greenham Common as the Amazon from the Oklahoma plains. All along its course, from Marlborough to

Reading, the Kennet flows in several beds and has innumerable side-streams and carriers. In places the valley is the best part of half a mile wide. But nowhere, I think, is it wider than in the Wilderness between Halfway and Kintbury, which is a mile long and perhaps 600 yards broad. It is thick woodland, virtually pathless, and marshy at all times of the year; the haunt of herons, grebes, water rails, teal, shelduck in season, spotted woodpeckers, reed warblers and grasshopper warblers. Otters there certainly were, but there wasn't much chance of coming on one, for it is simply not practicable to penetrate or wander about in that dense, boggy place.

I was still too little to do much in the way of specialized bird-watching, though I enjoyed seeing the moorhens, coots and swans on the open water. What struck me most forcibly on that first visit – the first of many – was watching the trout rising to the mayfly: and I'm pretty certain that that was what my father had brought me down to see. I saw my first trout for myself, without prompting. It was close in under the bank that we were walking up, and I had hardly noticed it before it startled and shot away into deep water.

My father pointed silently to a hawthorn bush overhanging the opposite bank of the river. I watched for perhaps half a minute, and was beginning to wonder what I was supposed to be looking at when the surface was broken, with a kind of unhurried intentness, by a rising trout. I saw the rings go radiating outwards and the whole circle of the rise float downstream until, diminishing little by little, it died away on the flow.

'Isn't *he* a splendid chap?' said my father. 'He'll do it again in a minute, I expect.'

He did, and this time I watched the mayfly drifting down on the surface, and anticipated the moment when the trout would rise to gulp it down. We remained sitting on the bank for perhaps ten minutes or more, and I found a point of vantage from which I could actually see the trout beneath the water, veering from side to side with flickering of its tail, sometimes allowing itself to be carried down a few feet before recovering its old position, yet always on the watch for the next mayfly. When it rose I could see the dark spots along its side, and once the dorsal fin broke surface as it turned to follow a fly a couple of feet downstream before taking it.

There were other footbridges – a bit out of repair and precarious, some of them – and on these we stood and looked down into the weed and the bed of the stream. My father showed me the difference between a grayling and a trout, and I learnt to recognize the chequered pattern of the grayling's high, long-based dorsal fin and the characteristic look of a grayling rise, different from that of a trout – or of a chub, for that matter. I remember I had a little, white, two-bladed penknife which someone had recently given me, and that while standing on one of the bridges I unluckily happened to drop it into the river. It must be down there still.

We took to going to the Halfway Wilderness quite often, for my father, though not himself a particularly keen fisherman (I expect he could have fished it if he had wanted to), saw that I was elated by the river and wished for nothing better than to walk the mile up its length to Wawcott and back on a sunny afternoon. One hot, still evening of high summer, we came upon a fisherman throwing a fly. This turned out to be a friend of my father, a celebrated fisherman named Dr Mottram. I watched fascinated as he splashlessly shot the light, delicate line and leader straight out to what seemed to me an incredible distance, let them drift down, recovered and re-cast. My father showed me the best place to stand when someone is casting – just behind his left shoulder. While we were there Dr Mottram rose, played and landed a trout, which he insisted on giving to us. He showed me how to pass reeds through the gills and carry it by them.

'Is he a very good fisherman?' I asked my father, as we went on.

'Dr Mottram?' he replied. 'He'd catch a fish where no fish was.'

'How d'you mean?' I said. 'Not really?'

'No; but you see, the thing is to find a fish and *induce* him to rise.'

Well, he induced me to rise all right. From that time on I knew I wanted to be a fly fisherman and bring home trout for supper.

But if I had lost my heart to the Kennet, with its great reed maces, its crowfoot and arrowhead and yellow water lilies (brandy-bottles) in the still pools, I still had another one to lose to the Downs. There are two ranges of Downs, one on each side of the Berkshire-North Hampshire area, the Kennet and Enborne valleys: the northerly, White Horse downs, which run westward from Streatley, south of Harwell and Wantage and on to Astbury and Liddington; and the southerly, Basingstoke-Winchester downs. It was to these latter that I always went with my father; or sometimes all five of the family would go. I can't remember ever to have done anything – anything at all – more delightful than walking on the crest of the downs, looking away into the purple, heat-rimmed edge of the horizon.

The downs, like Greenham Common, were a different country: different soil, grass, flowers, birds, and the land put to a different use. In those days, before the coming of the tractor, they were still mainly a place to graze sheep and train race-horses. Hardly anybody used to go up there except the shepherds, the race-horse trainers and their lads. The sunlight, the breeze and the stillness seemed intensified rather than interrupted by a grazing flock. Leisurely and unhurriedly they moved on across the grass, and every now and then would come the unresonant, cloppering tinkle of the bell round the neck of the bell-wether – the true sound of the downs on a hot afternoon – intermittent and unaltering as bird-song. Once, I remember, a shepherd greeted my father, ''Aft'noon, Doctor,' and then, after a few exchanges, rather tentatively, 'D'you like t'ave a look at this 'ere arm o' mine? 'E don't seem just right yet.' My father did so. I was well aware of standing orders – never show curiosity about patients or try to overhear consultations – and went to find another interest some way off.

God knows there were enough. The chalk itself always attracted me. The topsoil was shallow and friable, and the chalk subsoil was always breaking through, with or without the help of rabbits. You really could write – on a beech tree, for instance – with a lump of this chalk, although it was more scratchy than the sticks of chalk you bought in shops. Sometimes, though rarely, you might come upon a 'shepherd's crown'; a fossil sea-urchin. I still have three of these from those days long ago. One is a real beauty: about two and a half inches in diameter and an inch and a quarter thick; regularly shaped liked a heart, with the five lines of tubes clearly marked on top, as is the vent on the bottom. I. O. Evans, in *The Observer's Book of British Geology*, says of these, 'In the Chalk, they are so plentiful as to have been given folk names; the peasantry call the more pointed sea-urchins "shepherds' crowns" or "shepherds' mitres", and the flatter, broader type, shaped like a playing-card heart, "fairy hearts" or "fairy loaves".'

I soon found out that the chalk had its own flowers. The most beautiful were the wild orchids, which still bloom on the northward slope of Cottington's Hill almost as though in a terraced garden bed. Lady's slipper, too, flowered everywhere, as did the purple thyme. In season the cowslips grew thickly. I don't know anything nicer in the way of wild flowers than a big bunch of cowslips, and I rather think Shakespeare was of the same opinion, e.g., *A Midsummer Night's Dream*, II, 1, lines 10–16.

> The cowslips tall her pensioners be
> In their gold coats spots you see:
> Those be rubies, fairy favours:
> In those freckles live their savours:
> I must go seek some dewdrops here,
> And hang a pearl in every cowslip's ear.

Another flower I liked was the salad burnet. Since it was called the salad burnet I used to eat the leaves, supposing that you were meant to; but I've never really taken to them. They taste oily and rather hot. Milkwort there was, the flowers of which can vary with the soil from pure blue to almost white: and wild gentians, yellow wort, horseshoe vetch, dropwort, scabious, yellow rockrose and the beautiful purple-pink sainfoin: and everywhere, of course, the ragwort, covered with the yellow-and-black caterpillars of the cinnabar moth.

Downland woods, too, were different from those in the vale below. The beech hangers of the downs – dry, open-growing and airy, with no grass underfoot and the sunlight falling dappled and quick-moving through the patulous leaves – were quite unlike the damp Bluebell Wood, or the Sandleford copses of oak and hawthorn. The smooth-trunked, grey beeches, so thick about and standing so wide apart, pleased me simply by their huge size, even though they were no good for climbing. (You couldn't scramble up into them.)

It wasn't hard to learn to recognize the birds. The commonest and the most conspicuous were the yellowhammers. You could hardly miss them, for they seemed to have scarcely any fear of humans, and would sing out their little phrase from a hawthorn bush or a juniper almost at your elbow. There were cirl buntings too, but since in those days my bird-watching was spontaneous and largely uninstructed, I didn't distinguish between them and yellowhammers. The linnets I liked, partly for their song but mainly, I think, because (by English ornithological standards, anyway) the males are rather showy, with their deep pink breasts and foreheads. Best of all were the goldfinches. They forage along the downs in small flocks ('charms') feeding on thistle seeds, groundsel and the like. I defy anyone not to be stirred by the sudden, twittering arrival of four or five goldfinches, fluttering and pecking from one thistle to another. I remember calling out in delight 'Oh, Daddy, look!' and getting the wonted reply 'Aren't *they* a lot of splendid chaps?' Kestrels were not uncommon, and once I took one unawares, coming round the sharp corner of a beech hanger in time to get a close look at it sitting on a strand of wire, before it took alarm and flew away. What I chiefly noticed was the black band round the edge of the tail and the black spots, or speckling, all over the chestnut-coloured back.

Hares, too, were common in those days. In fact, you could hardly go up on the downs without seeing one or two. If you happened to be down-wind of them, and particularly if you could stand still in some sort of cover or half-cover such as a juniper (gorse doesn't grow much on the Hampshire downs), they would sometimes come quite near before suddenly realizing what you were and dashing away. The thing I have always admired in hares is their ability to rotate their huge ears through at least 180° and, I wouldn't be surprised, even a little more. In spring they caper in the open in a most arresting way, although I can't actually recall seeing them do this when I was a little boy. It is a courtship display, or so I have read.

The highest point on these downs is Beacon Hill, which forms part of the Carnarvon estate. There is still a public footpath up it from the A34 on the east side (or the Earl allows people to climb it, anyway) but in those days, before Hitler's war, there was a golf course below the hill, on the west side. It wasn't much of a course by exacting standards – the turf was spongy and the greens were slow – but from the age of about eight I used to enjoy playing there and it was novel and pleasant to be driven a matter of nearly two miles through the woods of Highclere Park. This is why, when I was a little boy, we always used to climb Beacon Hill from the west side, where the golf course was. You can't do that any more.

The fascination of climbing Beacon Hill was that on the top lay

– and still lies – Lord Carnarvon's grave. This is that Lord
Carnarvon who, with his faithful henchman Mr Carter, discovered
Tutankhamen's tomb. (In those days everybody used to pronounce
it *Tootang-Karmen*, and I still do.) We all knew the story: how the
findings were more wonderful than anything ever seen (though no
one had seen them as yet): how there was a terrible curse of the
Pharaohs on molesters of the tomb, which had carried off Lord
Carnarvon for a start: and that was only the beginning. Of course,
it wasn't my mother and father who told me about the Curse and
its effects; but Constance did, and Thorn the gardener, and several
other people in the village. It was common local knowledge.

Although there is a stone now, in those days the grave was
unmarked; I suppose because the ground hadn't yet settled, or for
some such reason. The site, perhaps five yards square, was
surrounded (as now) by high, stout iron railings and mown smooth.
In the middle the turf rose into the man-long hump of the interment,
at which I used to stare in numinous awe. There lay the Earl who
had been killed by the Pharaoh's Curse. This had all been his land,
and his great castle could be seen a mile away among the trees. He
had known the King, George V. Yet none of this grandeur had
served to avert the curse.

He had been such a nice man, by all accounts. There was an
anecdote current which I had been told as an example of the
manners of a true gentleman (and I have always remembered it).
It seems that at some midsummer before the Great War, Lord
Carnarvon was giving a fête in the grounds. There was a cricket
match, and a marquee had been put up, in which the Earl's tenants
were sat down to a generous feast. Lord Carnarvon himself was
strolling round, talking to people and making sure that everyone
was having a good time, when he came across an old fellow who
was addressing himself to a slab of ice pudding.

'Hullo, Giles,' he said. ''Hope you're enjoying yourself?'

'Well, my lord,' replied Giles, 'I don't reckon much to this 'ere
pudden. Why, 'tis stone cold.'

Lord Carnarvon picked up a spoon and tasted it. 'So it is!' he
said. 'What a shame! Smithers, take this away and bring Mr Giles
some of that hot apple pie.'

. . .

A good seven miles westward along the downs stood and still

stands Combe Gibbet. Although it was thought rather a long way in those days, we sometimes drove out there for a picnic. The story of the gibbet – what little we know of it – is a grim one, but even as a little boy I'd had it told to me. In 1676 two villagers of Inkpen, George Broomham and Dorothy Newman, were convicted at Winchester Assizes of murdering Broomham's wife and son 'with a staff' on Inkpen Down. The crime excited so much local horror and vengeful indignation that the pair were sentenced, exceptionally, to be hanged 'on the highest point in the county' (Hampshire), which by a coincidence happened to be the summit of Combe Down. (It's Inkpen Down on the north side of the ridge and Combe Down on the south. The summit is not quite 1,000 feet.) A double gallows was erected for the purpose and the pair were duly hanged. No one else has ever been hanged there, but it has become traditional to maintain the gallows. (I believe there is an obligation upon either the landlord or the tenant: I have been told which, but I forget.) When it becomes worn out by wind and weather it is replaced. The one there at the moment is quite recent, stout and good for years, I would say: but in the 'twenties, when I first went up there, the gibbet was old, the tall upright rifted and leaning awry, the lateral arms, not very long, rifted and tapered by weather. I didn't know it wasn't the original. I used to imagine the scene, two hundred and fifty years before; the jeering villagers, the hangman and his wretched victims in the cart, the horses blown from their long pull up, no doubt some dignified J.P. or magistrate in charge, the clergyman with his book, all in the stiff west wind along the down. How long did it take them to strangle?

And yet I have never heard that anyone has felt the place to be sinister or eerie. Certainly I never did. It is difficult to feel anything but delight and elation as you look northwards, out across the fields and woodlands of the Kennet valley to the White Horse downs fifteen miles away. Newbury today is spoilt, its former character and comeliness ruined, but in those days, sixty years ago, from Combe Gibbet you could see it, six or seven miles away to the north-east, a trim little market town of red brick, between the hospital on the south and, on the north, the Lambourn river flowing past Donnington and Shaw to join the Kennet north of the race course.

Ah, yes, the race course!

My father was doctor and surgeon to the Newbury races. This meant that when there were meetings our family received honorary passes to the members' enclosure and had lunch in the members' dining-room. To this day the smell of cigars always recalls to me the noise and tumult of the race course – the esoteric bawling of the bookies ('Two to one bar one! Two to one bar one!' 'I'll lay six to four the field! Six to four the field!'), the tic-tac men in trilby hats, standing on the high points of the grandstand as they flailed their arms in gesticulations whose recipients one could never make out in the crowd below; the electric tote flashing its figures as the bets mounted; the bookies' clerks, with polished brass boutonnières announcing their firms' names, scribbling on great clipboards and handing out bright-coloured, numbered tickets; the débris, as the afternoon went on, of those same, torn-up tickets littering the tarmac and the trampled, aromatic turf; the jockeys' names run up on a kind of hoist between two posts (Donohue, Wragg, Beery, Fox); the bowler hats (my father never wore one on any other occasion, though he did for a while when King George V died) and above all the beautiful, shining, lissom horses led round and round the paddock before the race, while the owners conversed with their overcoated jockeys. I knew Dorothy Paget by sight, and her colours (blue with a yellow hoop, cap yellow with a blue hoop), together with a few of the other famous owners of the day. I recall Golden Miller, that unbeatable horse, passing the post amid a storm of cheering, and Dorothy Paget leading him in.

Unlike going to the children's parties, going to the races was not frightening or disconcerting. There was more than one reason for this. First, nothing was expected of you. You didn't have to do anything in particular or talk to anyone you didn't want to. I was allowed to go anywhere I liked by myself, from the paddock to the top of the grandstand, and as I grew older my father often used to lend me his binoculars. I know what it is to be literally alone in a crowd. No one took any notice of a small boy edging his way between fur coats and cigars to the paddock rails, to watch Forbra or Limelight led past almost within touching distance. In a crowd of adults I remained solitary. I had my own bookie, though; a dark, toothy gentleman called Mr Bingham, who, from me, good-naturedly accepted sixpenny bets. (Several other bookies had refused.) Having placed the bet, I would climb to the topmost point of the stand, race-card in hand, there to identify the runners as they were mounted and then watch them led out and released to canter up the course to the start. The very sight of the bright racing colours was exciting. Through the binoculars I could make out the mêlée, walking to and fro down at the starting-gate. Then the bell would ring – 'They're off!' – and I would lean hard on the wall, elbows splayed and binoculars pressed close, watching my horse. Or sometimes, if it were steeplechasing, I would leave the members' enclosure by way of the gate onto the flat course, cross it to the steeplechasing course and take up my stand at the water-jump to see them go over. I have a memory of a dismounted jockey actually up to his neck in the water – the only time I ever saw it – but I was still quite small and remember no details. The horse must have refused, I suppose, and pitched him over its head.

In winter, at the steeplechase meetings, Newbury race course was – and no doubt still is – notorious for being bitterly cold, with cutting winds. Two or three great, open braziers, each about six feet in diameter and piled with glowing coke, were situated about the members' enclosure, and between races a circle of people two or three deep would form round them, stretching out their hands for warmth. It was near one of these that I saw, for the only time, King George V and Queen Mary; the only time, but it couldn't have been to much better advantage. It was known, of course, that they were coming to the meeting that day. I hadn't seen them arrive, although I had caught a distant glimpse of an entourage of grand-looking people up in the glass-enclosed royal box. One of the big braziers was sited round at the back of the members' enclosure, on the tarmac leading down to the paddock and the jockeys' changing-rooms. I was wedged in among people standing round this when I became aware of a stir. The crowd broke up and moved this way and that. Naturally, I moved too, and then, looking round, saw the King and Queen approaching. They looked exactly like the photographs of themselves in the newspapers; the King bearded and moustached, with the face of someone who – you would think – didn't smile much; Queen Mary tall and majestic, with a purple toque and a spotted veil. They paused for a few moments by the brazier, chatting quietly to two or three people with them, and then made their way down to the paddock. I can see clearly, in memory, the King studying his race-card as he walked away.

It must be remembered that in those days not only was there no television; there were no newsreels in provincial cinemas – films were silent, anyway – and royal walkabouts hadn't been invented (though I recall a charming, true story of the King and Queen walking in St James's Park and stopping deliberately to pose for a little girl with a box camera). To find yourself within spitting distance of the King and Queen was a terrific thrill for a small boy.

I said there was more than one reason for my feeling no nervousness of going to the races. We had, in effect, our own sitting-room – virtually private, and warm as toast on even the bleakest days. This was the race course hospital, a room about as big as a fair-sized drawing-room, situated just behind the members' grandstand and adjacent to the jockeys' changing-room. It had three beds made up with sheets and blankets; it had comfortable chairs and a roaring fire – and it had Nurse Lowe.

Nurse Lowe was exactly like a nanny from a Victorian children's story-book – Maria Edgeworth or Frances Hodgson Burnett. At this time she was, I suppose, in her fifties or even a little more. She was on the plump side, with gold-rimmed spectacles, rosy cheeks, white hair, a gentle voice and a beautiful smile. I'm afraid I was not always a very well-behaved little boy, but in Nurse Lowe's company it was easy to be as good as gold. Gentleness and kindness surrounded her like an invisible nimbus. I can't remember anything that we ever said to each other, but I certainly don't forget sitting by the hospital fire and talking to Nurse Lowe.

She used to knit and she used to darn. She had a great, open bag with her, full of socks and woolly vests and other mending. Her darning egg used to delight me. I haven't seen another for years past. It was about as big as a man's fist or perhaps a little smaller, and made of – or at any rate outwardly covered with – celluloid, I suppose (for plastics had not yet come on the market). It was bluntly ovoid; and one end was black while the other was white. The idea was that you put it into, say, the heel of a sock with the appropriately coloured end showing conspicuously through the hole to be darned. Then you held the whole thing clutched in your left hand and darned over the hole until the end of the egg was covered up. I felt that this was what the Americans call 'neat': I still think so. I wonder where that egg is now. People don't darn as much as they used to.

Sometimes Nurse Lowe would get a tip from a jockey – so would my father, for that matter – and give me a shilling or a florin to put on for her; for she was not supposed to leave the hospital. Whenever a jockey was brought in on a stretcher – sometimes unconscious, sometimes moaning or muttering curses in his pain – my brother and my sister and I had to look sharp and slip out quickly and unobtrusively, for we weren't really allowed to be there, and didn't want to get my father into trouble or to be ourselves forbidden to frequent the hospital at all. I remember once a jockey being carried in, his stretcher surrounded by two or three obviously important people in bowler hats, carnations and binoculars. My brother was the one who caught it for not becoming invisible quickly enough.

'Come, tumble out, boy, tumble out!' barked one of these grandees peremptorily.

I wasn't used to seeing my elder brother, who to me seemed almost grown-up, scuttling out of the way without a word. But that was what he did. 'Whoever's that?' I asked, as soon as we were both outside, somewhat disordered.

'Oh, that's old Baxendale,' said my brother with an air of patient toleration, rather as though he had been merely humouring the idiosyncrasies of the gentleman by acting in so undignified a way. Mr Baxendale (another patient of my father) I vaguely knew to be in some capacity or other the head of the whole race course and everything in it. I was appropriately impressed and somewhat apprehensive, but nothing more came of the matter.

My father – as I hope to make clear in the course of this book – although so grave and unsmiling in his manner, had a great gift of what one might term cryptic or veiled humour. This quality made friends for him among all manner of people who sensed intuitively this singular mixture of reserve with warmth and even mischief. One of these was the Comic Waiter.

I don't know by what system the race course authorities recruited staff like barmen, cooks and waiters for the race meetings. They would not, of course, have had a permanent staff, the meetings being relatively infrequent. I suppose they sharked up a list of lawless resolutes. (There spring to my mind the words used by some contemporary historian – Clarendon? – to describe the shortcomings of a Royalist army in the civil war: he says that it consisted of 'old, decayed tapsters and the like'.) No doubt a lot of the race-course people were engaged on a regular basis, as no doubt were my father and Nurse Lowe – and for all I know, Mr Baxendale. Anyhow, the Comic Waiter was always to be found on duty in the members' dining-room.

The Comic Waiter used to make a great business of serving my father. He would bring the steak (or whatever it was) and put down the plate not in front of my father but a foot or two away, in some convenient place. Then he would add the vegetables himself, commenting appropriately the while ('This cauliflower is certainly one not to be missed, Doctor'), and finally, having arranged everything on the plate to his satisfaction, would place it before my father, remarking something like 'There, Doctor; I think you'll find that'll taste remarkably good.'

My father used to play up to the Comic Waiter, rather as though they were a sort of duo in a music-hall sketch. He would ask him whether he had a horse for the two-thirty, express the hope that his feet weren't hurting him, or enquire whether the Stilton cheese was any good. ('Good, Doctor? Why, it won at Cheltenham only last week!')

Now one day my father and I were finishing lunch together in the members' dining-room by ourselves. I can't remember where the rest of the family were, but anyhow they weren't there. We had coffee, my father signed the bill and we made our way towards the revolving doors. As we approached them, we became aware of a stout, middle-aged lady who was, as they say, going on a whole piece. The recipient was the poor Comic Waiter, who was getting most of it, although the head waiter, standing near by, was also in the line of fire.

'I'm very sorry; I'm very sorry indeed, madam,' the Comic Waiter kept repeating. 'I'm extremely sorry –'

None of this contrition and apology was stemming the flow of the imperious lady, whom there was plainly no stopping. As we came closer I sensed my father's silent antagonism as he looked from her to the Comic Waiter and back.

'*And*,' she said, drawing herself together for another burst, '*and* they never helped me on with my coat or *anything* –'

'Serve you right, too, you silly old cow,' said my father, stepped into the revolving doors and was gone into the hurly-burly of the course outside.

I, coming behind, had just time to see the Comic Waiter clap his hand over his mouth, while the head waiter broke into a quickly checked guffaw. I went through the doors at once and fast, before she might take it into her head to grab me. Catching up, I said nothing to my father, or he to me; there was no need, really.

On another occasion my father had taken me out to the grounds of a big estate at Speen, on the further side of Newbury, to see the Police Sports. They were thrilling. The races were started with real pistol shots. The sack race was a riot, and so was the obstacle race. There were real Life Guards on their great, black horses, in full dress uniform of scarlet coats, shining helmets and breastplates. They did a musical ride and then formed into couples, face to face and side by side, for their horses to 'dance'. (They waltzed, I rather think.) I remember that I caused some laughter by saying to my father 'I think I'll be one of those when I grow up.'

The crowd was so thick and I was so small that it was hard to see. My father got hold of a wooden chair and planted it beside us, and I scrambled up onto it. I hadn't been there long when a man rather like Bairnsfather's Old Bill, with a clay pipe full of shag and string round the knees of his corduroys, got up on the bar along the side of the chair and balanced himself with a hand across its back. He seemed precarious, and I certainly felt so as we both began to tilt and rock.

'Gosh, this seems a bit wobbly,' I said.

'Oh, be it, son?' replied he companionably. 'Well, just you 'ang on tight –'

At this moment my father looked round and saw what was going on.

'Here, you get down!' he said. 'It's not your chair.'

The man got down, looking at my father with surly resentment.

'Nor it ain't the lad's chair, neither,' he said.

I felt ill-at-ease and embarrassed, caught in the middle of this exchange. I was out of countenance and didn't know what I ought to do.

'I suppose that's true,' I muttered sheepishly.

'Don't speak to him!' said my father brusquely. 'Don't have anything to do with him!' And with this he returned his attention to the track.

It worked, of course. The man said no more and edged away in the crowd. But the encounter taught me a lot. Silence and disregard, properly used, can be more effective than any amount of speech.

My father, like the old man in the folk tale, often had his own words for things. Some of these were simply onomatopoeic. I used to suffer, sometimes, from sneezing fits – probably hay fever, though I never thought about it. My father feared that this, if not controlled, might injure the mucous membrane in my nose by blowing it down into folds. 'I can't have any more of that *kasha*ming,' he would say reproachfully. The extraordinary thing was that that, too, worked. I usually found I could thereupon stop kashaming.

Crying, too, he disfavoured, unless there was good cause, such as a bang on the head, a blow on the funny-bone or any of the other accidents common in childhood. He didn't like you to cry for mental reasons only.

'I don't want any of that bad bowleting, my boy, when it's time to go back to school.' He was sympathetic, though, to your feelings. 'No one likes going back to work after a holiday,' he would say, as you struggled to hold back your tears. Or 'All good things come to an end.'

The car – or any car, for that matter – he always called the 'bouffam'. (In his letters to me he used to spell it 'bougham'.) 'I'm going into Newbury in the bouffam,' he would announce, 'if anyone wants to come along.' The word was in common use throughout the family, and I have gone on using it with my own wife and children and anyone else who has become an intimate friend. I always supposed that this, too, was onomatopoeic, imitating the shaking reverberation of a car's engine when idling, which was general during the early decades of this century. Years later, however – one day during the late 'seventies – I received from an American friend a page from a motor magazine: an article with the title 'Little Known of Bouffam/Bouffum'. It appeared that there really was a car of this name during the Edwardian decade, but it had ceased to be manufactured and, as the article said, little was now known about it. I have wondered since why my father should have adopted it as a generic term for any car, including his own, for to my knowledge he never owned one of the mysterious

Bouffams. During the Edwardian decade, as I have said, he had a De Dion Bouton, but all through my lifetime we had a series of Wolseleys.

A more useful word (because there is no single equivalent for it) was 'sadbit'. In the first place, a sadbit could be literally a 'sad bit': e.g., '*Uncle Tom's Cabin* is a book that's full of sadbits.' But it could also be a tragic conclusion, in reality or fiction. Here the advantage of the word was that it saved the speaker from having to go into distressing detail.

'Daddy, what happened to those kittens that Mr Cottrell said they couldn't be doing with?'

'It's a sadbit, I'm afraid.' Nothing more need be said.

'Splendid chap, Keats. 'Pity it was all such a sadbit.'

'Well, I think if Mrs Kennedy really means to go on with that idea of a cricket match it'll probably turn out to be a very sadbit.'

'If Ramsay MacDonald gets back in, won't that be a sadbit?'

But a sadbit could also be a person.

'Everyone's saying the new headmaster at the grammar school's an awful sadbit.'

'There were so many sadbits there that I came away early.'

Perhaps his best word was 'wugular'; and this, too, I have retained, never having come across any one word that covers all its applications. Like the Geordie word 'canny', it can mean all sorts of things. Wugular could mean anything from 'unusual' to 'dangerous' and from 'sinister' to 'sexually perverted'.

'It's Bank Holiday tomorrow,' he might say, 'so there'll be a lot of wugular chaps on the road. Funny fellows, comic men and clowns of private life.'

'I saw a wugular bird out at Highclere this morning. I'm not at all sure it wasn't a brambling.'

'I don't think I'd care to go there at night. It's a wugular sort of place.' This meant either a dangerous place or a place where you might be set upon, for my father had no superstitious fears.

'That Edgar Allan Poe must have been a wugular chap, I should think.'

Once, when I was about twelve, having intuitively sensed something I shuddered at, without understanding, about the second master at my prep school, I said to my father 'I can't help feeling, Daddy, that Mr Morris is by no means free from wugularity.' 'I'm quite *sure* of it,' replied my father, in a tone that precluded further speculation. When I grew older I came to realize that Mr Morris had been, as they say, as bent as a nine-bob note. He was a sadistic paederast, really.

At bedtime, there was always the hope that my father might come upstairs and tell me a story – for you couldn't depend on it. Often, in those days, if you asked an adult (not my father) to tell you a story, he (or she) would reply,

> I'll tell you a story of Jackamanory,
> And now my story's begun.
> I'll tell you another of Jack and his brother
> And now my story's done.

This was maddening, especially as you knew what was coming as soon as they started. But my father was, as he himself would have said, upsides with this. He told many stories about Jackamanory, a little boy who used to get lost in the town, or taken to the fair or a cricket match, or even to London. But Jackamanory, in the gradual and casual way of oral bedtime stories, came to be superseded by the episodic tales of Hedgehog.

If anything makes me realize that childhood is irrecoverable, it is thinking about Hedgehog. After all these years I remember scarcely anything that Hedgehog and his friends did. I recall that they had a cricket match, and on another occasion they went to the seaside. Everything they did was more or less trivial, homespun and not by any means cliff-hanging. There were no spies, chases, bombs or arrests. Looking back on them now, the stories seem a constituent part of their occasion; inseparable from the time and place where they were told, the nature and style of the person who told them and of the person who listened. My father's narrative manner was low-keyed and undramatic, pausing and conversational. His listener was fully receptive and uncritical, tired after a long day of childhood, relaxed after supper and a bath, happy with the kind of story which was familiar and singular to himself; and with the gratification of the story-teller being there, leaning with clasped hands upon the high brass rail at the foot of the bed. You were free to ask questions and interrupt. No, it didn't really matter what Hedgehog actually did, while the swifts flew high and screaming outside in the summer dusk or the gas fire quietly poppled in winter. I am fairly sure, from what I can remember, that he was ad-libbed. His evening adventure was ephemeral as the evening itself and the style of the telling became as familiar as the smell of my father's old tweed coat.

So then they would leave the door open with the landing light on, and I would set about going to sleep, often saying over to myself one of Constance's wonderful verses. Wherever can she have got them? It must, surely – it can only – have been from the Girl Guides.

> I went to the pictures tomorrow.
> I took a front seat at the back.
> I fell from the floor to the gallery
> And broke a front bone in my back.
> The band struck up but did not play,
> So I sat down and walked away.

'The following Sunday being Ash Wednesday, a meeting will be held in the vestry to decide which colour the wall shall be whitewashed. Admission free, pay at the door. Seats inside, sit on the floor. We will now sing –

'We went to the animals' fair.
 The birds and the beasts were there.
 The grey baboon by the light of the moon
 Was combing his auburn hair.
 The monkey fell out of his bunk
 And slid down the elephant's trunk.
 The elephant sneezed and fell on his knees,
 But what became of the monkey, monkey, monkey, monkey –'

There were others. One I remember proving so fascinating, later, to the boys at my prep school that I used to have to say it over and over again.

> There was an old man from beyond Japan
> And his name was Ching Ching Chinaman.
> His body was long and his legs were short

And this funny man couldn't walk or talk.
 Jing jang jorum, bibba labbalorum
 One cheer more for the hippy happy day.
 Go, go, go to the utty utty i,
 Tiddle-fi, tiddle-fi, Chinese doll.

They took him up to the top of the hill
And they rolled him down like a Beecham's pill.
They drove a cab to the Brighton pier
And they poured him out like a glass of beer.
 Jing jang jorum –

But I would be asleep.

IV

During the nineteen-twenties Newbury was a trim, self-contained little town – an ancient borough – a market centre for local farmers and the horse-racing people of the downs. It was on the Great Western Railway, and the journey to Paddington took exactly one hour. There was a market on Thursdays and a fair at Michaelmas, though even in my infancy this had already ceased to have much to do with the local economy and had become largely a matter of coconut shies and roundabouts. But the weekly cattle-market was important business, with its herds and flocks driven along the dusty roads into town and usually, in the evening, two or three (or more) drunk and disorderly fellows man-handled away by the police. (Resisting the police was quite as common then as now.) In adolescence, during the late 'thirties, I had no difficulty in recognizing Thomas Hardy's Casterbridge, even though Newbury hadn't actually got any sheep bleating within earshot of the magistrates' courtroom. In 1921 the population was 12,295: in 1931, 13,340.

One or more of the family went into Newbury daily. In those days deliveries to the home by butchers, grocers and drapers were a matter of course, and as I grew older I got to know the delivery boys, who could sometimes be inveigled into a quick game of darts against the kitchen fence on their way from the back door. Darts was the limit, though. ('Cricket? I'd get the sack!' said the butcher's boy when I suggested it one day.) Nevertheless my mother, delivery or no, liked to see what she was buying, particularly when it came to meat. There would be colloquies in the butcher's with beehive-haired Mrs Leach reassuring my mother, and calling upon 'Ar-*thur*!' (ginger-moustached, bloody-handed, his cleaver hanging at the belt of his blue, white-striped apron) to corroborate her. My mother

would pray my father's name in aid as a sort of frightener. 'Dr
Adams wasn't at all pleased with –' 'Dr Adams will certainly expect
–' In point of fact my father never ate a great deal and was not
particular what it was. As my mother knew well, her act was a
kind of charade. The Leaches, who were patients and had a
prosperous farm out at Thatcham, respected and valued my father
and wouldn't have dreamed of putting anything across him. All my
life, up to and during the Second War, we never dealt with any
other butcher. Now, the shop's long gone.

I first began 'going down in the town' with my mother while I
was still in a push-chair; though it was never a case of being made
to. You could come along or not as you pleased, unless you were
particularly required for anything, such as buying a new pair of
shoes or helping to choose a birthday present for someone like Jean
or Ann. There were three ways of covering the mile and a half.
You could walk; or you could go down in 'Mavis' (complete with
Cecil); or you could latch onto my father as he set out on his
morning rounds, usually about quarter to ten. What I liked best, in
childhood, was walking down – from Wash Common it's downhill
all the way – and then meeting my father, at about twenty to one,
at the South Berks Club and being driven home to lunch. The car
would be parked close by the Club, alongside the Roary Water, as
we called the white, tumbling outfall from the Hovis Mill. I was
always happy enough to wait, leaning against the high iron railings
and watching the turbulent Kennet foaming out from the mill ducts
below. There were three of them, round-arched and dark-mouthed,
though as a rule only two would be in use. The Roary Water was
exciting and frightening, like a ghost story, because you were safely
above it, and couldn't have got over the spiked railings if you'd
tried. But it was disturbing that the water came rushing so noisily
out of the dark. (I remembered this, years later, when I first read
Rasselas.)

One of my early memories is of walking hand-in-hand with my
mother along Bartholomew Street, when we saw coming towards
us a dirty, bearded man who was pushing up the roadway a home-
made handcart, a thing of soap-boxes and old pram wheels. This
was full of and hung about with dead rabbits. Their back legs were
tied together and as the cart rattled along their ears and poor, eye-
glazed faces swung and bobbed. The man, to leave his hands free,

had tied the shafts with a bit of cord under his armpits, and as he
went he was very deliberately skinning a rabbit with an old knife,
and tugging off the loose fur where he had got a grip.

I burst into tears; from shock, I think, as much as pity. It was,
of course, a piteous, ugly sight, but apart from that the man's
unconcerned, workaday air as he plied his knife made me realize
in an instant that rabbits were things, and that it was only in a
baby's world that they were not.

> It is the blight man was born for.
> It is Margaret you mourn for.

My mother did the best she could: but I reckon I grew up a lot
that morning.

Still, in those days there were plenty of living animals about
Newbury in which you could take pleasure. Donkeys, trit-trotting
with little carts, were quite an accustomed sight; so much so that
sometimes, before going down in the town, I would put a carrot in
my pocket, in case we met one. The cows, at close quarters, smelt
sweet and warm. But best of all were the horses – beer horses, coal
horses; Whitehorn the baker's horse, dappled brown and white, a
lighter, quicker fellow altogether, pulling his two-wheeled, box-
shaped, enclosed delivery van which looked a bit like a hansom
cab. There were fine carriages, too; Miss Myres and Miss Southby,
both patients of my father, drove everywhere by coach; Miss
Southby all in black, with an open-work, spotted veil and, of
course, gloves; their coachman was tophatted, his whip upright in
its stock beside him, tall as a spear. And it was by no means
uncommon to see men riding on horseback with their parcels slung
about them: they had been shopping. Gigs and traps, too, had
certainly not gone out. I remember a pleasant maiden lady, Miss
Spackman, giving me a lift one morning in her trap. I sat beside
her fascinated as the horse took its time over defecating less than a
yard before our eyes, Miss Spackman continuing to chat uncon-
cernedly the while.

But the best chap to meet, as my father would have said, was
the Water Gee-gee. The Water Gee-gee was very large, very white
and, as I remember him, covered with creaking, brass-decorated
harness. He wore blinkers, out of which he looked at you

benevolently before you gave him a lump of sugar. When he
stamped his hind hoof in the gutter it made a hollow, satisfying
snock! His job was to pull the big tank-cart from which water ran
onto the road out of perforations in a long, horizontal pipe at the
back. If I give the impression that he did the job on his own and
wasn't controlled by a man, it is because he gave that impression
himself. I suppose he'd done the job so often that he could do it on
his head without bidding. It was exciting to see the water jets
spurting onto the road and streaming down the camber, and then
to watch the gutter turn into a running rill, empty cigarette packets
and matchboxes floating along to the gullies and dropping in. We
didn't always meet him – no doubt he had his appointed districts
and areas – but when we did, I was allowed to stand and watch
him for quite a while. My mother seldom hurried, and possessed
the kindness and imagination to understand that a leisurely
encounter with the Water Gee-gee could make your day. I'm sure
she herself enjoyed it, too. It was always pleasing to be able to say
at lunch 'Oh, and we saw the Water Gee-gee'; as who should say
'We saw the Mayor.' I was really thinking not so much of
communicating my feelings, but rather of what I myself had felt.

The Mayor, in fact, was, as the Americans say, something else.
Alderman Elsie Kimber was a legendary figure in Newbury. She
came of the respectable family of Kimber the grocer's and was
middle-aged and unmarried. She had rimless glasses, wore a
heavily-skirted, brown belted garment, sandals and no hat, and she
rode a motor-bike. She was emancipated, bizarre, no fool and
excellent company, even to a small boy. To me it seemed entirely
natural that the Mayor should look somewhat unusual, as did, for
instance, Beefeaters. I vaguely supposed that that was what
mayors looked like.

To illustrate my mother's gift of identifying with children, I must
instance another time when we were down in the town together: I
suppose I may have been five or six. We were walking up
Batholomew Street from the southern end, by the railway bridge
(and Kimber's). In those days Newbury still had the sort of Thomas
Hardyesque atmosphere which I have been trying to evoke, and
there were still many dwelling-houses actually in the town, from
working-people's trim, small houses, fronting the street, to Dr
Hickman's beautiful house and garden (of which more anon) and

the Dower House, long since become business premises. People *lived* in the middle of Newbury because they preferred to. (It was quiet then, see.) We were walking past a row of neat little dwellings, near Vincent's the ironmongers, when suddenly, for some reason, I was greatly taken with the whitened step, the polished brass handle and gently gleaming panels which comprised a front door. Whoever owned it was obviously house-proud, but I didn't consciously think of that: I just felt I liked it.

'Look, Mummy,' I said. 'What a wonderfully good door for knocking on!'

'Why, so it is, dear,' answered my mother. 'A *very* good door for knocking on.'

I knocked on it with my knuckles. My mother knocked on it with her knuckles. We became absorbed.

'A *very* good door for knocking on !'

'Yes, yes!'

All of a sudden the door opened, and I had a glimpse of a lady in carpet slippers and an apron. But only a glimpse. My mother clutched my hand and together we sped away up the street – simply hared, as she herself would have said. Five minutes later we had forgotten all about it, and were watching a horse repeatedly tossing his head to get the last out of the bottom of his nosebag, while at each toss the chaff flew round his ears and the flies buzzed up in a cloud.

We were not, of course (ah! those class-conscious days), on visiting terms with tradespeople; you didn't ask tradespeople to tennis parties or anything like that. Nevertheless my father – and my mother – had many friends among tradespeople in the town, most of whom were always ready to oblige Dr Adams. One of these was Mr Tufnell (old Tuffy) and his protégée, Miss Rowle (Rowley, as everyone called her). 'Do you mean Miss Rowle?' snapped one of the lady assistants one day, when I asked for her. She (rightly) thought it disrespectful for a little boy to use the nickname. 'No, I don't: I mean Rowley,' I replied. And I got away with it.

Mr Tufnell was fond of telling how he had first come to Newbury as a poor boy with a shilling in his pocket. (That would have been in the eighteen-eighties, I suppose.) He was now the proprietor of a thriving newsagent's and toyshop, a tobacconist's and also of one of the town's two cinemas. I believe he was unmarried. So it was Rowley – dear, kind, unmarried, middle-aged, bubblingly cheerful Rowley – who ran the newsagent's, supplied us with newspapers and helped my father and my mother in all sorts of little ways. For example, on the strength of a telephone call she would pick up a prescription which had been made up at the chemist's, and it would be delivered with the newspaper next morning. Or she would take charge of a basket of shopping (Tufnell's was near both the club and the 'bus terminus) while my mother walked the length of Northbrook Street to buy something else. When I wanted to buy cigarettes (half a crown for fifty) for my father's birthday, Rowley would buy them for me, as I was, of course, under age.

The last favour which Rowley ever did for me was in 1946, at the end of the war. I had learned of the death of my dearest friend in Tunisia, and had there and then sat down in the College Bursar's office in Oxford and copied out his commanding officer's account of his death (no duplicating machines then) in my own hand. Returning to Newbury I gave it, weeping, to Rowley and she typed it for me.

Mr Mann was the floor manager at Toomer's, the ironmonger we favoured. He was middle-aged, tall and shiningly bald, in a long brown shop-coat buttoning down the front. He seemed just right for the arrays of smooth, flashing saucepans, spades and pails over which he presided. I liked the shop because it was spacious, light and full of hard, clean things which could be touched and even played with, without anybody minding. (They couldn't soil or break.) Also, it stocked exciting goods like clock golf sets and mousetraps (both box and break-back).

Mr Mann was another friend who was ready to do anything for my father, and I think with good reason. At one time he was not well and that, of course, is as much as I know about his illness, except that we can presume from the story that it was something internal, like rupture or hernia. He didn't seem to be getting any better and accordingly he wasn't confident in the treatment he was receiving or the doctor who was prescribing it. Being afraid, he spoke in confidence to my father and asked his advice. This was a ticklish situation, since he was someone else's patient and, if there really was no more that could be done, didn't want all the invidious trouble of changing doctors. My father connived at the secrecy.

One evening, after the shop was shut, he privily joined Mr Mann, who pulled down all the blinds of the display windows and stripped off. The big display window had powerful electric lights and here, among the trowels, frying-pans and mowing-machines, my father gave Mr Mann a full examination. All I know is that his diagnosis was a different one from the other doctor's, and that whatever ensued made Mr Mann better. One day, several years afterwards, I remarked to my sister that Mr Mann seemed devoted to my father. 'Oh, yes,' she replied, 'I rather think Father saved his life – or something like that.'

Mrs Mann was expert in making wine, and we used to come in for this in a considerable way. Much later, during the war, whenever I managed to get home on leave in summer, I used to fill my father's silver hip-flask with Mrs Mann's dandelion or cowslip and take it trout-fishing with me. It was extremely potent. You had to watch it, and I seldom, if ever, emptied the flask.

The most spacious shop premises in Newbury at that time were Camp Hopson's, who covered everything from haberdashery through men's and women's tailoring to carpets, upholstery and removals. (They still do.) As a little boy I was always impressed by the air of quiet, controlled activity and order, carried on by what seemed a great many black-clad, committed people intent on the tasks of the business; by the division of the place into different departments and the differences in atmosphere between each. The rooms seemed huge, extending back deeply from the street front almost like corridors, and the old-fashioned wooden counters very broad and solid.

In several of the departments there were 'overhead railways' which carried cash and bills from the counters to the central cashier's office at the back. When a purchase was made, the bill and cash were put by the shop assistant into a screw-top container, about as big as two fists, made to run along an overhead wire. This was then 'fired': a spring was released, the head of which struck the container and impelled it hard along the wire. It fairly flew off on its course, with a characteristic swishing noise which I can hear now, and you could watch its flight to the cashier's – a good, long way, too. Then, after a brief interval, it would return with the receipted bill and the change, arriving back with a loud 'ping' and a sudden stop. Sometimes there might be as many as four of these containers in flight at once, their frantic speed dominating the otherwise quiet department. I was always sorry to leave. I could have watched them for half an hour on end.

At times one would meet with the imposing figure of old Mr Camp, now well on in years, stout and impressive, an Elgarian figure with a dark suit, white hair and moustache and a rubicund face. He walked slowly, in a majestic manner, seldom speaking much. I realize now that he must have been born some time during the eighteen-fifties.

After the close-set chessboard of the haberdashery, the carpet department appeared vast – by far the biggest room I had ever been in. It was all open and unencumbered, with a large, low central platform on which carpets were laid out for display. It seemed as big as a field, and was filled with the true smell of carpets – the strawy smell of the new backing – as with the scent of grass. The carpet department was, I could sense, unique: there were no overhead wires and no money ever seemed to change hands. The shopmen were different, too. A few were 'proper' shopmen: others wore caps and green baize aprons. (They, too, of course, were in the correct uniform for their job.)

Yet another acquaintance of my father was Mr Gibson, a jeweller and watchmaker in the arcade. Mr Gibson was urbane and polite, a pleasant, courteous man; imposing, too, for he was on the large side and always wore a dark suit, with a waistcoat and a thin gold watch-chain across it. It was he who once said to me, quietly and positively, 'Of course, Dr Adams has got more brains in his little finger than all the other doctors at the hospital put together; only he can't get them over.' It was true: my father's reticence and practice of saying what he had to say and letting people take it or leave it confined those who liked and trusted him to such as had the sensitivity to perceive what lay within. He was often brusque, but he was usually right as well.

With certain tradespeople in the town his friendship was warmer, involving an element of the comical which drew him out of his customary gravity; and of these I remember particularly the Merry Mosdell and the True Messiah.

My father was always extremely careful about money. No doubt he had to be. For instance, he himself never used toothpaste, which he considered a waste of money. Using nothing but water and a toothbrush, he succeeded in keeping his teeth into old age. Although he advised me against toothpaste ('Only making some nasty old millionaire richer, my boy') he didn't actually prohibit any of us from using it. I've always preferred to use it myself, but I never asked him for money to buy it.

Another expense which annoyed him was that of having his hair cut. To have it done at home was not an option, since that would have been low class and bad form. The best hairdressers in Newbury charged about one shilling and threepence, as far as I recall – too much for my father, anyway. What he wanted was a working-class hairdresser who would nevertheless understand who he was and treat him accordingly. After a good deal of reconnaissance, he discovered Mr Mosdell.

Mr Mosdell cut hair at sixpence a time. He cut it most acceptably. He was a quiet man with a low, pleasant voice – I suppose he may have been about fifty at the time – and I think he was probably deferential to everybody as part of the job. His shop, complete with striped pole outside, was conveniently situated at the junction of Bartholomew Street and Market Street. In the window was a canary in a cage, and most months of the year the gas fire was on. The shop had a characteristic, warm smell; of shaving soap, bay rum and some kind of emollient jelly used for cuts or sore necks and chins. It was a cosy place, and I never minded waiting there.

I realize now that it was chiefly the *sound* of Mr Mosdell and his shop which has remained with me. Mr Mosdell had some handicap to one of his feet, which caused his movement round the chair to consist of a firm, hard step with one foot followed by a quick slide with the other. As he worked he talked quietly, with pauses between, and as a rule kept the conversation two-way by asking questions. My father, who liked and respected him, tended to become more fluent than usual.

Mr M. (in a low voice, spoken only to the customer in the chair): 'They've been saying, Doctor' (snip, snip) 'that it's very likely to turn out' (snip, snip) 'a wet summer.' (Bonk, slide.) 'What do you think?'

Dr A.: ''Shouldn't be surprised. 'Dare say it'll rain if it can.'

Mr M.: 'If it rains in July' (snip, snip) ''may clear up for August, and that'll be good for the holidays, won't it? I'm just going to take the clippers now, Doctor. Will you be going away yourself at all?'

Dr A.: ''Shouldn't think so.' (In fact, as I have said, he never went away.) Half-singing, 'Oh, I *don't* like to be beside the seaside.'

Mr M. (bonk, slide): ''Doesn't suit everybody. 'Gets very crowded these days, Doctor, don't you think?' (Soft susurration of clippers.) 'Sit down, Mr Inch; I'm just on finished with Dr Adams.'

Dr A.: 'Yes, I do. Waste of money as a rule, I think. Much better stay here.'

The snug shop, with Mr Mosdell's conversation, which was much the same to everyone, was another thing that made you feel grown-up, for your hair needed cutting like anyone else's, and at the end you were always asked if you wanted anything on it, even though you'd said no many times. (Well, you might have changed, mightn't you? And it made a polite conclusion.)

However, there was more than this to Mr Mosdell. He was a serious self-educator. I don't know whether or not he was a member of the W.E.A., but he certainly studied a great deal. I remember sitting in his chair one morning while he snipped away, talking knowledgeably about the Pharaohs and the culture of ancient Egypt. Yet there was nothing in the least boastful or pretentious about this. He certainly wasn't showing off, and I think the proof is that although at the time I had known him for some while, this side of him came to me as a surprise. I only hope I didn't show it, for I was a tactless boy.

He once told me a story of his youth. 'When I was a young fellow, a friend of mine and me, we used to go out most Sundays and walk to Reading along the Bath Road. About eighteen miles, I suppose. Of course, in those days there were no cars, no motor-bikes, nothing o' that. It was a nice country walk: we used to pick the flowers. We'd get to Reading in the late afternoon and there was a little café which was always open on Sundays. We used to have eggs and bacon and sausages and from there it was only a bit of a stroll to the station. We'd catch the train back to Newbury in the evening.

'One Sunday evening we were just finishing up at the café when Reg, my friend, says to me "You sure of the time, Bill? Only it feels later, somehow." We found my watch had stopped! Dear oh law! We fairly pelted down to the station, just in time to see the train going out. It was the only train there was.'

'Whatever happened, Mr Mosdell?'

'Why, we walked it; every step of the way. 'Took us all night; we were tired out already, you see. And of course we knew our parents would have no idea what had happened to us or where we were. Three times we were stopped by policemen that night. We got back home just in time to shave and go to work.'

That would have been, I suppose, in the 'nineties or about the turn of the century, when the Bath Road was still much as it had always been. It must also have been before Mr Mosdell acquired his bad foot, however that came about.

My father always liked to mention at home that he was going to have his hair cut. I think he reckoned he had a bargain, and he certainly liked Mr Mosdell's conversation. 'I'm going to see the Merry Mosdell after I've been to the hospital,' he would say, 'so I may be late for lunch.' And off he would set in high good humour, perhaps singing

> 'She was once my Twanky-doodleum, but now alas *she*
> Plays kissy-kissy with an officer in the Artill*eree*.'

Or again,

> 'I should like to meet 'im with 'is nice, new tart.
> Then hup would go Antonio and 'is ice cream cart.'

In time the Merry Mosdell grew old, and my father bestirred himself on his behalf. In those days it was not altogether easy to get into almshouses in Newbury if you had no church connections. I don't know about the Merry Mosdell, but my father certainly had none. He had been a boy at a Woodard school (King's College, Taunton) in the eighteen-eighties, and this had effectually turned him against church-going for life; though he habitually read the Bible, and during the war told me that he used to pray for my brother and myself. However, he had enough local influence to get the Merry Mosdell and Mrs M. appointed to a comfortable almshouse in the Newtown Road, and thus confirmed his good will towards another friend.

In 1946, when my father lay dying, I used to use part of the precious petrol ration to drive the Merry Mosdell the mile from the

89

almshouse to our home, where he would shave my father in bed. The talk was the same. Like bird-song, it didn't change.

The True Messiah was likewise a fine stroke of domestic economy. Brassicas, and vegetables such as parsnips and carrots, we never needed to buy; nor apples, for we ate our own. But exotic fruit had to be bought. Market day in Newbury was Thursday, and of course fruit was sold cheaper there than in the fruiterers' shops. The marketeers didn't deliver, but none the more for that. It was easy enough – yes, it was – to park the car in the market-place. The problem was to find a market fruiterer of quality, for of course more than one of them tended to sell inferior stuff mixed up with what you saw on top. However, fortunately my father discovered the True Messiah – and believed.

J. Messaias and Co. were an authentic London East End Jewish family business, with a regular circuit round market-towns of the south country. Unless you had yourself been entirely lacking in wit and humour, it would have been difficult not to develop a relationship with the two brothers.

''Ere, Doctor, I'll tell yer what. Yer go'er watch aht yer don't get this 'ere vitamin deficiency what they're all on abaht naow.'

'Do you suffer from it?'

'Never in yer life! You 'ave a coupla pahnds o' these 'ere oranges wot I bin keeping for yer special, Doctor, and yer'll keep yerself away from yerself. 'Be dancin' on the 'igh wire. Wrap 'em up fer the doctor, Joe. 'Ere, 'e can't carry that lot. Tike 'em across to 'is car.'

Bananas, oranges, lemons, tomatoes and grapefruit were what my father bought, together with pears in season. (We grew pears, but not always successfully.) Grapefruit were the latest thing; quite a novelty. For some reason it became my brother's job to 'do' them in the evenings before he went to bed. This meant cutting them in half, loosening each segment and then sprinkling on the sugar 'to soak in' during the night. When he had finished, he put them away in the cool, stone-shelved larder against next morning's breakfast. Yet somehow I never took to them; too bitter.

'Thursday,' my father would say. 'What d'you want me to get from the True Messiah? Dee-ee-eply *wai*ling, dee-ee-eeply *wai*-ailing –'

Like all the upper middle classes in those days, I was brought up to regard Jews as beyond the pale (have you actually *read* Bulldog Drummond?), but it didn't count if the Jews were (a) reliable tradespeople or (b) ladies and gentlemen (like the Behrends). As I grew older, it amused me to observe how my mother was able without – apparently – the least sense of inconsistency, to switch almost between two breaths. 'Mrs Somerset says those nasty Jews are building a lot more houses up at Donnington.' 'Oh, Daddy' (for she called him Daddy, as we did), 'Mrs Cohen rang up, and said Wendy seemed to be getting over the 'flu very well, but could you go in and see her this afternoon or tomorrow morning? She asked about Katharine: we had quite a little chat.'

Now that I have two Jewish publishers, a Jewish accountant and a Jewish literary agent, I feel I have unravelled this strange tangle in which I became unconsciously enmeshed during childhood.

Mr Dalby was an archetypal figure; and indeed I can never go into a greenhouse without remembering him. He was head gardener to that same, fearsome Mr Baxendale, at his fine establishment above the race course, on the edge of Greenham Common. Mr Baxendale was a patient, and it was while sitting in the car one morning in the drive outside his house, waiting for my father, that I first watched red squirrels. They came down from a cedar and scampered about on the grass.

Mr Dalby was always correctly dressed as a head gardener, in shirt-sleeves, brown waistcoat with watch-chain, and a brown bowler hat. He had a short beard, too. Towards me he was grave though kindly in manner. He must have been a north countryman, for I remember how oddly it struck me that he talked of 'cootting off the boods'. His long, knowledgeable conversations with my father, as they walked together through the greenhouses, made me realize that gardening is not a job or a hobby but a sacred responsibility (as to Adam and Eve). Years later, when I first became a householder in Islington, and encountered a neighbour – a barrister – who did nothing whatever to his back garden, it embarrassed me as an indecency might have. I did not avoid him, but I avoided all mention of the matter, which seemed inexcusable.

Mr Dalby was an expert on carnations. They grew for him in hundreds; scarlet, white, streaked, lemon yellow, pink and darkest red. Their scent, above the still, ferny pool for the watering-cans, also seemed coloured; opulent and sumptuous as oriental robes, intensely aristocratic yet in no way frightening (like the parties). It was at one and the same time natural, yet a smell of culture and wealth, so that one thought of languid, slant-eyed beauties with fans, leaning upon curved bridges beneath cobalt-blue skies, gazing down at the golden fishes half visible below their roof of water-lilies. One carnation does not possess this magical quality. It requires hundreds, blooming on the stem in humid, windless air.

The scale on which Mr Dalby was able to do things enraptured me. He had about twelve people under him. There were whole beds of penstemon and gladioli, banks of lilies blooming half beneath the trees, expanses of bright red salvias, whole hothouses full of great mop-head chrysanthemums. Through my father I had already learned to love roses: it was through Mr Dalby that I learned to love ferns. I had hitherto had little or nothing to do with ferns. The south country, unlike, say, the Lake District, has few wild ones, and what there were in our conservatory had never caught my eye beyond the primulas and cyclamen. Mr Dalby had fern-houses; and to me, with my penchant for a surrounding refuge, for seclusion and solitude, these were wonderful places. There were no colours; only the various ranks of varied green rising all around: no scents except the smell of moist greenery; no sound except the infrequent drip of a tap into water. I used to try to be left alone in the fern-houses. Then – or so it seemed – the singularity of each fern – the undivided fronds of a Hart's Tongue, the lacy, weightless quality of a Maidenhair – could impart itself. You had to keep still, as though you were watching birds; ferns spoke in low voices. They didn't come at you like orchids (for Mr Dalby had those, too. Yet somehow they didn't bowl me over; he sensed this and wisely refrained from dwelling on them).

Mr Dalby once gave me a maidenhair fern for a personal possession. It was a scion, for I remember him potting it himself. It grew and thrived, and remained healthily in the conservatory until Oakdene was sold in 1939. What happened to it then I don't know.

V

Six years old. 1926: the year of the General Strike. I heard and knew little enough about that at the time, even though we had just got a wireless. (I remember it had a lidded cabinet and inside it a small picture of a polar bear. No doubt some true radio buff will be able to tell me what sort of a set it was.)

Day by day, at winter's end, the big field across from Monkey Lane was ploughed – the field which led across to the Bluebell Wood. If you were in the kitchen garden or the paddock, you would hear the horses come jingling and clinking up to the top of the field, followed by the ploughman's cry of 'Log off!' Then they would turn the plough and rest for a minute, until he called 'Log on!' and off they would set on the four or five hundred yards back to the Bluebell Wood. They did this steadily all day, with the plovers wheeling and calling above them.

In what seemed to me the early morning (while the Marguerite bird sang), I would hear the village children going by – walking down Wash Hill to school in Newbury, well over a mile away. Sometimes odd, ragged groups of adults and children were to be seen going the other way, pushing rough, home-made handcarts on old pram chassis.

'Who are those?' I asked my mother.

'Those are the Penwooders,' she told me.

Penwood is an extensive tract of woodland in north Hampshire (most of it's still there), between the Enborne brook and Highclere. In those days it was common for poor people from Newbury to trudge the two or three miles up Wash Hill and out to Penwood to pick up and bring home as much 'firing' (e.g., *The Tempest*, II, 2, 185–8:

93

Caliban: No more dams I'll make for fish,
        Nor fetch in firing
        At requiring,
        Nor scrape trenchering, nor wash dish . . .)

as they could handle. Hence the handcarts. But when you think how quickly wood burns, it still seems sad that they should have found these expeditions worth the time and trouble. They had little, if any, coal to keep in the bath. I used to feel uncomfortable and guilty to see them go by. They were hard-faced and ragged, and I knew I didn't deserve not to be.

Still, the time had now come when I too at least had to be up at a reasonable hour. I was going to school — to the mixed kindergarten of the Newbury Girls' High School at the foot of Wash Hill.

The school, which charged moderate fees to the respectable Newbury bourgeoisie, was run by Miss Jane Luker and Miss Cobb. They were true blue-stockings in the tradition of Miss Buss and Miss Beale.

      (Miss Buss and Miss Beale
      Cupid's darts do not feel.
      How different from us,
      Miss Beale and Miss Buss.)

To a six-year-old, Miss Luker ('Old Jane') seemed a remote and formidable figure, inspiring awe and even fear by her reserve, her incisive manner and lack of humour. However, in the kindergarten I had little enough to do with her. The kindergarten mistress, Miss Binns, was a good teacher, with a kindly warmth to which we could all relate. She seemed 'one of us': she understood us. I owe her a lot, for with her I found that I liked learning and enjoyed the business of becoming literate, doing elementary arithmetic and finding out how to tell the time. My school-mates were either friends already – Jean and Ann were both in the class – or soon became friends. There wasn't a bully or an enemy in the lot.

Whom else do I remember from those days? Well, principally Miss Langdon, perhaps the most sheerly kind-hearted person I have ever known. Miss Langdon surely deserves to be recalled. She was the

Nature mistress, and she also taught us what I suppose must be called Divinity (Bible stories). In both these subjects she was, as far as I was concerned, completely successful; that is to say, she excited my interest by being herself committed. I can't remember anyone ever wanting not to listen to Miss Langdon. That, surely, is the secret of good teaching. She was gentle to the point of simplicity; rather like Mrs Do-As-You-Would-Be-Done-By; and because she expected us to be good, we mostly were.

I remember her bringing into class a thick glass tank half-full of straw, from which she enticed a fine toad onto her hand. It had never occurred to me to take a toad onto my hand; but now I was eager to – and did. Spiders, too, I handled happily; and once, a mole. (They don't bite.)

At one time, while I was in the kindergarten, I began, at home, to make a sort of 'collection' of butterflies. This could not have been more crude or useless. I simply caught the butterflies – cabbage white, peacock, red admiral, painted lady – killed them by pinching off their antennae and heads, and put them loose, all together, in a cardboard shoe-box. One day, when Miss Langdon came to tea, I showed them to her. Without actually saying an unkind word, she succeeded so well in conveying her pity and revulsion that I then and there gave up, and never killed another butterfly.

One day in class she was telling us the story of Abraham and the sacrifice of Isaac (Genesis, Chapter XX). 'And,' she finished, 'Abraham was *so* glad that God had said he hadn't got to sacrifice his dear son Isaac after all.' My friend Denis Hodder put up his hand. 'Yes, Denis?' 'I bet Isaac was jolly glad, too.' I felt that Miss Langdon – dear, kind Miss Langdon – had rather asked for it.

She was a great stickler for correct, clear, rounded diction on all occasions, whether appropriate or otherwise: my sister, up in the sixth form, once told me how she – Miss Langdon – was directing a school play in which some people had to be shut up in a locked cupboard. They were beating on the door and calling, under Miss Langdon's tutelage, 'Let – us – *owt*! Let – us – *owt*!' This, too, became a family catchword.

Singing we learned, of course: and here I remember one experience which had a great effect on me. One morning I was called up by Miss Binns and given a note to deliver to Miss Luker in her study. This involved walking the whole length of the school while classes were going on. The long corridor was empty and very quiet, but from behind doors and frosted glass walls, as I passed them, came murmurs which showed that lessons were in progress. It was like hearing the Niebelungs working underground: nothing to see, but evidence enough that hundreds of people were close at hand and concentrated.

Suddenly I heard, though from a distance, a louder sound; the sound of singing. As I approached, I could recognize the tune. In the silence filling the school, a class were singing 'Dashing Away with the Smoothing-Iron'. I stood entranced. It seemed unbelievably beautiful, like the song of angels.

All the brio of the song, its immediacy and delightfully happy melody, hit me as few other musical experiences have ever quite done. I stood and listened entranced. It was all just for me; or that was how it seemed.

> 'Twas on a Thursday morning
> And there I saw my darling.
> She looked so neat and charming
> In every high degree. *

'Now then, young Richard, what do you think you're doing?' It was Miss Muirhead, the gym mistress, on her way down the corridor. I hurriedly explained and then I, too, went speedily off.

I said I had no enemies; but perhaps I had a sort of one. Anyway, we didn't get on, and I reckon it was mostly my fault. Ruth Hubbard was a hefty little girl, a bit older than I. She was the daughter of our village policeman, and so bitter sometimes was our scrapping that I rather wonder, now, that he didn't step round and have a word with Dr Adams. Small children, of course, always tend to quarrel unless they are restrained; but Ruth and I would often go at it, restrained or not. I discovered that although Ruth was bigger and stronger, with her it was mostly tongue. She didn't punch much. However, the tongue could be mortifying and painful, as I knew from dealings with my big sister. I reacted to Ruth with anger and resentment. Usually it was I who got the reproof from Miss Binns, partly because I deserved it and partly because I was a boy. In those days boys were taught that girls were to be treated with courtesy, looked after and protected. (I hope they

* Cecil Sharp, No. 341. Captain Lewis, 1909.

still are, but Ah whiles hae ma doots.)

One day our lot were taken out for a nature walk. Miss Binns, not Miss Langdon, was in charge. We went along the Buckingham Road and so to the Enborne Road, with its gravel pits on waste land west of the Grammar School. Here the ground was rough, broken by low mounds of left-over gravel and corresponding pits full of stinging nettles and brambles. Yellowhammers and green-finches flew up from bushes and yellow-and-black cinnabar moth caterpillars throve on groundsel and ragwort.

It was here that Ruth and I began to quarrel once again. I can't remember what about; only that this time it was unusually bitter. It grew worse and worse, until I lost my temper completely. Reckless what I did, I took a step forward and pushed Ruth. What happened next had been no part of my intention. She staggered backwards, lost her balance, screamed and went over the edge of a pit into the nettles.

I was aghast. It seemed – and perhaps was – the worst thing I had ever done. Whatever would happen? Somehow Ruth scrambled out, sobbing bitterly. There was no fight left in her. Her face was all covered in white lumps, and her arms and knees too. I had never seen such a sight. She was obviously in horrible pain.

And now came something which I still feel to have been unjust. Miss Binns refused to take Ruth's part. 'It was *your* fault, Ruth,' she said. 'You started it.' I didn't think she had, but seeing which way the wind was blowing, I kept quiet. So did the others. All the way home poor Ruth was crying and pressing her lumpy face, but Miss Binns remained like flint. Ashamed, I had no more quarrels with Ruth for a long time.

Yet this episode taught me something else besides. When you think – or even if you feel sure – you're in the wrong, keep quiet. You may be lucky – even inexplicably lucky. If there is a judge and a ruler over you, you're under no moral obligation to blame yourself. The thing will be sorted out and if they blame you, then you can start, if you feel it, admitting wrong. But to *start* by admitting wrong – is wrong. You may not have been. You may have a natural tendency to think yourself in the wrong whether you are or not. Leave it, initially, to the judge, who is detached. (Unless, of course, you have reason to think he isn't.) I'm still sorry for Ruth: I think she was unjustly blamed, and considering her serious pain, unkindly treated (which was unlike Miss Binns). But perhaps I'm still wrong?

Martin Butcher was something else. He gave most of us the willies. No one could make him out. I think he must have been one of the unhappiest people I have ever known. Solitary, subservient and silent, he kept himself apart, even in playtime. He seemed life-defeated: there was no least go in him. Invitations to join in play he would quietly refuse. No one ever knew him to sing. When you could hear him – which wasn't often, for he seldom spoke – he had a low voice and a noticeable Berkshire accent, which put us snobbish little middle-classers off. The quality of his work was poor. At kindergarten level we weren't in competition, but you couldn't help knowing about Martin, from the way Miss Binns would look over his shoulder and say 'No, not quite like that, Martin,' or again 'Come along, Martin, don't copy Richard's book any more.' But he was sly and unscrupulous in his efforts to keep out of trouble, and would not only copy your book but, as though desperate, pinch your india-rubber to copy your later corrections. (We worked in pencil, of course.) The flesh-creeping thing about him was that he so obviously hated the whole set-up and was beyond any attempt to fit in or make friends. He lived in another world, where he simply suffered. Lacking all aggression, he had no resort but to keep his head down. We let him. It might, we felt, be Miss Binns's job to try to break the barrier and get him out. It certainly wasn't ours.

One episode I recall about Martin may, I think, throw a swift, momentary shaft into a murky woodshed. One day Miss Binns, going round the form to look at our work, stopped at Martin and said 'Not coloured, Martin? Where are the crayons you had on Tuesday?' In a low, expressionless voice he replied 'Dad took 'em away.' (We didn't refer to our fathers as 'Dad'.) It was, plainly, Miss Binns rather than Martin who felt embarrassed and anxious to end the conversation. What I have never understood – setting other considerations aside – is why, given that Martin's father had presumably agreed to send him to the High School, he should take away his crayons. But Martin's world was beyond guessing or comprehension.

He represented something new to me – something hitherto unexperienced. I suppose all of us – a few consciously but most unconsciously – felt the same. I had never before come up against someone who was openly unhappy all the time, as though that were his natural condition. Martin didn't try to do anything about his unhappiness; he merely endured it; for him it was normality. As a child of six or seven years old I had always, unthinkingly, taken it for granted that happiness was the natural condition of myself and all children – all those whom I knew, anyway. Martin was unhappy as a matter of course. In all actuality he had neither will nor power – so it seemed – to take a step to meet you. In such a case children feel no particular obligation. Faced with something they don't understand, they do their best to ignore it. If Martin had some strange gestalt of unhappiness, it was no business of ours to go out of our way to penetrate or mitigate it. The class distinction thing made it worse. Since we didn't fear him, his presence embarrassed and irritated us. We felt no particular pity for this poor creature who had nothing to say to us, whose home was, one could infer, very different from any of ours and who patently disliked his life. But beneath this – to me, at any rate – lay something more frightening. It was possible for a boy – here it was, before your eyes – to be wretched all the time and to have no way out. What *did* he want? What *would* he have liked? No one knew: he didn't know himself. He'd never known anything he liked. This actuality was disturbing and best avoided. However – as will be plain by now – I never, from that day to this, entirely got Martin off my mind. Things ought not to be like that for anybody: but they are. To come up against this – and instinctively to duck – is part of growing up.

Becoming literate was also part of growing up. I can't remember any particular moment when I realized that I could read – read anything I wanted to and read for pleasure. Nor can I recall any particular book as being the first I read. Nevertheless, before I was eight I had become a passionate reader. This was better than having to go to parties and getting into trouble for saying the wrong thing: better than the uncontrollable world of real people and their crushing remarks which often hurt so much more than they can have been meant to. A printed story was predicted. It was there, in the book, and my pleasurable task was simply to follow it, to experience it as though it were real, to seek it out to the end. Poetry was also predicted, but here there was the added delight of memorability. If you read a poem often enough, it stuck in your mind. The sound, the metre and the mood they generated were what came across to me. The meaning – the real meaning – often escaped me: it didn't matter. For example, a poem I discovered for myself and have more or less had on board ever since is Thomas Hardy's 'Friends Beyond'. The mood – and, unconsciously, the effect of the metre – seemed to me, at that age, kindly and reassuring. These nice, dead people were still around, talking to Thomas Hardy and not in the least frightening. The characteristic Hardyesque irony completely passed me by. But no doubt it would pass by any young child.

Reading was highly reassuring. It was the perfect escape – into other worlds which often seemed more valid and valuable than the real one. And no one found fault with you or blamed you for it: no, they were pleased to see you reading. And the thing that happened in books didn't evanesce, like last Christmas or yesterday's picnic. They stayed put, to become familiar, to be re-experienced as often as you wanted; and as they were dwelt on they grew in grace and power. Jim Hawkins was for ever and ever poised on the cross-trees. 'One more step, Mr Hands, and I'll blow your brains out!' That stuck all right. Or the Artful Dodger sidled across the road to the exhausted Oliver. 'Hullo! my covey, what's the row?' (The Dodger's dialogue throughout, culminating in his glorious appearance before the magistrates, has been a resource and solace to me for years. But again, the pathos of the Dodger's braggadocio escapes a child.) The permanence of books and the memorability of dialogue are well up among the most supportive things I have ever found. Becoming literate put me in possession of a new expanse, constituting a better bolt-hole than I could have dreamt of; far better than being behind the bedroom door at the Punch and Judy party. Words, and my own imagination, could open wider prospects and make the world more lucid and vivid – yes, and enjoyable – than I had known to be possible. Years later, when I was grown-up and living in Islington, I was privileged to pass this lot on to a friend, an East End boy. 'I never knew there *were* such books,' he said to me.

But there was a reverse side. I came upon it, of course, unaware: I couldn't have foreseen it. Stories and poems reflect all aspects of human experience, not just the pleasant ones. They include grief and fear. It didn't take long to discover that books could upset you a great deal. What was the first to do so? I don't know – I can't remember. Perhaps it may have been the heroic, self-sacrificing death of Elzevir Block (after years of undeserved imprisonment) at the end of *Moonfleet*. Ernest Thompson Seton was liable to upset you *passim*, without any warning at all. Scotty the hunter killed Krag, the Kootenay Ram. Raggylug's mother was pursued onto the ice, fell through it and drowned. The nest-building sparrow hanged itself in a loop of horsehair. Uncle Remus's stories of Brer Rabbit were usually delightful (I loved the dialect – reading it so as to hear it in my head), but did Brer Rabbit really murder Brer Wolf by pouring boiling water on him through holes bored in the lid of a chest?

Uncle Tom's Cabin was the book which upset me to the point of something approaching a small nervous breakdown. I can't recall now how the book came into my hands, but certainly no one in the family foresaw that it was going to have such a devastating effect on me. A child takes everything at face value and has no discrimination or standards of comparison. For what it was worth, I knew that *Uncle Tom's Cabin* was a book that *had* been read and taken seriously by enormous numbers of grown-up people, and that it had been influential in bringing black slavery to an end. I wanted to know what it could all be about. Obviously, this was a great book and something I was going to enjoy reading. It turned out a quite unexpected disclosure, a journey to levels of grief which I had never imagined. People laugh at little Eva now: she has become a symbol representing the worst kind of Victorian sentimental mush. A child, absorbed in the story, cannot see her in this way and has no mental equipment with which to criticize Mrs Beecher Stowe's outlook and narrative style. I found Eva's relationship with Topsy entirely convincing and unlike anything I had ever come across elsewhere. Eva's death came as a bad shock. It had never occurred to me that children died, and in trying to talk about it I didn't get much reciprocity from the parents of poor Robert. I had to weep and wonder almost by myself; although the housemaid, kind girl, was comforting.

There was worse to come. Simon Legree, his dreadful plantation and his two black torturers Sambo and Quimbo have never really left me. In an odd way it was all worse because I couldn't understand about Cassie. Why was she there? If I couldn't understand about Cassie, perhaps there were other, more upsetting things that I couldn't understand. But I understood all right about Uncle Tom, and I believed every word of it. I'm afraid I must have been a bit of a trial to the family for a day or two at least. To someone who tried to comfort me by saying 'It didn't really happen', I answered 'No, but I bet something like it did.' I had, after all, in effect been told that that was so.

Many years later, when I came to write *Shardik*, I found that the inexorable course of the story compelled me to create the character of Genshed. He had to be the most wicked, cruel man I could devise. Meditating, I concluded that in fiction there were really two kinds of wicked man: a rich wicked man, like Grandison in *Daniel Deronda*; that is to say, a man rich enough to be wicked without being physically violent. And a poor wicked man, like Mr Squeers. Genshed was deliberately modelled on Simon Legree, except, of course, that his victims were not blacks but children. The critic Edward Blishen, writing about *Shardik*, showed himself under the curious misapprehension that it was meant to be read by children, and accordingly warned all his readers not to let any child come near it. Well, I underwent Simon Legree as a child and, whatever the sentimentality of Harriet Beecher Stowe, he has remained with me these sixty years. Yet as a child it was less horror of Simon Legree which obsessed me than grief for Uncle Tom.

If you come to think about it, the relative naiveté and narrative simplicity of Mrs Beecher Stowe's approach to the reader were essential to my absorption and my passionate feelings of grief. I was eight years old: if it had been *King Lear* or *Jude the Obscure* I wouldn't have been able to take it in.

Worse than the grief emanating from stories and poetry was fear. Grief at least let you remain yourself, but fear could drive you distraught. I remember in particular one summer evening. I had gone to bed as usual, but was nowadays allowed to read until I was ready to lie down and go to sleep. I was reading the ghost stories of Algernon Blackwood (the books mostly came from my sister, who was generous in lending them and often left me simply to help myself from her shelves) and began upon 'Ancient Sorceries'. I don't know how long I took to finish it; an hour, perhaps. In the twilight the sinister, mysterious silence of the isolated little French town intensified round me and the people – the landlady, her daughter and the others – the people who turned into cats at night, came slinking into the tail of the eye and vanished, sometimes posturing, sometimes gliding round corners, never disclosing exactly what their menace was. That I did not really understand what I was reading about – witchcraft – if anything made the fear worse. It was something bad, something malign. Somewhere at the bottom of it was the Devil. At the top of it were the trance-like silence – *à cause du sommeil et à cause des chats* (I could work out what that meant, near enough) – and the half-seen, sidling cats. Conscientiously trying to go to sleep, I lay sweating, every now and then starting up with terror in my own familiar bedroom. I don't know why I didn't go downstairs to seek comfort. No one would have been cross: I would have been met with kindness. Yet somehow I remained there, helpless in the fantasy of the still town and the gathering cats.

A curious feature of all this is that in the story the witches – the cats – are not actually seeking to harm or physically to hurt the English visitor to their town. Their aim is to seduce him, to make him one of themselves; to effect, in some strange way, his transit into their world of the fifteenth century. It is rather the atmosphere of seclusion and mounting peril – the feeling of being helpless in a whirlpool – which is so terrifying. When my mother came up to bed, I suppose about quarter past ten, I was in a sorry state. She, however, was completely reassuring; she always was. Simply by her presence and her own natural separation from and sensible immunity to all such things, she could disperse the spectres and restore the senses to their proper command. The fear simply went away and, although it sometimes troubled me later, when I was alone, it gradually diminished and became diluted until I could cope with it.

Cruelty was upsetting in a different way. I have since learned that, setting aside all question of morals, conscience and what we would like to believe we think, we are all by disposition either sadistic or masochistic. That is, we identify naturally either with the tormentor or the victim. I identified with the victim, and how. In those days, the late nineteen-twenties and early 'thirties, only a handful of scoffed-at innovators knew anything about Freud and his world-changing discoveries. Nobody connected cruelty with sexual excitement. On reflection, this is surely an extraordinary state of affairs. What I am trying to explain is that in those days, incredible as it may seem to younger people today, sexual fantasies and imaginings were regarded as morally worse and much more unmentionable than cruelty. Sexual things simply 'didn't exist'. People pretended they hadn't heard you. You might acquire a bad reputation and people would drop you: I have known boys to whom it happened. Yet you could talk without causing embarrassment about cruelty – for instance, the well at Cawnpore in the Indian Mutiny. You couldn't talk about sex. The safety curtain fell immediately, like a portcullis.

What I am calling an extraordinary state of affairs is that this condition of the collective mind had brought about a stange moral inversion. I assume that most people today would agree that it is natural and harmless for people to entertain sexual thoughts – we all do, anyway – but that the idea of dwelling on cruelty is disagreeable; we wouldn't like to think that anyone we loved was prone to this. If it had been suggested to people in the nineteen-twenties that writing or talking about cruelty was at all connected with sex, they would have denied it vigorously and the person who suggested it would have been 'cut'. If they had actually come to believe it, they would have been overcome with mortification, because to them the idea of sex was far more embarrassing than the idea of cruelty. This seems strange now, but it was so: and consequently the whole nature of society was different.

In those days cruel but never explicitly sexual fantasies, bad enough to trouble any reasonably sensitive person, were a common feature of popular fiction. (As a matter of fact, there are some nasty and quite unnecessary things in *Humphry Clinker*, come to that; but in those days I hadn't read *Humphry Clinker*.) I was upset by things in R. M. Ballantyne, in H. G. Wells and in Conan Doyle, the last of whom, I still think, possessed a foully sadistic imagination. 'Sapper', too – a very popular writer of those days – can't be exonerated. And these writers were imitated in that regard by the lesser people who wrote for boys' magazines. Indeed, a certain amount of cruelty seemed almost obligatory in boys' magazine fiction, and often there was no mistaking the note of relish. People in those days not only knew nothing of sadism: they were also ignorant of the relevance and validity of fantasy to the psyche and to real life. Dreams were all rubbish, and fantasy was what Jung sardonically called 'nothing but': that is, a thing on its own, unconnected with the personality of the fantasist.

A lot of the nastiness just ran off the reader harmlessly. Most little boys aren't easily upset, and rubbish, being rubbish, soon evaporates. But when an author writes memorably and is himself as good as mad, like Edgar Allan Poe, it is another matter. Of course, I had no business to be reading Edgar Allan Poe at my age. It should have been kept from me. But my father was by temperament disinclined to interfere or put his foot down – what he lacked, as Mr Gibson had as good as said, was self-assertion – while my mother, though kind and understanding when you were troubled, didn't read books much and was not really conscious of them as influential and in certain ways larger than life. Little by little, I was becoming a compulsive reader, perhaps a trifle escapist, my rudimentary notions of self-respect to a certain extent tied up with reading. If a book enjoyed a high reputation, that was enough to make me feel that I at any rate hoped to read it. Sometimes I had to admit myself baffled. I could read *Oliver Twist, Nicholas Nickleby* and *The Old Curiosity Shop*, but I was defeated by *Dombey and Son* and *A Tale of Two Cities*.

Edgar Allan Poe gave me, as they say, the screaming hab-dabs. Were there really people like the man in 'The Black Cat'? I knew there were not – nor any like Montresor in 'The Cask of Amontillado'. These were creatures of a horrible fancy. But the force and credibility of Poe's narrative style reft you out of your world into his and held you gripped there. You had to read on. There is a deliberation and an absence of haste about Poe – some people might even say he is long-winded – which, if you are a submissive and conscientious reader, slowly enmeshes you and leads you step by step to the catastrophe. The trouble was that he wasn't pretending, like M. R. James. I felt that he himself believed every word of what he wrote. And even when the 'goodies' won, as in 'Hopfrog', the dénouement was so terrible as to leave me unnerved.

However, not all my reading (I'm glad to say) was as unsuitably advanced for my age as this; for a lot of the time I read undemanding stuff – honest tripe. The most enjoyable and memorable of these lighter books had been published during the first two decades of the century – before I was born: once again, they came from my sister. I wonder whether anyone reads them now. I fear not, for they are long out of print (in their beautiful, hardback, illustrated editions) and today children's books have become an industry: no one reads yesterday's much. But surely W. M. Letts's *The Story Spinner* would be worth reprinting? I still have my sister's copy of *Why-Why and Tom-Cat*, written under the nom-de-plume of 'Brown Linnet', and I hope my grandchildren are going to enjoy it as much as I did. Madeleine Nightingale's *Tony O'Dreams* has charm and humour, although as you get older you can't help but perceive its sugary sentimentality. Still, *Little Lord Fauntleroy* has plenty of that, and children still read it. They read Frances Hodgson Burnett's *The Secret Garden*, too.

Our edition of Edward Lear was the one illustrated by Leslie Brooke, and I don't think there could be a better. I still love the pictures. My mother used to read it to me (the actual title is *Nonsense Songs* and the publisher was Warne), and naturally it wasn't long before most of it had soaked in and I had it by heart. I can still run through 'The Jumblies', 'The Dong' or 'Uncle Arly' if I can't go to sleep. It's extraordinary how moving and memorable they are.

I have already mentioned my father reading *Dr Dolittle* to me. I understand that the Dolittle books are currently out of favour, on account, apparently, of the character of Prince Bumpo. It seems a pity to set aside a canon of some nine or ten books – though of varying quality, the last four being of little account, I reckon – which have a lot of merit and remain very readable to and by children. Their strongest characteristic, I think, is their buoyant optimism, even though this is often sentimental. For example, when the Doctor, Bumpo and Long Arrow defend Popsipetal against the Bagjagderags, apparently no one gets killed. Nevertheless, the books have consistency and integrity: they are nowhere false. Sentimental they may be, but they possess a decency and rectitude of their own, despite the lack of any spiritual dimension. And there is nothing amiss with the Doctor's passionate concern about the abuse of animals. He turned me against circuses, fur coats and other such evil things – for life.

Some of the most popular light reading for children during the 'twenties and early 'thirties were the *William* books of Richmal Crompton. The only thing wrong with William is that he went on too long; up to the Second World War, into it and beyond. He was overtaken by a changing world. He ceased to be what he had begun as – an amusing, topical, satirical and at times even damaging reflection of the 'twenties, the days of short skirts, motor-bikes and Oxford bags, bobbed hair and long cigarette holders. Ah, and the tramps, whom everyone feared and too few pitied; the disguised Bolshevik spies; the local amateur dramatic societies, and the Seaside, and spiritualism, and the earnest ladies and the Band of Hope! This is what gave the early William books their authenticity and their sting. William himself, of course, was a gratefully received anti-hero, in the spirit of the times. The great thing was that he was no prig. Of all things he detested a prig. I have, in the past, said in print that William – dirty, sceptical, cunning and ill-spoken - was a much-needed antithesis to Christopher Robin, but if this was so, it cannot have been deliberate, for the first William book came out in 1922 and *When We Were Very Young* did not appear until 1924. No, I think the irritation that created William and ensured his popular success goes back not only to Little Lord Fauntleroy, but also to the whole notion – late Victorian and persisting well into the twentieth century – of children as beautiful, innocent little creatures, whose charming world must not be touched with the rough hand of grown-up reality. Lewis Carroll had a gentle go at this in the *Alice* books: for example, Alice, called upon by the Caterpillar to recite 'You are old, Father William', comes up with a brilliant parody which has eclipsed the original. Yet Carroll himself, as he shows clearly, remained a member of the 'fairy creatures' school. *Sylvie and Bruno* is not easy to swallow nowadays. If Richmal Crompton was consciously reacting against anyone, it was probably Rose Fyleman ('There are Fairies at the Bottom of our Garden') and certain others like my Madeleine Nightingale, whose Tony O'Dreams is very starry-eyed and chivalrous.

After the First World War (though of course I knew nothing about this at the time) there was a general reaction against the accepted social values of pre-war days. It became fashionable for young people to be 'rather fast'. There was much media attention to cocktails, divorces, female independence, Noel Coward, Chicago gangsters, fast sports cars, very long woolly scarves and so on. People called each other 'Old Thing'. Along with these reactive features, society liked and bought William Brown.

He was a logical part of the whole reaction, Jung's archetypal Trickster in person. The memorable illustrations, by Thomas Henry, reflect this perfectly. They are idiosyncratic, exaggerated, cartoon-like, reminiscent of illustrations to *Punch* jokes. Above all, they are of the period, the time when the full-scale 'respectability' of Edwardian days and of the next decade were melting towards the 'thirties; talking pictures, charabanc outings, hikers and the Slump. The whole point of William was that he outraged respectability – vicars, visiting lecturers, poets, rich war profiteers and so on. That is the joke, time after time, and I could enjoy reading it all right – up to a point. The characters were, perhaps, rather puppets. The stories tended to be repetitive, and similar situations used to recur. The dialogue lacked the bite of 'Hullo! my covey, what's the row?' And the plots were often coincidental and contrived; you knew they were – like P. G. Wodehouse – but you went on reading, because it was easy. They indulged your laziness, really.

I think I would have to admit, if asked, that during my childhood I did become something of a book snob. I don't mean that I boasted about it – it certainly wouldn't have got me far with those about me if I had – but I did slip into the way of secretly giving myself credit for having read this book and that. (I thought I knew what was creditable and what wasn't: the credit depended upon what I had heard grown-up people say about a book. Whence else could it come? I knew I was just a learner.) I'm not at all sure that this 'snobbery' was my fault; and come to that, I'm not at all sure it *was* a fault. My sister, now seventeen or eighteen, had grown into a true scholar: that is to say, she had set her sights on academic distinction. She was head girl at Miss Luker's and soon going up to Girton. I admired my sister, and was very ready to accept her taste and guidance (though she never cared to read Dickens; Henry James was more her mark, and him, of course, I never even attempted). She would say things like 'Even little beastly Richard could read this, I should think.' (It might be Eden Philpotts, J. C. Squire or some such.) I would set about reading the book and determine to finish it one way or another. Usually I enjoyed it.

I believe that on balance the frame of mind I had is defensible. I wouldn't mind a child of mine reading for inward prestige (one did, I rather fancy), provided she wasn't just wasting her time and going cross-eyed with perplexity. I think that probably most people feel secretly proud of having read enduring books and a bit regretful about the ones they haven't read. Faced with the literacy of Sir Angus Wilson or my friend John Wain, I feel I have to some extent wasted my reading life: I wish I had read more. As to privately felt 'snob-value' reading in childhood, my defence is first, that everyone knows that it takes a certain amount of determination and persistence to read a book that extends you, and if you don't read books that extend you, you never learn or progress at all. Secondly, you have to get new ideas from somewhere, and open your horizon: also, you hope to develop a sense of style and to become able to distinguish between good writing and bad; between old writing and new, too, e.g., Defoe and, well – Alison Lurie. A child ought to feel himself in credit for having voluntarily tackled a book that stretches his mind and capacity. That's one thing. I *don't* approve of parents giving a child a book-list and pressing him or her to work through it. I know one man who has grown up a virtual non-reader on account of just that sort of thing.

I might add that for anyone considering an academic career, especially in the humanities, a developed ability in adolescence to read and grasp a book recommended by one's schoolmaster or tutor is virtually essential.

I don't know whether or not I was taking on too much when I accepted *The Pilgrim's Progress* before I was nine. It came about in this way. I had, of course, heard a lot about *The Pilgrim's Progress*: that was unavoidable. In those days most educated people would have been ashamed to admit that they had not read this enormously influential book. They would often quote from it, consciously or unconsciously, in daily speech. 'Now you mustn't get into a Slough of Despond.' 'Honestly, it's a real Vanity Fair down there.' Paul Fussell, in one of his books about the Great War, includes a passage about the influence of *The Pilgrim's Progress* on the war poets – Graves, Blunden, Sassoon, Owen, Rosenberg. After the Bible, it was the obligatory devotional work: I knew that. But I knew something else, too. It was a *story*; a story about a man and a journey. So if it was a story, you could read it. The way people talked, you ought to feel privileged to.

However, for some reason or other there wasn't a copy in the house; I don't know why. *The Pilgrim's Progress* finally came into my hands through Thorn the gardener. Thorn was a nice fellow – what used, in those days, to be called 'steady and reliable' – a chapel man and a teetotaller. (As I grew older my father used to let him take me to football matches: to watch Reading, who were then in the third division south, I rather think, and frequently lost.) Thorn used to read a good deal, and I would often find myself chatting to him, as he dug up potatoes or planted out wallflowers, about Sir Nigel and the White Company, or the Time Machine. One day he offered to lend me 'the most wonderful book in the world'. It turned out, of course, to be *The Pilgrim's Progress*, in a little, green-cloth-bound edition measuring perhaps four and a quarter inches square. I took it gratefully, noticing amongst other things that it wasn't very long.

It was full of pictures and conversations! The pictures were marginal, indenting the text. They were some sort of engraving, I suppose. Each was about half an inch square, and some were certainly frightening. I remember one of – is it Ignorance? – pitching over the sheer cliff in the thunderstorm. Apollyon was disturbing, too. But Christian always came out on top, ho! ho!

The doctrinal conversations, of course, were what effectively split the book in two, as far as I was concerned. The narrative I could follow easily enough and enjoy: it was highly imaginative and gripping. The conversations were rather wearisome, and I personally still think the book could do with fewer of them: they lack the invention, excitement and vividness of the narrative. All the same, I had determined that I was going to read the book, and through these dialogues I conscientiously ploughed. One day, my sister was kind enough to read some of it to me, and after reading a fair piece of one of Christian's doctrinal set-tos with the unworthy, suggested that we should skip it. I said no.

'But, Richard,' she protested, 'I could go on reading the same bit over and over again and you wouldn't even notice!' I still begged her not to leave anything out. I suppose it was a case of 'Don't treat me like an infant! Treat me like a grown-up!' Since I was so much younger than anyone else in the family, this was a constant feature of my childhood: I hated thinking that allowances were being made for me.

Katharine went on reading, and after a bit I realized that she *was* reading a passage over again and said so. To spot it was no credit to me: it was an obvious line: 'Do you think I am such a fool?' All the same, I decided there was a lot of sense in what she said, and for the rest of the book I went rather lightly through the dialogues.

I'm not sure whether *The Pilgrim's Progress* is worth reading when you're eight (though when I came to re-read it, some ten years later, I found I had retained the incidents of the narrative well), but I'm sure enough that it's worth reading. The story is unique – as far as I know there's nothing at all like it in English literature. It is memorably inventive and very well written; and it constitutes a kind of forerunner of the English novel. C. S. Lewis, Ronald Blythe and Sir Christopher Hill have said a great deal more in its praise. For a child, I think, its main quality is that it is about a hero who has thrilling adventures, and wins.

VI

It must have been about this time that I became aware that I had a godfather, and that he was a godfather both to admire and to like. His name was Colonel Richard Elkington, and I am named after him. He was a close friend of my father and lived out at Adbury Holt, a mile or two south of Newbury. A story remained popular in our family of how, one day at the Newbury races, my father was wearing a pair of brightly coloured socks, with which he was rather pleased, when Colonel Elkington came up to him and said 'Hallo, Flash Alf!' After this coloured socks, in our family, were always referred to as 'Alfreds'.

However, there was a whole lot more to Colonel Elkington than coming up with snappy cracks at the races. His tale is a strange one. I am not sure that I recall it with complete accuracy, but I will tell what I believe I was told. At the outbreak of the First World War, Colonel Elkington – a regular officer, of course – was commanding an infantry battalion. The battalion formed part of the British Expeditionary Force – the Old Contemptibles – and took part in the battle of Mons and the subsequent retreat.

One evening during the retreat, Colonel Elkington had carried out orders in placing his battalion in and around a French village, prepared to defend it. There was still a fair amount of light left when a German officer came to battalion headquarters under a flag of truce. (At the beginning of the war, there was less sheer hostility between participants than later: everyone has heard of the fraternization of Christmas, 1914.) The German officer suggested to Colonel Elkington that he might quite practicably re-position his battalion half a mile back, out of the village. It would, he thought, make no difference whatever to the battalion's strategic advantage (or to anyone else's near them), but it would make a lot of difference

Left: My father (above) aged about 35, with Uncle Ernest and the dog Esau. Circa 1905

Above: My mother with my brother John, 1913

Myself, aged 3, 1923

Below: My father on the lawn at Oakdene, circa 1932. Note:
(a) Climbing roses on the verandah pilasters
(b) Rats' dinner to right of my father's feet

Left: My brother John on the lawn with the cat, Mittens, circa 1934

Left: My mother and myself on the verandah, circa 1928

Far left: Matron Miss Adamson at the Newbury & District Hospital, circa 1927

A typical view of pines and heather on Greenham Common as it was before the Second World War. The Common was three miles long by a mile across, and virtually entirely accessible to the public

The Market Place at Newbury, circa 1912. It remained much the same during my childhood in the 'twenties and 'thirties, except that a few cars appeared

A typical reach of the River Kennet in the vicinity of Newbury. The wide water-meadow and deep verge of riparian plants are characteristic

Mr. Stow, circa 1933

Below: Myself, aged 10, as a schoolboy at Horris Hill, in 1930. (No self-respecting Horris Hill boy would have let himself be photographed wearing a school cap)

Bottom: The west front of Horris Hill, circa 1930

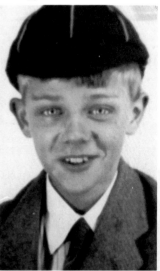

Mr. Liddell

Mr. Morris

Mr. Delmé-Radcliffe

Mr. McIntyre

Mr. Fussell

Left: Mr. Arnold, circa 1938
The quad at Bradfield, from the top of the Chapel
Tower

ΧΑΙΡΕΜΑΛΩΓΗΡΑΙΕΣΟΦΟΚΛΕΕΣΑΝΘΟΣΑΟΙΔΩΝ

The Greek theatre

'Oedipus Tyrannos' in 1937. Oedipus (John
Stewart) with the blind Teiresias and his
guiding boy, watched by the Chorus

to the village full of civilians, because as things stood the Germans were going to have to shell it.

Colonel Elkington, a humane man, thought it over and decided that the German officer was about right. As he sat thinking, no doubt he could see the girls and the children in the streets, making friends with his soldiers, as they always do. I don't know how long he had to make up his mind, but anyway he took the battalion back to a fresh position behind the village.

The result of this, at the conclusion of the 1914 campaign, was a court-martial. I don't know what the sentence was, but as the story was told to me, Colonel Elkington left the army. It may very well have been his own decision. He joined the Foreign Legion and served in it throughout the rest of the war. However, he was not without friends who knew his worth, and when the war was at last over there was pressure to get the case re-opened. Finally, the whole thing was reviewed and the Colonel was reinstated without a stain on his character.

The Elkingtons were a well-known local family and I have always felt proud of my godfather, who never failed, by the way, to come down handsome at Christmas and on my birthday. His nephew, Sir Richard des Voeux, commanded 156 Parachute Battalion at Arnhem, where he was killed.

Being a doctor's son, I naturally had a certain amount to do with the hospital, which was a mile away from our home, at the foot of Wash Hill. My father, of course, was always in and out, and not infrequently I might be with him. The hospital was a thriving one. Entirely privately supported, it was the pride of Newbury. Every ball, every fête, every Boy Scouts' melarky was in aid of the hospital. The doctors, the matron and the sisters were local personalities. It was an integral part of Adams family life.

My first memory of the hospital goes back to when I was very small – I think, three. I had a nasty earache and my father (ever mindful of Robert, no doubt) decided to take me down to the hospital, where I was put to bed. All the time, I seemed to be hearing a continual, disturbing whispering and susurration, as of leaves, which gave me no peace. Someone came up to me and asked 'Can you tell me in what way it hurts, dear – how you feel?' I replied 'There's a garden in my ear.' I had not experienced the last of that ear, as will be told.

The two senior sisters at the hospital were powers in their own right. Their names were Sister Tomlinson and Sister Dickinson – Sister Tommy and Sister Dickie. They were generally credited with a lot of medical wisdom, and the doctors used to remark humorously that they wouldn't dream of prescribing or doing anything for a patient without either Sister's approval. They were kindly dragons – my goodness, how they worked, too! – and to me, as I grew to know them, they seemed more and more like aunts. ('Hullo, young Richard; out of my way, now!')

But the nicest person in the hospital, and one of the fondest memories of my life – like Miss Langdon – was Matron Miss Adamson. She was, perhaps, rather an unexpected person to be a matron. She was then in her forties, I would now guess, with fine features and swept-back, white hair. She was quietly spoken and very gentle. Indeed, I never heard her raise her voice. To me she was, quite simply, a second mother. She was someone to whom I could tell everything (such as the Ruth Hubbard problem), and find her invariably understanding and kind. To me, of course, she, as Matron, assured, cool, slim and nice-looking in her dark blue uniform and flowing white head-dress, was a figure to be looked up to and trusted implicitly. The respect with which everyone treated her was plain to be seen. But they weren't free to come into her private room, as I was. She evidently liked me, and this meant a great deal, because a lot of grown-up people decidedly did not. I was spoilt, wayward and inconsiderate: but I was much less so with Matron, because there was something about her which made you behave as you should. The general atmosphere – even the characteristic smell – of the hospital, too, inclined a small boy towards a certain restraint. I knew well enough that this was a place where people came because they were ill – many gravely ill – and that my father's livelihood and working life were centred on it. It was a place to which to come and talk seriously to Matron: it wasn't a place to kick up your heels.

The hospital possessed great numbers of toys and games, and Matron used to let me play with these, and sometimes let me borrow them. I recall in particular a toy theatre, the like of which I had never seen. The cast were two-dimensional, on stout cardboard and properly jointed. At their backs were horizontal strips of sticking-plaster. In these you inserted one arm of a stiff,

T-shaped wire, the long arm of which extended out through a horizontal slit which ran the length of the stage half-way up the back-drop. With this they were manipulated from back-stage. I can't remember any toy ever giving me more pleasure.

Sometimes Matron would take me with her when she went round the children's ward. I would follow discreetly behind her as she went from bed to bed, speaking to each child in her low, gentle voice. My goodness, weren't those children just about glad to be ill in hospital? This was luxury. A lot of them had never known anything like it in their lives. They were poor, most of them, from homes in the courts and alleys of Newbury sixty years ago. They were in no hurry to get better – especially at Christmas-time. Shy and inarticulate, they mostly answered Matron in monosyllables, calling her 'Miss'. I remember her stopping by one bed and asking a little boy of about my own age to try to see whether he could keep his hands still. He couldn't, but she told him he was much better and going on well.

'What's the matter with him?' I asked Matron, when we were well past the bed.

'It's St Vitus's dance, dear,' she said. 'People who have that can't keep themselves still.'

'Will he get better?'

'Oh yes. He's better than he was to begin with.'

There was a singular quality about Matron of which I was intuitively aware, though I never thought about it much. It was simply a part of her self, as I came to know her; a kind of distance, of melancholy – the pensive gravity of a saint, one might almost think. It was as though there were some preoccupation – something untold which she never quite dismissed from mind. I believe I was possibly more sensitive to this than many grown-up people (I have never talked to anyone about it), simply because they generally spoke to her on some urgent matter or question of their own, while I, alight with affection, was nearly always waiting for what *she* would say to me. Would she have liked to have children of her own? Did the sort of things she often had to deal with upset her, I wonder? I can't tell – I never saw her after childhood. I'm glad I knew her: I've never known anyone who seemed at all like her; a lady out of Walter de la Mare, always more or less inwardly aware of some world beyond.

Many years later, I learned that Matron had died in a mental hospital.

It was during these last years of childhood – before I went to boarding school – that I became a film fan. These were the days of silent pictures – a new and important part of life in the nineteen-twenties to millions of people who had never known anything at all like the cinema before. Of course, those films are watched now with hindsight, in the light of the social tidal wave of the talkies of the 'thirties, the big luxury cinemas – the dream palaces – the great stars like Clark Gable and Greta Garbo. It must be remembered that people in the 'twenties had no idea that all this was coming, and found silent films wonderful enough. I can remember an old market woman, sitting next to me, utterly engrossed in *The Adventures of the Flag Lieutenant*. I can't recall who played the Flag Lieutenant, dashing and handsome – his name in the story was Dicky Lascelles – but they were all in China, and the English heroine was isolated, alone in her house and threatened by an uprising of evil Chinese. However, the Flag Lieutenant, of course, was on his way. As the film kept cutting from an Evil Face at the window to the heroine holding a phial of poison between her slim fingers and wondering whether the time had come to swallow it or not, my kindly old neighbour kept repeating 'Oh, Dicky, come quick!' and became quite ecstatic when, of course, he did. Not that I was any the less absorbed. I hadn't grasped, myself, that it was poison; and of course I knew nothing of the Fate Worse than Death, but when you're seven or eight you can easily become enthralled by things that are enthralling surrounding grown-ups; and anyway I knew at least that the Flag Lieutenant was coming to rescue her.

There was little glamour – in fact there was none – about those old silent cinemas. They were a great deal smaller than the new, purpose-built talking picture cinemas of the 'thirties. In many cases they were converted Territorial drill-halls, built in the Edwardian days of Kiplingesque patriotic fervour. The Everyman at Hampstead remains a perfect example. The seats weren't unduly comfortable and sometimes, in those smaller auditoria, you were conscious of a good deal of pipe and cigarette smoke in the air; but you were close enough to the relatively small screen. I remember that in the Picture Palace at Newbury there was an old-fashioned clock on the wall which was kept lighted by an electric bulb. It said

'Scruton's for Value' round the edge, and you had this in the tail of your eye all the time.

Then there was the three-piece ensemble, piano, violin and cello. Their job was to sit in an enclave below the screen and play music appropriate to the various scenes of the films, which had, of course, no other accompanying sound. They were very adroit, too. As I didn't listen consciously to what they played – I just took it as part of the story, as I was meant to – I can't say whether they had a large repertoire; but in after years I found that I was already familiar with things like the finale of the *William Tell* overture, the triumphal march in *Aïda* and the ballet music from *Rosamunde*. They seemed to have it all worked out. I suppose they must have had a private show to themselves before each three-day run. It can't have been too exacting a job, for in those days there were no continuous performances. There were two a day, I think; afternoon and evening.

The stories, in films which contained no dialogue except for occasional captions or titles, necessarily remained simple and straightforward. The endings were nearly always happy. This suited the mentality of most of the audience, who were unsophisticated compared with audiences of today. They were also – most of them – much more simply and uncompromisingly moral, and would have felt their self-respect damaged by watching anything involving adultery or promiscuity (but not the infliction of pain). A fair number of people did not go to the cinema at all, considering it immoral and a bad influence. One of these was Thorn, who would go only to Charlie Chaplin. This shows his excellent taste, for Charlie Chaplin surely remains among the most enduring figues from the days of silent films.

All manner of ingenious devices were used for the stories of films so that they could get by with a minimum of dialogue. There was a lot of miming, so that the acting now seems grotesque and laughable. The heroine would hold up her hands, open her mouth and shake her head in anguish: the hero would go down on one knee to her and clasp his hands: the villain went in for snarls, sidelong glances, sneers and so on. These contortions were conventions, accepted by the audiences of the day. The titles, when they came, were brief and simple. The one everybody remembers is 'Came the dawn.' Others might be 'As fast as possible!' 'Where is she?' 'The train is coming!' etc. I particularly remember the punch-line in a boxing film called *The Ring*, when at the end, the hero's brother, after the lost fight, said to him 'I knew you'd lose, so I betted on the other chap!' *Exeunt ambo*, with the winnings, to a quiet and happy life.

Douglas Fairbanks needed few titles. He leapt from balconies, fought five men at once, sword in hand, and so on. More than him, however, I enjoyed Harold Lloyd. Harold Lloyd was a typical, modern, nice young American, with a big smile, horn-rimmed glasses and check plus-fours. His was always the old, old story of the despised, silly fool who makes mistakes, but overcomes all hazards and wins the day. His own particular way of dispensing with dialogue was Danger. He would be the absorbed, monomaniac butterfly collector, net in hand, hunting a rare species out along a plank a hundred feet up, or along a girder which a crane proceeded to lift high into the air. I understand that he really did these vertiginous stunts himself, for in those days there were no specialist, professional stunt men and no trick photography. I like the memory of this probity: the audience believed that he hung upside-down by his ankles from a suspension bridge, or drove a car into a lake – and he actually did.

Bebe Daniels was a star of the silent days, too, before the introduction of talking pictures. I vividly remember one of her 'no need for captions' lines. It was swimming. The film was called *Swim, Girl, Swim!* At the climax, she arrived late for the crucial swimming race in a car. She dived from the roof of the car and off a bridge into the already-started race and, of course, won it.

But best of all, from my point of view, was Rin-Tin-Tin. Rin-Tin-Tin was an Alsatian, the wonder dog. His ploys were irresistibly gripping to an eight-year-old. He escaped from the villains' hide-out, where his master was held prisoner, and then led the police back to it; he guided the wounded, staggering hero across the mist-enveloped moor; rescued the heroine from burning houses or flooding mills; guarded lost children and so on. I could have watched him for ever and never minded that he usually did much the same things in every film.

In those days, apart from the thin accompanying music up front, below the screen, the auditorium was a great deal more still and silent than in today's cinemas – except for laughter, of course. As performances were not continuous, there was little coming and going during the show; there were no ice-cream girls or the like. I believe there were a few local advertisements, but they were slides. It was darker than today, and I remember watching the flickering, bright beam, a cone expanding from the projection-box to the screen, and marvelling at the miracle of moving pictures. It was not uncommon to hear someone reading the captions aloud, *sotto voce*, for the benefit of a companion who couldn't read.

Certification was lax, as far as I recall, and in practice anybody could go to anything. Parents exercised their own discretion. But I couldn't go alone, simply because the Picture Palace was right up at the other end of the town and it was too far. With the main film there was always an instalment of a serial which ended at a cliff-hanging point, to make you come again next week. Very often, of course, I couldn't come again next week, and hated missing the next instalment. Later on, in the 'thirties, when Boris Karloff started his fearful larks, it went for granted that I wasn't allowed to go. I've never seen *Frankenstein*.

I long to recall as much as I can from those days before I was nine and went to boarding-school, for in many ways they were the happiest of my life, an age of innocence so complete – that is, knowing no invasion or disillusion – that later on, in about 1949, I reacted with instant recognition to Dylan Thomas's poem 'Fern Hill'. I suppose it was easy at Miss Luker's – too easy, really – and there was little to contend with, there or at home. It seems that way in memory, but perhaps only because of the boarding-school contrast which followed.

I remember the old man, Faithfull by name, who used to come every summer, in late June, to scythe the long grass in the paddock. I loved the long grass – I still do – and it always seemed to me that with its scything the summer moved on to its second phase; hot and dry, with yellowing corn, midges and wasps and the cuckoo gone or soon to go. You couldn't chat to Faithfull as you could to Thorn; he'd just say 'Yes' or 'No' as he went on swinging his scythe, stopping every now and then to stand it up and whet it. The tall midsummer growth fell in rows; brome and melick, foxtail and cock's foot, sorrel and buttercup and moon daisies. When it was all done, I used to be allowed to have a hay party for my friends: we played with the hay in every way we could think of; hay houses, steeplechase courses, and who could build the highest pile. A day or two later it was all raked up and carted away: only the short grass left, and horseflies in it to bite your ankles through your socks.

You seldom or never hear a corncrake now; or a nightjar. But in those days they were nothing much to remark. I never actually saw either, but often heard corncrakes in the big cornfield on the other side of Monkey Lane. The nightjar I used to hear from my bed – a curious, sustained bubbling sound, almost like purring. He seemed to like the pine trees on the western edge of the garden, and was often to be heard there on summer nights.

I remember discovering that I'd at last got enough strength to be able to play the pianola alone, unaided. It takes a certain amount of muscle-power to push down the pedals – and to keep pushing them down steadily until the end of the roll. We had a whole ottoman full of rolls: I suppose my father must have bought them, along with the pianola, quite soon after his marriage to my mother in 1910. There were all sorts of rolls, which I played indiscriminately and enjoyed equally: a selection from *The Beggar's Opera*; from *Rose Marie*; from *Dancing Time*; 'If you were the only girl in the world'; 'Over There' (the American march); and, above all, Chopin and more Chopin. I came to know the waltzes well, without having any notion of their fame or supreme quality: I just knew I liked them. I used to play until my legs got so tired that I couldn't go on any more. Then I'd climb out of the drawing-room window – easier than going through the hall and out of the door – and perhaps, if it was high summer, pick a bunch of white jasmine for my mother from the bush growing up the end post of the verandah.

I remember the annual Two Minutes' Silence on 11 November. I dare say that anyone who hasn't experienced it as it was kept in those days will find it impossible to imagine. Whatever day of the week 11 November happened to be, the Silence was observed on that day. In London and the other main cities of the country, guns were fired on the stroke of eleven o'clock. Elsewhere, the wireless sufficed, or signals were given by the police, or by soldiers firing blank. Thereupon everything and everybody, wherever they were and whatever they were doing, stopped exactly as they were for two minutes, until the guns fired again. It was more than impressive: it was overwhelming. I suppose there can never have been anything like it: streets, cities full of people standing perfectly still and silent. Anyone who was driving a car, taxi or bus stopped the engine, got out and stood in the road with bowed head and hat in hand. In the shops, the assistant who was tying a parcel laid it on the counter and the lady who was paying for it put down her purse and stood opposite. Often, one saw tears on the faces of grown-up people.

I recall, one 12 November, seeing a photograph on the back of the *Daily Mail* of a taxi-driver in London having his name and address taken for not stopping his engine. It's occurred to me since to wonder at what point the policeman intervened and how the photograph came to be taken.

This universal observance (and enforcement) was based entirely on public feeling (and guilt for being alive). I doubt whether most people nowadays realize how enormous and appalling a shock the Great War was – and was universally felt to be. With the possible exception of the Black Death, it was by far the greatest disaster which has ever befallen this country. Our losses alone – over a million dead – substantiate that. This is not the place to try to summarize the economic consequences or the blow to the British empire. (I have, in effect, lived in one continuing economic crisis all my life: you feel the difference at once when you go to America.)

On the first day of the battle of the Somme in July 1916, far more men were killed than can ever have been killed on any one day before. I remember reading that at the close of the Allies' 1917 (Passchendaele) offensive, there was scarcely a family in England not mourning the loss of some member.

Within a few years, every village had its war memorial. Today they are often neglected – even defaced – and the people most impressed by them seem to be American visitors, who have more than once remarked to me on their ubiquity and the length of the lists of dead even in relatively small communities. The local names strike home – Tysons in the Lakes, Dyers in Somerset, Canes and Slococks in Berkshire. I particularly admire the memorial at Southend, Bradfield, Berks. This gives each man's rank, name, regiment or arm, the place where he was killed or mortally wounded and the date when he died. I believe this to be unique.

My generation grew up in the shadow of the Great War. Before I was nine I knew virtually all the significant place names – Ypres, Albert, Thiepval, Bapaume, Delville Wood, Vimy Ridge and so on. As I grew older I came to realize that the world has not been the same place since that war. In what respect? In a word, a universal sense of insecurity. Before the Great War, British people for the most part trusted their leaders, were proud of their country and believed in progress. Not any more. The general notion that leaders (and experts) are not to be trusted on any account, and that catastrophe is ever at hand, goes back not to the atom bomb but to 1914–18. I absorbed it unconsciously as part of growing up.

I remember the Christmas morning service at St Nicolas church in Newbury. This was a full-scale civic ceremony, which always used to impress me (and everyone) deeply. The church, which dates from the late fifteenth and early sixteenth centuries, is a very fine one, built for the most part with the fortune made by John Winchcombe, the wealthy clothier and wool merchant commonly known as 'Jack O' Newbury'. On Christmas morning, if you wanted to avoid being seated in some remote corner, you needed to be there in good time, for half or more of the nave pews on each side were reserved. A little before eleven the civic procession began. First came the Mayor, in his robes and chain of office, preceded by a mace-bearer. He was followed by the members of the Corporation, also robed, and the Mayor's guests, such as Ann's father, Mr Lester, head of the Newbury Waterworks, the squires of neighbouring villages, doctors of the hospital and any other local grandees the Mayor thought should be there. (My father used to be invited, but never went: I never once knew him to enter a church.)

Next came the British Legion, all in their medals and with two comrades detailed to present to the Rector their colour, to be laid on the altar. Several were disabled – blind or on crutches. After these followed a representative contingent, all in uniform, of every civic service; the police, the post office, the firemen carrying their shining brass helmets. A leash of nurses from the hospital would be there, conspicuous in white and blue. When everyone was seated Mr Majendie, the rector, would speak a few words of welcome and Christmas greeting and then we would launch into 'O come all ye faithful'.

I recall someone else who deserves record – the barrel-organ man. The barrel-organ man didn't come very often; perhaps once in eighteen months, or even more rarely. The barrel-organ itself I remember as a stout, solid affair – at least as big as a bath –

mounted on two wheels like a gig, with its own shafts and covered all over in stout, grey canvas, so that all you could see of the works were the pointer to change the tune and the brass handle you turned to play it. It was pulled by a donkey.

The barrel-organ man would simply come to the front door and start up. To hear him, wherever you were in house or garden, was to drop whatever you were doing and come running out. He talked little – perhaps he was Italian – but he always smiled amiably; and he would allow you to try to turn the handle yourself. I say 'try' because I never could master the knack of turning it evenly and regularly. The tune came out in jerks: but not when he played. It was a beautiful, unique quality of sound, a metallic vibrato. I wish I could hear it again. I wonder what it would be worth now.

The proper thing to give a donkey, of course, is a carrot; and much scurry there would be to produce some; from the garden if it was summer, and from the loft if it was winter. The donkey ate them with relish. Its lips were pleasantly flexible, warm and soft. The barrel-organ man didn't stay long. He took his hand-out and departed. I never liked seeing him leave. He was a rare treat.

I remember Mrs Griffin, the charwoman. Mrs Griffin looked poor as no one looks now. Her thick, black hair, which had certainly never seen a hairdresser, was fastened with hairpins in a bun at the back. She had no teeth and no false teeth. Her cheeks had a shiny, rosy colour – there was something a little gipsyish in her appearance – and she smiled a lot, to ingratiate herself, I dare say. She lived down in the town and used to come all the way up the hill on foot to scrub our floors. She scrubbed floors and she drank cocoa with her dinner and at the end of the day was paid half-a-crown. The job of taking it to her was usually delegated to my sister, who not long ago told me that she had never forgotten, in fifty years or more, Mrs Griffin's mumbling, effusive delight over her half-crown.

I remember, and I am not likely to forget, Marian Hayter. Colonel Hayter and his family were patients of my father, and lived out at Burghclere, not far from Colonel Elkington. There were two girls, Elsie and Marian, and two boys, Anthony and David. Anthony and David were the younger, about my own age, while Elsie and Marian were some eight or nine years older – about the same age as my brother and sister. Later, in the 'thirties, Elsie became an Oxford Grouper: and what happened to her after that I don't know. Marian Hayter was, by common agreement, the most beautiful girl for miles around. She did teach the torches to burn bright. Since then I have had the luck to meet some very beautiful women (including Virginia McKenna, Julie Christie and Raquel Welch) but I have never seen anyone – anyone at all – more beautiful than Marian Hayter. She fairly knocked you flat (even at the age of eight or nine); a perfect English blonde, golden-haired, blue-eyed, smiling, graceful in movement, softly rosy, with a kind of unselfconscious vivacity and poise which made you want to go on looking at her for ever. She later married the chairman of the Rootes Group. Good luck to him!

Anthony Hayter was one of the R.A.F. officers who escaped from Stalag Luft III in the famous and desperate wooden horse break-out. As is well-known, Hitler, in flagrant breach of the Geneva Convention, personally ordered that all escapers caught should be put to death. Anthony succeeded in travelling across Germany as far as Strasbourg. Here he was arrested by the Gestapo, who drove him out into a nearby wood and shot him.

. . .

For an eight-year-old the prospect of leaving home for boarding-school was a daunting one. I have always felt that the idea was not put across to me in a properly positive way. I had known for years – ever since infancy – that one day I was going, but I had also known since about 1928 that the time fixed was the Michaelmas term of 1929. However, this was changed, at almost no notice, to the earlier summer term. I don't know why, but I dare say it may have been a full quota of new boys already accepted, or something like that, which made my father agree to the earlier term. However, this was not the reason given to me. The reason given to me by my mother was that I had become too naughty and uncontrollable. If I were the parent of an eight-year-old boy, I certainly would not give him such a negative and dispiriting reason for so big and important a step in his life, even if it were true. I would contrive somehow to put the thing across to him in a positive way and do my best to persuade him to accept it willingly. However, if my dear mother had a fault, it was a moody inconsistency of temper. There were times when one could do nothing right. I can't remember what I'd done wrong when one day, round about the end of March 1929, she said 'As you're so naughty, I've decided to send you to boarding-school *this* term.' Of course, it had all been fixed well before that: my trunk had been bought and lettered, and clothes, socks and handkerchiefs put up together in conformity with the school list.

I tried pleading and promises to reform. But the sight of the trunk and other things brought home to me that this was a *fait accompli*. I remember, during that April, a feeling of mounting apprehension as the days went by, but not much else to mark the end of childhood.

On the afternoon of the day on which I was to leave, I slipped out alone into the garden and made a kind of ceremonial peregrination round the whole place, saying good-bye to the stables and the loft, the ruined pigsty, the herbaceous border, the hundred-yard-long hornbeam hedge; and to Bull Banks. The coming term was to last three months, and I would never have been away from home for anything like so long before.

I remember actually handling the grasses in the paddock and murmuring some sort of farewell to them. It was appropriate enough. For the next ten summers I was not to see the tall grasses changing their burnish under the midsummer wind; nor to take part in hay-making.

VII

Horris Hill was, and is today, an illustrious prep school of high standing, a worthy peer of its old sports-field rivals the Dragons at Oxford. In situation it is not a true hill, the buildings, grounds and playing-fields covering a slightly raised, rather bare upland a mile and a half south of Newbury, which I imagine must once have formed part of the brackeny, birchy wasteland adjacent to the west.

The school was built and founded in 1888 by a certain Evans – the first headmaster. His son, Johnny Evans, was, in his day, something of a national figure; first as an England cricketer and then, during the Great War, as an intrepid escaper from German prisoner-of-war camps. Later, in collaboration with one Major Harrison, he wrote a book about his exploits, entitled *The Escaping Club*. He made, I believe, three or four escapes, of which only the last, of course, was entirely successful; that is, he got back to England. For one of his escapes he used a file which was sent to him in a cake baked in Horris Hill kitchen.

During the Second World War, Evans formed part of an army organization in London whose job was encouraging and helping British prisoners-of-war to escape. In the course of his work he came in for criticism which need not be recounted here. Also, I have seen the argument expressed that, during Hitler's war, encouraging prisoners to escape was not altogether a good idea, since it brought about Nazi reprisals (such as the murder of Anthony Hayter and his friends).

Anyway, the foregoing makes clear that Johnny Evans (whom I sometimes saw on his visits to Horris Hill but, although his son Michael was an exact contemporary of mine, never actually met) was a courageous, games-playing, extrovert sort of man – a typical Victorian gentleman and Christian.

The headmaster of my day was Mr J. L. Stow, generally agreed to have been an outstanding prep school headmaster. He was chairman of the Prep School Headmasters' Association, to whom he was known as 'Daddy' Stow. At Horris Hill, however, he bore the homelier nickname of 'Stidge' (or sometimes 'Stygo').

Mr Stow was in every respect a strong personality. Even his gentleness and kindness were in some way powerful, like those of a lioness with her cubs. He possessed in a high degree the two essential qualities for a schoolmaster, warmth and humour; and he had a strong but pleasant voice. He taught well: in fact he was fascinating; it was positively enjoyable to be a member of any class he took. He was the form-master of the top form, of course, but he also taught math to the one-from-bottom form – no doubt as a means of getting to know the younger boys and size them up, for he was very keen on that. He knew every boy in the school – there were, in my day, ninety-four – by his Christian name.

Though neither tall nor particularly stout, he was a well-built, heavy, imposing man. (I never saw him run.) In my mind's eye he is always wearing a double-breasted, grey flannel suit and looking alertly about him from his brown eyes. (His manner was never abstracted or reflective.) He was continually among the boys and could converse with them good-humouredly and amusingly. He knew everybody's character and he knew everything that was going on.

He was – in that world, anyway – something of a larger-than-life character, generous and magnanimous of mind. He could be both emotional and intimidating. If he saw occasion (such as a fumbled pass in a school soccer match) he would burst out in a roar: 'Oh, no, no, *no*! Come *along*, now, for goodness sake!' which carried far across the field. I well remember how, playing in my first school match at home, I had the good luck to throw the wicket down from deep mid-off, running the batsman out. 'Well played, Dicky!' called out Mr Stow loudly. As good as an M.B.E. any day!

I often reflect, nowadays, how lucky I was to get four years of Mr Stow – to say nothing of his friendship in later life. From the ancient Greeks onwards, a fine schoolmaster has always been recognized as one of the greatest blessings which anyone can have. I had three, of whom Mr Stow was the first. He may have been a man of strong, turbulent emotions and even somewhat prone to angry outbursts, but he put them to excellent use, and he was liked and respected by everyone: the right man to have on your side.

Horris Hill was a school for young gentlemen, and there was much emphasis on the vital importance of truth, honesty and correct behaviour. Perhaps four or five times a term, on Sunday evenings after hymn-singing (of which more anon), Mr Stow would deliver what was known as a 'pi-jaw'. This might be concerned with all manner of matters – bullying, scatology (we knew nothing at all about sex, of course), behaviour towards the lower classes (kindly, polite, decided, firm and magnanimous), diligence, gratitude, how to show proper respect towards one's elders and betters and towards ladies, and so on. I recall how once he spoke to us about the wrongfulness of leading smaller boys into misdemeanour out of a desire to show off to them as being rather a devil. He showed how vulgar and unworthy of a gentleman this was, and then, with the most telling effect, quoted Matthew, Chapter XVIII, verse 6, 'Whoso shall offend one of these little ones . . . it were better for him that a millstone were hanged about his neck, and that he were drowned in the depth of the sea.' I've never forgotten it.

At times he could deliver a cutting rebuke without roaring at all. I had a friend called Pawson II, who had a habit of biting the skin on the sides of his fingers – unconsciously, I'm sure. One day, when he was doing it in form, Mr Stow took a minute or two to castigate the nasty habit and point out how objectionable it was. A morning or two later, the wretched boy was doing it again, while Mr Stow was expounding Virgil. He finished the passage and then enquired conversationally, 'Breakfast nearly over, Pawson?'

During my first term I was dreadfully homesick. Homesickness can be tantamount to a nervous breakdown – that is, you no longer care what anyone else thinks; you weep openly and so on. No one could have been gentler, kinder or more understanding than Mr Stow. He spent what seemed a long time in comforting me and talking to me privately. Later, one bit of this conversation came to be a standing joke between the two of us for years. Between sobs of misery I said 'Sir, can I say anything I like to you?' 'Yes, Dicky, you can say *anything* at all.' 'Well, sir, that Dickens this morning; I didn't think you read it very well.' This made me feel enormously better. We were able to talk about something other than my unhappiness, and Mr Stow had shown himself benign and humane.

I remember another incident worth relating. One summer evening Mr Stow was strolling round our dormitory, and by way of making conversation was asking each boy in turn how many runs he had made that day. 'Fourteen, sir,' said the dormitory captain. 'Well done, Michael,' replied Stidge. 'Ten, sir,' said the next lad. 'You must get another nought on it next time.' As he came closer to me, I felt apprehensive and horribly embarrassed, for I had been undeservedly lucky. 'And how many did *you* make, Dicky?' 'Sir,' I replied in a low, ashamed voice, 'twenty-eight not out.' Without a word Mr Stow extended his hand over the end of my bed. I crept forward and shook it.

Horris Hill was not a school of strong religious indoctrination, like an R.C. school or a Woodard. It was straight, unpretentious C. of E. in the manner of that time. There were school prayers morning and evening, consisting of a short reading from the Bible, the Lord's Prayer and the appropriate collects. On Sundays we walked both to matins and to evensong at one or other of the local churches, Newtown or Burghclere. Usually these were services for the school alone (we filled Newtown church, anyway) but on special occasions, such as Remembrance Sunday, we attended with the village people. We were disgustingly snobbish little boys, and I remember one of my companions imitating the Burghclere choir. 'Ten thaousand toimes ten thaousand . . .' Finally, on Sunday evenings, after divinity prep, there would be communal hymn-singing from the English hymnal. This was a popular institution. Everyone knew the tunes, and it was almost the only community singing we got. Small boys of that class are – or were – unthinking believers and in many cases deeply sincere about religion. I don't think we reflected with any intensity or fervour on the words, but some of the verses which come back to me now I wouldn't want any nine-year-old of mine to have on his mind.

> I sometimes think about the cross,
> And shut my eyes and try to see
> The cruel nails and crown of thorns
> And Jesus crucified for me.

Ah, holy Jesus, how hast thou offended,
That Man to judge thee hath in scorn pretended?
I, blessed Saviour, I it was denied thee.
I crucified thee.

I don't know how much effect this sort of stuff had on other boys, for we never talked much about religion among ourselves, but it shook me all right, and has left me all my life with a sickened horror of Christ's passion. Some years later, when I tried to talk to my mother about this, she dismissed it as 'morbid'. I could talk about it to my father, though. He understood and to a large extent shared my feelings; but he didn't tell me what to do about it.

I wish – and I dare say I am not the only person to have wished – that Christ had not died as He did. (Neither Mohammed, Buddha nor Confucius were put to death.) Nor can I see what good it did for us as Christians. I can see that Christ was the first martyr for Christianity. After all, He could have said to Pilate 'I won't do it any more: I'll go home and keep quiet.' That would have got him off all right, I think. (John, Chapter XIX, 12.) However, He preferred His integrity, and no doubt He was right in reckoning that His teaching would not be likely to endure if He showed that He valued His own life above it. 'But if you ask them' (the clergy) 'in what way the death of the Landlord's Son should benefit us, they are driven to monstrous explanations' (C. S. Lewis). The benefit must, I think, be accepted as purely transcendental in its nature. 'Almighty God, grant that the death of Thy dear Son may be effectual to my redemption' (Dr Johnson). However, my own greatest enlightenment and help in these difficult matters were to come many years later, first from Frazer's *Golden Bough*, but more positively and inspiringly from Joseph Campbell's *The Hero with a Thousand Faces* and *The Masks of God*.

However, I anticipate. Looking back now, I think the greatest benefit which I derived from Horris Hill was not doctrine (they didn't indoctrinate us with ideas: ideas are no good to little boys) and still less a religious atmosphere. (There was very little invoking of Christian values to support discipline: Mr Stow's reference to Matthew, Chapter XVIII, 6, was quite exceptional.) The benefit was a sound knowledge of quite a lot of the Bible. Thanks to Horris Hill, I have a pretty good grip of the synoptic Gospels (John came later), Acts, Genesis, Exodus, Joshua, I and II Samuel and I and II Kings. We didn't do the prophets or St Paul; too much for small boys. I think that these (expurgated, of course, after the manner of those days), comprised an excellent syllabus for nine- to thirteen-year-olds, and I have always been glad of it.

However, Bible Study was not pushed particularly hard at Horris Hill. There was divinity prep on Sunday evenings and a divinity period on Monday mornings. Apart from that, revision and preparation for the end-of-term exam were left to the discretion of the form master.

My introduction to the Bible itself (in contradistinction to the excellent *Baby's Life of Jesus Christ*, by Helen Rolt, which my mother had read to me, and the Bible stories told by Miss Langdon) was somewhat unusual. Horris Hill's syllabus for the academic year 1928–29 was the synoptic Gospels and the Acts; but I had arrived in the summer term, and consequently was plunged straight into Acts for starters. However, I already knew enough about Jesus's life, death and resurrection to have a reasonable idea of where we were and, as with *The Pilgrim's Progress*, I found it stimulating and exciting to think that I was reading, in the authentic, grown-up text, one of the great books of the world. I enjoyed the way of teaching, which, as well as explanation, was largely based on training you to identify, comment upon and remember memorable contexts. 'Silver and gold have I none; but such as I have give I thee: In the name of Jesus Christ of Nazareth rise up and walk.' 'Saul, Saul, why persecutest thou me? . . . It is hard for thee to kick against the pricks.' (Explain about donkeys.) 'And Gallio cared for none of these things.' 'Hast thou appealed unto Caesar? Unto Caesar shalt thou go.' As Rudyard Kipling said of *Uncle Remus*, 'The book was amazing, and full of quotations that one could hurl like javelins.' It's an admirable training in the appreciation of beautiful prose.

At the end of my first term, there was what was known as a 'massed divvers exam'. That is to say, the whole school took the same examination paper. The littler boys, of course, were not expected to do as well as the senior boys: they just did the best they could. I remember that the exam began with fifty one-word answers, the questions being given out orally – of which the first was 'Where were the apostles first called Christians?'

This divinity paper, to my own enormous surprise, turned out to be my first academic success. When the list went up, I was thirtieth out of the ninety-odd participators. The name of the top member of each form was underlined, and mine was above that of the top boy of the form above my own. Of course, my father was delighted, having been no inconsiderable biblical scholar himself; and remained one, too.

I should have explained earlier that Horris Hill and my home at Wash Common lay about a mile and a quarter apart as the crow flies and only about two miles apart by road. My father was the school doctor and of course I came in for a certain amount of ragging on this account – some of it rather spiteful. No doubt he got special financial terms for me, but I rather think there may have been other reasons behind his decision to send me to Horris Hill. We have always to remember the never-mentioned influence of poor Robert. If I was at Horris Hill, my father could keep an eye on me and if necessary even be there in a few minutes. Also, I know that he was not satisfied with the way in which the education of my brother (now sixteen) was turning out at Sherborne. John had gone to Sherborne prep school at the age of nine. My father had chosen Sherborne because it lay close to his own old home at Martock and he knew the district, the public school and its reputation. However, John had been unhappy there and had not done particularly well: nor was he getting on any better at Sherborne itself. He never seemed to act like a normal, happy boy. He was abstracted, self-conscious and preoccupied; worse, he did not get on well with my father, with whom his relations were always distant and cool. The two of them seemed to have little or no rapport. I think my father reckoned that, taking all things into account, there was much to be said in my case for a different boarding-school, nearer home.

Why not a day school in Newbury? the reader may ask. Don't be silly! Only lower middle-class boys went to day schools. If you didn't go to a boarding-school you weren't a gentleman, and on top of that you would grow up to be a wet and a weed. Worse still, you wouldn't be able to wear an old school tie and begin your career by being able to say 'I was at Wrykin' (or wherever). It

21 JULY 1929

DEAR MOTHER -

— —

Only nine more days
and I shall be home. We
played ~~the Newtown in~~
Newtown ~~yesterday~~ yesterday,
And Mr. Ashmore was
playing for the opposing
team. It is exams x this
week, and Bible exams
tomorrow. How is Percy?
Has he escaped lately?
I hope my garden is all
right? How is Emily?
~~Everyone~~ Everyone
is swotting for the Bible
exam tomorrow.
~~there is~~ there's no more

to day —

Richard

An elephant

would be an unthinkable social disadvantage, and reflect badly upon your parents. Such values were in those days unquestioned.

Horris Hill, whatever its merits – and they are considerable – was not and is not a beautiful place. The buildings are downright ugly – tall, gaunt, asymmetrical and horribly institutional in appearance. Although it is in open country, there is precious little pleasure in nature (or none such as I was used to) to be found in the grounds. A gravel playground adjoining what is called 'the lower field'; and an upper field which in my day was used only for nets, cricket, football and golf; a sloping pinewood on one side of the lower field and a thin belt of half-starved trees along the other; these were our confines. The whole place formed a bare upland, inhospitable alike to wild-flowers, birds and animals. Years later, when as an adult I visited the prep school called Elstree, near Woolhampton, to watch Horris Hill play them at football, I was struck by the charm and beauty of the place (it is basically a sixteenth-century manor, with delightful grounds) and could not help wondering how much influence the ugliness of Horris Hill and the beauty of Elstree respectively had upon those who unconsciously soaked up their environs during four impressionable years of boyhood.

Horris Hill's domestic facilities would strike any parent today with amazement. There were adequate water-closets, certainly, and wash-hand basins a little way off; but that was about all. On one side of the changing-rooms were some stone troughs, which you could fill with cold water to wash the mud off your arms and legs after football. However, this activity was neither supervised nor compulsory and few bothered with it. Everybody got one hot bath a week.

In the dormitories there were no taps; only carafes of cold water. Everyone cleaned their teeth into the same wash-bowl, to facilitate the task of the maid who came round to empty it and rinse it out.

Under each bed was a chamber pot, and these must have been emptied and cleaned by the maids as part of morning bed-making drill. In one corner of each dormitory was a lidded, wooden commode, for use by anyone who might be taken short in the night. I never knew one to be used; though during my time I knew three or four people to have involuntary 'accidents' in their sleep and beds.

In the mornings, winter and summer alike, there were cold baths.

In those days cold baths were a common institution of all boarding-schools. We'd have despised any school that didn't have them. (I believe Bryanston and Dartington Hall didn't: they were 'progressive' and *ipso facto* 'weedy'.) Two or three baths in the bathroom were filled with cold water and thither we proceeded in our dressing-gowns. You had to get in and out carefully, not to spill any water – a degree of deliberation which lengthened the nasty process. Cold baths, as well as evening hot baths, were supervised by the under-matron, Miss Archer, a spare, leathery, middle-aged, unsmiling woman who was universally liked and respected because she never raised her voice and was the same to everyone; firm, consistent and fair, and impossible to bamboozle. We never thought it in the least disconcerting to be naked in front of Miss Archer; and she herself was equally equable in the matter.

In those days there was much less fuss about nakedness. If some occasion, such as bathing, cold baths or the doctor, required you to be naked, you simply undressed without a second thought. Only ill-bred people were self-conscious about nakedness. As is well-known, Charles Dodgson (Lewis Carroll) used to photograph the little daughters of his Oxford friends naked, and they were delighted for him to do so, as he did it very well. Any innuendo about it would have been met with silence, raised eyebrows and an immediate change of subject: the offender wouldn't have been invited again.

Like most other people, I hated the cold baths. But from the school's point of view they had their advantages. To start with, Mr Stow didn't have to pay for hot water in the mornings. Secondly, they saved labour and were a quick, convenient way of getting ninety-odd boys up, washed and wide-awake. Thirdly, we never seemed to get colds and our general resistance to cold was good.

There was no electricity anywhere in the school. Downstairs there were gas brackets with incandescent mantles. Some had low pilot jets which burned all day, but these were only in relatively dark places such as storerooms, where they might need to be turned up at any time. At dusk, the pantry boy would go round the entire ground floor with a taper on a stick, turning on and lighting the gas. I still like to see a mantle, for instance on a Tilley lamp, take on its brilliant, dazzling glow: it tells of cosy snugness (not that we had any curtains), falling twilight and attention to books. I like the smell, too.

At Horris Wood, a house providing extra dormitory accommodation about three hundred yards away and situated just beyond the pine-wood I have already mentioned, there wasn't even any gas. As evening fell Vera, the buxom, pleasant, gentle-voiced maid, would light a whole battery of paraffin lamps and range them together on a tray. This she carried from room to room downstairs – hall and corridors too. Each had its place and each burned on until lights out. Sometimes one or another would suddenly flare and smoke, requiring quick adjustment from the nearest passer-by. These lamps had a smell all their own. It is one of pleasant associations for me, since I was – when the time came – happy at Horris Wood, as I will relate. Paraffin lamps at evening – that soft light, illuminating print, knitting or mending, but leaving friendly gloom in the room's corners – well, I'm sorry, reader, that you should have been denied the blessing of this gentle, homely change from the rhythm of the sun to the rhythm of nightfall. This is something vanished for ever, as surely as the dust on the hedges.

The routine of going to bed never varied. After prayers in the big schoolroom, a mug of milk and two biscuits were dished out to each boy. Then, after a reasonable interval, Mr Stow, standing at the big invigilation desk, would call out 'One!' The captain of One (always a second-year boy set over a new boys' dormitory) would lead his little file up to shake hands with Mr Stow, who said 'Good-night, Trevor', 'Good-night, Basil', to each. They would be followed by Two, Three and so on, until the last, Ten. The biggest dormitory had about twelve boys in it, but the two smallest had only four. The make-up of each was a cross-section of the school. The dormitory captain (whose responsibilities were vague but whose authority most certainly was not) would be a relatively senior boy, while the rest ranged gradually down in seniority to the 'dorm squit', who might be a mere second-termer. This system, on the whole, worked well, for it meant that you had some regular company other than your contemporaries, and that you learned how to deal with your elders (and, in due course, your juniors).

When you had said good-night to Stidge and climbed the stairs (sometimes with your biscuits still hoarded in your pocket) there would, in winter, be a single candle burning in each dormitory. (In summer, the fading daylight was enough.) Initially silence obtained, and everyone knelt by his bed to say his personal prayers.

The silence lasted for about three or four minutes and I never knew it to be abused. It was taken very seriously (though we never received any actual instruction about private prayer). Then a little, hand-held, tinkling bell was rung by the master on duty and undressing, tooth-cleaning and the rest proceeded. We got about twenty or twenty-five minutes for talk before being 'shut up' for the night. Reading, except on long lie-in on Sunday mornings, was not allowed.

To Horris Hill's lack of electric light I owe more than I can tell. Indeed, it may very well have been the greatest blessing of my life, for it was this which made me a dormitory story-teller. The shadowy, candle-lit dormitories of winter; or those same dormitories in the fading twilight after sunset; these were settings for a story-teller such as no electrically lit room could ever have provided. They possessed what Padraic Colum has called 'the rhythm of the fire' (the story-teller's rhythm, as opposed to the rhythm of the sun, the worker's rhythm). Often, at the beginning of term, a captain would ask his bunch, with whom he was not yet familiar, who could tell a story. It was unwise for the squit to volunteer; usually a boy of middling seniority would take up the business. As a rule the stories were homespun enough in narration – told conversationally, with little real sense of climax or flow. Still, I have since heard adult Irish and Scottish story-tellers with equally conversational and even bathetic styles. A true folk-tale teller is usually rather colloquial. Many listeners don't like a dramatic style of narration, especially from someone they know personally. It embarrasses them. They consider it pretentious and false. The dormitory stories nearly always lacked originality, too. They were likely to be paraphrases of Bulldog Drummond or Sherlock Holmes, or of some play the narrator had seen in the holidays or heard on the wireless. Ghosts were always popular, but were often laid on rather too thick. ('The door opened and in came a clanking skeleton . . .' Sometimes this sort of thing drew mocking interjections: '. . . who said "Good morning, boys: baths!"' – Miss Archer's invariable reveille.) All the same, good story-tellers did crop up from time to time. I remember how, when I was in Dormitory Seven, two boys called Wilkins and Meredith used to enact, vocally (we weren't allowed out of bed) nightly episodes of a whole serial play. It was about a stolen diamond, I recall, and continued, to much acclamation, for two or three weeks. At intervals the protagonists had to be in a car or an aeroplane, and another boy called Job – a nice chap who was later killed in World War II – was required to maintain continuously the *Brrrrr* of the engine. I didn't envy him. On the whole, dormitory talk could be amusing, informative and a lot of fun. You heard much about life in the school at levels other than your own.

You never knew what dormitory you were going to be in until, at the beginning of each term, you went upstairs to the locker-room and asked Sister. (Sister's name was Miss Wood. She was a strange, uncertain lady of emotional crushes and odd moods; she was not terribly popular. Looking back, I think now that her naturally passionate temperament was badly frustrated, poor woman.)

After some two years, at the age of about eleven-and-a-half, I became one of those selected to go over to Horris Wood. My dormitory captain of the previous term, S—, had been a bully and a beast: one of his devices had been to make you strip your pyjama-top off so that he could pour the hot candle-grease onto your back. Then you had to put your top straight on again. When you woke in the morning, the congealed grease tore the skin off your back.

I remember Sister Wood calling out across the crowded locker-room 'You're over at the Wood, Dicky!' I could have danced for joy; it was such an anxiety off my mind. I knew S— wouldn't have been sent over to the Wood: he was too senior. Either you went when you were about half-way up the school, or else not at all. Selection was entirely random. What was more, once you had gone to the Wood you remained there for the rest of your time.

Horris Wood was a soft option, and those who went there were, on the whole, envied. To be a Wooder set you a little apart, for it was a world of its own, with separate ways and a separate atmosphere. To start with, it was much smaller than Horris Hill, with only about thirty boys in five dormitories. Stidge was not the resident *genius loci*, but the third master, Mr Liddell (known as Twid). Twid could keep order all right, but he was unpredictable in his emotions. Most of the time he was gentle and kind-hearted to a fault – he hated punishing anybody – but he was apt to break out into sudden rages which could be frightening. The angrier he got, the less he could pronounce his 'r's', and I treasure a memory of my friend Jim Wilson imitating him with a cry of 'Oh, you howwible little bwat, can't you wealize it's a pawallelogwam?'

After evening milk and biscuits, instead of waiting to say good-night to Stidge, Wooders went off to the boot-room and put on overshoes, kept specially for them. These were not galoshes, but a sort of rubber-soled ankle-boot fastened across with a clip: I've never seen them anywhere else. Then you sallied forth into the night – starlight, fog, moonlight, rain, even snow, sometimes – to cross the three hundred yards to the Wood.

Matron-wise, the Wood wasn't run by Sister Wood and Miss Archer, either. No; it was run by May Gozzer – beloved, adorable Gozzer – whose regime was, I am inclined to guess, more motherly, kind, warm and indulgent than anything which a lot of those boys had known in their lives; I can tell you, many of the mothers I saw visiting on parents' days, tight-lipped, impersonal, unsmiling, fur-coated and lipsticked ('*Don't* do that, Geoffrey'), made me feel jolly glad that none of them was my mother. Gozzer was warmth and benevolence personified.

Her position as matron to thirty boys at the Wood – a sort of half-job – was typical of the kind of semi-official arrangement that could so easily be set up in those days when distances were greater, places more isolated, parents less critical and headmasters undisputed rulers of their own realms. The three Misses Gosling – Moggy, May and Ethel – were maiden ladies – patients of my father – who lived in a good, solid, Victorian house called 'Gorsefield' (or 'Gosfield' by the facetious) across the Common and about three-quarters of a mile from the school. They had the pleasant, sizeable house and they had a competence of sorts, left them by their parents, but it was too small for more than a modest establishment. They were of good family, but none of them had ever married (though the man who married May would have been lucky). Once, when I asked my mother why, she replied sardonically 'No one was ever good enough for them.' Now, appreciating my mother's own class background and marriage, I can see the force of her answer – an implied but very valid criticism of a silly social system. Be that as it may, the three Gozzers, though indulgently made a little fun of behind their backs, were popular and respected in the neighbourhood. They sometimes gave tennis parties on a court which was so mossy that the balls would hardly bounce, and at which they gave you 'lemonade' consisting of a lemon sliced up into a jug of water. They were dears. Ethel, the youngest, was deaf, and Moggy, the eldest, was an Oxford Grouper. But I am concerned now with May – 'Gozzer' to hundreds of Horris Wood boys of the 'twenties and 'thirties.

I don't believe Gozzer had any nursing qualifications and I'll bet she was paid next to nothing; yet I can't remember anything ever going medically wrong at Horris Wood. People got flu in the spring term – common in those days. Gozzer put them to bed in the sick-room, made them beef tea, spoiled them and fussed over them. My father came and looked at them and they duly got better. That was about the extent of it.

I suppose Gozzer – the tears come to my eyes as I write of her – wasn't altogether good for us, really. A matron needs to have some sort of authority, and Gozzer exercised virtually none at all. Yet bestowed upon her, as it were, like a nimbus, was the natural authority of a person universally loved. We all addressed her as 'Goz' as a matter of course. Once, Mr Liddell gave us a talking-to about it, but it made only a temporary difference. In any case, Gozzer didn't really care for Mr Liddell exercising much discipline. The punishment for talking after lights out was invariably beating (and with a cane, in pyjamas, that hurts a lot). Gozzer would, as often as not, get wind of Mr Liddell's intention to 'go round' after lights out to hear whether anything was going on; and when she did, she would tip off the captains of the dormitories. If it was to be a boy's birthday, others in the dormitory would let Gozzer know, and when she made her rounds to us in bed, with her tray of laxatives, medicaments, plaster and cotton wool, there would be 'celebrations' (known as 'celibries'). Gozzer, strictly against the rules, would give out butter drops all round (known as 'brown pills'). I have never known anyone – not even Miss Langdon – from whom sheer kindness and benevolence poured in such a stream. She loved to be kind. You could tell her anything: you could weep on her sympathetic shoulder. Perhaps, in that tightly disciplined world, that was her real secret. She loved us for the dangers we had passed, and we loved her that she did pity them.

If there came a point, as there sometimes did, when things got out of hand and something simply *had* to be put a stop to, she would go into a 'Goz fluster'. Speech would pour from her in a stream of unfinished sentences – 'No, no, no – you really mustn't – now stop, dear, stop – quite wrong – very bad for you, too – if

Mr Liddell got to know –' (We knew he wouldn't.) A Goz fluster always worked – calmed things down – simply because it was so embarrassing to see this charming lady out of countenance; we knew we'd abused her indulgence, and would pull ourselves together.

Gozzer's diction was very U and correct, in the Victorian/ Edwardian manner which even then was old-fashioned. She always dropped the final 'g' of present participles: So-and-so was 'charmin': he was comin' over on Saturday' etc. Perhaps he was goin' to play 'goff', for this was another of her turns of speech. People were liable to have nasty 'cawfs'. Marian Hayter was 'an awfully jolly girl'. I recall now that the Gozzers had a brother, known as 'the Major', who played tennis with a racket which had a fish-tailed handle. I've never seen another.

I cannot refrain from relating the story Gozzer once told me about her visit to Chartres before the Great War. 'We were goin' to see the Cathedral and then we were goin' on for a picnic and some fishin'. We got orf about ten o'clock and the only thing that was worryin' me was that we hadn't got anything to put the bait in, so it was messin' everything up. And then, as we were comin' out of the Cathedral, I saw this man sellin' bottles full of water, with round tops like jamjars. So I said to Ethel, "Look, the very thing for our bait!" So I bought two – although they seemed rather expensive – and poured out the water on the ground; and I was just puttin' the bait in when all these French people started makin' a terrible fuss and chatterin' away: we couldn't understand a word they said. But then it turned out that what they were sayin' was that it was holy water, and we had quite a business gettin' away from them. Well, how were we supposed to know about their silly old holy water?'

Poor Gozzer suffered from a spinal curvature. When I first knew her, this caused her to do no more than hold her head on one side, a little bent at an unnatural angle. My father explained to me in his usual brusque way. 'It won't get any better,' he said. 'It'll get worse.'

It did. As the 'thirties went on, Gozzer became more and more bent over, until she was bent like a hunchback without a hump. She had to give up Horris Wood, her boys and her sweet maid, the strong-armed Vera – who was worth any three other girls (and who lent me *King Solomon's Mines*). The last time I saw Gozzer was when I visited Gorsefield in 1949, to introduce my fiancée to her. It was a hot day. The door was standing open, but I rang the bell. After a few minutes May came half-running up the hall. She was literally bent double; almost to the ground. The top half of her body was horizontal, her right hand held out before her (to shake hands) and her face actually turned upward to greet us. Ethel was now permanently in bed downstairs, and wandering in her mind. She thought I was the bishop of Worcester and conversed with me accordingly. I cannot remember about Moggy. She may have been out. That day wrung my heart.

I never saw Gozzer again. She left me £25 in her will. I used it to buy a set of Staunton chessmen, carved by the famous Mueller in about 1885; ivory, the kings four inches tall. An awfully jolly thing, don't you know: I'm still playin' with it today.

But I was speaking of my initiation as a story-teller. The first night I got to the Wood I found that I was the squit in Dormitory One, which had only four beds. The captain was a certain Tony Priestley, a forceful but quite genial character with a reputation as a bit of a daredevil. The others were McCrum, a gentle, kindly, popular boy, and Geoffrey Hunter, who was later killed in the war. Sure enough, Priestley demanded from someone a story and I, seeing it was such a free-and-easy atmosphere and wishing to ingratiate myself, took the job on, squit or no squit. The story was the Breton tale of Peronnik and the Castle of Kerglas (Andrew Lang's *Lilac Fairy Book*). To my gratification it met with warm approval, and the following night Priestley required another. This time it was M. R. James's 'Lost Hearts'. I remember, at the end, Hunter asking 'But what *happened*?' I felt enough self-confidence to give him my sister Katharine's usual reply, 'Think it out'. 'Oh, I *hate* having to think it out!' said Geoffrey, who was inclined to be rather self-indulgent. But he didn't cuff my head for cheek, as he well might have.

The stories were insisted upon night after night. One way and another, they were dredged up from everything I had ever read. Sometimes, when Twid came round to 'shut us up' (it was always known as this, since there were no lights to put out: what happened was that the door was shut for the night; 'no more talking'), Priestley and the others would beg for another minute or two so that Adams could finish, and with this the good-natured Twid would often fall in. Sometimes he knew the story, since it might be 'The Monkey's Paw', 'The Bottle Imp' or some such, and would stay to hear it out himself.

By about half-term I could find no more stories to tell. I said as much, but this had no effect on Priestley. 'Adams, this is my watch, see? Slipper coming over unless you start in half a minute.' This, as Dr Johnson would say, concentrated the mind wonderfully.

In the end I was forced to make them up. There was nothing else for it. They had to have proper climaxes and conclusions, too. A thing on the lines of Frank Stockton's 'The Lady or the Tiger' wouldn't have done at all. I would find odd moments, during the day, to think about what I would try to embark on that evening. In the event it turned out not to be too difficult, for my audience were not over-critical, and by this time I had a tolerable standing. I remained in One for about three terms and, thanks to Priestley, his watch and his slipper, I never dried up.

But I did once get beaten for talking after lights out. It was all very sudden. I was finishing a story in whispers, to Hunter only, in the adjacent bed, when the door was abruptly thrown open and Mr Liddell, torch in one hand and cane in the other, said 'Who's talking in here?' 'I am, sir,' I said. 'Get out of bed: bend over: right over.' And so, with the torchlight playing on my bum, I received four. 'Next time it will be much harder,' said Twid, and left as sharply as he had come.

By our schoolboy code Hunter ought to have owned up too. After all, you can't be talking to nobody, and Twid should have thought of this and pressed enquiry. But what I believe now is that he hated beating people so much that he wasn't really thinking judicially and just wanted to get it over as quickly as he could. Mr Stow or Mr Morris would have got to the bottom of the matter.

Mr Morris was the Second Master. He was odd and frightening: at least, he frightened me – and a number of others, though not all. He looked as strange as he was, and it is clear to me now that he was perverted. He was about fifty, tall, the top of his head bald in the middle, like a tonsure in the sparse circle of grey hair. His long face had a drawn, ascetic look – a bachelor's face – with a high, prominent nose and wrinkled cheeks. He was loose-limbed and shambling. His clothes were the oldest and untidiest I have ever

seen on an adult; almost rags. His silent stare was intimidating
enough, but his anger was worse.

Bungey, as he was known, had a way of playing cat-and-mouse
which never failed to reduce me, for one, to trembling and
stammering incoherence (known in the school as 'Bungey dread').
Bungey dread was an involuntary, intuitive thing. Either you felt
(though sexually ignorant) that there was something queer and
frightening about him, or else you just didn't. (Most didn't.) He
would often begin in a low key. 'Talking: yes, talking. I rather
think you were. Perhaps you'd better stand up. And what were you
talking about, I wonder.'

'Sponge cake, sir.' (Titters. It always seemed to be something
that made you look absurd and ignominious; small boys have not
yet learned to lie or temporize under hostile questioning.)

'Sponge *cake*. Do you think it might enlarge your knowledge to
compose two elegiac couplets on the subject and read them to us
tomorrow morning?'

(Better than being beaten, anyway. But what on earth could be
the nearest Latin equivalent for 'sponge cake'? 'Spongia' was a
substantive, but it would need to be turned into an adjective,
wouldn't it? And 'cake' – er –)

A sudden roar from Bungey. '*Well*? Am I to wait here all day for
you to give me an answer?'

'No, sir. Yes, sir.'

'Hoity, toity, horrible mess!' (He really did say 'hoity toity': the
only person I have ever heard do so.) Approaches and picks up
ragged, ink-stained Ovid by one corner in finger and thumb. 'This
is your property?'

'Yes, sir. But I haven't written any words in it, honestly, sir.'
(One of the most heinous crimes you could commit was to write
English translations of Latin words in the margins of text books.)

'Did I say you had?'

'No, sir.' (Class now much enjoying the spectacle of an abject
demonstration of Bungey dread – the victim defending himself in
anticipation of an accusation as yet unmade.)

This sort of thing could sometimes go on for quite a long time.
I remember an incident which took place when I happened to be a
member of a dormitory situated just outside Bungey's upstairs
study. One evening, as we were undressing, three fairly senior boys

came up the stairs, grinning with bravado, halted outside Bungey's domain (he hadn't arrived yet) and announced to us, through the open dormitory door, 'We're going to get spanked.' Naturally we all felt, while waiting, a certain amount of vicarious tension. Eventually, Bungey came loping up the stairs, two at a time, strode down the passage and invited the culprits to step inside. For what seemed a long time we could hear only his low voice talking, though one couldn't distinguish any words. Then, suddenly, we heard him cry out, in a tone of impatience and excitement, 'No, kneel, kneel, kneel, kneel!' Then followed the sound of the blows. They told us afterwards that they had each been required to crouch upon the carpet, with their bare buttocks elevated, while Bungey beat them sitting in his armchair.

'Spanking', as we called it, had a kind of tabu aura around it. It was the subject of bated-breath jokes, little doggerel rhymes and so on, rather taking the place of sex jokes among boys too young to know about the latter. ('My son, my son, it must be done. Down with the trousers, up with the bum.') The instruments used were personal and various. Mr Stow used to spank on the bare buttocks with a thing called a fives bat, which is rather like a table-tennis racket but bigger, and longer in the handle. Bungey used to use the 'jack' of an old-fashioned wooden shoe-tree – the removable, handled bit that is thrust into the middle. He, too, beat on the bare buttocks. Mr Liddell, as I have said, used a cane.

For very serious offences there would be what were known to us as 'public spankations'. Of these, there were only two during the four years I was at the school. The first took place after a weak assistant master had entirely failed to control a prep which gradually dissolved into a general, anarchic rag. Everyone was wondering why the master was apparently doing nothing. In fact, he was taking names to report to Mr Stow. After evening prayers that night three of the principal offenders, picked at random, were told to come up to the front and take down their trousers. They were then beaten hard with the fives bat, before the eyes of the whole school. The second occasion was when three quite senior boys, members of one of the classes who were supposed to do their prep uninvigilated in their classroom, climbed out of the window and went for a night walk on the near-by common. As ill luck would have it, they ran into the Headmaster's brother, Sir

Alexander Stow, who happened to be taking a walk. Naturally, he reported them. They, too, were publicly spanked – five each with the fives bat. One thing about this I have never forgotten. Mr Morris's place at prayers was at the back of the big schoolroom where we assembled. During the pause while the culprits were taking down their trousers and Mr Stow had gone out of the room to get the fives bat, the silence was broken by the sound of Mr Morris shambling up the length of the room. He drew out a bench and placed it exactly at a right angle to the desk over which the three boys would have to bend. On this he sat down, leaning forward with his elbows on his knees and his hands together, with the air of a connoisseur who was not going to miss anything.

The junior masters were not allowed to beat, but an open-handed cuff across the head or even a kick up the backside were regarded by us as all in a day's work. Mr McIntyre, the veteran master of the new boys' form, refrained from cuffing, but used to grab people by the hair ('Ow, sir! Ow, sir!') and hold them forth at arm's length for questioning and derision. Notwithstanding, he was respected and popular, for he too possessed warmth and humour, and he taught well.

Everybody nowadays talks about the 'humiliation' of corporal punishment, cuffing and so on: but we never felt humiliated. A cuff was neither here nor there, if you knew it was merited. As for a spanking, you felt rather proud of having endured it well, and would hasten away to describe it in detail to your friends. I remember walking over to Horris Wood with 'Paddy' Ewart, on the evening when he had been one of those publicly spanked.

'Did it hurt, Paddy?' I asked.

'Yes, it did,' he replied in a casual tone. 'Quite a lot, actually.'

I knew that for him to say this it must have been agonizing.

The junior masters were virtually all young men in their twenties, some of them at a loose end, not particularly able and without any real sense of vocation. In the cases of some, it was apparent even to us that they were not particularly committed. Most stayed a few terms and then moved on to things like the Colonial Service, Australia or Malayan rubber. Mr Stow's nephew, referred to as Mr Monty Stow, was a permanency, but he was expecting to take over the headmastership in due course. It's surprising, really, how much we did learn from those half-interested young men and from old

Miss Jarvis. But one must bear in mind two factors. First, by modern standards, the syllabus was limited; and these were little boys, who were learning their rudiments; almost any reasonably intelligent grown-up could have taught them with the help of a good text-book. Secondly, there were rarely more than nine or ten boys in a class. I'm sure that it is to this pupil-teacher ratio that I owed my relative academic success – if it can be so called. There's nothing like a good start and the early inculcation of a serious approach. You couldn't help but attend and work seriously with only nine or ten people in the class and the master less than five yards away.

I was speaking, however, of the commonplace nature of punishment and physical coercion in those days; and here I must mention one exceptional figure, since with him alone (and one other, later, as I will tell) I have remained, as you might say, stuck – e.g., in dreams and in revenge fantasies after a few drinks. (My daughters, when they were little, used to say 'Strobe lights for Daddy's hate spot!') Mr Peter Delmé-Radcliffe was to all outward appearances a straightforward prep school master of the day – about twenty-six, tall, a good cricketer and intellectually perhaps a shade above normal, for he taught quite a senior form. He was completely humourless, with a cold, sneering, sarcastic manner which made him hated throughout the school. He handed out punishments right and left. He seemed to dislike everyone, including himself. I recall another, kindly master called Denzil Young, who was a personal friend of my brother, remarking to him once, during the holidays, that it was a great pity that 'Delmé' had ever taken up teaching.

One afternoon, I and eight or nine others were enduring a history lesson in which 'the Rad', as he was called, was expounding the feudal system. Having written 'King William' at the top of the blackboard, he was proceeding to illustrate how estates and manors were held by barons, knights and the like from their feudal lords. 'And Geoffrey,' he said, writing as he spoke, 'holds two manors of his lord Stephen.'

Sitting across the room from me was my friend Stephen Whitfield. I caught his eye and smiled. The next moment, in two strides, Delmé-Radcliffe was down on me, uttering I know not what about 'laughing in my class'. He repeatedly beat my head from side to side, first with the book he was holding and then with his open hand, until I was dazed, and fairly badly hurt. It seemed unreal, as in a dream. When he finally stopped, the class sat in a kind of stunned amazement. As I recovered, my sense of resentment and abuse actually led me as far as a kind of cryptic protest: I sat muttering 'Phew!' and looking from one companion to another. Everyone seemed shaken.

On another occasion I was seated two or three places away from Delmé-Radcliffe at lunch. (The masters sat at the ends of the long tables.) Speaking across the table to another boy, I said, 'I expect Monty will be there,' meaning Mr Stow's nephew.

'*Who* do you expect will be there, Adams?' interposed Delmé-Radcliffe.

'Sir,' I answered with some embarrassment. 'Mr Monty Stow.'

'Yes, well, now you'd better go and stand in the corner, Adams,' said Delmé-Radcliffe. 'I for one shall be better off without you for the time being.'

I duly stood in the corner until the meal was over and everyone had left the dining-room. Then Delmé-Radcliffe called me out to him and told me that I could spend the afternoon (it was a half-holiday) writing out 'I must not be insolent' three hundred times.

This type of imposition was a common punishment at Horris Hill, but the tariff was usually fifty times. A hundred times was regarded as severe. This was unheard-of and, to an eleven-year-old, mind-boggling. It was like being told to move ten tons of earth. I can't remember whether I said anything in reply.

To write 'I must not be insolent' in a fair hand takes about ten seconds. Allowing for natural pauses, one might perhaps say that five a minute would be good going. Remembering that this was an eleven-year-old and that the task was a long one, let us say he could hope to average four a minute. Mathematically the job should take an hour and a quarter (to do him justice, perhaps this is what Delmé-Radcliffe thought) but I remember it as taking rather longer than that. No one in the school had ever heard of three hundred times.

Enough of Delmé-Radcliffe: I've never come across him since. It was all due to a sense of insecurity, I expect, and no doubt he had his own troubles. But I wish he hadn't left a sort of lasting bruise on my memory. One ought to be able to overcome these things.

I've even known people who have achieved it in regard to the Japanese at whose hands they suffered, so I've really got no case against poor old Delmé.

Talking of injuries, I suffered three physical ones during my time at Horris Hill, and I think these are worth recounting, as they may make some parents realize how easily quite nasty injuries can be sustained by little boys at boarding-school. The first occurred while I was arguing about some nonsense with a slightly older boy – who wasn't, actually, a bad fellow, though rather uncertain and unpredictable. We grew more and more heated and may even have scuffled a little. Anyway, suddenly T— seized my thumb and bent it violently backwards. It threw me to the ground. It remained painful for a good week or two and got better only by slow degrees.

The second occasion, though nasty, was pure bad luck, with no malice involved. It was the last day of term – the day before breaking-up day – and we were all carrying our small personal belongings up from our lockers to our dormitories to be packed in our trunks. I had my things – writing-paper and envelopes, a box of dominoes, some crayons and so on – in a small pack, which I was holding on my back with a hand over each shoulder. As I entered the dormitory I was singing, and this tempted my friend Derek Seth-Smith, without the least unfriendliness and with a cry of 'Whoops!' to put out a foot to trip me. He meant me only to stumble, but unfortunately I fell prone. My hands being where they were, I could not put them out to save myself, and fell full on my mouth and chin. My lower left canine tooth drove into my upper lip, and my top left front incisor took a knock which I felt sure must have broken it. I screamed in shock, Seth-Smith began to whimper with fear, and both Gozzer and the master on duty came hurrying. I was bleeding quite dramatically and looking like Dracula, but a quick trip to the dentist in Newbury showed that nothing needed to be done. It was bad enough, though: I have had a hard little lump in my upper lip ever since, while the incisor has remained slightly wonky. I wouldn't care to tap it with a pen, for instance.

The third thing was just plain stupid, but it shows how unreflecting small boys can be. It happened before I had gone over to Horris Wood and while I was a member of Dormitory Four, the biggest dormitory at Horris Hill itself. One morning I committed some misdemeanour while Harrison, the captain of the dormitory, was still along in the cold bath room. The dormitory second, a boy called Meredith, decided to deal with me himself, and made me stand still, with my hands behind my back, while he boxed my ears. When Harrison came back he was told what had happened and said that he himself would now box my ears again, which he proceeded to do.

It is the truth, believe it or not, that it did not occur to me to connect this with what followed. A day or two later I began to have earache in my right ear. I was no stranger to earache, of course: once more there was a garden in my ear. I went up to Sister Wood, who felt that my father ought to have a look at it. He in turn decided that he would like an examination by a London specialist, which surprised and rather startled me, for in our family the general policy was to make light of indispositions and take them in your stride. He had a friend of student days at Bart's, a Mr E. D. D. Davis, who had become an ear, nose and throat specialist in Harley Street. So to Mr Davis – a little, dark, alert man like an Aberdeen terrier – I was taken, dressed in my best suit and pleased to have a day off in the middle of term. I can't remember much about it, except that he was very nice to me; but what followed was that I was taken home and kept a week in bed. All I knew was that I had seen on some piece of paper or other that I had 'otitis' (which means inflammation of the ear). When I returned to Horris Hill, I got teased quite a bit for malingering, and Mr McIntyre, having picked up the 'otitis', nicknamed me 'old osteophitis' (but it didn't stick).

It was not until years afterwards, as I was talking one day to my mother, that she told me that Mr Davis had said that I must have received a very severe blow to the head; and that Mr Stow, tackled by my father, had maintained that that was quite impossible. I think that it may have been at this time that the cooling of their relationship began: for a cooling there certainly was, and in his later life I often heard my father speak disparagingly of Mr Stow. Certainly, if Mr Stow had a fault it was that he would never hear a word against Horris Hill. For instance, the food (I now realize) was unimaginative and not good, but the slightest criticism – even a mere leaving on the plate – invariably brought Mr Stow down on the offender like a wolf on the fold.

The Horris Hill curriculum of those days would, I am sure, strike a lot of people now as, simply, incredible. Its purpose was to get as many boys as possible into Winchester. Other schools were not ruled out and boys who were obviously not up to the Winchester entrance were not sent away, but merely hived off to finish their time in a special form (no Greek) taken by Mr Liddell. Nevertheless, entrance to Winchester was what Horris Hill was all about. Before breakfast, fortified by cocoa and biscuits, we did forty minutes' early school, which was usually devoted to hearing or correcting last night's prep. The first period after breakfast lasted an hour and a quarter, and was devoted to Latin or, in the upper three forms, to Greek. This meant Kennedy's *Latin Grammar*, Caesar, Ovid and Xenophon. After this there was an hour's French, then an hour's break (nets in summer, puntabout in winter) and then another three-quarters of an hour's Classics. Into this lot English literature, divinity and poetry could be inserted at the whim and discretion of the form master – and that went for the setting of the evening's prep, too. After lunch, four days a week, there would be an hour's math, followed by an hour's history or geography – two of each every week. These were taken rather easy, since everyone knew that what really mattered was the Classics. I can still remember my gender rhymes to this day (and very sustaining they are, too).

> A, ab, absque, coram, de,
> Palam, clam, cum, ex and e,
> Sine, tenus, pro and prae.
> Add super, subter, sub and in,
> When state, not motion. 'tis they mean.
>
> Abstract nouns in "io" call
> Feminina, one and all . . .

One of the things that I enjoy in Benjamin Britten's *The Turn of the Screw* is the play made by the little boy, Miles, with the gender rhymes and the Benedicite:

> Amnis, axis, caulis, collis,
> Clunis, crinis, fascis, follis, bless ye the Lord.

All this, really, was the old Victorian classical education. Science, biology and any sort of technology were of no account in the education of young gentlemen. The general idea was that if you had a mind which could translate 'The Wreck of the Hesperus' into Latin elegiacs, then you had a mind which could tackle anything appropriate for a gentleman.

For 'gentlemen' was what mattered and no error. I have never, before or since, lived in such a class-conscious and snobbish atmosphere. Among the parents of these boys the snobbery was somewhat masked; the edge taken off a bit, as it were, by euphemism ('Well, perhaps that's not quite the sort of thing we . . .'), reserve, moderation and restraint. Among the boys it was open, articulate and undisguised, virtually the principal value in life. The Horris Hill word for anyone not considered a gentleman was a 'rustic'. This automatically included all workmen, shopmen, servants and so on; servant-girls were 'skivs', and no other word was in use. But beyond this distinction lay the finer business of penetrating disguise, pretence, imposture. Might someone purporting to be a gentleman really be a rustic? I came in for a certain scrutiny here, for my father was the school doctor – a sort of servant – and though I retained friends, I did not entirely escape calumny. Thank goodness! For that saved me from becoming drawn into – or at any rate from subscribing to – this scale of values. Recognize it I could not avoid doing – in the same way that one can recognize stinging nettles. Yet to this day I cannot help silently applying the criteria. Endorse them I never did. 'Your mater does the cooking, doesn't she, Adams?' asked a thirteen-year-old who was with me in the top form at Horris Hill. When I replied that that was so, he turned away with a snigger.

There were really two criteria. Speech, obviously: this had to conform to the southern upper middle-class norm, although a slight admixture of Scotch or Irish was acceptable in boys who might come from those parts. But clothes were almost as important. These had to be 'right'. For example, to wear a school cap in the holidays was really bad form, and I well recall the embarrassment and distaste made plain to me on this account when I once ran into two Horris Hill boys at Newbury races. To be convicted of acting like a rustic was virtually a *moral* condemnation. Indeed, it was stronger than several sorts of real moral condemnation. A single act, showing that someone had been a bully or a sneak, would be roundly condemned but fairly soon forgotten; yet to be a rustic would have been an ineradicable stigma. I say 'would have been' because I can't remember anyone at Horris Hill who actually *was* a rustic. (I expect Mr Stow saw to that.) This outlook didn't, however, rule out becoming friendly with the boot-boy, the drill corporal or the school carpenter. They were 'jolly decent rustics': i.e., they recognized the social distinction.

The other main ingredient of our society that I remember is, I reckon, universal among little boys at all social levels, never has changed and never will. In adult society, people commonly avoid contradiction, contention and argument, and refrain from correct-ing others. Boys aged nine to thirteen are unremittingly contuma-cious, contradictory and condemnatory, for ever squabbling, bandying words, picking bones and setting each other to rights. There had been very little of this at Miss Luker's. At Horris Hill it was incessant. I got to know the gentler, milder boys – Tim Reynolds, George Glossop, Tony Pawson – who didn't go in for dropping on everyone for any little thing, and made friends of them. But since you had to live in school society as a whole, nothing could keep you entirely out of the way of the sharp-tongued and the captious. On this account alone, prep school life is something one can feel happy to have outgrown. I have noticed that when one does occasionally run into old Horris Hill boys out of that generation – about 1927 to 1934 – they are not usually particularly forthcoming with happy memories.

My greatest comfort and pleasure during this time continued to lie with books. There was a reasonable amount of leisure in which you could read, especially on Sundays, which, in accordance with the system, were days of 'rest', i.e., inactivity. But over and above this, I devised a crafty scheme for reading during evening prep. One of the books with which we were issued was a very good verse anthology. I can't remember what it was called, but I wish I still had it. You could add this to the Latin grammar, math book and so on which you were taking from your locker to your desk for prep. Unless the invigilating master happened to be your own form master (and the odds were against it), he wouldn't know but what you had some verse to read or learn as part of your prep. With a bit of effort you could get the hour's prep done in three-quarters of an hour, which left fifteen minutes for reading the verse book. This was really supportive, a true escape.

O, young Lochinvar is come out of the West.
In all the wide border his steed was the best . . .

Whenever the moon and stars are set,
Whenever the wind is high . . .

Hamelin town's in Brunswick,
By famous Hanover city.
The river Weser, deep and wide . . .

'William Dewey, Tranter Reuben, Farmer Ledlow late at plough . . .'

Oddly, I became fond of the few Hardy poems in the book – 'This is the weather the cuckoo likes', 'When I set out for Lyonnesse', 'Christmas Eve, and twelve of the clock'. I knew nothing, of course, of the autobiographical and personal background to 'When I set out for Lyonnesse', but I grasped clearly enough that the writer had had some marvellous, transcendental experience; and that was sufficient. Hardy's standing as a fine poet needs no boost from me, but I think it lights up, as it were, a further corner of his genius that he made this direct appeal to a ten-year-old who didn't even know who he was or anything about him.

My greatest discovery at this time – the one which added a new dimension to awareness – was Walter de la Mare. I found in the school library a hardback copy (paperbacks hadn't been invented) of *The Three Mulla-Mulgars*, with the two coloured illustrations by E. A. Monsell. This was, in the event, to turn out to be one of the most important influences on my whole life, though of course I could have had no inkling of that at the time. I became entirely rapt, lost in the book. It seemed more real to me than my surroundings. There were no other books: this was the only real book. I was Nod in the snow, puny but nevertheless possessed of some strange, numinous power. Beyond the boring outward world this other, valid world of the imagination really existed; a remote, dangerous place, with its own animals, trees and plants, where all the inhabitants were animals (except Andy Battle, of course, and he, too, was remote; a shipwrecked sailor.

Me that have sailed leagues across
Foam haunted by the albatross . . .).

I put a friend, whom I judged to be likely, on to the book, and for weeks we conversed in references, proper names and quotations. We came within half a plank of worshipping Tishnar, but that would have been dangerous (and too revealing: we had no wish to hear her traduced).

Since those days I have read the book many, many times. Often I have set out to read it aloud to various people. My mother loved it, but I could never get my feeling for the book across either to my father or to my sister. Indeed, they teased me. This surprised and somewhat upset me. It was the first time that I had had the experience which I reckon that as we grow up we all undergo in one way or another. We find that even our intimates, and those we love very much, do not always understand or empathize with things which we ourselves feel deeply: either they don't feel them at all or else they see them differently. In the deepest recesses of the imagination we must expect to find ourselves often alone, separated even from our closest friends. (I was once in love with someone who hated Jane Austen.)

That wasn't, however, by any means all there was to Walter de la Mare during this time. One of the masters, Denis Fussell – may his name be blest for ever – had acquired the newly published *Poems for Children* (1930), comprising 'Songs of Childhood', 'Peacock Pie' and about forty other poems; and somehow the book came my way. By gum, some 'poems for children' those are! They flung open the door upon a numinous, night-blue world of incessant danger, wild beauty, loss, fear and death; no pretence or dressing-up (like M. R. James), but deeply felt and sincere, and all cast in words of storm, rainbow and wave. They struck into my heart the full realization of humanity's ultimate ignorance and insecurity in this world; and this has never left me, having since been endorsed again and again by just about everyone from Beethoven to William Golding.

> Who said, "Peacock Pie"?
>   The old King to the sparrow:
> Who said, "Crops are ripe"?
>   Rust to the harrow:
> Who said, "Where sleeps she now?
>   Where rests she now her head,

Bathed in eve's loveliness"? –
  That's what I said.

Who said, "Ay, mum's the word";
  Sexton to willow:
Who said, "Green dusk for dreams,
  Moss for a pillow"?
Who said, "All Time's delight
  Hath she for narrow bed;
Life's troubled bubble broken"?
  That's what I said.

VIII

My father's character was in certain respects oddly paradoxical. As I have told, with his time he was more than generous to his children. I spent long, happy hours in his company, being read to, walking in the country or simply accompanying him on his morning rounds. We never seemed to have too much of each other. In minor ways he, like my mother, spoiled me. Once, for example, I remember how I had been rather 'going on' for a day or two about how much I wanted a certain boxed game (I was very fond of indoor games) in which one 'caught' cardboard fish with small magnets on the end of miniature rods and lines. That afternoon I raised the matter again.

'All right,' said my father. 'Let's go down to the town now, and buy it.'

I was delighted, and was about to precede him out of the garden door that we normally used, when he said 'Let's go this way' and unexpectedly went down the hall towards the front door.

The game, wrapped in brown paper, was already stuck in the letter-box. We spent the evening playing it.

Yet this open-handed generosity did not extend to our education or our careers. My sister has since told me that when she got her entrance to Girton, my father wasn't at all keen for her to go up. He said he couldn't afford it, and it was only the formidable Miss Luker ('Nonsense, Dr Adams!') who coerced him otherwise. He used to say that he could never see the advantage of going to a university, since you were no better qualified when you came down. (He himself, of course, had gone from school to Bart's.) 'Much better get on and get a job.'

The funny thing was that if you asked him 'What job?' he had no particular ideas: he seemed to have no ambitions for the children he loved so much. I believe he would have been quite content for my brother and myself to take jobs, say, in a bank in Newbury (though, to do him justice, he paid for my brother to become a solicitor).

The real trouble was that he was not making a great deal of money; that much even a child could perceive, for during the early 'thirties our establishment began to dwindle, and went on doing so. Once, when I was little, we had had a gardener (Thorn), a cook and two housemaids. I can't remember the details, but gradually we came down to Thorn and one maid. ('Your mater does the cooking, doesn't she, Adams?') Yes, she did, and she did it loyally and well.

I had vaguely supposed that I would go from Horris Hill to Winchester, but as my last term approached it was clear that my father had other ideas. He reckoned he could get something reasonable in the way of a public school for less money, but he also wanted it to be not too far away from home. He meant to keep an eye on it. Casting around, he hit on the very place to suit him: Bradfield. He went over there, taking me with him, to meet and talk to the Headmaster. He liked the Headmaster and more than liked the look of the school; their business was soon done. I was put down for the Michaelmas term of 1933.

Bradfield lies on the Pang, about a dozen miles north-east of Newbury, in the heart of the Berkshire countryside and not far from Pangbourne. Like a pretty girl, the school has for a start a great asset in its favour. Both it and its surroundings are very beautiful. The school buildings are anything but compact, extending in a rambling way, from the south bank of the Pang up the hill known as Hogger, and covering more than a quarter of a square mile altogether. Open country lies all around, and out beyond the Pang, about a mile away, lies the extensive woodland known as Greathouse Woods. There can hardly be a more attractive school site in the whole country. The first-eleven cricket ground, known as Pit from the high banks which surround it on three sides, is outstandingly beautiful.

The place began in 1850 as a sort of choir school for the village – a kind of serious hobby, one might say, of the founder, a local gentleman called Thomas Stevens. By 1881 Stevens had in effect gone broke. He couldn't pay the staff, so he handed the place over to the then headmaster, Herbert Gray. Gray was to Bradfield what Arnold was to Rugby. During the thirty or more years (too long) that he was headmaster, he not only made the place solvent but built it up into a reasonable minor public school. Whitworth was the third headmaster to follow Gray and, although a limited man and in some respects even a little ridiculous, succeeded, largely by being a man of conscience and complete integrity, in keeping his staff loyal and even attached to him, favourably impressing parents and in general maintaining the standing of the place.

As is well known, Bradfield's unique feature is its Greek amphitheatre, constructed by Gray, during the late eighteen-eighties, from a disused chalk-pit, using the labour only of boys and locals. As far as I know, it is the only amphitheatre of its kind north of the Mediterranean. Here, triennially for the past century (except during the wars), an ancient Greek play has been acted in the original Greek. Gray himself, in his time, used to play the Choriphaios. The benefit and value of the Greek theatre and, simply, its power to influence for good and to confer happiness upon thousands of people – upon which I will expand later – have been another important feature of my life and had a great effect upon me. As I grew older it became – and remains – the best thing Bradfield gave me. To go there still brings its own singular delight. I am a Bradfieldian: this is my theatre – has been for more than fifty years – where I can honestly say that I have been more consistently happy than anywhere else. This blessing, however, was still to come.

I was the first boy ever to go from Horris Hill to Bradfield. (Now they go in numbers.) Many years later I heard (from John Moulsdale, a kind of Bradfieldian Mr Chips) that Whitworth, meeting Mr Stow at some sort of academic get-together, said 'Well, Stow, so you're sending me a boy at last.' 'A very peculiar one,' replied Stow.

For a boy in the top form at Horris Hill to take nothing more than the Common Entrance exam to a school like Bradfield was felt to be almost – if not quite – a discredit. Neither Mr Stow nor Mr Morris, of course, said anything to imply this, but my form-mates did – plenty. I had no recourse but to bear this as best I could. The way things turned out – and in the light of Nicholas Monsarrat's account of Winchester at that time in his autobiography, *Life is a Four Letter Word* – I can only feel very thankful that I went to Bradfield.

However, it would have been a strange new boy of thirteen who could have arrived at any idea of this. In those days life at Bradfield was – by modern standards, anyhow – harsh. At least, it was harsh at the bottom, though I was to find out later that it was not so harsh at the top. The academic work was all right – I came top of my class during my first term, and was told by the form master (that same John Moulsdale) that I ought really to have been placed in a higher form – and so were the games. But over and above these was the fagging, which was severe. This fell into four categories, of which the worst was house-room fagging. House-room fags were organized in gangs of four – a head fag and three others – who were 'on' twice a week. (The Sunday gang had only Sundays.) Their job was to sweep and dust the house-room (where all but the most senior boys lived when not in class or at games) in the evening, before prep. They had twenty minutes in which to do it. This doesn't sound bad, but in practice it was murder. To start with, the brooms were worn and wobbly-headed from hard use, and the damp rags for dusting smelt sickly-foul. Twenty minutes wasn't time enough for the job. The fags (not allowed to take their coats off) worked like demons, all of a sweat. The brooms raised a choking dust which hung thick in the air like fog and fouled your hair, your neck and your clothes. Afterwards, you could cough or blow your nose and the mucus would actually be black. The raised dust settled on the tops of the lockers and on the windowsills and undid the work of the fag doing the dusting. Bigger boys cursed you for the trouble you were causing. At last it was time to stop, though it could never be time to be done. Then came the crunch. The head of the house-room – not a prefect, but next in line – inspected the work. If he decided it was inefficient – and, like most jacks in office, he was usually hard to please – he could punish you – either the head fag or the whole gang. The punishment might be learning verse, or it might be doing an extra fag – that of someone else who had given better satisfaction. For consistently bad fagging – say, three times in a row – you were beaten by the junior prefect.

Then there was bell fagging. You were bell fag for the day about three times a term. This meant listening out of the window for the school bell and, on hearing it, running, fast, to ring the house bell (in our house, a war-time relic, the bell of a submarine, *B. 10*). This wasn't too bad, except that you were stuck with it all day and couldn't settle to much else. You had to be 'there', listening out. Study fagging was much more of a bore. There were two fags to each prefect's study, and they had to sweep and dust it, wash up the tea-things, clean the prefect's shoes and so on, in addition to their other fagging duties. It left little free time for the junior boys.

Finally, there was the practice known as a fag call. A prefect could enter the house-room and shout 'Fag!', whereupon everyone with less than two years' seniority had to run and stand in front of him. The last one to arrive was landed with the job – going to buy Mars bars, etc., from Grubs, or carrying a note to a prefect in another house. It wasn't a fair system, because the boys with lockers at the far end of the house-room stood the least chance.

Punishment by prefects for breaches of rules was common. A few years ago I met a contemporary at the Old Boys' annual dinner, and we began swapping memories. 'It was fascism, really, wasn't it?' he said. I could only agree. If a prefect at Bradfield told you to climb up the wall, you not only climbed up the wall damned quick, but you thanked him kindly for not kicking your bottom while you did so. The house was forever full of people learning verse, writing essays so many pages long, picking up rubbish from the gutters of the road leading down the hill, or getting up early to call prefects in their beds at some ghastly hour. A beating in the dormitory was a not uncommon event. The house prefects were allowed to beat only with the heel of a shoe. For a serious offence, the head of the house could beat you with a stick. Later, as a young officer in 1941, with Hitler at the gates and all on the hazard, I had to learn that British Other Ranks were not going to stand for the sort of discipline which had been the order of the day at Bradfield.

The school regime worked on the privilege system. As a new boy you had no privileges at all: as you gained in seniority you acquired some, and then more. It was a privilege to brew up on a Primus, to put your hands in your pockets, to whistle or sing, to wear a pullover, to call another boy by his Christian name. There was a whole host of sartorial privileges – brown shoes, coloured colours, tassels on mortarboard hats – for we all had to wear mortarboard hats and gowns – and heaven knows what else.

But the worst one was the prohibition on 'bitching'. Bitching was school slang for horseplay, but the term extended to any unbridled behaviour whatsoever. To push another boy was bitching; to take a hop, skip and jump or to swing from the branch of a tree was bitching. I remember a boy who was judged to be bitching by kicking a tin can. The rule against bitching was rigorously enforced, and the punishment was always beating. This meant that until you were in your third year, you couldn't let off steam anywhere at all (apart from games), and even in your third year only in the house-room: and these were healthy boys of thirteen, fourteen and fifteen.

In writing of Delmé-Radcliffe I said that with him and with only one other I have remained mentally stuck. This other was my housemaster, Mr B. M. Arnold. There was no way in which Mr Arnold and I could have hit it off. He was a most rigid and insensitive man, with no natural inclination towards literature or the arts, and a martinet who enforced the strict rules with no flexibility at all. His great obsession was with 'leave'. For any out-of-the-ordinary activity, such as attending a College society meeting or going, when bidden, to see another master during prep, you had to ask and receive leave. If you were a hair's breadth out of line – if you went early or came back a minute late – he would be on it like a knife, and any attempt to defend yourself only drove him into a terrifying rage. He was himself a distinctly limited man: he taught only lower school forms, and the general view (later corroborated to me by John Moulsdale) was that he had got his job only because Mrs Arnold was a close friend of the Headmaster's wife. 'Rather an unfortunate appointment, really,' said Moulsdale.

Mr Arnold had been a major in the Gunners during the Great War, and this – not his rank, but the war – he invoked incessantly. We must all be like the fellows who fought in the war, we must be worthy of their example, we must never give up but always fight on, etc. I can't remember ever having a conversation with him in which he showed any real receptiveness or sensitivity. On one occasion he quite literally shouted me down and punished me with stoppage of all leave for a month (to the fury of my form master) for something I hadn't done and given the opportunity could have proved I hadn't done. The trouble was that he could be very alarming in confrontation and there was no reasoning with him. His nickname was 'The Freezer' – to 'freeze' meaning to quell with a fixed, hostile and intimidating stare. I can never forget that freeze: it was like waiting for a hand-grenade to go off.

The harm was negative. To go to a public school and *not* to have a wise, understanding housemaster is to be deprived of something which ought to be a blessing and a major influence for good. The greatest single factor (for good or ill) in a boarding-school education is the boys' relationship with their teachers, which ought, ideally, to remain potent; a helpful, warm memory in later life. (Hence the public status of 'Mr Chips' as a kind of archetype.) When I saw, a few years ago, in the West End, a successful and long-running play, called *Another Country*, about a public school in the 'thirties, I was struck by the feature that the cast contained not one master and that no sort of relationship of the boys with the masters was ever touched upon. Yet this is what public school education is all about. The staff should be gurus, wise advisors, liked, respected people whom you feel you want to emulate. A universal situation like this is, of course, impossible of achievement in real life, but nevertheless it ought to be possible to bring about some of it, with some masters and some boys, some of the time. A housemaster whom you both fear and despise (as one grew older one could not but despise Mr Arnold – not, perhaps, for his conduct but certainly for his want of sincere interest in the arts) is a misfortune. In Arnold's time The Close (the name of our house) were reckoned a rough bunch of hobbledehoys. There's no doubt that a lot of us were – philistines – and Mr A. did nothing to remedy this. I doubt he was ever aware of or thought about it. But I will say one thing for him. At least he was conscientious and took the job seriously, according to his lights. He visited the sick, got round the dormitories and talked to people.

What I always felt and still feel about Bradfield at that time (and this is borne out by contemporary friends) was that the actual teaching – with certain honourable exceptions – was not up to much. In those days, a public school was a relatively remote, secluded microcosm. Parents were discouraged from poking their noses in. The media never turned their beams that way. It never occurred to headmasters and others to make public appearances (there was no television, anyway). In those enclosed communities, a master with good reasons for not feeling further ambition, having found himself a niche, could gently grow older and more eccentric in peace and quiet. The pressure of public examinations was nothing like what it is today. Far fewer parents and pupils thought in terms of a university, and for those who did, the universities were not difficult to get into, provided parents had the money. Quite a few of the masters at Bradfield were old shellbacks, some of them distinctly eccentric and certainly not people to push a boy on and devote themselves to getting the best out of him. This to a certain extent includes the Headmaster, for though a decent fellow, brisk, and knowledgeable about the staff and the school (he made an excellent first impression), he couldn't teach for toffee. In point of fact he *didn't* teach: he merely waffled. I don't think he prepared his lessons at all. (And he had no sense of humour.) Fortunately, however, I was later to come under the influence of two quite exceptional masters, who changed my life.

I have said enough to show that life for a junior boy (a fag) at Bradfield in those days was not only not very pleasant, but also a considerable strain – the academic work, the organized games and runs, the fagging – about as much as you could physically cope with.

Unlike Horris Hill, at Bradfield there was no allotted time for private prayer. And there was no sex education; none. Yet any kind of sexual crime was very severely punished. In a homosexual relationship – and there were plenty – the bigger boy might possibly be 'asked to leave'. Some of these relationships were touchingly sincere and helped both participants to find a bit of happiness and pleasure amid the rigours of College life. During my third year, when I was just sixteen and beginning to make a bit of a mark in the school by my writing, I got to know a senior boy in another house; Anthony Jacobs, the editor of the school magazine (in which some of my poems appeared). Reader, I married him; well, something like that, anyway. This was the rain-drenched summer of 1936, about the worst on record; day after day of rain, making games impossible. Anthony and I were blissfully happy. He was so considerate, so unselfish, so kind and even-tempered a lover that I can only asseverate, after all these years, that that was one of the happiest love relationships of my life. I myself was not moved to sexual activity, but I loved being desired by Anthony; I loved gratifying him; and I loved talking with him and being with him. He was himself of unconventional disposition; no mean poet, as well as being a fine musician and singer and a splendid actor. In short, he was excellent value and very good for me. His influence helped me enormously and I was proud to be his lover. That summer he played Feste in *Twelfth Night* in the Greek theatre. It was a notable production. I missed him like hell the following term, after he'd left. He went up to Cambridge and then became – with his beautiful speaking voice – a radio actor with the B.B.C.

I think the bad feature of the Bradfield regime was that it set out to hammer you into the deck, and in many cases didn't lift you up again. No doubt it is a good thing for boys to 'have the nonsense knocked out of them' ('Not fit to command until you've learned to obey'), but Bradfield had the effect of leaving me without any initiative whatever in objective life. It's safest to obey; it's safest to do what you're told; it's safest to take no offence, never to criticize and not to answer back. It's safest to defer to authority and take no chances. Let others take the decisions.

The only area of my life not affected in this way was the realm of the imagination, which remained untouched by the regime. In the realm of the imagination I move surely and independently, ready to take the initiative and to select and reject on no advice but my own. I know where I am and what I'm doing and have no apprehension. ('You shut up: I'm doing this.') Well, perhaps it was all for the best. Who can tell? But I think it's a great pity that the concept of self-respect was virtually omitted from that public school system of the 'thirties. Unless you came to be a prefect (which I never did) you couldn't really have much in the way of self-respect. Like Doolittle in *Pygmalion*, you couldn't afford it. You had to go in for lying, evasion and abject subservience. Getting round the fetters on your raw physical energy and your sexuality called for cunning and duplicity. I, of course, was no stranger to the unscrupulous. (The begonias.) But at Bradfield this developed into a policy of dodging and avoidance almost like that of Solzhenitsyn's Ivan Denisovich – except as regarded the academic work and the games, like fives and swimming, at which I wanted to excel.

I think it is worth recording one particular thing – a good and valuable thing among all the dreariness – which happened during my first term. The form I was in, known as Lower Shell B, had in its curriculum one period a week with the music master. What he did with us was entirely up to him. The music master was a quiet, reserved man called John Alden (who, as I was later to learn from Anthony Jacobs, on the whole disliked the system and most of the Senior Common Room). Alden's principal notion for the weekly hour was to have a lasting effect on me. Towards the end of term a string quartet were coming to give a concert at Bradfield, and Alden's idea was to familiarize us with the works which they would be playing. This he did partly with gramophone records and partly on the piano. He did it very well. By the day of the concert the principal subjects and the construction of the movements were clear enough, at any rate, to me. It was an excellently chosen programme: Haydn's Opus 64, No. 6, in E flat; Mozart's K458 in B major (the *Hunting Quartet*); and the Ravel Quartet. The whole business was a complete eye-opener to me: I had known nothing whatever of the construction of movements or how to listen intelligently to music. Of course, for a thirteen-year-old it was only scratching the surface. But it was a true start – a first step – an escape – into a valid fantasy world of solace and delight. Music is the most sure and splendid, the most estimable of all fantasy worlds – if indeed it is a fantasy world and not the only real one. Apart from anything else, that term's work with John Alden and the concert itself left me with an abiding love of the sheer sound of a string quartet. And there were Beethoven, Schubert, Brahms, Dvořák, Bartok and heaven knows who else to come. That's what I call education – adding new dimensions to life.

After two years at Bradfield things began gradually to improve. In the summer term of 1935 I took School Certificate, got seven credits (not very difficult) and next term, at fifteen and a half, got my remove to the upper school. I pressed strongly, on my own account, to be allowed to become a history specialist, and so found myself back in a class of no more than nine or ten people. My first academic year there, 1935–36, was pretty disastrous and boded little good to come. The study of history and the writing of historical essays require a particular kind of mental discipline and application, and neither John Moulsdale (who taught the English history) nor Whitworth (European) got this across to me at all. I wasted my time, really. By the end of the summer term of 1936 I didn't look like any sort of university entrant, and the Headmaster said as much on my report. (Not that my father cared.) However, in another sphere I had come under yet one more of the important and lasting influences on my life.

I have spoken of the 'old shellbacks' who formed the hard core of the Senior Common Room. However, few of these taught at fifth- and sixth-form levels. (They wouldn't have been able to.) A lot of the higher-level teaching was done by clever young masters who were on their way through – up the career ladder to appointments at more illustrious schools. Such a one was Mr James Hunt, whose speciality was Classics, and whose form was the Classical Fifth.

The upper-school system at Bradfield was that when you began to specialize you were hived off for your special subject – historians to Moulsdale and Whitworth, modern linguists to Monsieur Le Grand and so on. However, your actual form, for all official purposes, was held to be the form in which you did English literature. This, for me, was the Classical Fifth and the master was Mr Hunt.

At this time Mr Hunt would have been, I suppose, about twenty-six or thereabouts. (He completed his career as second master at Rugby and, now retired, teaches Classics extra-murally at Cambridge.) His teaching style was free-and-easy to a degree quite unknown both to Bradfield and to me. All the same, there was no disorder in his class. Anybody was free to say anything and there was a lot of banter and laughter, but he couldn't half teach English literature. I had, of course, already made some acquaintance with Shakespeare (*The Tempest* and *Macbeth*) and had read a fair bit of poetry on my own account, but now I found myself in the hands of a born teacher of outstanding talent. Mr Hunt made you feel that nothing was more exciting or mattered more than English poetry. Chaucer, John Donne, Gray, Cowper, Keats, Shelley, John Clare; and that controversial contemporary whose name was steadily growing, T. S. Eliot; Auden, Spender, MacNeice. We had to read them aloud. We found ourselves required to write sonnets, rhyming couplets, limericks, ballads in the Border style, short lyrics. We were asked to give individual assessments of poems out loud in class. I had never received such exciting and stimulating teaching in my life: I had not imagined that teaching *could* be like this. That 'other world' which I had frequented alone – the world of Walter de la Mare and Thomas Hardy – now opened wider every week, and was frequented by others; notably by Mr

Hunt. Life was beginning to make sense in a new way.

With personal poems, Mr Hunt was always ready with friendly criticism and advice. I made, through him, the acquaintance of Hal Lidderdale, the boy (before Anthony Jacobs) who edited the school magazine. Although three years older than I, he was quite ready to let me come to his study and talked to me like an equal. I learned a lot from him. I remember being arrested with delight by his repeating from memory of 'Take, O take those lips away'. I had never read or heard it before. Here is a short poem of mine which found its way into the school magazine about that time.

Profunda

Fathomless are the things which are known by instinct,
    not by reason.
The flaring of a flame, the fly-fall of a leaf,
The tinkling of a nail that rolls along the road.

Things fathomless as glass, and soundless in their sound
    as water breaking over stones:
The sound of apples falling to the ground,
The sound before a shot is fired,
The sound of clocks before they strike the hour.

Sights to the eye like skimming trout in shallows.
The butterflies, whose wings flash in the sun:
The opening of a bud which knows not why it opens:
We know not whence we come.
They know not who they are.
It knows not how it came to be.

Now that I look back on them, the generosity and tolerance of Mr Hunt amaze me. After College tea in the evening I (no more a fag) and like-minded others were free to stroll down to his lodgings by the Pang, to listen and talk about poetry and literature to our hearts' content. Sometimes I was late for prep, and then Mr Hunt would give me a note, which Mr Arnold, perforce, would have to accept grudgingly. ('What is it that you do, exactly?') I fear I must have let my contempt for him and his house show a little too plainly. The truth was that while I had hitherto endured what I had supposed to be the only life at Bradfield, I had now discovered another – life in the Classical Fifth, life under the aegis of Mr Hunt and, increasingly, among friends in other houses. Had I only known, however, I'd seen nothing as yet. The following academic year, 1936–37, was to blow a hole in my psyche a mile wide and change everything for ever.

IX

Meanwhile – that is, during this time of the mid-'thirties – things were changing at home. My sister had graduated very well in history at Cambridge – she got a Second in the first part and a First in the second – and was now teaching. One of her first appointments was at Exeter, and once I accompanied her when she drove down there in her rather Toad of Toad Hall-like Fiat (an open tourer); a terrific trip for those days. (It was actually she and not Mr Hunt who first put me on to the avant-garde T. S. Eliot.) To me she didn't seem any more absent from home than before, since she, like myself, was based there in the holidays.

My brother passed his Law Finals honourably, winning something called the Berks., Bucks. and Oxon. prize, and became articled to a solicitor in Newbury; John Louch, a distant relation of the family. These academic successes by one's elder siblings were a bit daunting. I certainly didn't look like doing anything comparable, but at least no one suggested to me that I had to.

I now have no alternative but to include in this story something painful and distressing. It didn't distress me personally at the time, but all the same it can't be left out. During these years of the mid-'thirties my father gradually took to drinking too much whisky. I have often, since then, wondered why. After all, he had a fine intellect (including a delightful sense of humour), a beautiful home, a loving and faithful wife and three children of whom two at any rate had done well at the outset of their careers. Reflecting today, I think I understand. First of all, I am told – it is common knowledge, is it not? – that doctors, as a profession, are somewhat prone to drink. It is largely to do with the continual exposure to anxiety, sorrow and grief unavoidable in a doctor's life. ('And could I have saved the patient?') Together with this, my father had grave money worries. I think he had really had them, more or less, ever since he had bought our beautiful home and garden and set up what was perhaps, for our means, a rather ambitious establishment. Then, he had been in his forties. Now he was in his sixties and no doubt the strain of the job, the scarcity of money, the pressure of competition from younger doctors and simply the weight of the years had begun to get him down. (But the whisky, which I would estimate at roughly half a bottle a day, must have cost quite a bit.)

I sadly fear that in this situation my poor mother didn't take what I would reckon to be altogether the right line. Though not teetotal or puritanically down on anyone having a drink, she had, with reason, a fear and horror of its effects in excess. She had been brought up a Methodist; and as a young nurse in her twenties in Bath had come to dread Saturday nights, when the battered wives and beaten-up pub fighters were brought in. I need hardly say that my father was never violent or even noticeably different in his manner. Nevertheless adults (if not I) could tell that he was drinking. My mother reacted with anger and condemnation, where perhaps a more sophisticated woman might have taken a different and helpfully sympathetic line. I don't know: how can anyone judge after all these years? Whenever she found the half-bottles of whisky – in drawers or elsewhere about the house – she would take them away. This meant, of course, that further ones would be locked up in the triangular Jacobean cupboard (the Marie Stopes cupboard – I have it now) to which my father alone had a key. Naturally, my parents' relationship suffered, though they never quarrelled openly before their children.

I, at sixteen, was largely left out of this – I mean, it wasn't mentioned to me by my mother, sister or brother – but naturally I couldn't help perceiving the disapproval of my mother and also of my brother. My own reaction was one of sympathy with my father, simply because I had always liked and respected him so deeply. I thought of him as the head of the family and it seemed to me that it wasn't for his children, at all events, to start judging or blaming him. It also seemed to me that my brother appeared almost glad to have a valid reason for censure, but now I think that was unjust. Anyway, I wasn't prepared to say or do anything that would damage my relationship with my father, which meant everything to me, as I believe it did to him.

In point of fact our relationship deepened during my last two or three years at Bradfield; partly, I suppose, because my father felt lonelier (and had less and less work to do), partly, perhaps, because he felt that I was one person who wasn't critical of him, and partly because I was developing new interests and activities in which he liked to play his part. In 1936 I won the school poem prize with a sequence of six sonnets dedicated to him (Mr Hunt's comments and criticism had been crucial), which of course pleased him very much. I was developing as something of a swimmer (100 yards breast-stroke and water polo), and my father liked to come to the matches. Quite often, too, on summer afternoon half-holidays, he would bring the car to some agreed rendezvous about a mile from College (no danger of running into Mr Arnold, who would certainly have made a fuss and whom my father had come to dislike) and we would walk and talk together. I had formed an interest in wild-flowers, and managed to get an award for my pressed collection in the school natural history exhibition.

But the best thing of all during these teenage summers was my father introducing me to fly-fishing. He himself, on the tennis court, taught me to cast, and after a bit I could do it well enough to have a stab at the water. That already-mentioned patient of my father, Mr Bertie Tull, who lived below Greenham Common, owned both banks of the Kennet for a considerable distance below Newbury, and thanks to his generosity and kindness I had access to virtually unlimited fishing – what with the side-streams and carriers, as much as a boy could possibly fish over during a long summer day. To start with I caught nothing but dace, but one evening I got a 3-lb. chub, and then, some evenings later, my first trout, which my father landed for me. From then on I was hooked for life.

The river was unstocked and untended, for Mr Tull was no plutocrat. No one else fished it. It was really a water-jungle, very different from the weed-cut, trim, lawn-mown and well-stocked reach of the Kennet which crook't age fishes nowadays. Any trout (or grayling) you came across were wild, and you could be justifiably proud of getting one out, for the weeds were never cut and there were sunken branches, tree roots and goodness knows what else. During the summer holidays I would sometimes spend all day on the river. I saw otters (though not often), herons, kingfishers and dippers, and one hot afternoon in a heat-wave I surprised among the rushes a badger, which thirst must have driven down from the woods to drink. Since those days I have fished in Connemara, Wales, New Zealand and Virginia, but never so idyllically and happily as during those far-off, pre-war, adolescent days on the Kennet below Greenham.

At this time, too, I took up chess. Either chess exerts a fascination over someone, or else it doesn't. Anyone who plays chess will understand my stout Cortez-like excitement as I realized that I had come upon an illimitable, inexhaustible world – the miraculous parenthesis of the chess-board. I had no dreams of becoming outstanding – that, I knew from the outset, would have required a dedication like that of a concert pianist, and even then I probably wouldn't have what it took. No, I just wanted to play chess with grown-up people better than myself and learn to become a decent club player. (This is just about what happened, actually: I finished up in my forties playing 6th board for the Department of the Environment.) I applied myself to chess books. In those days the great name was Capablanca. He was known by repute to everyone, including those who didn't play chess at all – to the man on the Clapham omnibus, as they say. I bought – at least, my father bought for me – Capablanca's *Primer of Chess* and *Chess Fundamentals*, and took my coat off to them. Another vaunted chess writer of those days – now, I understand, no longer regarded – was Eugene Znosko-Borowsky, author of *The Middle Game in Chess* and also of an attractive little book called *How Not to Play Chess*. (The first maxim it contained was 'Avoid Mistakes'.) I joined the Newbury chess club and there made some interesting friends. Another new dimension.

The members came from the respectable Newbury bourgeoisie. The top board was Mr Godwin, the tax inspector. Then came Mr Tom Webb, a grocer; Mr Franks, a tailor. Old Mr Bradfield, who was deaf, smoked a very smoky pipe, wore a black velvet skull-cap and took so long to move that he never finished a game. They were all very kind to me ('*I'll* give you a game, young doctor') and by degrees I improved. I remember the moment when it consciously entered my head that with a little more application and effort I might be able actually to beat some of these nice men. Then, one evening, something really exciting happened.

I was playing Black against a certain Mr Bance, one of the better players in the club. Mr Bance always adopted a rather off-hand manner when he played me, as though he were obliging me but not trying terribly hard. (No doubt this was true.) Whenever I played a bad or disastrous move – and this was all too often, for I hadn't as yet assimilated the basic ideas I was later to learn from the great Nimzovitch – Mr Bance would whistle disconcertingly and then proceed to put in the boot. However, this evening I was directly attacking his king in the middle game, with a combination of pawns, two knights and the queen. All of a sudden I saw – well, I thought I saw – that if I sacrificed my queen (which his king would have to take) it followed that I could mate him in two moves with the knights alone. I looked carefully at it. Surely it couldn't be so? There must be a snag. I went over it again and again and could see no flaw. I sat so long that Mr Bance became a little fidgety. (We didn't use clocks.) At length I realized that if I didn't essay the sacrificial attack I would be kicking myself for the rest of my life. I moved the queen and said 'Check!' Mr Bance looked at the set-up briefly, shrugged his shoulders and took the queen. He had clearly not seen what I had. I was now committed: there was no point in further deliberation. I moved one of the knights and said 'Check!' Again he hesitated only for a few moments before moving his king as I had foreseen he would have to. No apprehension clouded his brow. I made the third move, with the other knight, and again said 'Check!'

There followed a pause. At length Mr Bance said in a somewhat bewildered voice 'It's mate, isn't it?' 'Yes, sir,' I replied. 'I think it is.' 'Phew! That was pretty smart!' said Mr Bance. He was generous, too. He mentioned it to more than one member. But I didn't note down the position: I wish I had, though I think that to have done so there and then would not have been good form. I've never been able to recover it by memory.

I don't mean that this was a great turning-point in my development as a chess-player, or anything like that. Mr Bance often thrashed me subsequently, and I went on making silly mistakes, despite Eugene Znosko-Borowsky. But it was a taste of glory. I knew now that a thing like this could sometimes be done, and furthermore I had done it – once. I have never done anything like it again, but it's the kind of thing a chess-player doesn't forget.

One friendship which I made at the club – a strange one, I suppose, though it never seemed so at the time – has remained a warm memory. Dr Hickman (another well-known Newbury name) was at this time well on in his eighties, with a white beard, a piping voice and one lens of his spectacles smoked. He had once been a colleague of my father (who was twenty years younger) and lived in the middle of Newbury, in a beautiful old town dwelling-house on the corner of Bartholomew Street and Market Street. He lived alone, attended by two devoted, middle-aged maids (or housekeepers). He knew who I was, of course – when my father picked me up from the club the two of them would usually chat a while; and soon he gave me an open invitation to drop in at his house any evening I liked, to play chess. Of this I often availed myself, as much for the pleasure of his company and the charm of the surroundings as for the chess.

His parlour was neat, snug and wood-panelled, with numerous bookshelves and a coal fire. On the mantelpiece, under a small glass dome, stood a clock, about five or six inches high, made to look like an open book, with the hour on the left-hand ivory page and the minutes on the right. The right-hand pages, which were sprung, were held in retraction by a small metal claw: in the course of a minute this claw itself gradually retracted, until finally it released the uppermost right-hand page to flick over and join the left-hand pages, its reverse side showing the hour. Upon each hour, of course, the reverse side changed one on. I have never seen another clock like this.

Outside the French windows (also timber-framed) lay the long, walled garden, parallel to Market Street. White beehives there were, and dahlias, golden rod and antirrhinums, the bees droning and drowsing among them. You couldn't hear any traffic. I would be let in by the housekeeper ('Doctor's in his room, sir') go along the passage and open the parlour door. Dr Hickman would be reading – some small-print, Victorian book – holding it up high to the light and peering through his smoked lens. He would look up. 'Oh, it's you, young Richard. All right, you know where they are: get 'em out.' And I would go to the cupboard.

He played very much for fun. If I pondered too long, he would say, 'Come on, man, you're not playing for pound notes!' He had, indeed, the reputation of having been an impatient man in his day.

I grew to be more than fond of him. We had some great games in that Victorian parlour; and I heard some interesting reminiscences, too, for he had been born as long ago as 1849.

In 1938, during my last year at Bradfield, I learned that he was ill and abed. A week or two later came one of my father's characteristically brief communications. 'Old Hickmaninov has been gathered to his fathers, and I am sure he is glad of it.' He had left me his beautiful twenty-inch square board and his chessmen. I still have them. A label on the back of the board says 'Hickman'. It shall remain there.

Reader, after his death that beautiful, eighteenth-century house was bought by a 'redeveloper', razed to the ground and the garden obliterated by concrete. A petrol station stood on the land for some years, but now the whole neighbourhood has been once more redeveloped and the site of Dr Hickman's house and garden form part of the broadened highway of Market Street. There were no 'listed buildings' in 1938.

It was at about this time that my father gave me a bit of our garden in which to grow my own roses. I chose them carefully and he and I drove all the way from Newbury to Waterer and Crisp, beyond Reading, to buy them. Traffic lights had just been introduced in Reading. My father, over thirty years a motorist, had never seen traffic lights and he ignored them, simply looking right and left as he had always been wont. It was a hair-raising run, but I never said a word.

As a new dimension the roses were a great success. I sprayed, manured and learned how to prune. I well remember the first bunch I brought in to my mother, and how delighted she was. I can recall the names of several, but not all of them: Mrs G. A. Van Rossem, Madame Jules Bouche, Portadown Fragrance, Shot Silk, Etoile de Holland, Ivanhoe. I had a Paul's Scarlet Climber, too. Some of these names seem to have dropped out of catalogues nowadays, but others, like Shot Silk and Etoile de Holland, are still going strong.

Life in Mr Arnold's house at Bradfield had now become something from which I derived nothing at all and to which I felt I owed nothing. True, I fenced, played fives and swam for the house, but as I enjoyed these sports and they were organized to some extent on a house-competitive basis, I couldn't really do otherwise. I knew my housemaster would never make me a prefect, and I determined to try all I could to make him look a bigger fool for not doing so than he could make me look by depriving me. And so began the academic year of 1936–37, with no Anthony Jacobs and myself a distinctly dim, unproficient member of the History Sixth.

X

In their small classroom below the miniature rifle range (and not far from Mr Hunt's digs by the Pang), the History specialists found themselves facing a dark-haired, olive-skinned, slightly stout young man, rather good-looking, with a pointed nose and large brown eyes. He spoke pausingly, choosing his words or his next phrase with care, yet always incisively and directly. This was Richard Hiscocks, newly appointed to take over both English and European history at sixth-form level. He was also form master of the Classical Sixth, since he was to teach English literature at that level, too.

From the outset it was clear that Hiscocks was taking the job – and his pupils – very seriously indeed. He had obviously prepared each lesson carefully beforehand, and his style of teaching was deliberate and lecture-like. There were none of the sallies, badinage, quips and laughter which formed part of Mr Hunt's classes. Indeed, as we were to find out, if Mr Hiscocks had a fault it was that his sense of humour was a bit limited. Sometimes you could almost see him weighing up a joke he'd been told before deciding whether to laugh or not. To any red herring introduced by a member of the class he would respond courteously for a sentence or two before closing further irrelevance with his famous phrase 'Still we – er – can't discuss that now.' The Classical Sixth had a song, which went to the tune of 'You Can't Do That There 'Ere':

> Oh, we can't discuss that now.
> Oh, we can't discuss that now.
> Anywhere else we'll discuss that there,
> But we can't discuss that now.

Here was a change indeed from the Headmaster's dilettante, half-informed waffling! You could hardly take notes fast enough as Mr Hiscocks, in his gown and characteristic pose, leaning on the newel-post at the foot of the little flight of stairs which led down into the classroom, talked about Wallenstein and Gustavus Adolphus, or Archbishop Laud and the Covenanters. What with several other people needing them, you had a hell of a job to get hold of all the books he told you to read for your weekly essays. It was easier to buy some of them, like Tanner's *Constitutional Conflicts*, since there was usually only one copy of anything in the school library.

The big surprise came when Hiscocks said that he wished to see each of us tête-à-tête, at his own digs, for an hour every week, to return and talk about our essays and discuss our future work and progress. These, in effect, were tutes, as at Oxford or Cambridge. (Oh, *wouldn't* Mr Arnold be pleased, I thought: an hour out of prep once a week!) His subjects for essays were enigmatic and challenging. 'Is it right that Cromwell's statue should stand outside the House of Commons?' '"To the King's [Charles II's] coming in without conditions can be attributed all the evils of the reign. (Clarendon)" Discuss.' 'When examiners ask these questions,' explained Hiscocks, 'they're *getting* at something in particular. They want to see whether you grasp the vital point and can say – er – what they – er – want you to say.' Many were the private colloquies and puzzlings over what he wanted us to say: but after a bit we began to get the hang of it.

At the end of the first week he rated me so severely for the poor quality of my essay that he almost had me in tears. 'I don't think that represents an adequate standard of work for a sixth-form boy.' 'Oh, sir!' 'No, I *don't*.' And he proceeded to do something which none of his predecessors had got around to before. He began actually teaching me how to read for, prepare and write a historical essay. I dolefully poured out my heart to Mr Hunt, but he told me it was high time, and would do me nothing but good.

Gradually – very gradually – my essays improved. So did my enthusiasm. I began to realize that my lukewarm application and attention during the previous year had been due largely to the tepid quality of the teaching, and to not having been taught in the first place how to set about history as a specialized subject. Hiscocks was like a refiner's fire. (One or two people actually dropped out.)

He lived for the History Sixth. There was no subject in the world so rewarding and noble as history. But its proper study – and entrance to Oxford or Cambridge – required a whole, all-round man, and to this many-faceted matter Hiscocks addressed himself with no less ardour.

When it came to English literature, our travels in the realms of gold were so unforeseeable as to blow your mind. We read *Edward II*, *Tamburlaine the Great*, *The Winter's Tale*, *The White Devil* and *The Duchess of Malfi*, Shakespeare's sonnets, *The Shoemaker's Holiday*, *The Knight of the Burning Pestle*, *Philaster*, *Samson Agonistes* and – yes, we did – *The Ascent of F.6*. (I read the part of Ransome's mother.) In this sphere Hiscocks was less dogmatic than in teaching history. You were expected to have ideas and to voice them. He himself was very receptive of ideas from the form, and would often admit that he hadn't thought of that, and allow it to be pursued for a while.

He was keen on lecturettes. Members of the History Sixth would be allotted subjects to which to devote special study and on which to give short addresses to the class. I remember speaking – or doing my best to speak – on 'James I and the Spanish rapprochement', 'Shaftesbury and the Oxford Parliament', and 'Aspects of eighteenth-century music'.

For it must not be supposed that Hiscocks, in his sense of responsibility to his pupils, stopped short at history and English literature. That wouldn't provide fodder enough for university scholarship general papers. He had a gramophone with an enormous horn (the latest thing in those days) and on Sunday evenings anyone in the Sixth was invited to go to his rooms, listen and talk. From the National Gallery he ordered hundreds of postcard reproductions on a sale-or-return basis, and these were passed round and discussed in class. You were free to order those you liked, and encouraged to build up a collection. (This was how I first became acquainted with Gauguin, with Kandinsky and with Matisse.) I still have some of them. 'A painter's – um – true job,' said Hiscocks, 'is to make people see ordinary things in their true reality and as they have never seen them before. Now take the – er – seventeenth-century Dutch painters: Pieter de Hooch and – er – bricks, for instance . . .' Many years later, I was to travel in the Tahitian islands and find out that Hiscocks had spoken even more sooth than he knew. Gauguin painted exactly what is there to be seen.

Architecture we studied, and Hiscocks organized expeditions to Winchester and Oxford. I volunteered for a lecturette on Norman, and in the course of preparation found myself standing in a kind of daze in the north transept of Winchester Cathedral, and later actually moved to tears in the tiny, forlorn church of Avington beside the Kennet near Hungerford. As no book could, the austerity of Norman architecture told of a bleak, bare, northern world where the wind was cold, stones weighed heavy and vaults were round-arched and square in plan, because there was no other way in which vaults could be constructed.

It was at about this time that a series of articles by J.M. Keynes appeared in *The Times*, embodying his innovatory ideas on national economics and a policy for avoiding booms and slumps. Hiscocks cut these out and made me read and digest them thoroughly. 'It always makes a favourable impression, Adams, if you can answer a question on – er – economics.'

Every week Hiscocks had a period devoted to current affairs. Each member of the class was allotted a subject – the Far East, Germany, Domestic Affairs and so on – and was required to comb the respectable daily newspapers for items and make his week's report to the class. I wasn't very good at this (my subject was the Near East) and tended to be slangy and facetious in my reports. Hiscocks corrected this tendency, and I learned the value of speaking precisely, with dignity and an air of authority, when addressing an audience (or a panel of examiners).

You'd wonder how on earth we got through all this, but we did; to be continually stimulated and excited, and to feel your capacity and abilities growing in directions you had never imagined – such experiences are commonly agreed to confer pleasure. Hiscocks may sometimes have been a little pedantic and humourless (another of his pet phrases, which everyone could imitate, was, 'What's the – er – significance of that, Smith?' – or whoever you were). But as in the case of General Montgomery, like Hiscocks or not (and I did, very much), he was the right man for the job. I was naïf in those days and had no ideas whatever about my own future. I was entirely content to work for Hunt and Hiscocks, to swim and play fives for the school, to write poetry and to find myself at last out of the house-room and sharing a study with two boys I liked. It was as demanding and vivid a present as ever I have known.

.   .   .

I must now digress a little, in order to fulfil my earlier commitment to say more about the Greek theatre and its effect upon Bradfieldians.

Practically all British schoolchildren today have some acquaintance with Shakespeare. They read and act him at school. They study one or more of his plays for examinations. In recent years the admirable practice has grown up of producing the set play for the year in London and elsewhere, and the students are taken to see it. If you were to go enquiring among adults in a public bar on a Saturday night you'd probably have quite a job to find anyone who didn't know *something* about Shakespeare. (Who Shylock was, for instance.) Shakespeare is part of the general scene as he is not in America.

This means that everyone, as a matter of course, thinks of drama in terms either of the proscenium arch or the Elizabethan open stage, or both: and drama itself they think of as something essentially secular, intended to move swiftly, to exploit suspense and to be as realistic as the confines of the stage and theatre will allow. (Shakespeare spends a lot of *Henry V* in lamenting that he can't be more realistic, and the same point comes up a good deal in *The Knight of the Burning Pestle*.)

Ancient Greek drama springs from entirely different sources, is based on entirely different concepts of drama, moves slowly, excludes action on stage, is religious and not secular, verges on the ritualistic and is deliberately subject to various strict conventions. The audience all know the story, or it is assumed that they do. The topography of the stage is different from that of modern theatre, the relationship of protagonists, chorus and audience is a formal desideratum and the playwright's objects are different. I won't enlarge on this any more – it would take pages, anyway – but an excellent novel to which I recommend the reader is Mary Renault's *The Mask of Apollo*. This will give anyone a reasonably firm grip on the social background, the conventions and the nature of ancient Greek drama in its day.

Quasi-ritualistic in form, controlled by accepted conventions and essentially conceived and written as a series of episodes divided by choruses: these characteristics are integral with and follow from the ground plan of the Greek amphitheatre itself – σκηνη, ὀϱχηστϱα and surrounding βαθϱα. The whole set-up constitutes a different dramatic world, the product of a different society and having a different purpose from that of Elizabethan, Jacobean or later European theatre. Most people in this country go through life without realizing this at all, or having any notion that ancient Greek drama is a vital part of the European cultural heritage. But Bradfieldians take this in through the pores – they can't help it. In the summer term when a Greek play is on, it dominates and takes priority over everything else. Most people, including those not connected with the play at all, become familiar with it. A lot of people watch it in rehearsal and go to see it twice or even three times.

Yet how authentic is it? The answer must be, only to a limited extent. For a start, we are not ancient Greeks and theirs is neither our society, our religion nor our language. Again, we don't know how spoken ancient Greek sounded, or what their music or choral dancing was like. How much sense of involvement had the audience? I'd say a lot. They clearly had the sense of being reft out of themselves (catharsis), for we are told that the audience were terrified by the Eumenides, that pregnant women miscarried and heaven knows what besides. I have always admired Kenneth Tynan's proposition that drama consists in showing what people do when they become desperate. This certainly applies to ancient Greek drama, but whatever transporting feelings the ancient Greeks had, we can't really share them today. The Bradfield Greek play, however beautifully and sensitively directed and performed, can only take place, as it were, in a glass case. *We* are not worshipping Dionysos.

And yet, to feel oneself part of this singular tradition of Bradfield; to know the great plays themselves – *Agamemnon*, *Antigone* (as Hiscocks would say, one of the most – er – significant works in western literature), *Philoctetes* (another such), *Alcestis*, *Oedipus Coloneus*, the *Bacchae*, *Hippolytus* – to have seen and heard these performed in what must be – the theatre itself included – at least a respectable approximation to the original performances – this can only be counted a tremendous benediction, something always to feel grateful for. A true sense of the form and nature of ancient Greek drama – a visual knowledge – this is the privilege and heritage of Bradfieldians. And it's just about unique to them, too, apart from a few classical masters, dons *et hoc genus*.

I was lucky: there were two Greek plays during my time at Bradfield; the *Agamemnon* of 1934 and the *Oedipus Tyrannus* of 1937. Since then I have seen about thirteen Greek play productions – probably in total as many as any Englishman alive. They have had a lot of effect on my own work and on my way of thought as well.

In the bye years there was Shakespeare. Oh, wasn't there just! The Greek theatre, with its fine acoustics and enormous acting area, including the orchestra, the audience and even sometimes behind the audience, is ideal for this sort of drama. I'm sure Shakespeare would have loved it. As I have told, in 1936 *Twelfth Night* was produced, and in 1938 *A Midsummer Night's Dream*. This was my introduction to the latter play, and since then I have never seen a production informed by more sheer magic. The Oberon (Michael Halstead) was splendidly regal and sinister. The Puck (John Hopewell) seemed not human, a half-malicious gnome-creature of mischief and witchcraft. Peter Quince (Alan Helm) and Bottom (Tony Dallas) were side-splittingly funny. The whole story seemed to unfold under a kind of green, arboreal spell, and to this the music, specially composed by Cecil Woodham, contributed a great deal.

In 1939 the production was *Romeo and Juliet* (there were no girls in those days: all parts were played by boys), and although I had left by this time, I came to see it. I can only say I'm glad I did. My friend Euan Straghan was an outstanding Mercutio. Since then I've seen a lot of Shakespeare at Bradfield. Two particularly memorable productions were Charles Lepper's *Hamlet* and *The Taming of the Shrew*.

Without the Greek theatre I could not possibly have received anything like such an education in drama. I can only repeat, I have been more consistently happy in Greeker than anywhere else at all.

.   .   .

Now we have come to the Michaelmas term of 1937. By this time no thinking person over fifteen could fail to be conscious of Hitler. The country was split in two. There were people, even as late as now (and they included the Prime Minister, Neville Chamberlain, and quite a lot of his Government and back-benchers) who believed that Hitler could be bought off and war averted. They thought that the major threat was Russia, both on account of its great power and because twenty years before it had had a left-wing, Communist revolution and was committed, by Marxist and Leninist doctrine, to the destruction of capitalism. At all costs, thought the British right-wingers – the appeasers, as they became known – we must avoid a repetition of the horror of 1914–18. Even Hitler couldn't be so crazy as to want that. If we can do a deal with Hitler, there could be a strong Anglo-German alliance (plus France) and Germany will be our bulwark against the 'Bolshies'.

Up until the Munich crisis of September 1938, this was, as a matter of fact, a tenable view. But the whole argument rested on a false premise – namely, that Hitler could be trusted to keep a promise, that he too didn't want war and knew when to stop.

The left wing were diametrically opposed to all this. They consisted of the thinking working-class and the intellectual left – which of course included Hunt and Hiscocks and all readers of *The New Statesman and Nation* and the *News Chronicle*. On the whole, this lot were in sympathy with the Russian regime of Stalin, upon the true cruelty and horror of which they were completely misinformed. They thought Russia really was a country where there was true class equality and where working-men, through nationalization, had freedom from capitalist exploitation. They wanted us to be allied to Russia and, while we were about it, to take a reformist leaf or two (as they supposed) from Russia's book. They saw Hitler, quite correctly, as a cruel tyrant and an untrustworthy international crook, with whom sooner or later accounts would have to be settled.

So both sides were partly right and partly wrong. Chamberlain was tragically wrong in thinking that we could do a deal with Hitler, but right in thinking that the one thing the people he represented wanted to avoid at almost all costs was war. (He also knew we weren't armed and ready.) He was also right that Soviet Russia was a potential danger.

The Left were entirely wrong about Russia but entirely right about Hitler. They were also right in thinking that their own Tory Government was ready to give Hitler a great deal too much (such as Czechoslovakia) in the hope of avoiding war. They thought that if we'd stood up to Hitler and Mussolini earlier, over the Rhineland (1934) and Abyssinia (1935), we'd have stopped later trouble. They were right.

It's no part of the purpose of this autobiography to chronicle the politics of the time: but the point I want to stress is that from now on (about mid-1937) my generation lived in the knowledge of Hitler and the apprehension of war. It was 'business as usual', but always with that grim thought at the back of everything. My sister, that hard-headed realist, was under no delusions and consequently neither was I.

By autumn of 1937 I had become one of Hiscocks's star pupils. This had really happened because we suited each other. More mature boys, who had already formed ideas about what they intended to do, didn't really care for Hiscocks, and even ridiculed him in a quiet way: though not to his face, of course. They thought he was too imperative and ardent, and expected too much. I was as putty in his hands, but this does not mean that I didn't try to use my own mind. 'I'm not – er – altogether convinced of that, Adams.' (One of the rare smiles.) 'Convince me.' And I would proceed to try; sometimes successfully, sometimes not. Certainly Hiscocks could be a gauleiter, and one got to know where his sympathies (what Shakespeare would call his 'affections') lay. When he spoke of Stein, Hardenburg and Scharnhorst and of Turnvater Jahn, a kind of light would come into his eye and his discourse would wax extra warm, which was more than it did for Mazzini or even Garibaldi.

The information that I was lined up by Hiscocks to sit for the various Oxford and Cambridge scholarship examinations, with the first lot coming up early in December, had no particular effect on me; not of excitement or apprehension or anything else. I didn't even start thinking 'If I get an award – If I don't get an award –' I didn't think ahead at all. If this was something that Hiscocks wanted done, then I'd better get on and do it. I ought, of course, to have been able to talk it all over with my housemaster, but as for all practical purposes I hadn't got a housemaster, I simply left everything to Hunt and Hiscocks.

As the time drew on, Hiscocks's preparations were meticulous. We did bona fide three-hour papers for real. Since available time for these was a bit limited, we also did 'mock-ups', in which we were given a sample exam paper, required to choose four questions and to précis verbally what we would say and how. We did viva voce interviews, with Hiscocks pretending to be three dons. In all this my housemaster played no part whatever, except to be awkward and disobliging about the leave I had to get from him in order to fulfil Hiscocks's programmes.

Meanwhile, my dear father had become very ill. I have never known exactly what his illness was, but it must have been some kind of breakdown consequent upon his drinking. The opinion of my sister and brother, who took over the administration of the family's affairs, was that as I was safely away at Bradfield and in view of the impending exams and also of my deep attachment to my father, the more ignorance I was left in, the better. I was not told either that he was delirious or that his life was in danger. However, Mr Arnold – though inadvertently – soon dispelled most of this happy ignorance. It so happened that I now had a minor responsibility in the house – that of reporting to him nightly the names of those who had been absent from any meal that day. (They always had leave and good reason: no one would want to cut a meal. But this was the system.) Every evening at this time, when I went into his study to report, he would immediately ask 'How's your father?' This at first surprised, then disconcerted and finally alarmed and upset me. Well meant, I'm sure. I used to reply 'All right as far as I know, sir.'

That early December I set out for Oxford in fairly thick snow. The journey involved a bus from Bradfield to Reading, and thence a train. As I came under Tom Tower, clutching my suitcase, and got my first sight of Tom quad, it naturally startled and excited me greatly. Oddly enough, it didn't daunt me. Rather, it had the opposite effect. I thought, I had no idea that Oxford was like this. I know what I want now, all right: I want to come here – not necessarily to Christ Church, but somewhere. (My sister had already warned me 'Whatever you get, I don't think you'll be able to go up to Christ Church; too expensive.')

Dining that night in Christ Church hall – reached by way of the glorious staircase – reinforced my feelings. If this was what Oxford was like, then I was going to get to it. The sight of so many strangers – the other candidates – didn't unnerve me. I don't know why: it wasn't in character. (Mr Punch.) Apart from natural courtesy, I maintained a certain reserve. One little incident I recall. A fellow opposite me leaned across the table and said 'Would you moind passing the moist sugar?' Golly, I thought, a rustic! Competition from a rustic! I'll show him! This unworthy thought at least served to raise my morale. (I had never heard the term 'moist sugar' before: later I told my mother, and after that we always used to talk about 'the moist' in inverted commas.)

I wasn't offered anything as a result of those exams, although I learned afterwards that I had been considered for an exhibition at Merton. (The group of colleges involved was, I think, Christ Church, Oriel, Merton and Corpus Christi.) But I enjoyed doing the papers. This was for real, and it was encouraging to find that I *could* do them; and if I was any judge, do them reasonably well. Some of the results were posted up before we left Oxford. I remember hearing this while I was chatting among a little group of other candidates, and was unwise enough to enquire where the list might be seen. 'Oi wouldn't wurry!' said the moist sugar chap banteringly. Well, he must at any rate have had some money, that moist sugar chap, for next year he was up at Christ Church as a commoner.

I didn't feel particularly dashed by not getting anything, and Hiscocks had nothing but praise when we went over the paper together and I told him what I'd tried to say. The next scholarship exam was for Worcester College, on its own. The college was lucky enough to be second in line that year – to have second pick of the candidates. Hiscocks was calm and assured. 'The – er – field will be much clearer now, Adams.'

It so happened that at this time I stumbled into another of my periodic and virtually unavoidable rows with Mr Arnold about some slip-up over leave to go to a school society meeting, or something like that. It was his way not to impose a penalty or punishment at the time of the offence and be done with it, but to go on remembering it against you and accordingly to withhold the next two or three requests you might have to make. 'Well, in view of what you've done recently, I don't see why I should give you leave to go out on Sunday, do you?'

A little before I was due to go up again for the Worcester scholarship exam, I was suddenly summoned by the housemaster. 'Mr Hiscocks wants you to go and see him this evening. I said I had no alternative but to refuse permission.' Here he became a little incoherent. 'Your recent conduct – you people – But you've *got* to go, it seems,' he spat out, like a man thwarted beyond endurance. 'Somebody from Worcester College, or something.' I waited. 'You'll be back by quarter to eight and if you're not back by quarter to eight you'll be beaten. Is that clear?'

'Yes, sir.'

I got down to Hiscocks, who was openly frustrated and annoyed that I couldn't stay as long as he wanted. I was apprehensive of the housemaster's anger and threat, and made it 'twenty to eight', to be quite sure. 'The person from Worcester' turned out to be an old boy named Jimmy Gilman, a friend and fellow-historian who had gone up to Worcester the year before. (Did Mr Arnold know this? If not, why not? If so, why didn't he tell me?) Hiscocks had actually got Jimmy to come and give me the low-down on the dons of Worcester, their predilections, fads and foibles. He did so, most penetratingly and helpfully, for half an hour or more, until I felt I had cut it as fine as I could and must race back to the house. Mr Arnold did not, of course, bother to enquire whether all had gone well.

I had one final briefing from Hiscocks a day or two later. He had nice rooms, down at Lord's Farm, some way from College, but muddy of access in winter. Just as I was leaving to go out into the snow, he turned his head and looked at me over the back of the sofa. 'Do well at Worcester, Adams. It's a nice place: you'd like it.'

From the very start there was something propitious about the Worcester enterprise. The College, the beautiful quad, Dr George Clarke's library building, the gardens approached down a tunnel (like Alice), the lake, the playing fields – everything delighted me. As luck would have it, they lodged me in the De Quincey rooms – the finest undergraduate rooms in College. It was still bitterly cold, but when we got into hall the next morning, to start on the first paper, I found my place was near the fire, the only source of heat in the big room.

The papers might have been made for me. It was almost uncanny. 'Examine the Spanish connection as a factor in the reign of James I.' 'What restraints were placed upon the power of the monarchy at the Restoration, and how effective were they?' 'Estimate the contribution of Prussia to the defeat of Napoleon.' 'Compare and contrast Mazzini and Cavour as leaders of the Risorgimento.' Time was the only problem, and the invigilator had to stand over me and begin 'I'm afraid –' before I reluctantly parted with my European history answers.

The English essay was a brute. There was only one subject and no more. 'Character and intellect'. It wasn't my sort of thing at all, but I had an honest stab at it. ('Never start writing for at least an hour, Adams: longer, preferably.')

The general paper came last, on a dark, freezing afternoon. I couldn't believe my eyes as I read through the questions. 'Write a short appreciation of *one* of the following styles of English architecture: Norman; Early English; Decorated; Perpendicular.' 'Must epic deteriorate as civilization advances?' 'Of what use are museums?' 'Compare any two of the following:- Bach and Handel; Reynolds and Gainsborough; Keats and Shelley; Trollope and Dickens.' And there, at the foot of the page, 'What measures would you take to avoid a slump?'

As it fell out, this exam spanned the end of term at Bradfield, so I was returning home direct from Worcester. My mother, who loved to go out in the car whenever she could (she didn't drive), had been driven to Oxford by Thorn to take a look round, have tea and return home with me. She was early – the exam hadn't finished – but in spite of the cold she set out to have a walk round the College. As she was thus engaged, in some way or other she ran into and became acquainted with the medieval history tutor, Vere Somerset. Vere Somerset was a bachelor, at this time in his mid-forties, I suppose: something of an aristocrat (a connection of the family of Beaufort) and passionately fond of music. As I was to learn, he enjoyed arranging social occasions for his students and getting to know them. My mother, who had been a pretty girl, was always up for a little light flirtation, and what with my father's illness and our financial decline, must during the last year or two have come to feel rather deprived socially. Anyway, she and Vere Somerset took a shine to each other, and it was he with whom she had tea. A little later, in the early evening, I underwent a fascinating viva voce. All I can remember of it is that they were plainly well-disposed towards me, and that I had a friendly altercation with Mr Pickard-Cambridge, the distinguished philosopher, about the merits of Tchaikovsky as a composer. (I was pro-Tchaikovsky: Mr P.-C. courteously suggested that in time I would get tired of him. I can't say that I ever have.)

We were home in time for dinner, and I found my father coherent and convalescent. I knew intuitively that he had stopped drinking whisky (I expect he had been badly frightened), but he was ready enough to go two hundred yards up the road with me to the village pub and have a beer or two. We didn't talk about his illness, but I could tell he was as glad to see me again as I was to see him. He had retired from work, and I had the feeling that now that he would soon be recovered, he was likely to find time hanging on his hands. My brother was at home, but my sister – now teaching at the Frances Holland in London – hadn't yet arrived for Christmas.

I didn't have to wait long for news from Worcester. A day or two later my mother received a short letter from Mr Somerset in his own hand. It said how much he had enjoyed their meeting at the College, and then went on to tell her that it was intended to elect her son to an open scholarship the following day. In a P.S., he added 'I enjoyed your son's remarks on Keats and Shelley.' (I can't remember saying anything very original.)

Here was a go! My kind, serious-minded, responsible brother at once began worrying his head about ways and means. The scholarship (Worcester awarded two history and two classical scholarships annually) was worth £100 a year. At that time, it was generally reckoned that a student could manage in a modest way on about £240 a year. Where was the other £140 to come from? My brother set about the business of applying to the County Council for an auxiliary (county) scholarship.

A day or two later came the official invitation from the College, offering me the scholarship. It was necessary for me to accept formally in writing. At the same time arrived my sister – the arrival of whom I had been awaiting eagerly.

I had always respected and admired my sister. Her own fine university achievement had made me dare to hope that one day I might be able to manage something of the sort. During my time at Bradfield, although I had achieved certain academic successes, she had never spoken a word of praise or congratulation. At last, I thought, I knew why. It was because, as I now perceived, these had been relatively trifling, parochial matters, not really worth remark by a scholar of her standing. She had been waiting to see whether I was capable of doing something worthwhile in the real world. Now I had. Now, at last, she – the only knowledgeable, discriminating person, apart from Hiscocks and Hunt, whose praise was worth having – would say what she had been keeping back for something that really deserved it.

She showed up in her usual door-slamming, kick-off-your-shoes style. I waited happily while she had a drink and a meal. Afterwards, while she was reading the paper, my mother said something about the scholarship.

'Well,' said my sister, 'I do think someone might have taken the trouble to ring me up and tell me.' A little later she went out somewhere. She didn't allude to the matter again.

It still hurts, after all these years. But little by little I came to realize that her saying nothing was due not to deliberate unkindness, but to a sort of emotional inhibition which made it impossible for her to find or to come out with words of warmth or compliment. There are people – they are usually clever people – who have this limitation. Years later, I was to work for a brilliant civil servant, David Nenk, in the Ministry of Education, who had the same impediment. Anyway, my mortification was eased by a telegram which arrived that evening. 'Congratulations and best wishes Hiscocks.' (Nothing from Mr Arnold, of course.)

My brother's representations to the Berkshire County Council were successful. They awarded me a grant of £90 a year. The other £50 would be found somehow. I rather think Aunt Lilian came down with the ready. Good for her! The more immediate question was whether I should now leave Bradfield or remain there until the end of the summer term. Once again, I had no views of my own and was quite content to wait until others had decided for me. My sister and Hiscocks met and talked it over: their decision was that on balance I would gain more by staying at Bradfield. Hiscocks remained of the view which he had put into writing for the authorities at Worcester. 'As a historian he is immature but capable of good work.' ('It's always better, Adams, not to – er – lay it on too thick.') I could do with two more terms of Hiscocks.

I had no objections. As the winner of an open scholarship, I now rated the privileges of a full blood; that is to say, in all respects those of a house – though not a College – prefect. This was certainly one step towards putting down the housemaster. I began to meditate on other possibilities. Two were open to me during the coming Lent term. I could try to get my fives colours and I could try to win the Denning, as it was called – the College prize for English literature.

Both were distinctly chancy. The fives team consisted of only two pairs, which meant that, logically, only four people stood to win their colours. Michael Paine, the head prefect of the Close, was an outstanding athlete and easily the best fives player in the school. He had taught me virtually all the skill I had – really because he wanted a decent partner for the house to win the fives doubles cup. (He himself would win the singles.) In another house there was a boy called Henry Joy whom I knew I couldn't beat. That left two places, and the aspirants were myself and two other boys called John Hoare and David Martin. What actually happened in the event was that I began that term in the College second pair with John Hoare; then David displaced me; but towards the end of the term, David went sick and I played the last two or three matches in his stead. Exceptionally, the term ended with five colours, Paine, Joy, Hoare, Martin and myself.

The Denning was recognized as an arduous business, on account of the work involved and the hot competition. No one *had* to enter for the Denning prize: you chose to do so only if you coveted glory. There were several set books – novels and poetry – on which to be examined, and there was also a paper on general knowledge of English literature. This was unusual inasmuch as it was held in the College library and you could go to the shelves and look up anything you wanted. It was a matter not of memory but of what you knew.

My principal competitors were a boy called Francis – no mean poet – and an even better poet named Michael Rivière, who had a really keen mind. After all this time I remember only two things about the syllabus. The first is that one of the set books was Sir Thomas Browne's *Religio Medici*. This happened to be one of my father's favourites. He bought me a beautiful annotated copy and himself 'talked through' the book with me. That was one paper on which I surely knew what song the sirens sang. The second is that the general paper included a question something like 'Write an appreciation of any distinguished Victorian poet.' I waded in with Tennyson, on whom at the time I had a great crush. I remember quoting 'Lady Clara Vere de Vere' as evidence that he possessed a social conscience! Heaven knows how I won the Denning, but I did.

The pleasant thing about these last two terms at Bradfield was that no one – not even Hiscocks – was particularly demanding about work. Nothing more could really be required of me, and by this time I had absorbed enough proficiency to satisfy without taking too much trouble. This was largely, of course – as it is with any job – a business of knowing what to concentrate on and what didn't matter. (No wasted energy.) In leisure time there were plenty of exciting discoveries to be made, such as Gerard Manley Hopkins and – a novelist who was currently hitting the high spots – Ernest Hemingway. Mr Hunt was engaged to be married to a charming girl called Catharine Cohen, who sometimes took me out in her car on wild-flower expeditions. I was always hoping that we might find a rare orchis, such as the Bee orchis or the Military orchis, but we never did: and indeed I never have. The twayblade is the best I have ever done from that day to this.

One hot summer night in July, a few days before the end of term, I was lying in bed in my 'single' (senior boys had single rooms) when the door opened quietly and a low voice said 'Adams, are you awake?'

It was Michael Paine. What on earth? I thought. It was out of the question that Paine, of all people, could come to another boy's single for sexual reasons.

'Yes,' I replied in some apprehension.

'Then let me congratulate you,' said Paine, 'on being awarded your house tie. Good night.' And with this he shut the door and departed.

The award of a house tie at Bradfield was nothing to do with seniority or with being a prefect. A prefect did not automatically merit it. In fact, only a minority of boys who became prefects were awarded their house ties. Conversely, it was possible, though rare, for someone not a prefect to be awarded it. Prefect or not, you had to have distinguished yourself outstandingly at work or games or both. I seem to recall that Martin Ryle, later Sir Martin Ryle, the great astronomer, had the award before he was a prefect. The tie was in no sense a consolation prize for not being a prefect. In fact, as I have explained, in a certain sense it was more illustrious than being a prefect. I rather think that at this time there were only about four in the Close (including Paine, of course).

I wonder who exactly was behind this? I have never known. Did

Paine persuade the housemaster, or did the housemaster himself undergo some change of heart? Subjective reactions are strange. Little in my life has given me more pleasure and satisfaction. I still have the tie and sometimes wear it when I go to Bradfield.

I must be fair to Mr Arnold. Before I left he spoke warmly and kindly to me, and he wrote nice things on my final school report. Poor chap, he was trying to do his best, I expect, and conscious that he'd got the job only because of his wife's pull with the Headmaster. Well, he was lucky in one respect: he got what Pallas Athene promised Odysseus. 'From the sea shall thy death come, the gentlest death that may be.' He was fond of sailing, and often went to the Channel Islands. One day his boat – ship – whatever it was – was anchored a little way out, and he was rowing ashore in the dinghy. As the dinghy glided up to the quay it could be seen that all was not well. The housemaster sat dead at the oars.

XI

Munich. The name resonates, a name of unease, foreboding and, retrospectively, shame. What can I add to all that has been said on the subject of those terrible days during the high summer of 1938? Only this: that whoever you were, business-man, bobby or bootblack, it came piercing into your personal life like no other occurrence for nearly twenty years past. There was going to be a war: there wasn't going to be a war: there was. The news obliterated everyone's personal preoccupations, rolling over them like a fog. It was like driving along an open road and suddenly coming upon a terrible accident, with flashing lights and peremptory policemen.

I was only eighteen, but old enough, when Mr Chamberlain came back to London waving his piece of paper, to feel two things. The first was that while he was clearly fooling himself, he didn't fool me and he didn't fool a lot of other people. It was too good to be true. Did he really suppose that Hitler, after taking the Rhineland, Austria and now the Sudeten areas, was going to stop at that? If he did, he could only be the victim of wishful thinking. I remember laughing bitterly at the cartoonist David Low's summary: 'The Führer gave his solemn promise that there would be no further trouble until next time.'

The second was that I felt ashamed. I had been brought up to feel pride in Britain – in the British Empire. Britannia ruled the waves. No one could dictate to Britain. But now they had. Underneath all the waffle about 'negotiations' remained the fact that Hitler had demanded, with threats, the Sudeten areas. We had begun by saying 'No' and had ended by saying 'Oh, all right'. And we had sold Czechoslovakia, a country which *had* been ready to fight. We had sold them without any representative of theirs being present. Of course, I had no reliable knowledge – no one had, really – about our preparedness for war. Even today, people are still arguing about whether or not we could practically have gone to war in 1938. But I believe that if we had felt sufficient determination, we probably could. The main reason why we didn't was an imponderable: we didn't want to, we weren't in the right collective state of mind, and everyone over thirty or thirty-five had memories they couldn't bear to face, of the Great War of 1914–18.

All the same, after Munich everyone felt virtually certain that there *was* going to be a war. The only question was when and how it would start. Hitler's taking over of the whole of Czechoslovakia early in the following year should, as far as our honour was concerned, have been the *casus belli*. All it seemed to give rise to, however (as a friend of mine remarked), was a lot of casus belli-aching by Mr Chamberlain. He had been made to look a fool. His piece of paper was worthless, his credibility gone. All his defenders could say now was 'Well, 'e done 'is best, didn't he?'

I remember someone writing of the American Confederacy of 1861–65 that its whole life was war. The whole period of my life *in statu pupillari* at Oxford was passed in preparing for war, in war itself or in its exhausted, threadbare aftermath. This certainly made unique – each in its own way – the two periods of time, before mobilization and after demobilization, that I spent as an undergraduate.

When I went up to Worcester in October 1938, the life of an Oxford undergraduate, even a relatively impecunious one like me, resembled that of Evelyn Waugh and not that of Philip Larkin or Kingsley Amis. It must be hard for a modern undergraduate to imagine. You were required to have your own silver and glass, for you were going to do a lot of eating and entertaining in your own rooms. During the two winter terms, Michaelmas and Hilary, you had a coal fire in your sitting-room as a matter of course, and it was part of your scout's job to bring up the coal. In the mornings, round about quarter to eight or half past seven, your scout would enter your sitting-room, clear out the dead fireplace, lay a new fire and light it. Then he would lay the table for breakfast and boil the electric kettle. After this he would carry in a can of hot water, enter your bedroom and wake you (if you needed waking). He would put the can in your wash-basin and cover it with a towel. While you were getting up he would go down to the kitchen and bring up your breakfast under a dish-cover; eggs and bacon, kippers or whatever you fancied, together with toast and all the milk you reckoned you would need for the day. This concluded the proceedings for the time being, but later on in the morning he would 'do' your room, make the bed and empty your overnight piss-pot. Similarly, you had lunch brought up to your rooms – whatever you ordered – while tea – crumpets, anchovy toast, cucumber sand-wiches, cake, biscuits, etc. – you ordered on a prepared slip of paper: and that lot was brought up, too.

Dinner was in hall; and if I remember correctly, you had to dine in hall a minimum of four evenings a week. For this, of course, everyone wore gowns. The scholars sat at their own table, just below the dons' high table on its dais. Each scholar, in rotation, had a week of reading grace before everyone sat down. The grace was in Latin and of considerable length. I have it by heart and can repeat it now. The scholar who read grace for the week also had the duty of reading the lesson during the short daily service in chapel at 8.15. (You had either to attend chapel or else answer morning roll-call in one of the lecture-rooms for a minimum of four mornings a week. You also had to attend one service in chapel on Sundays.)

Dinner consisted of four courses – soup (or fish), meat, pudding and a savoury. To drink you could order anything you liked (charged to your battels) but for some reason no one ever ordered wine. Nearly everyone drank beer, though a few drank stout or cider. These were served in the beautiful College silver tankards, dated either 1715 or 1745.

The custom of 'sconcing' was honoured very much in the observance and not often in the breach. Certain offences were 'sconceable': being improperly dressed, mentioning a living woman by name, using bad language (e.g., 'damn' or 'bloody'), singing, or speaking more than three consecutive words in a foreign language. The decision whether or not a man should be sconced lay with the senior member of the table. A sconce, or lidded silver tankard, held three pints. It could be filled with anything the culprit liked – almost always beer – and was charged to him. He drank as much as he wanted and having done so, passed the sconce to his left. The next man then drank likewise, and so on until the sconce was empty, whereupon the lid was closed. Very occasionally, the culprit might 'floor' the sconce, i.e., drink the lot at one go, and if he did, it was chargeable to the man who had sconced him. I saw it done only twice.

'Do well at Worcester, Adams. It's a nice place: you'd like it.' I did, from the start. Apart from having your own money to spend (I had £10 per eight-week term) and going to bed (or not) whenever you liked, the first thing that filled me with a rush of surprised, unexpected delight was that everyone – to put it simply – was nice. Gone were the boors and morons up with whom, *inter alios*, one had had to put at Bradfield. Here, everybody seemed to like, or at least to respect, Shakespeare, Mozart, Rembrandt and Co., and was ready to talk about them all night if you liked. Some writers about Oxford, e.g., Evelyn Waugh and John Wain, have laid it on thick about the bullying and wrecking ways of the hearty set, but although I can remember a few people at Worcester who might be thought of as a bit philistine, I recall them only as being very likeable in their own way and never doing anything rough or violent at all. Everyone seemed quite ready for your company, and to dislike anybody was simply not done. Within the first day or two there was a stream of callers to my rooms. 'Do you row/play football/fives/squash/tennis/golf/hockey?' 'Would you care to join the Conservative Club/Labour Club/Liberal Club?' 'Are you interested in Eastern mysticism, classics, music, poetry, jazz, archaeology, birds?' There was a society for everything, and to join it you didn't have to be any good.

Apart from societies and their organized activity, people were always in and out of one another's rooms. You could drop in on anyone you knew and unless he was working he was always glad to see you. Tea would be made and conversation pursued. Groups of friends would sit up half the night, discussing, arguing or listening to music. Mostly, people found their 'set' and lived in it, but the society was fluid and a common interest was enough to make a friend. The big difference from a public school – apart from the circumstance that we were all a little older – was that everyone *wanted* to be up at Oxford and found the easy, unregimented life most congenial. In a word, everyone was happy. I have always gone along with Max Beerbohm's witticism: 'A university is a place where all the nonsense that was knocked out of you at school is gently put back in again.'

So far as girls were concerned, we saw none or few. All the colleges, except the four women's colleges, were exclusively male. Most people didn't bother themselves about girls, and for those who did (such as myself) it was a stony and difficult road. One way or another you could probably, if you wanted to, get to know one or more girls in the women's colleges: I, for example, was able to invite round to tea a rather beautiful White Russian girl whom my sister had taught when she was at the Frances Holland. Natalia might have proved a good thing, since she was more emancipated and less conventional than the average female student of the day. However, she showed herself rather too much emancipated for my purposes, since she proved to be in love with someone who wasn't at Oxford at all, and after one term went down and married him.

I became acquainted with one or two other girl students, but it was clear enough that sex was something they simply didn't want to know about. In those days, it was out of the question for any respectable girl to go in for sex with anybody to whom she was not married or at least engaged. You might just possibly achieve an exception to this rule (that was why you kept trying), but if you did, the girl would almost certainly start pressing you to marry her, and if you refused break off the relationship. I personally never knew of any 'affairs' (as they were called) involving sex (my own or those of friends) which didn't end, sooner or later, in recrimination and regret on the part of the girl (unless they ended in marriage). I suspect (in the face of assurances to the contrary) that in a lot of cases things may not be all that different now.

The rules applicable to girl students were strict. All female visitors had to be out of College by seven in the evening, and had to be in their own colleges by eleven, unless they had special leave, which was not lightly granted. As far as we ourselves were concerned, if your scout found your bed unslept-in, he was supposed to report you to the authorities. What happened then I don't know, for I never came across a case myself.

The set-up regarding pubs was a strange one. The rule was that no undergraduate was allowed to drink on licensed premises. This meant all pubs as well as the bars of hotels. In practice, of course, we all did go to pubs, and this was where the proctors came in. The proctors were dons of the university, serving in rotation in this disciplinary capacity. In academic dress – dark suits, white tie, flowing gown and mortar-board hat – they perambulated the city in the evenings, accompanied by 'bulldogs' – two bulldogs per proctor. The bulldogs were selected from among the younger and fitter college servants. On duty they wore dark lounge suits and bowler hats.

When the proctorial team got to a pub or bar that they were going to raid, the proctor would stand outside and the bulldogs would go in. If they saw one or more people, recognizably undergraduates, drinking, a bulldog would approach and ask courteously 'Are you a member of this university, sir?'

'Yes, sir.'

'The proctor would like to see you outside, sir.'

The bulldogs waited politely while the victim 'drank up'. They then accompanied him outside and he went up to the proctor, who again said 'Are you a member of this university, sir?'

'Yes, sir.'

'Your name and college, sir?' And, when this had been noted down, 'Will you please return to your college now, sir?'

Within the next day or two, the culprit would receive a summons to the proctors at the Bodleian Library, and report thither in academic dress, white tie, cap and gown (known as 'sub. fusc.'). For a first offence you were fined £5. For a second you paid £10, and for the third you were rusticated – sent down – though not permanently: probably for the rest of the current term, or for the whole of the following term.

The system was a kind of elaborate game, only with real forfeits. You were not held morally to blame for having a drink in a pub (you could drink yourself silly in college, as long as it was on college drink), but the whole charade was taken seriously by the authorities and perforce by us too, for a £5 fine was no joke. If you fled from the proctor, the bulldogs' job was to chase and catch you. A good runner could sometimes get away, but it wasn't often attempted.

The odds were against being caught in a pub (I never was), but the official ban on having a quiet pint, together with our enforcedly celibate state, meant that we lived the delightful life of undergraduates in a kind of artificial, half-unreal society. Since virtually everybody had come up straight from school and had never lived as an adult in society, we accepted these restraints unthinkingly and as a matter of course, just as we accepted the 'gate fines' system.

Gate fines worked like this. At five past nine every evening Great Tom, the big bell at Christ Church, would be rung 101 times. When it stopped, college gates were closed. It was all right to be out of college, but when you came back you kicked the heavy door and the porter came and opened it. Then you had to write your name in a book in the porter's lodge. If you came in before ten, you were charged a penny on your battels. Between ten and eleven, it cost you (I think) threepence, and between eleven and midnight, sixpence. After midnight you couldn't be admitted; or if you were, you were in trouble. However, you could clandestinely climb into college if you knew where and how, and people constantly did this. I often did, and was caught only once (I walked right into the law tutor), for which I was duly fined by the Dean.

It was during these two academic years, from October 1938 until June 1940, that I made the warmest and deepest friendships of my life. I will just mention here – to get it out of the way – that I personally never came across any homosexuality at Oxford. As far as my set were concerned, that was something that no one felt inclined for.

There weren't many wealthy undergraduates up at Worcester. It wasn't a wealthy college; rather, a beautiful and admired though unpretentious one. Everyone I knew lived on relatively little money – no champagne parties, no cars, or dinner parties at the Mitre. My £10 a term – enough for beer, the occasional meal out and for hiring punts on the river in summer – was probably, I think, about the average or perhaps a trifle below. Once, when I stayed up an extra two days at the end of term to give a friend moral support through a dicey exam, my mother rebuked me for such unjustifiable extravagance and bade me come down forthwith.

As I have said, Worcester elected four scholars a year, two classical and two historical. The two classical scholars of my year were Kenneth Irwin and Frank Schumer. The other history scholar was Alasdair Christison.

Irwin, from King's College, Canterbury, was a gentle, quiet, self-effacing fellow, of a pious disposition and inclined – at this stage of his life, anyway – to be a little lacking in humour and to hackle up if his leg was pulled. He was not a friend of mine, since he didn't care for a pub and was not particularly outgoing or warm in manner. At the beginning of the war he was a conscientious objector, but later he saw things differently. Indeed, the war years changed and matured Kenneth. After the war he revealed himself as much more human, and we became better friends.

Frank Schumer, from Giggleswick, was one of the most delightful people that I have ever known in my life. Warm, amusing, clever, bold in manner – nay, well-nigh swaggering – he played rugger for the College and acted in the O.U.D.S. When he discovered that I wrote poetry, he became a just and perceptive critic, very ready to talk about it. Among other things, he was a member of the University Air Squadron, which had premises down on the Cherwell. I sometimes went there as his guest, and I remember how, one perfect summer evening, we sat with our beer on the grassy bank and poured a libation to Isis as we talked about Gray and Collins. During our first term, Frank fell in love upon sight, not acquaintance, with a strikingly beautiful girl student called Barbara Horsfield, who used to come to lectures in Worcester hall. He was a handsome, dashing fellow and I'm rather surprised, looking back, that he didn't get anywhere with her. Anyway, by Guy Fawkes Day he had reluctantly given it up as a bad job, and I remember him getting drunk in College and moodily tossing one lighted firework after another, like spent matches, into the Pump quad outside the buttery. He wore his heart on his sleeve if anyone ever did, and was always up to something flamboyant, such as shouting 'Arms for Spain! Arms for Spain!' as the Dean was crossing the quad. (The Dean, Colonel Wilkinson, was notoriously reactionary and right-wing.) Frank's well-known and much imitated chuckle – 'wer-her!' – at anything mischievous was often on his lips. He, perhaps, more than any of them all, typifies for me the world that disappeared in the war. He was likely, had he been set on, to have proved most royally.

Alasdair Christison, my fellow history scholar, became the closest friend I have ever had. He was the only child of a small-time garage proprietor in Jesmond, Newcastle-on-Tyne, and had been at Dame Allan's School, Newcastle. He was intensely proud of being Scottish, though he had none of what is too often wrongly thought of as the Scotch character, being warm, generous, full of wit and humour, and anything but pedantic. It was he who first alerted me to the magic of Montrose. In appearance he was stocky and very dark, with black hair, a pale complexion, great dark, brooding eyes and so strong a beard that he sometimes had to shave twice a day. He was a true Celt, imaginative and sensitive by nature, quietly spoken and inclined to indolence. 'I could sleep my life away,' he once said to me. On another occasion, when asked by the Senior Tutor why he hadn't read more in the vacation, he answered 'Well, chiefly laziness, I'm afraid, sir': which caused the Tutor to remind him that it was in the power of the College to withdraw his scholarship. Indolent he may have been, but he had a remarkable brain. He told me that before he came up for the Worcester scholarship exam, his school had been in two minds whether to put him in for history or for mathematics.

We pursued our friendship and our passionate enjoyment of Oxford modestly, for we had little money, no social connections and no particular ambition to 'get on' in games or in undergraduate society. We listened to a great deal of music together, sharing many happy discoveries. I remember particularly the March evening when Mr Pickard-Cambridge took us as his guests to the Holywell music rooms to hear Schubert's *Octet*. It bowled us over, of course: but when we began to stammer our thanks to Pickard-Cambridge, he replied (in his squeaky voice) 'Oh, my dears, haven't you heard that before?' After we had left him, we went for a walk down the Isis towpath to Iffley Lock in the full moonlight. A skein of swans flew over, their wings sounding the characteristic 'whaup, whaup'. The scene possessed a kind of resplendent melancholy entirely in accord with the Schubert we had heard.

.   .   .

A winter night, late in 1939. Alasdair and I are strolling idly back from a meeting of the Classical Society at Christ Church, having listened to an amusing paper about Odysseus's trick of shooting through the axes. Our way lies down St Michael's Street, and as we pass a house near the corner with George Street, the sound of someone playing Chopin most beautifully halts us in our tracks. We stop and listen, unmindful of the cold, and when the player ceases applaud vigorously. He comes out and asks us in. He is a Polish refugee, middle-aged, lonely, none too coherent in English. He used to be a musical journalist. He gives the impression of having lost everything but Chopin. He goes on playing, and after a time plays some of his own compositions, including a mazurka written in deliberate imitation of Chopin. 'But dis is not – oh – Chopin, 'e is not for imitating.' It is the first time either of us has met a refugee Pole.

.   .   .

It is a blazing morning in June. We have a tutorial with Vere Somerset at ten o'clock, and are strolling, demure and gowned, in the shining College gardens, dew on the grass and the lake rippling in the sunshine. We are arguing about Henry II, but soon Alasdair's conversation turns (by association with another Henry II) to Mary, Queen of Scots, and her lovers, Rizzio, Bothwell, Darnley, and to the Babington plot. 'The poor fool will never cease till she lose her head.' Alasdair is soaked in Scottish history, a new world to me. He goes on to talk of the Covenanters, of Montrose, Alasdair Macdonald and the great victory at Inverlochy, 'a dawn trumpet from the hills'; of youth hostelling in Scotland and of the well-known warden, the Scots-Italian Don Capaldi. 'The warrden doesnae approve o' people who get up ower airly in the morrn.' After a time he begins singing to the ducks.

> 'There was a wee cooper that cam' fra Fife,
>   Nickety nackety noor na noor.
> And he has gotten a gentle wife,
>   Hey wully wallachy hoot John Doogle alleyn quo
>   rushety noor na noor.'

It takes some time for me to learn this so that I can do it fluently. We lie on the dewy grass of the cricket field, protected by our gowns, and play clouds in the sky, like Hamlet and Polonius, until nearly ten. On the way back, we decide we ought to be recognizably Plantagenet for this tutorial, and deck ourselves with sprays of flowering broom from the herbaceous border.

Mr Somerset greets us as friends should greet on a June morning. The scent of the broom begins to fill his warm, sunny room. Soon Alasdair is quietly defending Henry II against Becket. On the Papacy, Mr Somerset resorts to Funck Brentano and other authorities. His scout, Eton, comes in with coffee. Outside the window a blackbird is singing in the Provost's garden. I am thinking that we might well pick up some sandwiches and beer from the kitchens and the buttery, get a punt and have lunch on the river.

.   .   .

It is a summer evening in 1939, the last summer of peace. Toscanini is conducting all the Beethoven symphonies, week by week. Not many of our little set possess wirelesses, but mine (hired) happens to be one with a really good tone, and four or five of us have met in my room for the weekly broadcast: Alasdair, sitting at the wide-open windows, looking out on the darkening gardens and the huge copper beech almost up against the wall; Arthur Klingler, a big, handsome Bavarian, sprawled on the carpet, smoking his pipe, with which he is forever tinkering with a little bunch of probes and sprays like a small pocket-knife: Clifford Scorrer, neat and dapper, a fine pianist, rather High Church and soon to become an ordinand; Peter Townsend, a quiet fellow with a passionate social conscience, a Quaker and an incipient sociologist: and Victor Warren, a tubby, red-haired, good-natured, easy-going friend. Tonight Toscanini is conducting the fourth and fifth symphonies. Perfect happiness and contentment fill the room. How could anything be better than this? Yet only a few days ago we have been to a meeting where veterans from Spain – Tom Wintringham's people – have spoken of the Nazi support for Franco and the inevitability of the coming war with Fascism. Forget it – forget it for a little, as the slow movement of the fourth symphony rocks on in its affirmation of joy and seligkeit.

.   .   .

Alasdair and I, with a few friends, are having a pint in the Turf Tavern, back of Hertford, before dinner in Worcester hall. The beautiful scent of lily-of-the-valley drifts in from the garden outside, as we sit and chat in the snug parlour. The talk is of Durham Cathedral, which I have never yet seen. Alasdair describes the unique beauty of the Galilee chapel. Someone else speaks of Chartres, which hardly any of us have seen.

After a while it's time to go. The others precede me out into Hell Passage. I loiter behind to talk to the pub cat and tickle its ears. The others walk straight out into a proctor and all have their names taken. With the connivance of the landlady, I hide in a cupboard and escape.

The proctor has difficulty with Alasdair's name. He explains it as 'Christ, is, on.' The next day, down at the Bodleian to pay his fine, he is reprimanded and told that if that was intended as a joke, it was a joke in very bad taste. Alasdair, five pounds poorer, reckons this to be adding insult to injury. He was not trying to be funny at all.

. . .

Four of us are punting on the Cherwell, with a picnic in a hamper and a four-pint stone bottle of cider trailing astern. We have come upstream from Magdalen Bridge and now we are playing with the little Marston weir at the end of Mesopotamia. Arthur Klingler drives the punt head on into the weir again and again. At last he drives it in so forcefully that the punt is flooded, cushions and all, and nearly sinks. We are all soaked. There are only about two inches of freeboard. We daren't move. We let the punt drift down to the island below the weir and, under Arthur's Bavarian direction, scramble out, haul the punt ashore ('One, two, three, *heave!*') and turn it upside down to drain it.

The picnic is soaked through. We make the best of it in the May sunshine, nibbling on the bank. Everyone's soon more or less dry. 'You know,' murmurs Alasdair meditatively, 'what I like about these sandwiches is their subtle flavour of Thames Conservancy.'

. . .

It is late winter. We have had a lift in a don's car out as far as Great Tew. We walk in the gardens of the manor which was Falkland's, and I speak of the first battle of Newbury, of the burial mounds on the battle-field, and of how Falkland rode into the gap and was shot down. The sombre yews and box hedges seem entirely fitting to thoughts of Falkland and his circle, virtually rusticated to Great Tew by the obtuse foolishness of Charles I – ever a bad picker – who called Falkland to office only when it was too late. 'I shall be out of it all by nightfall,' Alasdair quotes.

We've left our return rather late. We discover there isn't a bus. Anyway, even if there was, we've hardly got a shilling between us. Alasdair says never mind, we'll hitch-hike. On the country road to Oxford it's already dark, and no lighting. A lorry comes grinding along – they went slowly in those days – and Alasdair bends down low into the headlights, almost under its wheels, thumbing for a lift. The lorry pulls up and we have a friendly lift back to Oxford. I've learnt something. This is the first time I've ever hitch-hiked. It won't be the last, to say the least.

. . .

It is getting on for midsummer, 1939. The O.U.D.S. are rehearsing
The Tempest in Worcester gardens, with Leslie French directing and
playing Ariel. We lie lazily on the grass, watching. The Prospero –
Robin Benn, of Exeter – has a magnificent presence and a beautiful
speaking voice.

> 'You do look, my son, in a moved sort,
> As if you were dismayed: be cheerful, sir.
> Our revels now are ended. These our actors,
> As I foretold you, were all spirits . . '

Neither Alasdair nor I have as yet seen *The Tempest* on stage. The
lake makes a perfect background, and they have built a large model
ship which glides across the view at a distance of about fifty yards.

Later, at evening rehearsals, it is discovered that the swans are
attracted, like moths, by bright light, so that when the goddesses
in the masque arrive by barge across the lake, the swans swim
behind of their own accord, creating an effect which astonishes
everyone, including the director.

> You sunburned sicklemen, with August weary . . .

This marvellous line casts a fascination over me, so that I feel I
could come to every performance just to hear it spoken.

At the end, Prospero really does 'drown his book' in the lake as
they sail away for Milan.

.   .   .

A chilly March afternoon on the Isis. Torpids week is in full swing,
and the Worcester first boat has been making bump after bump.
This is the fourth day and they are confidently expected to bump
again.

Alasdair and I don't ourselves row, but we have run with the
Worcester boat every day so far, and are about to run again now.
We form part of a little group of Vigornians (Worcester men)
clustered on the towpath a little below the New Bridge. The minute
gun has gone, and we keep glancing at the second-hands of our
watches. The fellows in the Worcester boat – *Ann of Oxford Street*,
after De Quincey's girl-friend (he was up at Worcester) – have
taken off their scarves and sweaters and are bending to their oars.

The boatman holds the stern steady on a boathook, but ready to cast off in a few seconds' time. Looking downstream, we can see the long line of other college boats similarly tense and ready. People begin chanting 'Ten, nine, eight, seven . . .'

The gun goes and instantly everything is in turmoil. The boats are cast off. The Worcester stroke sets a tremendous initial pace, to gain speed at the outset. We need to get right away from the boat behind and start gaining as quickly as possible on the boat in front. Everyone on the towpath is shouting, barging and stumbling over one another in their haste to keep up with the boat. 'Worcester! Worcester!'

In and out of other people's feet: in and out of other people's coat-tails and pink-and-black scarves we veer and dodge, always keeping up with the boat a few yards away to our right. Under the New Bridge and on upstream into the Gut. There's a man on a bicycle – the coach – whose job it is to fire his pistol once when we are within a canvas of the boat in front, twice when we are bow to stern and three times when we are overlapping. Our cox is swaying forwards and backwards, shouting to his crew. 'One – out! Two – out! Three – out!' We're gaining. The pistol goes once, almost in my ear, so that I'm deafened. 'Worcester! Worcester!'

Alasdair trips and almost falls into the water. I grab him just in time and we pound on up the Gut. Some of our followers, winded, have dropped out now and the going is easier. The coach on the bike yells at us 'Get out of the bloody way!' Two guns! We're bound to bump now. We're nearing the top of the Gut, where the towpath curves away to the left. In a few more yards we shan't be able to keep up with the boat: anyway, I'm blown.

The pistol goes three times, and the little following group, with what's left of their breath, become hysterical. 'Three guns, Worcester! Three guns!' Our No. 2 oar is almost fouling the rudder of the boat in front, anyway. Our cox steers to port. Their stroke can't row now, because our bow is into him. Their cox raises his arm in acknowledgement of the bump. The oars, winners and losers alike, slump in their seats, dead beat. The coxes steer the boats in to the right bank – only a few feet away – as the boat behind comes past. 'Well rowed, Worcester! Well rowed!' This is our fourth bump in four days. There will be a bump supper – the crew dining on High Table in dinner jackets with pink facings –

with a bonfire to burn the boat and all the concomitant mayhem involved. Meanwhile, Alasdair and I set off for College in the early dusk, intent upon crumpets and anchovy toast.

.   .   .

October 1939. War has broken out during the long vac., but in a way it is almost an anti-climax, for in the first place everyone more or less knew it was going to, and in the second place nothing much has changed, except that everybody has been issued with gas-masks. We are now in the eight months of the 'phoney war'. Hitler has conquered Poland in the first Blitzkrieg, and is left unhindered to prepare his next step. Upon the outbreak of war all undergraduates were enrolled as 'potential cadets' and were instructed not to join up, but to await instructions. Alasdair and I, in our second year, are supposed to be reading for a 'war-time degree', to be conferred at the end of the summer term of 1940. How much good will it ever be to us, we wonder.

The new academic year brings a fine crop of friends from among the freshmen scholars: William Brown, one of the classical scholars, a slim, pale, spidery Yorkshireman with a deadly wit; Mike Seale, from Fettes, a rather dashing, silk-scarf-wearing lady-killer, like Brian in Terence Rattigan's *French Without Tears*: and George Revnell, known as 'Robey', from a fancied resemblance to the great comedian. (It's his eyebrows, really.) Our little set has expanded to absorb the new-comers. Everything, including the academic demands of the tutors, has become rather lax, as though both work and College discipline (such as it ever was) were now felt to be somewhat irrelevant to the mainstream of life. Arthur Klingler, of course, is no longer with us. We know he was anti-Nazi, and feel sorry for him, trapped on the wrong side.

Today, fifty years later, as I write, old St Ebbe's has gone for ever: all the area between Folly Bridge and the Botley Road has been 'redeveloped'. No doubt this is a social change for the better, but those of us who used to frequent them will never forget those narrow lanes round the old castle, and the quiet little pubs where Gown met Town and made friendships on Town's home ground. The Jolly Farmers, so much frequented by us that we were often invited to play in the Aunt Sally and shove-ha'penny teams, is still there, but not Paradise Square as it was in those days. And not Billy Iles the landlord, either, or Stan Roberts the taxi-driver, or

Hilda Brown the Walton Street landlady, who used to play shove-ha'penny in silk gloves.

One summer evening in 1939 Clifford Scorrer was having a quiet pint in the Aunt Sally back-yard of The Jolly Farmers when a Town friend came dashing out to say that the bulldogs were in the pub. There was one stationed outside the yard gate, too. Clifford lay down full-length under a bench against the wall, and three good ladies from among the regulars sat in front of him with their skirts spread. The bulldogs walked through the yard, but found no 'members of this university'.

. . .

A keen night soon after Christmas of 1939. Although we don't yet know it, we have entered upon what is going to be the great frost of early 1940 – weeks of snow and bitter cold. The stars sparkle and the east wind blows piercing sharp across the High, the Broad and the Giler.

Alasdair and I are sitting on a hearthrug, close to the fire, in the Turl Street flat of Baptista Gilliat-Smith. This is really a kind of undergraduate *salon*, frequented by people who like to think they are poets or artists. I have taken to coming here since some of my poems have been accepted by John Waller, a Worcester graduate who edits his own magazine, called *Kingdom Come*. Baptista, a free-lance artist of considerable ability, designed the cover. She is sitting beside me.

There are about seven or eight people in the room, and all but two are sitting round the edges, since the gramophone is on and a rhumba is being danced in the middle. The music is exotic, repetitive, rhythmic, hypnotic. The couple are dancing apart – not embracing, as was usual in those days – but facing each other, close together, reciprocal, smiling, eyebeams intertwined.

The man is Baptista's fiancé, George Murre, a Syrian. He is a good dancer, of striking appearance, tall, quick-footed, black-curled, olive-skinned, dark-eyed, as Mediterranean as they come. The very figure of grace and virility, he is improvising his footwork as he sways and twirls opposite his partner. It is well-known – indeed, it is at the moment plain to be seen – that Baptista is nuts about him.

His partner, pretty, dark-haired, slim, expensively dressed, getting on for thirty – quite old by our standards – is a woman so notorious in Oxford that the Vice-Chancellor has exercised, exceptionally, his statutory power to forbid her to reside within the city. Millie lives out at Marston, and has to sleep there, too. It's about all she does do there, though. She spends all day and every evening in Oxford, often until after midnight, in the undergraduate world, moving from one casual love affair to the next. They last her three or four weeks, as a rule. Millie, herself of humble origin, once succeeded, some time ago, in getting married to a wealthy but dissolute and barmy undergraduate. Their incessant, violent quarrels, which as a rule seemed to take place in semi-public places such as the Cornmarket Hotel, led at length to a tarnished divorce and a financial settlement for Millie which has left her with more money than she really knows what to do with. What she likes is inexperienced undergraduates, but it never takes them long to discover how far she is out of her depth with people possessed of even a relatively modest intellect.

Let it not be supposed, however, that what Millie offers is sex – or at any rate anything beyond embraces and kisses. Sex hadn't really been invented in those days. Obviously, a statement like that needs qualifying, but I cannot be bothered to do it. Anyone who lived then as an adolescent knows what I mean. Though unquenchably hopeful, undergraduates did not really expect to have sexual relations with their girl-friends.

To be perfectly candid, I think that most of us, if our bluff had been called, would have felt weak at the knees and only vaguely and theoretically knowledgeable about what we had to do – let alone about the all-important business of playing it right emotionally, of oneself feeling spontaneously the proper emotions. The whole thing was too rare, too fraught, too unfamiliar. As I have said, most people simply didn't bother with it at all. Alasdair didn't. 'I'm a non-starter,' William Brown used to say. He didn't actually add that it made life a lot easier, but the remark implied it. To persevere, you had to be ready to be humiliated and also to be driven by an inward demon, for all the lie of the land was against you, and there was no one experienced to whom you could talk – not your parents or your tutors or your adult friends.

One bitterly cold afternoon in the Hilary term of 1940, I came back to College to find that Millie had filled my rooms with flowering mimosa. The scent of mimosa has had that association for me ever since. Like Sir Andrew Aguecheek, I was adored once, too.

I don't think she did me any harm, beyond pleasantly wasting a lot of time. She hadn't really the capacity to effect a grip on what you'd call a mind. She looked nice, though, and I don't remember her ever being spiteful.

The frost went on until everything – walls, flowerbeds, fences – was like rock. Worcester lake was so hard frozen that the gardener had a job to keep a patch open for the ducks. I learned to skate. Everyone who couldn't already skate learned to do so. There were distinct advantages. No strangers could come into the College to skate – and you can't really conceal skates and boots – unless they had been invited and were accompanied by a member of the College. Every afternoon, the west end of Beaumont Street would get quite frequented by girls with their skates, hanging about in the hope that somebody would invite them in. Worcester men used to go out and look over the talent. The ice, of course, became crowded until the early darkness fell. Does a pretty girl ever look better than when she's skating?

The most delightful skating, though, took place among ourselves at night, by moonlight. Four or five of us – Alasdair, Clifford, Frank Schumer, myself and one or two others – Cullen Powell, perhaps; Jim Sharp or Victor Warren – would have a couple of glasses of College port after Hall (Fonseca '12? Graham '20?) and then wander down with our skates to the glistening, deserted lake. The moon shone bright. We were in College: we could skate all night if we wanted to and none to say nay. Everyone else seemed to have had enough for the day, but not we. I suppose we could have ordered hot mulled claret to be brought down, but it didn't occur to anyone. Clifford – always the sprucest of us at any time, and never more so than in his tan skating boots, plus-fours and tartan scarf – took off from among the frozen-in branches of the great, overleaning, chain-supported horse chestnut on the south bank, zipped down the length of the Provost's garden, turned in a half-circle and came back even faster. Alasdair, in old flannel bags and converted football boots, joined him, and the two cavorted and pranced while William Brown took photographs. Soon there were half a dozen of us out on the long lake shaped like a boomerang – each arm some eighty to ninety yards long – and all across the bare gardens rang the sound of skates upon deep ice. I remember how once we sang catches as we skated. I see Alasdair approaching, flickering in and out of the long shadows of the leafless boughs, starting 'See, Bob, see, the play is done. Milady's chariot, run, boy, run.' I hear the others joining in and Clifford squealing 'I've lost my watch! I've lost my watch!' until, having forgotten how to bring it to an end, our voices trailed off and we came in to sit side by side close by the ilex – that very ilex from which Ariel had leapt to obey Prospero. We had health and energy enough to skate till midnight and after; until moonset, once. Then we would repair to Clifford's rooms in the New Building and he would play us Beethoven while Alasdair made the tea. (He never really trusted anyone else to make tea.)

Why no one was ever disciplined over Alasdair's party I have never understood. This, too, took place on a winter's night and the secret planning was matched only by the suicidal cheek which brought the revels to an end. We decided that nothing would do for us but to have a barrel of bitter standing broached in the bedroom. And it must be illegal, of course. It never even occurred to us to enquire whether the College buttery would supply us. (I'm sure they wouldn't have: not a barrel.) No, no; we hied away to The Jolly Farmers and propounded our scheme to Billy Iles. It all worked. We bought from him what I believe is known as 'a pin' or, as Billy called it, 'four 'n 'alf'. (Thirty-six pints doesn't sound much for a party, but we meant to have some bottled as well, and anyway, we had to tailor our prank to the smugglable size of the barrel.)

The pin fitted snugly into a sugar-crate, which was carefully fastened down and ticketed 'Books: with Care'. Someone even found a Blackwell's label to stick on. Then the crate was loaded into Stan Roberts's taxi and driven by Stan his very self to the gates of Worcester.

Alasdair, in his second year, had some of the nicest rooms in College: 10:3 (the third set on Staircase 10). Immediately below lie the De Quincey rooms (the ones I had had for the scholarship exam), from the tradition that they were occupied by Thomas De Quincey when he was up. If so, he was extremely lucky: I spent much time, both before and after the war, in negotiating with the College authorities to try to get those rooms for myself, but never succeeded. Stan Roberts, actually assisted by the suitably tipped assistant porter, carried the laden sugar-crate up to 10:3 and then left us to our own devices. We got the barrel into the bedroom, but I can't now remember upon what we supported it: we had no proper cradle, of course, but something efficient was improvised. The spiling and tapping were carried out, and we reckoned the beer would have settled well enough by that night.

Undergraduate beer parties differ little from one another, I imagine, though perhaps, if one held in 1892 must have been rather different, at least in appearance, from one held in 1940, a similar difference might apply to one held in 1990. I don't recall much about the early stages of the beer-up in 10:3, except that Alasdair was got up as Groucho Marx, whom he could simulate extremely well, especially with the adjuncts of a painted black moustache and an unlit cigar. 'The Dean? Why, the first time I met him I swept him off my feet.' His eyebrow work was particularly good. In the sitting-room was a conspicuous sign, devised by Mike Seale, pointing the way to the bedroom and reading 'To Ye Pysse-Up: Refills'.

Now it so happened that this term the occupant of the De Quincey Room was one Dr Kiernander, a don belonging to a non-Oxford academic institution which had been evacuated to Worcester as part of the general exodus from London marking the outbreak of the phoney war. Dr Kiernander had not exactly endeared himself to Worcester – or to us, anyway – during the Michaelmas term, and as the beer flowed more freely, imaginations ranged and songs were sung, it occurred to William Brown and Jim Sharp, with natural spontaneity, that bouncing on the floor might be an effective way of reminding Dr Kiernander of the Vigornian presence vibrant above him. His name became adopted into those songs which are traditionally sung at undergraduate beer parties.

> So, balls to Dr *Kier*nander, *Kier*nander, *Kier*nander,
> Balls to Dr *Kier*nander, dirty old sod.
> For he's kept us waiting while he's masturbating,
> So balls to Dr *Kier*nander, dirty old sod.
>
> The other dons, to stop his frolics;
> The other dons, to stop his frolics . . .

William's lean, angular frame was well suited to bouncing. He spun and twirled like Ravel's Scorbo: he seemed to be in three places at once, while the further corners of the room were kept in bouncing continuum by Alasdair, Mike Seale and myself. The lights shook and the coal fell in the fire. As people paused breathless for a rest, I felt stirred to improvise, though the tune was not mine but something of Arthur Askey's which swam into my head.

> Poor Kier*nand*er, whatever can he do?
> He wakes with a fright in the middle of the night
> And the ceiling's falling through.
>
> O-oh, poor Kier*nand*er, the noise becomes obscene.
> He hurries hence in self-defence
> And goes to fetch the Dean.
> O-oh, poor Kier*nand*er –

But that, in fact, it forthwith transpired, was exactly what Dr Kiernander had done. Colonel Wilkinson, the Dean of Worcester, was suddenly among us. Voices trailed off and silence fell. We noticed that Dr Kiernander was not among those present, and we thought none the better of him for that.

The Dean paused for a short space, but all he finally came out with was 'This party will now disperse.' His eye then fell upon 'To Ye Pysse-Up: Refills'. Following the direction indicated, he reached the bedroom and stood gazing at our broached pin on Alasdair's chest-of-drawers.

'What's this?'

'That, sir,' replied Alasdair, trying to look a little less like Groucho, 'is the cause of the trouble.'

I remember trying drunkenly to insist that the onus of any blame was equally mine, but all the Dean said was 'Go to bed, Adams.' I didn't, however. We adjourned to someone else's rooms, got hold of some more beer from somewhere and continued in a rather less unbuttoned style.

The following morning we saw our pin, now empty and bungless, lying well out on the central lawn in the quad. This turf was sacrosanct. There was a standing fine of half-a-crown for anyone observed walking on it by the porter, Sergeant-Major Bryant, ex-Grenadier Guards.

How it had got there we never discovered. Somebody went and

distracted Bryant's attention while Alasdair and I hauled the barrel off the grass and back up to his rooms. Later, we returned it to Billy Iles. As I have said, I have always been puzzled that the Dean took no further action. He must have guessed that our barrel was contraband and besides that, I wouldn't mind betting that we must have cracked the ceiling below. Perhaps he didn't much care for Dr Kiernander, either.

. . .

That spring we made an expedition down the underground Trill Millstream; we did. In fact, I reckon I must be one of the very few people who can have traversed the length of the Trill Millstream three times. As is widely known, the originator of this exploit was T. E. Lawrence who, when he was up at Oxford (Lincoln), decided that the stream was probably navigable and went down it successfully with a companion, a torch or two and a loaded pistol 'in case of rats'.

I have no idea what has happened to the Trill now that old St Ebbe's has gone and so much of south-west Oxford has been redeveloped. The topographical set-up used to be this. The Isis runs from north to south past the west flank of Worcester, under Hythe Bridge and on down to St Ebbe's. It then makes a right-angled bend to the east and so reaches Folly Bridge and Christ Church meadows. Its course forms, in fact, an arc of ninety degrees. This arc used to have a chord, and the chord was the Trill Millstream, which ran out of the Isis into an arched brick culvert just below the north-west corner of Paradise Square, and ran eastwards underground to emerge at the south-west corner of Christ Church and thence back into the Isis. The tunnel was of arched brick all its length, and I remember it as being about five or six feet wide – the water surface, that is – and the water as fairly fast-flowing – about two or three miles an hour – and three to four feet deep, with a firm bottom. It was not a sewer, but various storm culverts entered it along its length (as I shall recount). The opening at the upstream end was covered by a timber door which was in effect a top-hung hopper and not locked. You only had to pull it up to get in.

I would very much like to know what sort of craft Lawrence used. As will be told, I have good reasons for wondering. For our first expedition we took two canoes from Magdalen Bridge and

South-West Oxford in 1939

paddled them upstream. William Brown and I were in one and Alasdair and Mike Seale in the other.

I am nervous by temperament, and when I was young I would sometimes, in fits of bravado, enter upon hare-brained exploits and then, later, wonder what the hell I had got myself into and why. As the wooden door swung up and we shone our torches into the pitch-black tunnel, I felt much more like going back than going on. However, no one else said anything to that effect and, having bumped and scrambled the canoes in, we began floating down.

The door swung down behind us and we were now entirely dependent for light upon our torches. Our voices echoed in the cavern. No effort was involved in going down, for we were simply drifting with the current. However, we found ourselves having to take note of two features. First, the height of the progressive sections of rounded brick tunnelling above us varied. In some places they were only about two-and-a-half or three feet above the surface of the water, while in others they were a good five or six feet. Going through the lower lengths you had to duck and stay ducked, and you couldn't always see for how far, for there were curves. Secondly, at intervals the tunnel above water level was crossed by stout iron pipes with diameters of about five inches. These also involved ducking, while in addition several ran across so low that we had to force the canoes hard down in order to get them under.

This was what finally buggered this first expedition. I don't know how far we'd gone down (the total length of the stream was perhaps 700 yards) when we came to an extra low pipe under which the up-curved prows of the canoes simply would not go. We got out into the water, standing waist-deep, and did all we could to force one of them under. No good. Then we even had a shot at lifting it over, but that was no good either: I've forgotten why; perhaps the roof was too low or the canoe was too heavy. (One of us had to hold the torches.) There was no help for it. We had to go back. Going back was, of course, harder work. We didn't use the paddles much: we put our hands to the roof or the walls and shoved. There was nothing much to it, and eventually we re-emerged at the Paradise Square entry.

However, I felt annoyed and frustrated. To have been baulked in this way was maddening. Once I was dry (it wasn't much fun paddling back to Magdalen Bridge and then walking back to

Worcester in soaking wet clothes) I put in some time thinking it over. The answer came over the first pint of the evening. A canoe would not go under that pipe: but a punt would.

William said he'd had enough of it: he thought honour was satisfied. However, Mike and Alasdair were game, and felt, like myself, that a punt was surely the answer. So the second expedition, three men strong, set out from Magdalen Bridge one afternoon about a week later.

Everything seemed to be in the bag. We entered the tunnel as before – more self-confident now – and drifted smoothly down. It was no problem at all taking the punt under the pipes – it had so little freeboard – and when we came to the pipe which had baulked us before we slipped under it easily, lying prone. On we went, and at length – oh, whoopee! – saw a glimmer of daylight ahead. This brightened and approached, and we found ourselves at the downstream egress of the Trill from under the south-western walls of Christ Church.

And here, if you'll believe it, was where we once more came unstuck. At its very mouth, the stream curved in a right-angle between its brick walls, and this the punt could not negotiate: it was too long. Again we got out into the water and tried everything we could think of; we pushed, pulled and heaved. The frustration was extreme, for several feet of our bow were actually out of the tunnel and protruding into the daylight. We turned the punt on its side and yanked and dragged, but nothing would get it round that very last bend.

Like the Duchess of Malfi, we felt we could curse down the stars. I was in such an unreasonable state of emotional mortification that I was all for leaving the ruddy punt where it was and going home. Heaven knows what Round and Faulkner, at Magdalen Bridge, would have had to say, but I was past caring. It was Mike Seale who pointed out that obviously the College authorities would be told: punts cost a lot of money. We would indisputably be for the high jump. We had no alternative but to go back up the stream.

At this point Alasdair said he was going home; he was soaking wet and already had a cold from last time. This was so entirely out of character that I have never quite understood it. Alasdair's courage and sterling endurance we had seen for ourselves many a time. What I think now is that he meant exactly what he said, no more

nor less. He feared possible illness; he knew himself to be no coward
and that our opinion of him was so high that he could afford this
indulgence. In fact, we didn't think ill of him: we knew him too
well. And besides, we all thought that all that Mike and I were in
for were a couple of uncomfortable, tedious hours and that would
be that.

As Alasdair left us and headed for St Aldate's, a cloudburst
began. The rain simply belted down. Well, we thought, at least
we'd be out of that. With some little difficulty we dragged the punt
scratchily free from the walls on either side (we'd jammed it pretty
tight in our efforts to get it round the last bend), climbed in and
began the upstream journey, Mike in front (i.e., at the stern) and I
behind.

Pushing the heavy punt upstream was fairly hard work for two.
I cut my hand on a projection of brick and Mike said his palms
were getting scraped. The torches, after the manner of these battery
jobs, were dimming, and besides that, we had to leave them lying
propped in the punt; we couldn't direct the beams because we
needed both hands for shoving.

After a time it seemed to me that the current was getting faster.
I could hear it chattering against the sides of the punt, and also it
seemed to be offering more resistance. I thought, too, that I could
see the water level minutely rising, although it was hard to be sure
in the dim light and without averting one's attention from shoving
to take a good look.

However, quite soon a good look became unnecessary. From
ahead of us there sounded a heavy splashing and falling of water,
quite different from anything we had heard on the way down. Soon
we arrived at the reason – or reasons. Cascades were spouting into
the tunnel from inlets in the upper sides and the apex of the arched
roof. The Trill was a storm-water sewer, and under the present
cloudburst outside, every gutter in St Ebbe's was pouring water into
it.

Several of these inlets we had no alternative but to pass beneath,
for they were directly overhead and the tunnel was too narrow to
permit avoiding movement to either side. The punt took in water
along its length, from stern to bow, though not enough to bail. We
grabbed the torches, held them clear and shoved on.

I now bethought me of a jolly eventuality. The water was rising

– how fast and for how long? As I have explained, the arched roof ran in sections, some high, some low. Suppose we were to find ourselves in a high one, but unable to get forward or back because the water had risen too high in low ones ahead and behind. Well, but what to do about it? We'd already left some pretty low lengths behind us. I felt myself entering into a state of panic, for we were progressing so slowly – and were so tired – compared with our previous progress down.

Mike was admirable. Perhaps his apprehension of possible danger, more cool-headed than mine, was also more accurate, for to be quite honest I am not at all sure to this day how much danger we really were in. Could the millstream fill to the roof? If so, for how long? Could one wait safely in a high-roofed section until the level subsided? I doubt we really were in danger: but the torches were failing, the water was very noisy in a nasty, echoing, sepulchral way; pushing seemed increasingly hard, and painful too. At times like this you find out what you've really got at the bottom of you, and I fear I hadn't much. But Mike had.

I don't know how long it took to get back to the Isis: perhaps half an hour or forty minutes. It was still raining as we came out and turned off the wilted torches. We rested a while and then set off downstream for the Cherwell and Magdalen Bridge. There was a bit of reproach about the sodden cushions, but of course we attributed this to the rain – correctly. On the way back to Worcester we dropped into the Turf and each drank two double brandies, which had no intoxicating effect whatever. I wonder why: I suppose there must be a medical or physiological reason connected with stress.

Also, I still want to know in what sort of craft T. E. Lawrence successfully went down the Trill Millstream. If it wasn't a punt or a canoe, then what was it?

XII

What, meanwhile, of my home and my family? Since October 1938, when I went up to Worcester, things had changed much, and for ever. After recovery from his illness and retirement from medical practice, my father had in effect abdicated from his position as head of the family. He now left decisions to others, and acquiesced in them. From an emotional point of view this meant little enough either to my sister or my brother. Katharine, teaching, was now twenty-eight and had not been living at home – except now and then – for some time. John, who was twenty-six, still lived at Oakdene but, as I have explained, had never had a warm relationship with my father. Emotionally, he stood to lose little or nothing from my father's diminution. I think that, although he never said so, he thought that my father had failed in his family duty and responsibilities – as indeed he had – and that for this reason he felt contempt and resentment, but little sympathy. He could feel little sympathy because he had never kept my father's company for enjoyment or from any sense of affinity. My father's merits left him cold, while his failings irritated him. He thought, too, that he had let my mother down; for John, undemonstrative though he was, had always been devoted to my mother. He felt resentment because responsibility for the family's economics, which were in a bad state – indeed, well-nigh desperate – had now devolved upon him, so that he had had to take on a rotten job, someone else's balls-up. Always pessimistic by nature – a great smeller of rats and discoverer of flies in ointment – he now had only too good cause for shaking his head and wondering what would become of us. I owe him much gratitude, in this worrying situation, for always doing everything he could to help me and never showing anything but full support – no envy – for my going up to Oxford.

Although I was too young, too self-centred and irresponsible to realize it at the time, he had a pretty rough ride, inexperienced as he was, with his new family responsibilities; and he did well. I thank him much.

For me, of course, this was a time of adolescent expansion, although for the rest of the family it was a time of harsh retrenchment. My father – he must have had a bad fright – now drank nothing stronger than beer, and not a lot of that. During these final years of the 'thirties he gradually began to assume the ways of an old man. He didn't know what to do with himself: he often said he wished it was time to go to bed, but when he went to bed he would say he wished it was time to get up. He thought ill of the state of the world – and God knows it was fully as bad as it could be – and largely gave over initiative and any sort of personal purpose or direction. Whither, indeed, could he go? He had no work and no money. While I was still at Bradfield he had derived vicarious enjoyment from my success, but Oxford he could not relate to, though he came over there to see me when I asked him. The last thing I wanted was for him to drop out of my world, and in the vacations we still enjoyed a good deal of our old relationship. It was different, though, for I was no longer a child and he could no longer be my guide and mentor, for at bottom – though he never said so – his heart was not in what I was doing. I know now, too, that he must have regarded the impending inevitable war as a terrible threat to his children and also the end of his world; as was no more than the truth. He was not a stout-hearted man by temperament and the fire had been knocked out of him. Yet I could still keep warm at the ashes.

Some time round about midsummer of 1939, when he was sixty-nine, my father was advised that he must have all his teeth extracted, or else incur further grave illness. He submitted. I well remember his return home on a beautiful June afternoon, when Arthur Klingler, my Bavarian friend (who was staying for a week or two of the long vac.), and I were practising trout casts on the lawn. I called out and asked him how he was. He replied 'Sans teeth, sans eyes, sans taste, sans everything.' Yet in those days I had little real feeling and was short on empathy: I felt sorry, but I didn't really set myself to imagine what it must be like to have all your teeth out, or what it would do to your state of mind. God forgive me.

My brother and sister had now decided that there was no alternative to selling Oakdene and installing my parents in a smaller, more economical house. After looking at a few, it seemed to them that the best course would be to move into Thorn the gardener's cottage, which was already ours. (The Thorns, of course, would perforce be leaving us anyway.) It would need a bit done to it, but not much. So during the summer of 1939 Oakdene, my beloved and life-long home, was put on the market. Like most people who have ever sold a house, my brother has spent the rest of his life regretting that we didn't get more for it. He had a true sense of responsibility, yet he was by temperament someone for whom nothing ever went quite right.

Oakdene was sold, a few weeks after the outbreak of the war, to a middle-aged couple called Balfour, who could not have been nicer to deal with or to have as neighbours. Mr Balfour, not to mince words, was a gentleman, of the same family as Arthur Balfour, the Edwardian Prime Minister. He was cultured, friendly, extremely loquacious and a pleasant man to deal with. Mrs Balfour was also pleasant enough, but had her own ideas about what she wanted to do with the property. Now, I personally began to feel one disadvantage of moving to the Thorns' adjacent cottage: you had to stand by – without a word, of course – and watch what she did. And what she did, principally, was to fell the trees. Oakdene's three acres contained plenty of trees, and several of these had individuality and had in effect been landmarks in our lives. We knew every tree in the garden, of course. I could draw a map, now. I have never been able to understand Mrs Balfour's motive in felling the trees, for having felled them she did nothing more to the sites. She felled the three silver birches along the crest of Bull Banks, and she also felled the Spanish chestnut – which made even my brother wince and express regret. Then she dug up the circular rose garden outside the dining-room windows: but she didn't convert it to something else. She just dug it up and left a mess. It all seemed very odd; but we never quarrelled with the Balfours.

I personally left Oakdene – for the last time – for Oxford in October 1939, and returned to the cottage at the end of term in December. I found living there not unpleasant, even though we were a tightish fit. My brother had enlisted, earlier in 1939, as a gunner in a territorial artillery regiment, the Berkshire Yeomanry, which mobilized upon the outbreak of war. During that winter he was stationed on Newbury race course, where he had a pretty rotten time (it was a very hard winter).

The cottage was comfortable and snug enough: I accepted the situation contentedly. The only thing I couldn't quite get used to (though I never said so, of course) was the rather explosive gas geyser for hot water in the cold little bathroom (a lean-to), which took about half an hour to trickle you a bath.

It was in this cottage that my father spent the last six and a half years of his life. I'm afraid he cannot have been happy, although he never showed as much in his dealings with me. I myself, at nineteen, was young and foolish and full of my own doings. It honestly never once occurred to me that we had come down in the world.

It may seem astonishing – even incredible – to a reader that it should not have exercised my mind that the family fortunes had failed and that my father, quite contrary to anything that 'Dr Jarge' could have foreseen or imagined when he left Martock for Newbury with his bride in 1910, was ending his life in failure and straitened circumstances, with the local reputation of a dried-out alcoholic. I didn't feel regretful, or in the least ashamed of my family. The reasons, I now think, were three. First, the war had an obliterating effect upon private and personal troubles. Everyone's feelings at that time were primarily concerned with the war. I remember an amusing song of those days, popularized by the comedian Jack Warner, called 'Didn't you know? There's a war on', in which the imaginary verse-by-verse protagonists, each of whom would normally have been more than justified in complaining or even in extreme anger, were always met with the bland rejoinder 'Didn't you know? There's a war on' (e.g., the returning husband finding his wife in bed with another man, etc.).

Secondly, my parents themselves never said anything to me to suggest that they had any regrets or were at all sorry for themselves.

The third reason was my own temperament, which rendered me more or less immune to considerations like 'What are people thinking?' or 'Have I got as much money, or social standing, as that fellow over there?' My life was really centred upon four things:

my love for my father; my friends at Oxford – friendships more enjoyable, productive and rewarding than I could ever have imagined; my work on the history syllabus, which I found enormously enjoyable and gratifying; and fourthly my imaginative life, which was in certain respects more real to me than reality.

I had always had a lot of fantasy in my life – as far back as I could remember. Once it had been the kingdom of Bull Banks, its halls and state rooms secluded among the laurels; a land-locked realm, deriving its attributes largely from King Arthur and peopled with knights, whose enemies were foxes. Later, at Horris Hill and under the influence of films and of writers like Sapper and Dornford Yates, Bull Banks had become a gay, fashionable city-state of sport and pleasure, its celebrities, my companions, forever playing cricket or football matches or dancing in champagne-flowing night clubs (like those of Ralph Lynn and Winifred Shotter; Bertie Wooster; Marlene Dietrich). At Horris Hill I had found that this Bull Banks carried so much conviction and included so much detail that other boys revealed their own fantasy countries (and one or two, I suspect, hastened to invent them). A few years ago, walking along the Embankment by Charing Cross, I ran into a friend from those days, and as we chatted, recalled those kingdoms – his and mine. 'Ah,' he said, 'but you had the ends much better tied up than I did.' Certainly a great deal of my time and mental energy went into the fantasies, which in my infancy compensated for solitude and at boarding-school for boring features like Mr Morris and Mr Arnold.

Not the least of the wonderful things about Oxford was that it happily accepted and took on board even your fantasy potential – whoever would have thought it? – developed and transformed it, blending it with magic oils, with sounds and sweet airs that gave delight and hurt not. Christopher Isherwood found exactly this at Cambridge, and wrote about it in his autobiographical *Lions and Shadows*. Alasdair, like Isherwood's friend Chalmers ('*Already* the crowds begin –'), would find phrases suggesting themselves as we listened to music. I recall how we derived, as surely as ever did Swann from the 'petite phrase' of Vinteuil, a peculiar and personal meaning from the *Leonora No. 3*. (Alasdair used to sing, '*I* think, he *soon*, will *really* be quite free.')

Indeed music was the great, the principal releasing agent, acting like some miraculous catalyst to bring upon us trance and ecstasy, to release from within headlong excitement and frenzies of communicative speech. We were often transported and borne away by music, as on the night when Pickard-Cambridge took us to hear the Schubert *Octet*. Arthur Klingler struggling like a wrestler with the additional handicap of having to express himself in English ('This man Mozart . . . he is more great than is possible'); William Brown hardly able to contain himself in patience until the end, to tell us that one of Sophocles's choruses had exactly such a rhythm; Frank Savory – the only trained musician of us all – intently following a Schubert trio with a pocket score; Alasdair saying nothing at all until he was pressed and at last coming out, Celtic fashion, with something so pregnant yet enigmatic that everyone felt an immediate response and none could find a reply. How lucky, how supremely blest for the nonce we were, waiting for Hitler in the silver sunsets that still shine across Worcester of an evening!

I suppose that in all our elated foolishness, nothing was more intense than the cult of Chopin, out of which grew leagues-long forests of fantasy. Up to a point it was I who was responsible for this, for it was I who bought the records, one by one, and I who placed on the dresser in my room a portrait of Chopin between two green wax candles in pewter candlesticks. I even persuaded the domestic bursar to let me repaper my room in a light green, faintly shot with orange. However, you can't propagate a cult by yourself. There have to be devotees. ('Everyone rapt in his own fantasy,' as Alasdair said.) Clifford, William, Arthur Klingler and the rest of us would immerse ourselves, night after night, in Chopin, while snow fell deep or moths flitted in from the scented garden through the uncurtained windows. Our pianists, for the most part, were Cortot, Rubinstein and De Pachman. I still have the records, but seventy-eights don't work properly on a modern machine, and in any case I have good and sufficient reason to prefer not to open the door any more upon the heartbreak of Chopin. Yet on those nights when the dragonfly hung poised over the abyss (yes, I know the man said 'butterfly', but I think dragonfly's better), none of us would have paid attention to a voice that told us that this truth was evanescent and would one day become irrecoverable. 'Phaeacia's been discovered: it can't be undiscovered.' It can; and candles – even spiral-fluted, green ones – can burn out. This all happened so long ago.

. . .

During my last pre-war term at Oxford – the Trinity term of 1940 – something more than delightful, a true and splendid blessing, overtook me. This occurred while France was falling and our army was escaping in near-rout from Dunkirk.

The tenth of May was – still is, I suppose – my birthday. I had arranged to give a party in The Jolly Farmers, and a lot of people were coming: not only my Worcester friends, but Baptista's crowd and the *Kingdom Come* magazine lot, and some of the university swimming club (I used to swim, after a fashion), and Hilda Brown, Stan Roberts and other town friends. The beer was to flow like the Kennet.

My scout, Bill Money, woke me as usual about a quarter to eight on a perfect May morning. 'Good morning, sir. Many happy returns, but I don't know about the day. Them buggers have gone into Belgium and Holland.'

I took this in as best I could. 'What d'you reckon will happen, then, Money?'

'Anything could happen, sir. Anything at all.'

But now, just at the start – the first day of the German attack – there was not a lot more to be learned from anyone -- even the wireless – than Money had told. It wasn't that we weren't concerned or that we didn't take it seriously. We were simply waiting to see what would happen. None of us, of course, imagined that France would fall. Inasmuch as we thought at all, we vaguely supposed that some situation would develop not dissimilar from that of the 1914–18 war. Anyhow, it was lovely weather, and I wasn't going to let the Jerries – or even the thought of them – interfere with my twentieth birthday. I did a morning's work on the French Revolution and after lunch went on the Cherwell with Mike and Alasdair. None of us was apprehensive, even though what was happening was never entirely absent from our minds.

My party at The Jolly Farmers was a great success. No one had ever thought of giving a party in a pub before. I can't think why not: it was the easiest way imaginable to give a party. You simply handed the landlord a capital sum and told him to serve the company free until it was exhausted. Both bars and the Aunt Sally yard outside were well filled. It was more distinguished undergraduate company than I normally kept, partly because, student-like, people had brought other people along. I remember asking William Brown how many he thought were there. 'If all the people,' he replied, 'who've come to this party were laid end to end, I shouldn't be at all surprised.' However, nobody was rowdy or violent and nothing got smashed.

In the middle of it all, someone came bursting in with the news that Chamberlain had resigned and Mr Churchill had become Prime Minister. It seemed wonderful and the whole party stood and cheered. At that time we had no notion, of course; of Churchill's stature as a statesman or of what he was going to achieve. This was before the fall of France, before Dunkirk. But there had for some time past, throughout the whole country, been a general feeling that Chamberlain was not suited to be a war leader and that since Munich he had lost credibility. He had not prosecuted the war with confidence or vigour. This attack of Hitler's had at least done one thing: it had shown conclusively that we needed someone other than Mr Chamberlain. All we knew of Churchill – as yet – was that he had been consistently anti-Nazi for years, that he was pugnacious and that he really hated Hitler. Anyway, we felt that any change, with this crisis now upon us, could only be for the better. So we stood and cheered beerily, as the sun of the tenth of May 1940 set upon St Ebbe's.

One unforeseen result of this party was that I was asked to quite a few more myself. As I have explained, none of our little set had money (my party had been paid for out of birthday money) and we certainly didn't go in for socializing in fashionable, Lord Sebastian Flyte society. But one thing undergraduate society was not was snobbish, and several people who had come along to my party felt like reciprocating. Besides, I had apparently made a bit of an impression as 'the chap who gave a party in a St Ebbe's pub', which was regarded as stylish and original.

At more than one of these parties which I went to, I noticed one particular girl who struck me as very attractive. I had no idea who she was, and didn't ask anyone. She was not conventionally pretty, but with all the bloom of youth upon her she was most striking. She had dark hair, an unusual, sensitive face and a very graceful way of moving, light and quick. She seemed to radiate energy, laughing and responding to her companions with such readiness and warmth that I, watching, felt my heart turn over. She carried herself with so much assurance, I thought, that she was obviously an experienced socialite, a regular Oxford party-goer quite out of my star. So I leaned against the wall with my hands in my pockets, and gazed and reflected, as she burst into a peal of laughter at some crack I couldn't hear, how lucky some people were to have access to girls like that.

For the demon, this last twenty months, had given me little peace. Natalia Galitzine had been followed by various disappointments, including a girl home student who, in my arms, said 'No, Richard, you're deceiving yourself: *you* couldn't want *me*.' It was a compliment of sorts, but it was all too disappointingly true. And when, determined nevertheless to persevere, I pressed my suit, 'You mustn't say things like that to me, Richard.' A little while after Brenda, I became a very platonic friend of Betty Sants, the girl who was a friend of Ralph Glasser (the Gorbals boy at Oxford) and who later died, after a bicycle accident, at the end of a coma of more than a hundred days – one of the longest comas, I believe, known to medicine. Betty was a jolly good sort, but not what I was looking for. Then there was a pretty, blonde girl, named Bertha, in the gramophone record shop at Newbury, who at my invitation came over to Oxford to be taken on the river. I don't know why it didn't work, but it didn't. I could only, regretfully, agree with Alasdair: 'I've never yet seen you with a girl and thought you looked like a couple.'

One summer evening in the prime of Hitler's weather, as his tanks forged on through France, I went to a party at Wadham, given by a young man called Hector Bruce-Binney. Hector Bruce-Binney was an undergraduate with a great deal of money, who was sedulously cultivated by John Waller for the reason that, though lacking any literary talent, he was ready to put a lot of it into *Kingdom Come*. His rooms at Wadham were expensively got up and rather overdone in an incongruous mixture of styles – his own idea. (I remember stars on the ceiling, but little else.)

I had come alone, but there were quite a few people there whom I knew. I chatted and moved about. Suddenly I saw, leaning on one end of the mantelpiece, the girl with dark hair; there was no one with her.

I strolled across and began some sort of conversation. She had the most wonderful voice, a contralto which came arrestingly from her slight, trim frame. And her manner was warm; so responsive that I needed all my self-possession to look as though this sort of thing was nothing new to me. We fell easily into talk. She asked me to get her another drink, and I could see that she was someone who enjoyed drinking. In fact, she enjoyed her*self*. Energy and animation fairly blazed out of her – a jolie-laide of nineteen or so, Jung's *kore* personified.

She told me she was the daughter of a don at Exeter (College). Her name was Jennifer Tomkinson. She was not a student.

The room was hot, crowded and full of smoke. (In those days everyone smoked.) We were chatting happily, with no least self-consciousness (the curse of the young): Jennifer's company seemed to dispel anything of that sort. As for me, I felt that all this was too good to be true. I also had the feeling that it was taking place without my volition, as though a boat were gliding downstream with the current. Something had happened. For the first time a girl – a girl I had had an eye for and now, on acquaintance, found wholly delightful – was showing me that she thought me attractive too.

After a time I suggested that perhaps it would be nice to go outside and walk in the garden. Jennifer readily agreed, and we slipped out unnoticed. The May evening was serene, Wadham garden tranquil, cool and beautifully solitary. We came to a great copper beech and spontaneously I looked it up and down with the eye of the tree-climbing child I had been only a few years before. It was a cinch.

'Would you like to climb that tree?' I asked Jennifer.

'I'd simply love to.'

I was still to learn that Jennifer seldom refused any reasonable proposal, as long as she liked the person it came from. Reciprocity, as the Americans say, was her middle name. We addressed ourselves to the tree, I going up first, partly so that I could pick the holds and give her some help from above, and partly because I thought it would be a bit embarrassing for her to have me looking up her skirt. As far as I was concerned it was easy climbing, bough after bough, but Jennifer, lacking about three inches of my height, couldn't always quite reach the branch above and was glad of a hand. Her enthusiasm, however, remained undented.

At its top the tree formed a sort of little arbour, a firm place to sit enclosed by sprays of leaves. I reached it, turned, gave Jennifer both my hands, drew her up beside me and kissed her warmly and with confidence. She responded ardently, and when I released her set about kissing me on her own account, looking into my eyes and laughing at my astonished joy. Yet she, too, seemed in a little amazement. Intuitively, behind my flood of desire and happiness, I sensed that this girl was not the sophisticate I had supposed, but someone more or less as inexperienced as myself.

I can't recall how long we stayed at the top of the tree – if indeed I ever knew – but when we came down we didn't go back to the party. We went out to a meal somewhere or other, drank some beer in a pub and together strolled down towards the Parks.

'D'you feel like a couple?' I asked Jennifer a little tipsily.

She looked perplexed. 'But we've had a couple already.'

It seemed a splendid joke. I explained. 'I'd like to meet this Alasdair of yours,' she said. 'Tomorrow?'

Walking back to Worcester down Beaumont Street, I knew beyond doubt that I had attained to a different state of being. There was no catch in it: it had happened and this was what it was like – reciprocated love. Then and there I determined that, come what may, I wouldn't do anything that could possibly forfeit this radiant blessing I had stumbled upon. I could still feel her touch upon my cheeks and my wrists. Everything seemed so amazing that I vaguely thought there was something I ought to be doing about it; but no, there was nothing to do except wait until tomorrow.

I needn't have worried. Jennifer was to be my girl and no one else's for a long time to come – as we reckoned time in those days. She loved me as much as I loved her: but it was some while before I could believe it, before I became convinced. At a distance she had seemed such a smart girl, so elegant, so self-possessed, so much surrounded by polished undergraduate friends. And so she was: but there was a paradox in it. She was not experienced, not canny, not the girl my timidity had suggested. What I had thought poise was really nothing but self-forgotten, happy spontaneity. For she was a great one for forgetting herself, was Jennifer. She could enter into just about anything going as naturally as a child, and she had a Cleopatra-like quality of making anything becoming which came from herself. 'Oh, bloody bugger!' she would say happily, tripping over the punt pole, and it seemed not a teenage mannerism but perfectly natural and acceptable. (She didn't do it too often, you see.)

My friends took to her immediately, and she to them. Mike Seale in particular, a handsome boy somewhat resembling the young James Stewart, was very much taken not only with her vivacity but in particular with her beautiful voice, and would question her again and·again simply for the pleasure of hearing her speak. She was entirely at her ease with Alasdair, William and the others, for she was a girl who was used to being admired and, like Yum-Yum's moon, there was not a trace upon her face of diffidence or shyness. The great thing about Jennifer was that she never put on any sort of act. She had come by magic and magic she remained.

All through those bright summer weeks, while the Germans smashed their way towards Paris, the two of us were about as happy together as it is possible to be. I remember a garden party one evening out at Garsington, where some acquaintance said to me 'Richard, what's happened to you? You've changed in some way.' I dallied with my golden chain and, smiling, put the question by. Hilda Brown, the Walton Street landlady at The Jolly Farmers, also took a great liking to Jennifer, who made her laugh. One day the two of us hitch-hiked to Newbury – hitch-hiking was easy with Jennifer – but my father didn't warm to her. I don't know; with hindsight, could he have been jealous? I know now that parents often are. But for once I didn't care what my father thought. This was perhaps the happiest quality of my relationship with Jennifer; my own unwavering certainty. There were no second thoughts, no unwelcome discoveries. I knew what I wanted and this was it. She clearly felt the same.

What did she do for me? For in love there must be mutual conferral and a feeling that the other has qualities not your own. Quite simply, Jennifer was a totally different kind of person from me. She did not go in for passing exams (or want to do so). She had no particular ambitions. She was certainly not a stupid girl – anything but – yet she was not academic, not particularly well-informed and did not try to be. I was a striver, but Jennifer, for all her bright energy and eager reciprocity, was lazy and self-content. Nor was she given to deliberation. There was an immediacy about her – about her reactions and her whole style – which suited her very well. Indeed, she enjoyed a youthful lightness of heart verging on the irresponsible. Yet God knows that one thing those times needed was lightness of heart, and the ability to put by the terrible things that were happening; for our time to take part in them had not yet come. It would be a fair criticism for any serious-minded person to say that we were nothing but playmates – Peter and Wendy – and that the relationship was childish. So it was, to the extent that we had no notion of marriage and that physical love – apart from kisses and caresses – didn't enter into the picture. Desire did, certainly, but in the manner of those days, fifty years ago, Jennifer was apprehensive of so serious a step.

JULY 30, 1924.] PUNCH, OR THE LONDON CHARIVARI. 131

Bashful Bride (on honeymoon). "NO—NO MORE KISSES NOW, GEORGE. AND—DO BEHAVE! WHAT EVER MUST THAT COW THINK OF US?"

It must be remembered that, while today a young couple who are continually together and obviously fond of each other are not only condoned for making love but virtually expected to do so and even thought rather odd if they don't (hostesses put them in the same bedroom, etc.), in those days all social pressure was very heavily the other way – heavily enough to give any girl second thoughts. Girls were brought up to think it cheap and contemptible. To be known to sleep with a lover most certainly didn't do *any* unmarried girl, however independent, any good (see, e.g., Dorothy

L. Sayers's *Strong Poison*). An eighteen-year-old virgin, living at home with her mother, was more than fully entitled to have qualms and to feel that it was a risk simply not worth taking. Risk? Of what? Of possible pregnancy, but, apart from that, of the most almighty row imaginable if the truth were to come out. I had, of course, met Jennifer's mother – a delightful person with a warm sense of humour and fun – and I knew that she felt in no doubt that we would stop short of physical love. That was why she allowed Jennifer so much freedom and why she was always so nice to me.

If Jennifer herself was in two minds – as she was – I was quite ready to accept the situation. This surprised me. I had thought I was ruthlessly, single-mindedly carnal, and it was rather pleasing to discover that I valued Jennifer's inclinations more than my own selfish will. Besides, I could see that if she was only going to be full of regret and guilt afterwards, it would be ruinous to all our pleasure together to set out to overcome her reluctance. She was very good for me as things were: for she was the very Antipodes of Hiscocks (who would not, I sensed, have liked her much). There was a wholeness, a feminine roundness (as opposed to a male sharpness), a completeness, about Jennifer. She didn't compete or toil in the spirit: she simply existed. There was an admirable humility about her, for despite being if anything too conscious of her limitations, she was the best-tempered girl in the world. In fact, now that I come to think of it, though I once or twice saw her reproachful, I never once saw her angry. It wasn't her style. I hadn't heard about Jung in those days, but if I had, I might have mused on one of his cracks: 'Man seeks perfection, but perfection is incomplete. Woman seeks completion, but completion is imperfect.'

Our happy summer went on, while the world ran ruinward. The Germans, advancing at the rate of thirty miles a day, reached the channel at Abbeville. Older people – including Bill Money – shook their heads and said that this was worse than anything they could remember. The exact succession of the days and disasters escapes me now, but of course I remember Dunkirk. Quite a few of our evacuated soldiers were brought back to Oxford. They were to be seen around, and you could tell them by their air of battered exhaustion, even though they had been fed and rested. Among them came a Worcester friend of mine, J. D. Evans, a man a year senior to me, who had joined up at the outbreak of war the previous year.

J. D. told me that the Germans had to be seen to be believed. He said he had personally seen what looked like a solid wall of tanks appear over the crest of a slope. 'And we'd got no effective weapons to oppose them.' He also said that being dive-bombed by Stukas was most demoralizing. Again, we were not equipped to hit back. It sounded bad. I was, of course, ignorant in these matters and still a mere child – young for my age, I think – yet I shared the feelings and faith of everyone throughout the country. Somehow or other, it would all come right in the end. Later, George Orwell derisively summarized the British attitude: 'Anyway, England is always right and England always wins, so why worry?' I won't say we weren't worried, but I never met anyone who thought we should sue for peace. Apparently Hitler thought we were going to: the very idea shows his limited comprehension. My mother used to say 'You mark my words, dear. That Hitler – he'll come to a bad end.' It's easy enough, now, to say 'Yes, of course,' but it didn't seem like that at the time, I can assure you.

The term ended. The University authorities had arranged what they called 'special examinations', on the results of which they awarded 'war-time degrees'; although, as I've said, we all doubted how much use they would be later. However, this was no time to be thinking of such things. The storm was up and all was on the hazard. At least I got a distinction in the special examination, for which the College gave me a prize – a handsome copy of the letters of Keats, stamped in gold with the College crest.

Memories are vague. I remember, having come home, driving to Newbury station, about mid-day, to meet a train, though I don't remember which of the family was on it. I was standing on the platform when I heard behind me two soldiers talking. One said something to which the other replied 'What, 'ave the French packed it in, then?' 'Yeah.' 'Bloody 'ell, that's a go, ain't it?' My feelings were exactly those expressed by Louis MacNeice in his poem on the debacle: 'Something twangs and breaks at the end of the street.' France's capitulation was a dying fall; it made a small, contemptible, paltry sound. Nevertheless, it left us all with the feeling that now we were in real trouble.

My calling-up papers arrived in the post. The thirteenth of July was my date to report to Aldershot. At the outbreak of war I, like the majority of undergraduates, had been interviewed at Oxford and asked to state my preferences. I had had one firm idea, based on what I knew of the First World War: anything rather than the infantry. If they were giving me a choice I would darned well exercise it.

My first option had been for the Navy. However, the Commissions Board (or whatever they called themselves) at Oxford wouldn't grant this. They said that I was 'a potential cadet' and that the Navy was already over-subscribed with such. My next choice was the Fleet Air Arm, but this also was denied for the same reason. I could feel the infantry lapping about my ankles. In desperation I asked what about the Royal Army Service Corps? (Here I must give my sister due credit: it had been her shrewd suggestion.) Yes, into that I could be mobilized as a potential cadet, at the end of the summer term of 1940. I would receive instructions 'through the usual channels' in due course.

As the day drew nearer, my personal world seemed to disintegrate piece by piece, in a mundane and undramatic way, until I was left, in effect, stripped and bare. Our little Worcester set dispersed to the four corners of the British Isles, well knowing that within a matter of weeks we would be setting out again for barracks, aircraft stations and shore training establishments: for Catterick, Portsmouth, Down Ampney, Tidworth and the like. Any possible return to Oxford certainly did not lie in the foreseeable future. Books were taken to Blackwell's or Thornton's and sold for whatever they would fetch. Sheets, pillow-cases, towels, dinner services, glasses, pictures – all the things that normally stayed put during the vac. – had to be packed up to go home.

Alasdair's tea service was Northallerton china; nice, capacious cups and saucers decorated in bold red and deep blue. I'd drunk tea from them many a time. 'I can't see any point in carting those all the way back to Newcastle,' said Alasdair. 'Take them to Newbury with you; they can stay there till we all get back.'

A last pint in the College buttery, farewells and tips to our scouts, another last pint in The Jolly Farmers and Oxford was left behind indefinitely; except for Jennifer, for there were still three weeks or so to run and she and I were determined to meet a few more times before I disappeared into the khaki belly of the whale.

Arrived back at home, I felt foolish doing nothing all day, even though it was my last chance for a long time. Everyone was doing something. So I went and joined myself unto a citizen of that country, and he sent me into his fields to feed swine. In point of fact, I went to work on Captain Cornwallis's farm for two or three weeks (and that was the first money I ever earned). Swine were certainly involved, for on my first day one of the regular labourers, a fellow named Tucker, gave me a sacking apron and told me to hold a piglet upside-down by the back legs, gripping its head between my knees while he castrated it with his pocket knife. I set my teeth and fettled myself, but when I actually had the piglet in position, its back against my stomach, squealing blue murder, and Tucker opened the blade of his pocket knife with his front teeth, I said I couldn't go through with it. (I doubt I could now.) Tucker closed his knife without a word and we started doing something else, but a little later he remarked 'You're not the first one to turn that job in, Richard.'

Most of the time, though, it was haymaking. I never learned to use a scythe, which I would have liked, partly because the hay was cut by revolving blades and horsepower, and partly because no one had the time to teach me. I raked the hay into field-long windrows by means of a horse-drawn, automatic rake. The tines bumped behind you, picking up the cut hay and pulling it along. As you came up to the end of each windrow you had to judge the right moment to pull a lever which lifted the tines and released the hay to lie in the row. Bennett, another of the men, let me carry on for a couple of hours and then suggested politely that perhaps I'd like to hand over to him. During the lunch break he asked 'D'you know what the old mare said to me, Richard?' I had no idea. 'She asked if you could go back on the rake s'afternoon.' There was a general laugh. I learned, that day, that a horse soon weighs up whoever is behind it (or on it, for that matter) and if it's allowed to, will take advantage of the inexperienced to idle. On my second spell I took care that the mare became brisker.

It was at this time that the L.D.V. (Local Defence Volunteers) were formed, which later became the Home Guard. Every able-bodied man who, for one cause or another, wasn't in the armed forces joined up, and there was no reason why I shouldn't. (No one ever thought of women volunteering, although the A.R.P. was full of them.) We certainly were a scratch lot – no uniforms, of course, and no military weapons. All we could really do was keep a night-long watch at points all round the local countryside, in case Hitler's parachute troops turned up. They were confidently expected ('Reckon 'e's bound t'ave a go somewheres or other') and anyone who had a shotgun was determined to make good use of it. It was a great time for rumours and for 'My brother knows a man in Whitehall who was saying –'. Everyone believed for certain sure that in Holland the Germans had dropped parachutists disguised as nuns; so they probably would here. I imagine real nuns must have had quite a difficult time getting about on their lawful occasions.

I was given the odd and rather superfluous job of riding round our sentry posts on a bicycle in the middle of the night, so that I could be challenged and subsequently confirm that everyone had been where he ought to be. (I had no wireless, of course: no one had.)

It was only a week or two after midsummer and the nights were short. I remember, towards the end of one such night, wheeling my bicycle while I walked with two or three others along a country lane, on our way back to Wash Common and dismissal after the night's duty. It was still dark – or darkish.

'Won't be long now, then, 'Arry,' said one of my companions to another. 'There's th'old lark startin' up, 'ear 'un?'

It was indeed a skylark on the wing. I had not known before that they sense the dawn and make their first song-flight in the darkness shortly before light comes into the sky. This knowledge was my most valuable – indeed my only – gain from my short service in the L.D.V.

Now there was hardly a piece of my civilian life left. I'd said good-bye to Jennifer; and to the few people in and around Wash Common who might possibly notice I was no longer about, including Jim Spencer, publican of The Bell. Packing's not much of a problem to someone on his way to join up. Extra socks, ditto underclothes, handkerchiefs, pyjamas and a toothbrush and tooth-paste were about the size of it. In those days, in theory at least, a man was supposed to be able to join the Army with nothing but what he stood up in and be completely 'all found' by the quartermaster. Issue kit included a safety razor but, oddly, neither pyjamas nor a toothbrush. So a soldier was officially acceptable sleeping in his shirt and pants and never cleaning his teeth. Is he still, I wonder?

The thirteenth of July came. All in the hot, sunny afternoon my mother and father came down Wash Hill to see me off from Newbury station. I was to go by train to Reading and change for Aldershot. The train, when it arrived, was a little diesel more like a large motor-coach. I got in, waved good-bye and, as we departed, sat down. I made up a triolet, though not a very good one.

> With that he lit a cigarette
> And sang to keep his spirits up.
> He thought "It will get tougher yet."
> (With that he lit a cigarette.)
> He said "The footlights flicker up,
> The house-lights dim, the stage is set."
> With that he lit a cigarette
> And sang to keep his spirits up.

Although, as my sister was for ever telling me, I was too much addicted to self-dramatization, even I could hardly have over-dramatized, within myself, that summer afternoon departure from Newbury on the diesel train. It was carrying me away not only from my childhood and adolescence, never to return, but from an entire society and way of life, from everything I had experienced and come to know as familiar. The world would never be the same again.

XIII

Arrived at Aldershot, I got on a bus which seemed to be pointing in the right direction and, as we set off, asked the conductor where might be No. 1 R.A.S.C. Training Centre. ''Ow the 'ell d'you expect me to know?' he replied. This was my first experience of the 'Ask a silly question' syndrome. I was no longer Dr Adams's son or a scholar of Worcester. I was a stranger mug who seriously expected civilians to know about military topography. But then, whom could I ask? A policeman, a soldier? What did other people do? I got out my papers to have another look at them. At this moment some kindly passenger said 'What's the barracks, son?' They were called, I now saw, 'Buller' (one of the more unsuccessful generals of the Boer War). I was told where to get off the bus and which way to go. I arrived, was directed to some building or other to check in and found others doing the same.

For those who have not had the pleasure of going to Aldershot, I had better try to describe it. Of course, this was fifty years ago, but it's all still there – or most of it. Before the nineteenth century, soldiers used to be accommodated by being billeted, in larger or smaller groups as practicable, in the homes of local civilians or anywhere else that was thought suitable. This was, of course, an untidy and unsatisfactory system in several respects – difficulty of transmitting orders, quarrelling with civilians, lack of discipline, robbery and so on. It was the Duke of Wellington who promoted the idea of barracks, so that soldiers could be concentrated and disciplined in places where military interests and values did not clash with civilian ones. In addition to barracks in most county towns, special concentrations grew up in what were judged to be suitable places, e.g., Aldershot, Bulford and Catterick. Bulford, of course, is on Salisbury Plain, where soldiers can train and manoeuvre without getting in too many people's way. It is easy to see why Aldershot was favoured. It is an easy journey to and from London and it is largely surrounded by land of no use for farming – heather, silver birch and pines, that sort of country. Some of the outlying barrack blocks are actually among the heather.

The barracks – I only got to know Buller, but no doubt they are all much the same – possess a uniquely bleak and dispiriting quality, something like workhouses or the precincts of old, Victorian hospitals. I would guess that they were built between about 1840 and 1880. You would not be terribly surprised to see Privates Mulvaney, Ortheris and Learoyd come round the corner, with pillbox hats, swagger canes and big moustaches. The barracks are neither town nor country. Civilians have no haunts nor business there, and there are no trees, no flowers or grass, no shops and no pubs. Birds are restricted to sparrows. Between the red-brick barrack blocks, married quarters, guard-rooms, offices and training sheds lie bare, level areas of asphalt and featureless, straight roads. The centre of each barracks is the barrack square, about 40,000 square feet of open hard-standing, where people drill and drill and drill. The square is a sacred place. You cannot walk on it (assuming you wanted to) except in the way of duty. You may not smoke within about a mile of it. (I quote Corporal Edwards.) A barracks is like a naval ship; there is nothing there but what is necessary, utilitarian and practical. This, in my day, meant that there were no baths and no showers. The barrack blocks were all exactly the same, consisting of a large, rectangular room with a floor of polished (and that means polished slippery) boards, about thirty iron beds and lockers and a lavatory and some wash-basins at one end. To live in such an environment day in and day out, seldom going anywhere else, you have to adapt yourself, like an evolving animal, and become conformed to your surroundings.

In the 1914–18 war, as far as I can make out, people were frequently commissioned as officers straight out of civilian life. If you could pass as a gentleman you could pass as an officer. But as the casualties mounted, officers were often promoted from the ranks. R. C. Sheriff's *Journey's End* portrays what was no doubt a typical set-up in many companies. The company commander, Stanhope, is a gentleman and a veteran (though pathetically young). His second-in-command, Osborne, is an ex-schoolmaster, also a gentleman. Lieutenant Hibbert is a somewhat pseudo-gentleman, Lieutenant Trotter is a promoted Other Rank, not a gentleman, and 2nd Lieutenant Raleigh is a boy straight from his public school.

In Hitler's war the set-up was rather different. At the outset the *Daily Mirror* and other newspapers declared that all promotions to officer should be by merit from the ranks. Everyone should initially have to join up in the ranks. The Dean of Worcester, Colonel Wilkinson (who had been a Guards officer and an aide to General Plumer in the 1914–18 war), head of the Oxford University Officers Training Corps, maintained openly and stoutly that this was rubbish and a waste of time and money. If someone was obviously officer-material, he should be sent straight to an Officer Cadet Training Unit (O.C.T.U.). Colonel Wilkinson did not really get away with this and it did him little good, for it was much remarked upon that although he held his appointment as head of the Oxford O.T.C. all through the war, he never received any honour in recognition of his services.

However, Oxford, Cambridge and some other universities were enabled, as it were, to meet Colonel Wilkinson half-way. Undergraduates who joined the University O.T.C. had (as we have seen) a say in what they should be mobilized into and also had their calling-up date deferred so that they could take special examinations devised more or less *ad hoc*. What was more, although they were not called up as cadets, they joined the ranks as 'potential cadets' and were put into special training squads with others like themselves. It was in such a squad – Brander Squad – that I found myself that mid-July. Who Brander may have been I am not at all sure, but it is of interest, though probably only a coincidence, that a 'Brander' is mentioned by Kipling as a commanding officer in one of the Mulvaney-Ortheris stories.

In Evelyn Waugh's *Men at Arms*, Guy Crouchback joins the Royal Corps of Halberdiers as a 'probationary officer', along with twenty others. Apart from the fact that we were not 'probationary officers' but 'potential cadets', Brander Squad's daily life and régime were very similar to Guy Crouchback's. I suppose there were about thirty of us. We lived in a barrack-room (though a few of us spilled over into unoccupied married quarters) and messed in the communal Other Ranks' mess-room. Apart from messing, however, we really had little or nothing to do with the other Other

Ranks, except for our squad commander, Corporal Edwards, and the various N.C.O. instructors who took us for weapon training, P.T., anti-gas and so on. We lived among ourselves and this made all the difference.

Corporal Edwards was a regular, about twenty-five, I suppose. I think it is greatly to his credit that he was able to act naturally and be his rough self, yet impose his authority on us and command our liking and respect. He pushed us hard in those long summer days, when the asphalt turned sticky and the bonnet of a lorry became too hot to touch. After all, his own standing and promotion depended on whether we were a credit to him. But he was no bully and he never had recourse to any authority but his own. He had a sharp sense of humour, he talked with us off duty and got to know us and he shared with us the life of the barrack-room. He instructed us in how to get a high shine on a pair of army boots, how to iron battle-dress trousers until they had a knife-edge crease up to the top of the thigh, and all the rest of the bullshit. He had an impressive stock of regulars' catchwords and sayings, one or other of which could be applied to almost any situation. 'By Jesus, you blokes want to get some service in.' 'Get a grip of it!' 'Don't touch 'im, 'e'll break.' 'Well, fall down with it, then!' 'Lot of bloomin' joskins!' ('Joskin' is a regular soldiers' term for a recruit.) 'That belt's bloody milo.' (No good at all.) 'Jesus wants you for a sunbeam!' Initially, we were all a bit shocked by Edwards's casual taking of the name of Jesus, but the good fellow meant not the least harm by it, and after a few weeks we used to do it to each other, in inverted commas, as it were. 'By Jesus, Dicky, you'll never get by with that rifle.' I started as 'Dicky', but one day Edwards said we were all Goons, except me, and I was 'The Jeep'.★ After this everyone called me 'Jeep'. I had never had a nickname before and liked it.

★ 'Popeye the Sailorman' was the hero of a pre-war strip-cartoon (published in this country by the *Daily Mirror*), who acquired enormous physical strength by the internal application of canned spinach. He was accompanied by a female, named Olive Oyl, of dubious charm but indisputable fidelity. He had a friend, a smoothly self-possessed scrounger and rascal named J. Wellington Wimpy, who lived on hamburgers for which he never paid. This is why hamburgers became popularly known as 'Wimpys'. It is also why Wellington bombers became known as 'Wimpys'.

Popeye had another loyal follower called the Jeep, a little creature about the size

And what did we do for those two months, from July to September? We bashed the square. Crikey, did we bash that square? We did foot-drill and arms-drill and platoon drill, up and down and round and round the square and the adjacent drill-shed, while the sweat ran off us in streams. I can't remember that we ever did this in shirt-sleeve order. What I do remember is that we had to keep our battle-dress jackets buttoned to the neck and the two hooks-and-eyes, at the top, fastened all the time. You had thick khaki close round your throat from morning till night, and a thick khaki shirt underneath that. Off-duty, too, whether in barracks or going down-town, in shop or pub, all the time, you had to be clipped up to the throat. If one of the barracks N.C.O.s, who knew you, happened to see a clip undone, you might get away with no more than a roar of 'Sun-bathing, eh? Do it up!' But out of barracks, a stranger red-cap (military police) would be quite likely to put you on a charge – or threaten to, anyway. This would not improve the prospects of a potential cadet.

In some ways it wasn't a bad life. You had no cares or responsibilities apart from your boots, clothes, rifle and bedspace; the food was quite good and as our drill and bullshit steadily improved, Edwards became positively avuncular. He was, at bottom, as contemptuous as we of the continual orders to 'bump' the barrack-room floor till it shone, highly polish both our pairs of boots and so on. I remember him, one evening, giving way to an outburst. "'Ighly polished! 'Ighly polished! That's all they thinks about, 'ighly polished! 'Ere, I'll tell you what! If a bloody Messerschmitt come over, they'd want it 'ighly polished!' This took our fancy, and the highly polished Messerschmitt became part of Brander Squad's folklore.

We all got very fit on sunshine, plenty of food, no worries and vigorous work: but by jingo, it was a hard day we did and no

---

of a cat, which could presage the future, if asked, by sticking up his behind to indicate 'Yes' and squeaking 'Jeep, jeep.' This is why, later on in the war, when the American troops began arriving in numbers, their light, open-sided vehicles became known as 'jeeps'.

Popeye suffered intermittently from the hostile attentions of 'goons', whom he always thrashed, of course: these were great, clumping, stupid, malicious creatures, rather like Norwegian trolls. This is why German soldiers were called 'goons'.

mistake! Reveille sounded at five o'clock a.m. By ten past five – it didn't matter how you were dressed: shirt and trousers were enough – you had to be out on the asphalt to give your name to the N.C.O. taking roll-call. Then there would be various things to be done: shining the taps in the washroom and so on, bumping the barrack-room floor and folding the blankets (no sheets, of course) until they were entirely uniform. After breakfast, the first hour's drill of the day began at eight. Then would follow weapon training (Lewis gun, Bren gun, anti-tank rifle, bayonet, etc.) under Sergeant Tierney, a caustic but humorous Irishman with a biting tongue. There would be P.T. in the gym. – really arduous – followed by anti-gas instruction from Corporal Pryor, a Yorkshireman whose nickname was 'Moosty ha-a-ay'. ('Now phosgene 'as a pro-nounced odour of moosty 'a-a-ay.') More drill, followed by instructions on, perhaps, badges of rank, by Edwards. ('You, Jeep, badger ranker brigadier.' 'Three stars, corporal, in triangular formation, surmounted by a crown.' 'Yeah, three piss-pots, eh, surmounted by – you, Anderson, badger ranker major-general.')

About every third night we would have to provide four men for guard duty, under an N.C.O. who might or might not be Edwards. Three men, each in turn, were sentries outside the guard-room, with two spells each of two hours on duty. When the guard were inspected at guard-mounting at quarter to six in the evening, the smartest man of the four was appointed 'stick man'; the softest job. He had to go to the cook-house for the cocoa, wash up the supper, carry messages (if any) and so on. The trouble with guard duty, apart from the boredom of four hours as sentry, was that you never got any sleep. You might manage to doze, but somebody or something was always bumping about, or clattering or talking in the guard-room. You went sleepless back to the following day's square-bashing.

Whenever we sat down during the day – for a gas lecture, or a talk from the Padre or the M.O. (on V.D.) – most of us simply could not help falling asleep, and the N.C.O.s were relatively easy on this. I learned how to sleep while looking as though you weren't, but very often the N.C.O.s were in almost as bad a case as we were. Sleep in the barrack-room tended to be fitful, too, on account of interruptions. If you could get six hours in, you were darned lucky.

The interesting feature of this régime was that it included scarcely anything that a regular recruit's training would not have included in, say, 1935. We knew nothing of the course of the war and hardly ever saw a newspaper, much less an officer. We learned nothing about the Germans or about motorized transport (although we were R.A.S.C.). We did have, I think, two days on the rifle ranges, where, we were told, we had acquitted ourselves well. Otherwise we lived an almost barrack-enclosed life, among instructors whose way of doing things had remained virtually unaffected by the war. It was, as I say, an easy life after the intellectual demands of Oxford, and at least all hardships were shared in common. We were lucky, too, in that we had no one objectionable in the squad. No one was malicious and no one was hated.

One day I found myself on some sort of coal fatigue with an old sweat, a regular. (I say 'old': I suppose he may have been forty.) Whatever we had been told to do – I can't remember what it was, now – was plainly silly and ill considered, involving about twice as much work as was necessary. After a while the old soldier said to me 'I'll tell yer what, lad. This is a right balls-up.' I said I heartily agreed and we toiled on. About five minutes later he remarked 'This is the biggest balls-up since Calonso.' 'Why,' I asked, 'what was Calonso?' 'Well, I don't rightly know,' said he, 'but that was the biggest balls-up there ever was.'

This intrigued me, and later on – much later on – when opportunity offered, I put in a bit of research. The result was interesting. Colenso (*sic*), according to the *Encyclopaedia Britannica*, is a village in Natal, about sixteen miles from Ladysmith. It was the scene of an action fought between the Boers and the British under Sir Redvers Buller on 15 December 1899. The British lost. I suppose my old sweat might have joined up in 1920 or thereabouts. He must have acquired the name orally, as a proverbial term in the regular army for a military fiasco.

For part of the time – quite a few weeks, as I recall – that we were at Aldershot, there was a prisoner in the guard-room. We would come across him when we were on guard duty at night, and sometimes by day on the square. What he had done I never heard – probably overstayed his leave, I expect – but my Lord, was he atoning for it? He appeared a very ordinary sort of man, medium height with sandy hair, and he was always, or nearly always, in a state of desperate exhaustion, gasping, glassy-eyed and half-oblivious. He was taken out on the square in full equipment (no rifle) and drilled – often at the double – from morning till night by the regimental police. It was terrible to see, for he was being tortured, in effect. Even now I can hear the N.C.O.'s voice sounding through the guard-room window: 'Left-right-left-right-left-right-left-right-left-turn, double march, left-right-left-right, mark time. Come on, pick 'em up!' Eventually the man would be marched back into the guard-room and would collapse, panting and pouring with sweat, on one of the cots. He never spoke. I have never seen anyone in a similarly dreadful state of suffering and exhaustion: and while he was still trembling and huddled, the time would come for the next spell outside. His life can only have been a nightmare that never stopped.

In the end, he broke a bone in his foot, marking time, and they took him away, to be seen no more – by Brander Squad, anyway.

We had one day out from the barracks about once a week, when we were put in a bus and taken out to the Tank Obstacle. Hitler was still expected at any time and part of the plan of defence was to dig a ditch across the whole of southern England deep enough and wide enough to constitute an effective anti-tank obstacle. All available personnel worked one day a week on this job. Here we *were* allowed to strip: we stripped to the waist and worked in pairs, shovelling aside the already dug earth. It was a notable sight, the long line of the great ditch and the stripped, toiling men stretching away into the sun-haze, glistening with sweat.

By this time enemy aircraft (including highly polished Messerschmitts) had begun to appear over England, and every platoon or squad on the Tank Trap had to detail two men for anti-aircraft duty, sitting and waiting beside a Lewis light machine gun mounted on a tall tripod, pointing upwards and capable of being turned in a full circle. Except that the sun was hot, and you had no shade, this really was a soft option, and I was delighted to find myself detailed for it one August morning. I took with me on the bus my *Complete Works of Shakespeare in one volume* – the same that I had been given under Hiscocks at Bradfield. (I still have it, though coverless.) I spent the long, hot day reading *As You Like It*, which I had never read before. That play still recalls the tank trap, the dirt flying and the clink and glitter of the shovels in the sun. No enemy aircraft ever came.

I said there were no baths or showers in barracks. There weren't; and by this time, reader, you may have inferred that this deficiency was rather boring. It was; but there was one mighty solace and refuge, may God bless her eternally, Miss Daniels' Home. Who Miss Daniels was I don't know, but to her everlasting credit she established her Home in Aldershot for the comfort of the brutal soldiery. Here you could have a hot bath, even if you did have to queue for it; and, I think, it was free. And you could follow it with eggs and bacon for about one shilling and sixpence – for in those early days of the war, rationing had not yet begun to bite, and there were still plenty of eggs, bacon, bananas and chocolate. Many a comforting hour of an evening did I spend at Miss Daniels' Home, clean, replete and ready to appreciate the interesting variety of Victorian religious pictures on the walls. Is it still functioning, I wonder? I hope so.

I think I know how starlings must feel. One retained, of course, some sense of individuality, but at bottom you genuinely felt yourself to be primarily a particle of a group. Brander Squad's luck or good or bad treatment were yours, and even letters from home didn't really dilute this feeling much.

Like Guy Crouchback and his fellows, we used to chant aloud, en masse, the rhythms of obedience to drill orders. '*Ow*-pen Or-der: *March!*' Edwards would shout, and the squad, responding, would yell: 'One, one-two, stop: *up*, two, three, shuffle!'

Once, half the squad disappeared, quite literally, for about five days. It happened in this way. Our normal daily training routine was always liable to interruption on account of 'the exigencies of the service', which during that summer meant flap in one form or another; in other words, an emergency due to the real or supposed activities of the enemy. It was usually some form of nocturnal stand-to, but this particular jamboree went several times better than that.

One fine morning, Company Sergeant-Major Byrne told the good Corporal Edwards that Brander Squad were required to provide a guard for a train full of ammunition parked on a siding somewhere in the locality. We weren't told where: nobody was ever told where anything was in those days, and all place names on roads, stations and signposts had been obliterated or removed.

Something between twelve and sixteen of us altogether were detailed off. Edwards stayed behind with the remainder (which included me) while the guard embussed – rifles, bayonets, gas-masks, tin hats and full equipment – and departed for their unknown destination. They would be gone, we were told, for at least twenty-four hours.

They were: and for longer; and yet longer. After two days we began to speculate and wonder. The rumour was that the train had vanished, taking the guard with it; and apparently – or so it was whispered – no one in Buller Barracks, not even that distant and lofty presence, the rarely glimpsed Captain Cousmaker, knew where.

Three days passed. Brander Squad now had a distinct sense of amputation. Our hard-won, supple, homogeneous flexibility had been dislocated. We continued, as best as we could, drilling and stripping down the Lewis gun, but the truth was that the N.C.O.s didn't really know what to do with us. For all sorts of purposes, half a squad is like half a novel; viable in a way (e.g., *Weir of Hermiston*; *Edwin Drood*), but essentially deficient and dissatisfying. There came to be longer and longer spells of 'Fall out for a smoke' or of bumping the barrack-room floor.

One blazing afternoon, as we were bumping away on boards already as bright as a mirror and slippery as a skating rink, there sounded a trampling of boots in the entrance up by the washroom, and in came the guard, trudging in ones, twos and threes, greeting no one and looking at nobody, like people who have had more than enough and can't really believe it's over. I remember Frank Espley and Bob Young walking boot by boot past my bedspace without a glance or a word; and Frank leaning his rifle against the wall, sitting down on his bed and beginning to unlace his boots with an air of distance and detachment from everyone. Their unforced aloofness, the guard, conferred on them a kind of authority ('Much too good to tell to you brutes,' said Stalky), and it was only after a while, and that by means of patient questioning, that we learned the full story.

You must understand, for a start, that any guard – even a single night's guard – is a great bore and no joke. As I've said, you never really got any sleep beyond a light doze. You can't take off your equipment or sit down to a meal. The two-hour spells of sentry-go

– two hours out of every six – are tedious and wearisome. Frank Espley & Co. had had four or five days of this, all day and all night.

Why had they vanished, none knew where, not even their company commander? The answer lies in the bitter disposition of the time. In that war, the entire public was conditioned to become security-mad, and in all earnest did so. Lovers did not tell their girls where they were stationed. Every vicar, waiter and tea-lady was under suspicion as a possible fifth columnist.* Invasion was an imminent reality which everyone expected as surely as rain. 'Not *may* – they *will* come!'

Now in these circumstances an ammunition train is no fun at all; and as the time passed, the R.E. officer commanding that particular train became more and more conscious of the fact. He felt sure the Germans must know its whereabouts. That kindly old girl who had brought a tray-full of cups of tea for the lads down her garden: how much did she know? Come to think of it, her wireless aerial looked odd. Probably by this time the entire neighbourhood knew it was an ammunition train. What if a Dornier, escorted by two 'ighly polished Messerschmitts, were to come blazing and bombing down the railway track so plainly visible from the air? Enemy aircraft were over England every day now. A train stationary for several days in a siding, with sentries all round it, was asking for trouble; a natural sitter. And if it went up?

Eventually the officer determined that action was no more than his plain duty. He went to see the local Rail Transport Officer (or R.T.O. – also an R.E.), and succeeded in getting a movement order for the train. As few people as possible should know where it went. The R.A.S.C. guard need not know; they could just as easily go on guarding without knowing. Of course, Buller Barracks should have been told, but somehow that got overlooked. The train departed westward by night, taking the guard with it. They never knew where it stopped, although Frank Espley told me later that he thought it was some lonely spot in east Dorset. All they really knew was that long before they were relieved, they had had more than enough. What struck them as the last straw was that in addition to

---

* Fifth columnist. During the Spanish Civil War, the Fascist General Franco said that he had four columns advancing on Madrid and a fifth column inside the city. The term became proverbial for a spy or traitor.

sentry duty, two people were required continuously on the ack-ack Lewis gun. No enemy aircraft came, however.

We ended those thrill-packed two months with a passing-out parade like you never saw. A new colonel, Colonel Bolton, had just taken over the barracks and this dignitary actually had the gall to send Brander Squad – Brander Squad! – off parade to make themselves smarter, saying he would see us again at three o'clock that afternoon. Edwards was incensed; his Brander Squad, whose glitter shone from beyond the horizon like the aurora borealis! Angry and resentful, we got down to work again in the barrack-room, Brasso, boot-polish, flat-iron and blanco. ''Ere, Jeep,' said Edwards, 'give me them trousers. *I'll* put a crease in 'em such as 'e'll *never* check.' And so he did. I think it was Idwal Pugh who asked Edwards, very dead-pan, if he thought we should commandeer a couple of stretchers and four members of another squad to carry us severally onto the square.

Well, we did pass out, and learned that about three-fifths of us had been selected to go on to the O.C.T.U. at Boscombe. I was one of the lucky ones, but somehow (I felt without being told) only just. In those days I looked so slight and thin, with blue eyes and very fair hair – anything but a soldier. Still, this was not the Army, but the nation in arms. I felt sorry for Brander friends left behind. They remained potential cadets, but had to go back to square one and do another two months. In the event, however, they nearly all got to O.C.T.U. and ended up as officers; a decidedly mixed blessing, as I was to learn.

XIV

The O.C.T.U. consisted of the Burlington Hotel at Boscombe, together with one or two smaller local hotels pressed into service as billets. The physical conditions were a lot better than Buller Barracks: there was constant hot water and we slept only four or five to each hotel bedroom. If you weren't on guard, you could go into Bournemouth any evening you pleased – pubs, dance-halls and restaurants. Yet somehow, as that hot high summer slowly turned to a perfect late September, I personally felt almost as though Aldershot, with its leafless asphalt wastes and polished barrack-rooms, had been a holiday. In a way it had. For the first time in years I had not been required to use my brain: physical obedience (though often exhausting and arduous) was all that had been required. Life in Brander Squad, now broken up for ever, had been island life. You only had to do what you were told, very little intruded from outside, and if there were discomforts – shortage of sleep, sweating in hot uniforms – at least they were borne and shared in common. Brander Squad had lived in isolation, surrounded by Other Ranks with whom it had had very little to do. Here, you had to become a human being again: you were credited with an intellect, upon which demands were made. As a cadet, distinguished by your white cap-band, you were expected to be smart and correct even when off the premises. A bad slip-up – drunk, say, or late back when out on a pass – and you ran a serious risk of being R.T.U. – returned to unit, which would mean the end of your hopes of becoming an officer. In brief, although life was more comfortable at Boscombe, it was not nearly so colourful and amusing as Aldershot. Brander Squad I find I remember with affection, but not the O.C.T.U. There were compensations, however. Within the month I found myself at a symphony concert in Bournemouth and seriously involved in a conversation about Brahms. This sort of thing, paradoxically, made you homesick for Oxford by being a poor second-best, whereas Aldershot had been a foreign land and a challenge to overcome.

The weather, however, remained idyllic and nearly every day we found ourselves either weapon training on the sunny cliff-tops or carried out by bus into the New Forest for tactical exercises, with lunch in a pub thrown in. This was how we came to see at first hand a fair part of the Battle of Britain. The main battle, of course, was taking place further to the east, but on many days enemy aircraft – Dorniers and Heinkels – flew over Bournemouth and the New Forest and were engaged by our fighters. They flew in formation, sometimes escorted by their own fighters, and the Spitfires would dive upon them, their exhausts leaving long white plumes across the blue sky. The bursts of fire were very short, usually only a second or two, for a Hurricane or Spitfire could use up all its ammunition in about fifteen seconds. Oddly, I can't remember ever to have seen an aircraft brought down, no doubt because the total length of time during which we watched, although sensed vividly and with great excitement, must have been comparatively short. I recall that more than once the instructor N.C.O.s had to tell us to pay attention to them and not to the air fighting.

Night alerts – air-raid warnings – were common. Most nights the sirens would sound and soon after, sweating in our stuffy rooms behind the black-out screens, we would hear the Germans coming. They made a distinctive and unmistakable noise, for they used to desynchronize their engines with a view to making it more difficult for our people to locate them accurately. '*Wow-oo, wow-oo, wow-oo,*' they went, and then we would hear our own anti-aircraft guns barking sharp and quick, like vixens. Soon, however, the Germans would have flown on towards the Midlands or to Bristol. They weren't concerned to bomb Bournemouth, a seaside residential town with no industry. Towards morning they would return on their way back to France. They would have lost formation by now and there were often a few stragglers. One night, as we lay tossing and turning on our mattresses in a small hotel right next to the beach, a solitary plane unloaded three bombs which it must have been unable, for some reason, to drop earlier. We heard them whistle – a descending glissando, high to low – and then burst in the sea a little offshore. This, except for V1s and V2s in London, was the only time during the war when I personally came under anything that might be called enemy fire.

I remember the night the Germans went to Coventry: that was the biggest raid so far mounted, and one of the biggest of the war, although later Germany itself underwent far bigger ones from the Allies. The distinctive wow-wowing seemed to go on interminably. Lying in the dark, lit only by the glowing points of our cigarettes, we speculated where on earth such a force could be bound for. We'd heard nothing on that scale before. Next day, we learned of the frightful destruction in Coventry and of how the King, woken and told of it, had driven there from London, arriving as the dawn broke.

A lot of our time was spent learning about the innards of lorries, under instruction from soldiers who had mostly been drivers in peace-time. I wrote and asked my mother to send me a boiler-suit. It duly arrived, very new and very blue. After parade one morning I put it on and rather self-consciously joined the others in the big garage. My instructor, a nice fellow called Norton, pantomimed brushing me down with a clothes-brush and then blowing dust off my shoulders. I made sure, that morning, that that boiler-suit got well covered in oil and grease.

My sister came down to see me one week-end, and we went to Poole, to Corfe Castle and to Wareham, where the marble effigy of Lawrence of Arabia lies in the little Anglo-Saxon church. She was soon to take up a war-time teaching place (in lieu of a master) at Tottenham Grammar School, and to become an air-raid warden in Belsize Park. Katharine had a far more dangerous war than I; she served through nightly air-raid alerts in London for more than three years.

As December drew on, I found myself pondering rather anxiously on the now imminent prospect of becoming a subaltern. Thanks to Mr Arnold, I had never held a position of authority in my life, and had no practical experience of enforcing a moment's discipline, let alone of carrying responsibility for the proficiency and behaviour of others. Apart from the scouts at Oxford and friends in pubs, I had almost no experience of what are (or were) loosely called 'working-class' people. I vaguely supposed that all would be made plain in the fullness of time. Anyway, I reflected consolingly, I would have a sergeant and some corporals. They'd tell me what to do.

We began to busy ourselves with officers' clothing. We were measured for and in due course fitted with our service dress. After the rough battle-dress to which we had become used over the months, it felt strange. I remember one of our lot, a rather tough Glaswegian called Bill Coutts, saying it 'felt like wearing bloody pyjamas.' Then there were our pristine Sam Browne belts, on which we set to work with new-boy enthusiasm to make them glitter like russet glass. By now, of course, we were all completely inured to polishing brass and leather, and could sit companionably over it for an hour at a time, chatting or listening to the wireless.

There was no formality about our being commissioned. 'They' simply wished us good luck and we put up our pips and went off on a week's leave before reporting to our new units. It felt most peculiar to be continually saluted as you walked down the street. I was at first surprised that soldiers really did salute me; but they did. 'I'm so sorry for poor Richard's arm, going up and down like that all the time,' said Jennifer to her mother. I suppose I should have felt proud to be an officer, but all I felt was rather nervous. After all, we hadn't had to strive particularly hard over our commissions: we'd joined up, willy-nilly, as 'potential cadets' and been put through a system more or less on a conveyor belt. We hadn't as yet had experience of service in a real military unit in any capacity, let alone as officers.

My posting was to C.R.A.S.C. Northern Ireland. Only one other member of Brander Squad was down for the same destination, and that was Frank Espley. Espley, a Cambridge man, though of the same age and inexperience as myself, had advantages which I certainly didn't grudge him, since he was amiable and I liked him and had always got on with him well enough at Aldershot and at the O.C.T.U. His home was on a south country farm, and this had given him, during his adolescence, plenty of experience in dealing with working people, right down to gipsy casual labour. His appearance, dark and rather handsome, inspired confidence and he had a general air of competence and self-possession. Though he had never intended to join the army in peace-time, he was really, by temperament, a born officer. We always remained good friends. I was to see him promoted to captain within a year and to feel that he certainly deserved it. We lost touch, but three years later, right at the end of the war, we met again in unexpected circumstances.

1941 was the most inactive period of the war, and the inactivity imposed a strain on both morale and discipline. The Germans had chased the British army ignominiously out of Dunkirk before defeating and then occupying France. The United Kingdom was not in land contact with the enemy anywhere, except in the Western Desert. Japan had not yet entered the war. The whole country was full of our soldiers – unit upon unit – who had nowhere to go and nothing to do except 'training' – which was just killing time, really. How on earth were we ever to get at the enemy on the European mainland? Our Navy, of course, remained an undefeated bulwark against invasion and Hitler, during the autumn, had lost the Battle of Britain. America was still on the touch-line, uncommitted. It looked like stalemate.

In spite of all Churchill could say to the nation, morale was inevitably rather low. The men, as a whole, were 'browned off' and hadn't as yet acquired any confidence in our military leadership. There was certainly no wish for peace, but equally there wasn't much more than a deep, unreasoning faith in our cause. It would all come right somehow; but how, exactly? No one knew, and in the meantime everyone objected to polishing boots and buttons and having nothing worthwhile or constructive to do. A lot of the men were only too ready to 'take the piss' out of new and inexperienced officers. I was twenty, and slightly built, with fair hair. I felt apprehensive.

But I struck lucky. Frank and I were posted to a relatively large R.A.S.C. unit specializing in petrol supply. It was stationed at Langford Lodge, a big house and grounds on a peninsula half-way down the eastern coast of Lough Neagh. It was a major's command and there were about fifteen officers in the mess altogether. Frank and I were each given command of a platoon – or 'section', as they were called – of some forty men, with about twenty Bedford three-ton lorries.

This was where I fell in with Sergeant Tuckey – easily the best thing since Corporal Edwards. Sergeant Tuckey was a regular, aged about thirty. He knew the platoon thoroughly and had them in full control. He had the reputation of a bully, but it was only his manner: more bark than bite. The whole unit, or 'Petrol Park', as it was termed, had served in France and come out of Dunkirk. They considered themselves experienced soldiers and, as far as I was concerned, they were.

Naturally, as the weeks went by with the trivial round, the common task, Tuckey and I got to know each other well. He ran true to type. He was out of the same stable as Corporal Edwards and the other Aldershot N.C.O.s. You knew exactly where you were with him and he possessed that greatest merit of a colleague, consistency in all circumstances. The regular army, with its injustices and humiliations, had taught him cunning, patience and equanimity. In moments of disappointment or mortification, Sergeant Tuckey would invoke a generic being rather like Santa Claus, Jack Frost or John Bull, known as 'Sailor Vee'. 'Oh, well, Sailor Vee, sir,' he would say, as we learned that two of our lorries had become unserviceable, or that the people supposed to relieve us would be an hour later than we had originally been told. In time, I personally found Sailor Vee a great help in army life, and I continue to feel grateful to Sergeant Tuckey for his gruff but fundamentally kindly indoctrination of a green subaltern of twenty.

My platoon – 'G' section, they were called – had been given to me as a soft option: Frank's 'D' section were a bit rougher, though not as rough as some of the others. 'G' section consisted largely of ex-territorials: decent, respectable men, from the London suburbs mostly, with a sprinkling from Sheffield and Shropshire. Any fool could have commanded them, for they gave no trouble. I set out conscientiously to learn their names and something about them as individuals. It wasn't difficult, for they were ready enough to talk. Indeed, my only handicap was that their previous platoon commander, Billy Moisson, who had brought them out of Dunkirk and was still with the Petrol Park as headquarters subaltern, was an exceptionally nice, kind-hearted young man whom they had all liked very much and whose departure they regretted. I couldn't hope to step into his shoes, and I spent some time trying to think out how best to make use of my assets (if any). I was supposed to lead this platoon, which meant that they were supposed to feel some sort of regard for me. But on what grounds? They knew quite as much about lorries as I did – rather more, some of them. Games might have helped, but in this sphere the unit was deplorably inactive. It amazes me, now, that in all the months I spent there I never saw an organized game of football or cricket. Yet the situation we were in cried aloud for it, and it could easily have been arranged.

I arrived at my own answer without any conscious resolve, and the contention I experienced and the way in which I was subsequently justified by events now strike me as rather amusing. This rather egregious, thinking and literate platoon (orderly room lance-corporal types, a lot of them: any old soldier will know what I mean) were short of reading matter, for a start. I lent them what I had – Hemingway, Kipling, E. M. Forster – and discussed it while I was supposed to be invigilating maintenance on the lorries. I lent the *Spectator* and the *New Statesman* too (there was nearly always a despatch rider going in to Belfast who could buy them) and discussed the articles in them with individuals. After a bit it dawned on me that soldiers in a democratic army ought to be stimulated to think and to express themselves. They ought to get together to do this: but they had nowhere. The only roofs over their heads were their Nissen hut billets and the N.A.A.F.I. However, there were plenty of rooms up at Headquarters – Langford Lodge itself – including the Padre's 'quiet room'. Having obtained the Padre's agreement, I organized a discussion one evening on 'The British situation in Ireland'. This was a success, and I was able – though taking care not to overdo it – to score a few unassuming points through knowing a bit about Gladstone, Parnell, the Easter rising and what not. It was certainly a breath of fresh air for 'G' section. They revelled in it. By this time I had come to like them and identify with them so much that I was more than ready to defend my notion to anyone from the C.O. downwards.

The next occasion was a bit more provocative. One of the members of 'G' section was a rummy sort of cove by the name of Driver Hopkins. He had been deliberately wished upon us by headquarters (having arrived from God knew where) because they reckoned that he could do least harm in a bunch like 'G' section, as opposed to some of the Glasgow/Liverpool/Bolton sections. All I knew about Hopkins was that he had some sort of bad reputation as an agitator. There was a file about him up at headquarters which I wasn't allowed to see, and even Billy Moisson wouldn't talk about it. To this day I have no idea exactly why Hopkins was regarded as potentially explosive.

I soon found out for myself, however, that his general demeanour on parade was unexceptionable. He was as good as anyone else at carrying out the chores of the dismal day. His manner was perfectly reasonable: indeed, propitiatory, for he usually spoke to me or the N.C.O.s with a little smile on his face. He gave no trouble, and I soon perceived that he exercised no influence whatever on 'G' section, disruptive or otherwise. Even Sergeant Tuckey couldn't positively diagnose him as 'bolshie'.

Yet he was known to harbour bolshie ideas. That was evidently part of the mysterious label which had been pinned on him. He was some sort of left-winger who was opposed to 'the system'. In what way, I wondered. I very much doubted that Hopkins, from what I had now seen of him, could either appeal to or defeat in argument honest young bourgeois like Driver Dooley, Driver Hutcheson or Driver Portway. I decided that it would be a good idea to let him have his head in public. It would call his bluff: it would tend to defuse the mystery about him.

By now my discussion group was attracting a certain amount of attention in the mess. No one ever called me to account officially – neither the C.O. (a rather ineffective man with little influence or power of leadership) nor my company commander, Captain Roope. But Theo Overman, the senior subaltern, shook his head. He disapproved of Other Ranks being encouraged to read the *New Statesman*. He also thought – which was true – that I was an inexperienced and rather flighty young officer, prone to unorthodox and flyaway ideas. I always got on perfectly well in the mess, however, and no senior officer was prepared actually to forbid the 'G' section discussion group in principle. (They couldn't, really, if you come to think about it.) The distrust was more of what the group might actually be being encouraged to talk about and of how I might be running it. Billy Moisson, out of sheer personal anxiety for his beloved 'G' section, attended one or two meetings, and so did Captain Roope.

The Hopkins meeting turned out a damp squib. The subject was how far the U.K. would be justified in taking invasive action to foil a German invasion of Eire. Hopkins, speaking first, unwisely adopted the line that Eire was capable of defeating a German invasion on its own. He could not be taken seriously. I was disappointed: I had been rather hoping he would at least put up a show.

In the middle of all this contretemps, the powers at G.H.Q. (London) set up the organization called A.B.C.A. – Army Bureau of Current Affairs. The soldiers were now to be *encouraged* to learn about, think and talk about the war and its politics. Social affairs, too, they were to be stimulated to discuss, under the guidance of their officers. Weekly brochures were to be issued to platoon commanders, containing information about the Nazis, the Far East, American society, plans for after the war and so on. These would be used as bases for discussion. The whole thing was to be co-ordinated at commanding officer level. What it came down to was that my ideas were fully and entirely vindicated. I had enough sense, however, to refrain from saying so.

About this time I also floated and gained recognition for what came to be called the 'Stranger Prince' idea. Quite often during these stagnant months, an odd hour or two per week would be spent in teaching groups of our R.A.S.C. men – sometimes a section, sometimes a company – something a bit out of the ordinary; the 36 Mills grenade, it might be; the Thompson sub-machine gun, or some specialized knowledge that some officer or N.C.O. happened to possess. (We had a corporal who had been invalided out of a Commando unit, and an officer who had worked for Mercedes-Benz in Germany before the war.) My idea, such as it was, was based on my observation that usually the men would listen with more respect, interest and attention to a stranger than to their own officer. As a matter of fact, Frank Espley and I had been using this ploy between ourselves for a while before it caught on. It worked quite well within the unit, but it worked best of all if you could co-opt a real 'stranger' – an officer from another unit. 'Now we're very lucky to have here with us this morning Dr Morton, who's come specially from' (Belfast or Omagh or whatever) 'to talk to us about tropical diseases, of which he's had first-hand experience.' Then next week one of our people would go and talk to Morton's lot, about the Liverpool docks or something.

Late in the spring of 1941, 'G' section had a welcome bit of luck to break the monotony of camp life. You have to understand that we were all fretting – pining – for real work. We wanted our lorries and ourselves to be used in earnest, not merely maintained and 'ighly polished day after day. In the sort of conditions we were, the true distinction was not between work and play, but between meaningful activity and boring inactivity. Any Lakeland sheepdog feels the same: they obviously like being put to use and are eager for work. What 'G' section got was the so-called Seskinore detachment.

Early in 1941, it was determined by the High Command that a fresh division should be moved into Ulster, its various units to be stationed throughout the Counties Omagh and Fermanagh. The quartermastering part of this was, of course, a big job and its details were to be arranged and controlled by a captain quarter-master from his own H.Q. in the barracks at Omagh. Naturally, he needed a fleet of lorries, and so informed C.R.A.S.C. at Lisburn. What he got sent to him was 'G' section. As far as I remember, we got about two hours' notice to get packed up and ready to drive the seventy or eighty miles from Langford Lodge to Omagh. It was, of course, a matter for jubilation to be selected to go. I wonder, now, that our O.C. didn't send Frank Espley. He would have been out and away the best subaltern, but perhaps my section had slightly the better N.C.O.s and blokes.

Seskinore is a village about six or seven miles south-south-east of Omagh, in the County Tyrone. Here there was a small R.A.S.C. supply unit (not motorized), commanded by one Captain Slater, to whom I duly reported 'G' section that evening. Details fail me in memory, but I do recall that the way things eventually turned out was that I messed at Seskinore, while 'G' section were billeted in a bunk-bedded parish hall in Omagh. They thought the whole set-up was a riot; the best thing that had happened for months. So did I.

Three-spired Omagh was a pretty place at that time; a remote little county town almost at the end of the world, with King Billy prominent in every home (you can take a white horse anywhere) and the pubs full of porter. The natives were more than friendly, the soda bread was excellent and 'G' section were declared to be great fellas, surely.

The quartermaster was a nice old regular called Captain Milner. I liked him, and he and Sergeant Tuckey took to each other at once. Every morning, with notebooks at the ready, Sergeant Tuckey and I would report to Captain Milner, to learn what he wanted done. The deliveries consisted of chairs, tables, bunk-beds, cupboards, lockers, mattresses, mats and all the rest of it, to be loaded at X and driven to Y the same day. For labour we had a detachment of the Pioneer Corps; and it was in this area that I had a little squabble with my section. 'G' section drivers didn't reckon to join in loading and unloading: they reckoned to sit and smoke in the cab while the Pioneers (mostly foreign refugees) got on with it. I disputed this and finally, faced with muttering by the N.C.O.s, rolled up my sleeves and did some fair spells of loading myself. I can guess what happened when my back was turned, but as long as it wasn't, the drivers helped to load.

This was the first time in my life that I had had to organize anything on my own, and it wasn't altogether as easy as it may sound. The miscellaneous loads had to be worked out and the necessary number of trips and lorries. All you could go by was empiricism: there were no loading tables, and anyway the items were very various. Some of them were fragile, too. The destinations were all over the place; anywhere at all in the Counties Tyrone and Fermanagh: Ballygawley and Newtownstewart; Fintona, Castlederg and Lisnaskea; Dromore, Strabane and Aughnacloy; Augher and Clogher and Fivemiletown. There weren't enough N.C.O.s to escort each individual run, which might involve anything from six or seven lorries down to a single one. Private soldiers (drivers) weren't supposed to be able to read maps and so couldn't be held responsible if they got them wrong. Sergeant Tuckey and I would work out the most economical route by which a corporal on a motor-bike could conduct four, five or six lorries to different destinations, dropping one off here and two off there. Then the drivers and pioneers had to be fed, by arrangement. We had to do our best to calculate the duration of the various jobs, so that Driver Limbrick or Driver Seabourne could be reckoned to be able to get back from job A with enough time left in the day to get reloaded and do job B. Inevitably, there was a fair amount of what von Clausewitz calls 'friction'; the many little hitches that interfere with the smooth working of the machine. Driver Petherick arrives at his destination to find he is seriously expected to reverse his lorry up three hundred yards of impossibly muddy boreen. He doesn't fancy a dose of wheelspin: he refuses. The pioneers refuse, not unreasonably, to hump the load. Something has to be sorted out. Driver Harris has blown a gasket near some God-forsaken place called Drumquin. Captain Milner isn't quite right about the relative proximity of X to Y, and must be tactfully told, with, if possible, a constructive suggestion about what's best to be done. Driver Portway has hit a dog/pig/donkey/goat, and the owner, be Jasus, is declaring it has him fair destroyed and where's the lieutenant at all?

As the days went by, the light lasted longer and the weather improved, Sergeant Tuckey and I found that we carried in our heads cognitive maps of Tyrone and Fermanagh, including the better pubs. Captain Milner was pleased with the work and said so. I had become reasonably proficient on a motor-bike, and would sometimes take a convoy myself or else ride round to half a dozen destinations to make sure my drivers were not being messed about by some twit of a stranger N.C.O. I began to feel that I really knew 'G' section and was capable of using them to the best advantage as a technical tool. As for 'G' section, they hoped it would never end. They were a good lot: I was still too inexperienced to realize what a good lot they were. Throughout the Seskinore detachment, not one man was put on a charge and only one man collected a minor punishment.

Driver Mallett it was, of all people: biddable, reliable, polite, intelligent, pleasant-spoken, impeded from a stripe only by a certain diffidence in his ways and manner. One morning, on parade, as Sergeant Tuckey and I were walking up the back of the front rank, Tuckey remarked, on his own initiative, 'You want 'aircut, Mallett.' 'Sergeant.' That day, however, turned out an unusually busy one, with several of our lorries out late, and Mallett didn't get back from Coalisland until after supper-time. The following morning found him in the same crinite condition. ''Aircut, Mallett,' said Tuckey. ''Shan't tell y'again.'

But once more the exigencies of the service kept poor Mallett out until a late hour. This time it was a broken-down motor-cycle to be taken back for repair to headquarters workshops at Langford Lodge. (We had a workshops fitter with us on the detachment, a good fellow named Kliskey, but of course there were limits to what he could effect on his own.) In Mallett's position, I'd have got a mate to get to work with nail-scissors and a safety razor, but anyway he didn't. Next morning on parade I saw what hadn't happened, but decided to leave it to the sergeant, as he'd shot first. I moved on up the rank as Tuckey, in a low, confidential voice, began 'Now you listen to me, Lady Godiva –'

But all Mallett got was cleaning the N.C.O.s' motor-bikes.

One evening, when I had left my little Austin staff-car parked outside the billets while I held an N.C.O.s' meeting, I came out to find that Turner and Beach – two big, strong men – for a joke had lifted it, fore and aft, onto the pavement. I took this as a signal compliment. My relations with the section were now such that I was considered fair game for a harmless practical joke.

.　.　.

It was during this spring that something much less funny for me took place. I had been writing to Jennifer regularly and at great length, while the weeks extended into months. I wish I had those letters now, for there would be a lot of forgotten stuff in them: like the time of heavy snow when we shovelled the railway line clear at Crumlin; and the hot summer day when I swam from Langford Lodge out to Ram's Island, in Lough Neagh, about a mile, with Frank accompanying me in a dinghy. Jennifer, however, had seldom or never replied to these letters. I wasn't really surprised or troubled in mind, for one thing because I knew she was only about three-quarters literate and for another because I knew her to be lazy and inconsequent. I had no reason to suppose she wasn't glad to get my letters or that she didn't enjoy reading them as much as I enjoyed writing them. I was already looking forward to my first spell of leave.

The letter which at length came from Jennifer wasn't very long – probably shorter than this synthesis of it. It told how, a few weeks after Frank and I had left for Ulster, she had met an R.A.F. Pilot Officer trainee – a flying cadet, in fact. He had found her no less charming than I had. She had fallen entirely and all-absorbingly in love with him. They had become lovers and were to get married. She had just heard that he had been killed in training: she didn't say how. She couldn't bring herself to write more. She was very sorry. Her mother would write and tell me more.

I don't think many people can have been confronted with a situation like this. Some girls, of course, would have written a 'Dear John' letter as soon as they were sure of their own mind. In that event I would have known what Jennifer had felt (and done) weeks before her lover died. But that wouldn't have been like Jennifer. She always used to let life slide. This was like – no, not like: it *was* – being introduced to an unknown man who, although dead, still had the power to cut you out. Of course I felt sorry for him and very sorry for Jennifer. But equally, of course, my sorrow was qualified; by knowing that Jennifer had been this chap's lover as she had not been mine; by the fact that he was dead; and by not being able to help feeling that I ought to have been told something sooner. (True, there had been no actual obligation on Jennifer to have told me anything at all, but a responsible girl would have done so.) What ought I to do, I wondered. There wasn't much to be done, except to reply to her letter with appropriate sympathy and hope that perhaps one day we might meet again as friends, etc. I did that, but of course it expressed little or nothing of what I really felt. I felt forsaken; or could it be, discarded? From my point of view, it didn't really make much difference that the poor chap was dead. Dead or alive, the fact remained that obviously Jennifer couldn't get back to feeling about me as she had formerly. She wouldn't be around again for a long time, if ever. The only sensible thing to do was to forget her by a deliberate act of will. (Her mother did write; a sweet letter, full of understanding, but of course it made no difference.)

In Captain Milner's office at Omagh there was an extremely pretty A.T.S. girl, who typed and answered the phone. Her name was Kaye McNulty and her home was in Belfast. She was delighted to be asked out to dinner by a real lieutenant.

For me, our relationship was the equivalent of the 'good long holiday abroad'. I wanted to be taken out of myself, and was ready enough to let Kaye and the relationship take us whither it would. It took us to bed, which was nice. Also, as every young man knows, it is gratifying to be seen around in public with a conspicuously pretty companion. Kaye was an Ulster girl, and this helped things along no bounds, since she knew the country well and enjoyed showing it to me. It created what I needed – a new world.

The Seskinore detachment, like all good things, came to an end and 'G' section had to return to Langford Lodge. However, my relationship with Kaye was by no means fatally affected. She seemed to get week-ends off very much as though her job had been on a peace-time footing, and often it wasn't very difficult for me to get a twenty-four-hour pass. I couldn't, of course, keep things secret from my friends in the mess. One Saturday, when Kaye and I were having a drink in the lounge bar of one of the hotels in

Belfast, some of my fellow subalterns happened to drop in. They left me in no doubt of their admiration for Kaye. Theo Overman, who used to devise topical lampoons to be sung in the mess when the beer was flowing, added another stanza to his version of 'There ain't no flies on Auntie'.

Verse: Oh, there ain't no flies on Dicky,
On Dicky, on Dicky.
There ain't no flies on Dicky
And I will tell you why.
To Seskinore the 'G' men went
But with the A.T.S. his time was spent.
Oh, there ain't no flies on Dicky
And that's the reason why.

Chorus: Oh, there ain't no flies on Dicky, on Dicky,
There ain't no flies on Dicky
And I will tell you why.
He turned the key and locked the door.
The room was number five-oh-four,
So there ain't no flies on Dicky
And *that's* the reason why.

Kaye took me to Enniskillen, and we walked by the solitude of Lough Erne in a long, calm evening, the great, empty expanse of water still as any pool, while a red sun smouldered and failed out of the sky. Kaye said she felt that if I threw in a sword, a hand would appear from the water and catch it by the hilt. Another time we went to Londonderry, walked round the walls and stood where Governor Walker had stood in July 1689, when King Billy's relieving ships broke the boom.

We went to Newry; and to Newcastle under the Mountains of Mourne, and climbed Slieve Donard in the rain. Once, having got a three-day pass, I took Kaye, wearing a mendacious wedding-ring, into the republic. We stayed at Collooney in the County Sligo, and walked out to Lough Arrow.

Before the end of 1941, however, I had become inwardly impatient with this static soldiering, which seemed to hold out no prospect of anything more active or exciting. A reorganization of the R.A.S.C. had resulted, *inter alia*, in the abolition of so large and bulky a unit as the 'Corps Troops Petrol Park', which had really been better suited to World War I than to World War II organization. It was split up, and in the process, to my grief, I lost command of 'G' section and became an officer in a smaller unit, the 3rd Corps Troops Petrol Company, stationed on the Maze race course. Frank Espley was not one of those who came with us, and inevitably he and I lost touch with each other. Sergeant Tuckey was still with me, and the two of us were given command of a completely 'green' section, straight out of recruits' training depot. They weren't a bad lot, and after a few weeks we began to feel reasonably proud of them, and they of themselves. The trouble lay elsewhere; in the person of the commanding officer. I had better give him a pseudonym.

Major Trill was a regular officer, and very young indeed to be a major. He was not yet twenty-four. He was a tall, fair young man, intensely assiduous and lacking in any sense of humour. It was a small mess – not more than nine officers in all – and there wasn't much opportunity to keep clear of him. We had several tiffs, for he was inclined to be thin-skinned, conscious of his age, and also, as a regular, reckoned to larn us a thing or two before he was done. With nearly a year's experience of commanding a platoon on active service, I did not take kindly to this. There were other reasons, too, for feeling that Ulster had become a back-water for an officer who had gained some experience. The war in the Western Desert had begun in earnest. Wavell had defeated the Italians in his campaign of 1941, and only the fulfilment of the British obligation to divert troops to fight against the Germans in Greece had prevented him from forging on into Tripolitania. Greece had fallen to Hitler and then the German airborne troops, at enormous cost in casualties, had invaded and taken Crete, coming within half a plank of defeat in the process. By December 1941 Operation Barbarossa, the Wehrmacht's attack on Russia, which had begun in June 1941, had brought the Germans to the very outskirts of Moscow. During the same month the Japanese made their attack on Pearl Harbour and America entered the war. The first months of 1942 saw the high-water mark of the Axis, while at the same time, in February, Singapore fell to the Japanese. I am bound to admit that I personally was fully expecting Russia to be defeated, after which, no doubt, Germany would find itself ready at last to invade

England. I had changed my original state of mind of being determined to avoid the infantry. I now reckoned that it was up to everyone, in the desperate straits we were in, to be ready to do something active. If you were going to be killed anyway, you might as well be killed fighting the enemy. At least it would be preferable, or so I thought, to continuing to kick around the Maze race course under the dubious command of Major Trill.

How was one, however, to get transferred to a more active role? It wasn't so easy. As an officer of a specialized arm (e.g., Signals, Engineers, Ordnance, R.A.S.C., Gunners, etc.) one could not simply leave that arm and transfer to another. To do so (it was reckoned) would be a waste of all the training (and experience) that had been lavished on you by the army.

While I was pondering the problem, I got a spell of leave and spent some two weeks at home; and it was here, round and about Newbury, that I first clapped my eyes on the newly-formed Airborne Forces. I was by no means of a sceptical temperament in those days: indeed, I was romantic and impressionable to a degree, and the sight of the red beret and the flamboyant blue and maroon pegasus flash excited me and went straight to my heart. This was the answer! I would volunteer for Airborne Forces! There were Airborne R.A.S.C. as there were Airborne Gunners, Sappers and Signals. I would transfer in my capacity as an R.A.S.C. officer.

Even this, however, proved very difficult. The Airborne Forces certainly had their talent scouts out in Ulster as in England, Wales and Scotland. One could put in for an interview, and I did. But they were, understandably, rather careful about whom they took, and at twenty-one I had no particular qualifications to recommend me, except that I was fit and willing. There were plenty of other people volunteering for no better reason than I; because they were browned off. Also, in those days I was under weight for my height of about five feet eight inches. One of the specified requirements was that the weight should 'correlate normally with the height'. In short, I didn't seem to be able to get the Airborne to take me on.

By midsummer of 1942, I had had as much of Major Trill as I could stand. He plainly felt the same. I felt – I still feel – that he had begun to lie in wait for me, as it were, and drop on me for anything he could. My general feelings were almost identical to those of Charles Ryder at the beginning of *Brideshead Revisited*. I felt disillusioned and thoroughly bolshie. Finally, finding myself one fine day 'on the mat' to the Major for what seemed to me no reason at all, I had the worst row of the lot and finished up by demanding an overseas posting. He was by no means unwilling: he had had enough of me, too.

It was in late July or early August of 1942 that I found myself in a draft of unattached R.A.S.C. officers forming at a depot in Halifax. We were all strangers to one another: I knew nobody. However, before leaving the Maze race course I had been given a tip by another of the subalterns, Johnny Lund. 'I rather think,' said he, 'that there's a friend of mine on that draft, a chap called Roy Emberson. If he's there, I should latch on to him if I were you. He's a good bloke, and doesn't give a hang for anyone.'

XV

Roy Emberson *was* on the draft at Halifax, and proved to be a man after my own heart. I lost no time in getting to know him. He was about twenty-three or twenty-four. His appearance was in his favour: he was a likely-looking, handsome young man, with light-brown hair, brown eyes and a fresh complexion. The thing which struck me almost at once was his air of relaxed, unassuming self-confidence. In those war-time days, almost all young officers (and older ones) were living in unaccustomed circumstances and conditions, among people with whom they wouldn't have had much to do in peace-time. This insecurity often led many (including myself) into assuming one sort of air or another for the benefit of strangers – the tough man of few words, the man who seeks advantage by excessive courtesy, the detached man whose real thoughts are elsewhere, and so on. There was nothing at all like this about Emberson. He struck you as being quietly self-possessed and entirely himself. He didn't put on any sort of act – you felt – because he didn't need to. At the same time he wasn't detached. He was shrewd and alert. He seemed poised and in accord with his surroundings. He was secured as much by his limitations as his qualities. Nostalgia and sensitivity couldn't find a toehold anywhere in him. Privately, in my own mind, I nicknamed him 'Harlequin': but just at the moment he was a Harlequin without a Columbine – though on the lookout, of course. Without being loquacious or self-assertive, he was debonair in manner, an adventurer, as it were, by temperament rather than by resolve. He seemed cheerful and carefree; an amusing, refreshing person to be with. During the months we spent together I never once heard him raise his voice. His favourite word of approval was 'genuine': 'a genuine sort of bloke'. He was certainly that himself.

After a day or two of each other's company at the depot, Roy and I found that a natural third had become added to us. This was, as Roy put it, 'a long slab of an Irishman' called Paddy Gibbons. Tall he was, and a little older than either of us, with a noticeable touch of the brogue and a gently teasing way with him. I began to feel that the trip to the Middle East was going to be better fun than I had expected.

Round about this time the whole draft, of whom there were about thirty or so, received a briefing from some major who was technically in charge of us. The only thing he said which mattered – or that I remember – was that on board ship we would be four to a cabin. He said that those of us who had already formed groups of two or three should foregather on one side of the room, while the rest, who hadn't, should stay where they were. The already formed groups were then to 'pick up' their complement from among the rest, just as teams are picked up at school. ('We'll have Smith.' 'We'll have Jones' etc.)

Now it so happened that the Adams–Emberson–Gibbons group seemed a shade unlucky in the choosing order. We were the penultimate group, and when it came to our turn there were only two people left. One was a gloomy, unlikeable man called Cairncross (that is not his name) whom nobody cared for. The other was a mere child of a subaltern, patently immature and shy, who had not summoned the savoir-faire to make any friends or to 'put himself across' at all. The wretched two stood and waited while we conferred in a corner.

'Take the boy,' said Paddy. ''Got to be better than Cairncross.'

After some hesitation, Roy and I agreed. We said we'd have the boy, who seemed glad not to be left the absolute last. I felt sorry for Cairncross – I who was no stranger to humiliation – but he had rather brought it on himself.

Our 'boy' turned out to be called Giles. He was known, he said, to his friends as 'Piggy' (but gave no reason for this). Piggy Giles proved an excellent fellow, honest, kind-hearted, good-natured and obliging. I think we all felt the better – more secure and more equal to the unforeseeable hazards of our impending journey – on account of the four-square team we'd now formed. I can't remember that during the ensuing months we ever had a serious disagreement among ourselves; but we pulled each other out of several holes, and avoided a few more because it became known that we were mutually supportive. I remember how one night a burly, aggressive fellow called Murphy got drunk and began trying to pick a quarrel with me. He became discouraged, however, when it was made plain to him that there were four of us.

I wouldn't mind having those months over again; not only for our travelling adventures, but simply for the enjoyment of the comradeship of 'the gang of four'. I've never experienced anything quite like it since, for it was in its nature a product of the strange journey we were on, with all its new experiences and unforeseeable encounters.

We sailed from the Clyde. Our ship was called the *Nea Hellas*. She was a Greek passenger ship which had been at sea when Italy fell upon Greece, and had at once sailed to put herself at the disposal of the Allies. She formed part of a big convoy, escorted by destroyers. Our voyage took place at the height of the German U-boat campaign – the Battle of the Atlantic. It was quite on the cards that one or other of the convoy ships might be torpedoed, but in the event none was. We weren't apprehensive; we felt confidence in those distant, greyhound-like destroyers we could watch from the deck, speeding around us and signalling to one another.

The food was excellent. Furthermore, this was before the days when all troopships went 'dry'. There was a considerable amount of drinking aboard the ship – among the officers, that is. A lot of people were overspending their pay, and I recall a poker school, consisting mostly of R.A.M.C. officers – doctors, in fact – in which disconcertingly large sums changed hands. There were no women on board; not even a nurse.

We sailed far out into the Atlantic; almost to within sight of America, a steward told me. This was to elude the U-boats. Then we returned eastwards and so came at length into tropical waters and to Freetown, Sierra Leone, where we remained for a few days. It was swelteringly hot, and humid as a Turkish bath. No one was allowed ashore. The garish little town was half-concealed by rolling clouds of vapour, and above it hung the mountainous forests, matted, shaggy green – greener than anything I had ever seen – like a shapeless giant sprawling prone, head hung down over the minuscule men and their tiny boats dotting the harbour. The still, green jungle looked vast, dwarfing everything else, rendering humanity itself futile. It must have looked no different to the first Portuguese navigators. I was glad when we left and sailed south for Cape Town.

At Cape Town, we knew, we were going to disembark and in due course board another ship to sail up to Suez. There would be shore leave while we were waiting. The prospect was exciting. The ship's stewards spoke highly of Cape Town: it was a great place to have a good time, and September was the best of all months to be there. We received plenty of gratuitous advice about shops, restaurants, clubs, etc. I have always remembered Roy Emberson's reply to this. 'Just give me Cape Town,' he said. 'I'll do the rest.'

One morning very early, I was surprised – and rather annoyed – to be woken in my bunk by Roy. His *sang-froid habituel* seemed for the moment to have left him. He was urgent and animated. 'Come up on deck, Dicky. *Now!* You've *got* to see it!'

It was easier to do as he said. We all went up on deck. The ship was lying in Table Bay. Some way off was Cape Town itself, dusky in twilight. Beyond and above rose the long, level line of Table Mountain, dominating everything below. Behind it and up to the zenith, the whole sky was aflame. The cirrus clouds looked like great crimson brush-strokes, flake upon burning flake. We were arched over by this luminescent, glowing vault. The steep face of the mountain, still in shadow, and the fiery sky formed a setting for the smokeless, motionless city itself, its buildings slowly revealed as white – white upon white – bigger and smaller blocks of white, as the light grew and fell upon them, first the shoreward and gradually those on the farther slope. Upstanding to the right was Lion Rock, itself a smouldering red.

This was our first sight of the famous city where none of us had ever been before; the city which, in prospect and our imagination, promised every sensuous pleasure attainable by young men. The four of us stood together, breathing the scented air wafted from the shore. Hibiscus? Frangipani? Gardenia? Bougainvillea? I didn't know then which were scented and which weren't, and didn't care, in that silent resplendence. ἥβαν, I thought, ἥβαν μετα των φιλων. This was what it meant! We had been led to expect something exciting and beautiful, but nothing approaching this.

That morning, as we lay to in the bay, I composed a lyric for the occasion – one purposely devised in Embersonian idiom.

Roy Emberson's Song about the Cape

Heads down, forwards! Sweet and low!
The white town shining like a fall of snow.
All the land of evergreen,
Royal with sunlight, rich, serene;
Everything you've never seen.
Now the shore leave's through, and so
Where's the girls? What do you know?
Rock it out, boys, let it go.

Tonight the war is gilt and gloss,
Crimson flowers and Southern Cross.
On the Mountain, cloud-mist swirls:
Harbour-lights a nest of pearls:
All the drink and all the girls.
Come on, lads, let's see you move!
Don't it grip ya, ain't it smooth
On the batter, in the groove?

When the Stukas rock the floor,
Boy! You'll wish you'd drunk some more.
When the grade gets really tough,
Think your lust was slight enough.
Get stuck in and grab the stuff!
Soft, sweet Cape and all that's there,
Flame hibiscus, golden air,
Country for a millionaire!
And tomorrow's grey and rough.

Later that day we went ashore, equipped with passes which were valid until two a.m.

It was that very evening, in Cape Town, that I made, by pure luck, one of the enduring and truly rewarding friendships of my life. It came about like this. At that time, with troopship convoys bound for the Middle East not infrequently putting in at Cape Town, the native British (in contradistinction to the Boers) were all keen to show hospitality and warmth to Allied soldiers. A considerable crowd of people were waiting actually on the harbourside to welcome the soldiers as they came ashore and invite individuals to their homes. As officers we, of course, hung back from this amicable melee; but we were soon told of other arrangements which had been made for us: namely, the Convoy Dance.

At that period of the war – when the Middle East Force (though we didn't know it, of course) was being heavily reinforced and built up for the El Alamein offensive – whenever a convoy stopped at Cape Town, all officers were *ipso facto* invited to what became known as the Convoy Dance at a big country club called the Kelvin Grove. Kelvin Grove is – or was at that time – a beautiful place, with a dining-room, a ballroom, bars, a swimming-pool, extensive gardens – the lot. In my memory it remains – for I went there only once – rather like the wonderful place where Le Grand Meaulnes found himself at the magic party. All that needs to be said is that all four of us found ourselves having the time of our lives. Roy Emberson remained, as usual, of self-assured and quiet demeanour, but I reckon even he was pleasantly startled. The girls were as delightful as the gardenias and the moonlight. There can be few places as beautiful as South Africa in September.

It was getting on for late in the evening when I, strolling happily along a corridor near the ballroom, came upon a pretty, dark-haired girl in her mid-twenties. I passed the time of night.

'Have you seen the Secretary anywhere?' she asked me.

'I'm afraid I wouldn't know him if I saw him.'

'Well,' she said (she had a very pleasant, rather firm contralto voice which suited her well), 'it's like this. Earlier this evening, I gave a bottle of gin I've got to the Secretary and asked him to look after it for me, and he locked it up in the safe in his office. If I could only find him, I could get it out.'

I should explain that in those war-time days, if you were lucky enough to get the chance to buy a bottle of gin, whisky, etc., you latched on to it tight and made damned sure nobody snitched it. There wasn't much more, you see.

I gladly joined the girl in her search. Her name was Muriel. (It wasn't, actually.) Her family lived in Cape Town: that is to say, her mother did; her father was dead, but she had two elder brothers. As we went on conversing, it became clear to me that this was a cultured, educated lady; a bit different from Roy Emberson fodder. I took off my Harlequin mask, dropped my Harlequin persona, told her my name was Richard (not Dicky) and steered the conversation on to T. S. Eliot. We got on well.

'And what's more,' said Muriel, 'my brother's a *real* poet. His poetry's published by Faber.'

This was a time – the 'thirties had, indeed, been a decade – when Faber and Faber were the avant-garde publishers of the widely read and successful poets of the day: Eliot, Ezra Pound, Auden, Spender, Isherwood (not a poet), MacNeice and others. In those days contemporary poets were more widely read than they are now, and their names were names to conjure with.

'Who is he?' I asked, wide-eyed.

'George Shaw,' replied Muriel.

This gave me a considerable jolt. I knew the name of G. D. Shaw (which I've been asked to alter) well enough, for it appeared among the Faber poets whose books were listed on the backs of the dust-jackets of the poetry of Eliot, Auden and the rest; however, I hadn't as yet read any G. D. Shaw, for my funds at Oxford had been a bit limited for buying books, though I was up-to-date in possession of Eliot, Auden (*Look, Stranger* and *Another Time*) and MacNeice (*Plant and Phantom*). And here was G. D. Shaw's sister, talking to me and looking for a bottle of gin. I was only twenty-two and had never met any of the recognized modern poets, but was myself full of aspirations; and furthermore, had been starved of any real intellectual company for more than two years past.

Muriel Shaw has remained one of my dearest friends. We were never lovers and never looked to be: but how much wisdom, understanding, support, discriminating advice, sensible criticism and warm encouragement I have received from Muriel during the past nearly fifty years I cannot begin to measure.

We duly found the Secretary and the gin, tracked down Roy and the others with the girls they had met, and went on to a night-club. When we parted, Muriel left me her address and telephone number; the other girls did the same and dispersed to their homes. (This was long before the days when even a Roy Emberson could expect to sleep with a girl the first night he met her.) It was now after two a.m. – no good going back to the ship – and the four of us began to look around for somewhere to sleep.

We came to a hotel and went in. But we had fallen into a common error of strangers in Cape Town – that of assuming that everyone was friendly. This particular hotel turned out to be very

Boer. Only the night porter was around, and he was hostile and unhelpful. No rooms, no nothing. This annoyed Roy, who finally said he was going to sleep there anyway, and laid himself down on a sofa in the foyer. Paddy and Piggy followed suit. The porter said he would call the police. Roy said Let him. At this point I had nasty visions of Boer policemen returning us in handcuffs to O.C. Troops on the *Nea Hellas*, and, having failed to persuade any of my friends to join me, set off on my own.

The porter followed me. He didn't try to restrain me or grapple with me. He simply followed me wherever I went. We wandered out for miles into the suburbs. It had now grown fully light. Finally I got a few yards in front of him and pulled myself up and over a high fence. This defeated him. I found myself in somebody's garden and walked out of it into the road. Then I strolled back into town, had breakfast at a hotel and after sitting in the sunshine until about ten o'clock, telephoned Muriel.

Muriel said Would I like to come and see her, and off I set. We spent a delightful day at her home and addressed ourselves, amongst other things, to the matter of my pass from the ship, which had now, of course, expired. It said two a.m. all right, but it bore yesterday's date. With infinite care we went about erasing that date so that no one could possibly perceive that it had been interfered with. We used a penknife, scraping very, very lightly. We used breadcrumbs, too. It reminded me of the bit in Edgar Allan Poe when the chap says it took him a whole hour to open the door of his sleeping enemy's bedroom and put his head round it. Finally we put in today's date, counterfeiting the adjacent writing very deftly and using a similar pen. No one could have detected the forgery. After that we went swimming, lay on the sand and talked about Yeats.

That night, after dinner, I swaggered up the gang-plank and presented my pass to the two military police sitting behind their table in the waist. One of them checked the pass, ticked off my name on his nominal roll in the ledger and handed the pass back to me. I had gone a few yards when he called 'Sir.'

'Yes, Corporal,' I said, turning back.

'I wouldn't wave that about too much, sir. Today's passes are blue, you see.'

I found the other three already back in our cabin.

'Ah,' said Roy, 'the Cape Town Harriers! 'Had a good run?'

I told them. 'And what happened to you?'

'Why, we stayed put, of course,' said Roy. 'What d'you think?'

'And *did* they call the police?'

'Yes, they did.'

'And what happened then?'

'Well, the police asked "Have they been violent, or used bad language, or broken anything?" And these geezers said No, we hadn't; and the police said "In that case, we're not interested. They've committed no offence." So we hung in there till about seven-thirty and then went off to breakfast.'

They must have been British, as opposed to Afrikaans police, I thought. However, Roy's judgment had been proved right yet again, and I felt appropriately foolish.

A day or two later we all left the *Nea Hellas* and went into camp at a place called Retreat. We went on enjoying Cape Town for about a week or more, until we were required to embark once again, this time on the *New Amsterdam*.

The *New Amsterdam*, a Dutch ship still staffed by the Dutch, had, like the *Nea Hellas*, sailed to join the Allies when her country was attacked by Hitler. She was at this time one of the largest and most luxurious liners in the world. She had no escort from Cape Town to Suez: she sailed at 25 knots in irregular zig-zags (which were perfectly all right once you'd got used to them). We were very comfortable on board and nothing eventful occurred as we went north.

We came to Suez, and thence to the big base camp at Gineifa. We were still able to stick together – an almost incredible circumstance in the Army – and had a tent for four. We knew that our comradeship was bound to be nearly over: postings would be coming in for us almost any day now. We had already been hauled up, one by one, and quizzed about our past experience and any specialist knowledge we might possess. It had been noted – though for all practical purposes it was a mere technicality – that I had spent all my time as an officer in units which were supposed to be concerned with petrol, or P.O.L. (petrol, oil and lubricants), as the Army called it. In fact I had had no specialized experience of the storage and transport of petrol.

One little incident of this time has remained in my memory. One evening, in late twilight, the four of us were having a few drinks at a café on the shores of the Great Bitter Lake. It was late October. The El Alamein offensive had begun a day or two before; we knew something big was happening, but news was still confined – as far as we were concerned, anyway – to talk and rumour.

As we sat chatting in the almost gone light, we became aware of a living creature on the sand near-by. It was sandy grey. Its body was flattish, a disc about as big as the palm of a human hand. It had spindly legs about as long as human fingers (you could imitate it with your hand) on which it walked, or crawled, slowly, in a stilt-like manner. Since voyaging, many years later, to Morea in the Tahiti group (where they abound) I have decided that this was a species of land crab. They are nocturnal, and live in shallow holes in the sand, to which, under the impact of light, they retreat, scuttling, rather as cockroaches do. Roy Emberson, our imperturbable, self-possessed soldier of fortune, evinced an almost cringing horror of this crustacean, and moved hastily out of the way as it came on. To him it bodied forth an epitome of the whole nature of this vile, dirty, nauseating country (we'd all had intensive gyppy tummy – diarrhoea – on arrival, of course) and several hours later he was still saying 'I wish I hadn't seen it.' We had yet to encounter centipedes (akrebah), scorpions and (I, at any rate) the biting flies of the Negeb Desert. I doubt whether land crabs can hurt you: I have never given them the opportunity.

One night, a chance-met acquaintance (and I'm going to name him: he deserves it) called Lieutenant G. W. Reid asked whether I could lend him a book or two to pass the time. I lent him my first editions of Auden's *Another Time* and Louis MacNeice's *Plant and Phantom*, and never saw them, or Reid, again. This cured me of lending books. 'What, lending books at twenty-two, A clean upstanding chap like you? –'

The good Lord compensated me. One morning I wandered into the N.A.A.F.I and there came upon a dog-eared little stash of battered books, paperbacks and others, for lending to the troops. Browsing and furrocking, I picked up a dingy, smallish volume, bound in what had once been light-blue. It was *Emma.*

I had never read *Emma*; or any of them, for that matter. It was like a revelation. I was glued to it a few hours later, when my posting came through. I was to report to Pal. Base in Jerusalem. In those days Jerusalem was in Palestine, a British-controlled country.

It didn't much matter to me where I was posted, as long as I could go on reading *Emma*. I felt sure the N.A.A.F.I. wouldn't miss it, so I knocked it off. It anaesthetized me against the final break-up of the gang of four. Piggy's posting had come through at the same time. We all said very English, casual good-byes to one another and went our ways. I can truly say that I little thought how those months of transit would remain in my memory locked for year after year. They had given me almost (though not quite, as I will relate) the best time I ever had in the army.

XVI

I boarded the north-bound train in vague preoccupation.

'A bad thing! Do you really think it a bad thing? – why so? –'

'I think they will neither of them do the other any good.'

'You surprize me! Emma must do Harriet good:'

We came to Ismailiya and ran on along the length of the Suez Canal. We reached El Qantara on the border, where Arabs ran up and down the platform shouting 'Eggiz, George! Eggiz an' bread!' 'Money change your money!'

'Oh! what a sweet house! – How very beautiful! – There are the yellow curtains that Miss Nash admires so much.'

On along the Mediterranean coast, on a railway which no longer exists; on to El Arish and Khan Yunis, all sand and white, chow-like, vagrant, ownerless pie-dogs, the kind that licked Lazarus's sores, I expect.

'Walk home! – you are prettily shod for walking home, I dare say. It will be bad enough for the horses.'

Gaza and points north. Never a stream to be seen along the narrow coastal strip. We came to Ramleh and Lydda, and here, for some forgotten reason, I got off the train and went up to Jerusalem by military lorry. Human nature is so well disposed towards those who are in interesting situations, that a young person, who either marries or dies, is sure of being kindly spoken of.

At Pal. Base, in the King David Hotel (blown up and destroyed by the Irgun Zvai Leumi in 1947) I presented my credentials and was posted to a Petrol Depot sited near the ruins of Ashkelon, on the Philistian Plain, not far from Gaza.

'What's Gaza like?' I asked the orderly room sergeant.

'Well, it's like all these wog towns, you know, sir: couple of shit-bins and a camel.'

I spent the night in Jerusalem before travelling back south.

'Oh! but indeed I would much rather have it only in one. Then, if you please, you shall send it all to Mrs Goddard's – I do not know – No, I think, Miss Woodhouse, I may just as well have it sent to Hartfield –'

No. 2 Petrol Depot was, in effect, nowhere. It was a camp of Nissen huts and petrol stacks on the bare plain. It had a major O.C., a captain and three subalterns, of whom I was one.

The plain truth is that for the next year and more I did, in effect, nothing. For all military purposes I might just as well not have been there. To this day I do not know with any clarity what was the precise function of No. 2 Petrol Depot. It certainly was not to maintain a regular supply of petrol to the advancing 8th Army, for at that rate it would have been humming, and it was not. There was a branch railway line leading away to the main line (the one I had travelled up), but only about four or five times during the year I spent at Al-Jiyah (as the place was called) were we required to load a train with petrol cans for the desert.

Our petrol all came by pipeline from Iraq via two mysterious staging posts known as Mafraq and M4. Most of this Iraqi petrol went direct to Haifa, but it kept us topped up as well. We stored bulk petrol in tanks, though not very much of it; and this went out to local recipient units in Bedford tanker lorries – a regular but small business. And then there were the storage stacks, which was what the depot was really all about. At intervals on the face of the open plain had been dug about twenty shallow pits, each about half to a quarter of an acre in size. These were roofed over with corrugated iron and stacked with the standard four-gallon containers known as 'flimsies', filled some with petrol and some with diesel. They *were* flimsy, too. They were almost of the consistency of foil: you could easily dent them with your hand. And of course they were prone to leak. Inspecting for and removing 'leakers' was a continual chore: and only marginally worthwhile, too, it always seemed to me, for of course you could spot only the ones on top or on the edges of the stacks. If you have a stack of cans numbering twenty by twenty by ten high, you can conveniently inspect and get at only 780 out of the 4,200 – a few more on the top, perhaps, if you're conscientious enough to tilt the outer ones and look in. The raison d'être of 'flimsies' – which were universal throughout the Middle East Force

– was that they were cheap and disposable. (Beaten flat, they came in handy for all sorts of jobs – surfacing, patching, roofing and the like.) Throughout the year 1943, however, they became more and more widely recognized as wasteful and more trouble than they were worth, because they were so frangible in handling and spilt as you poured from them: also, in stacks, the lower ones tended to buckle under the weight of those on top. As the 8th Army advanced westward, they captured plenty of Jerricans, the stout, lid-locking, lipped-for-easy-pouring, grooved-for-firmer-stacking cans of the Germans. Soon the British were making them in imitation, and by the time the Normandy campaign opened in 1944 they were universal. (But by then I was no longer in petrol.)

'The stacks' required us – the R.A.S.C. personnel – to have along with us no fewer than three very different sorts of people. The first were the white, dog-handling military police. There were about eight of these, lance-corporals mostly, and there were two to each dog – Alsatians. The dogs, I was told, were trained by some civilian genius in Haifa. They were impressive; instantly obedient, coats sleek and shining, fangs gleaming. They had been trained to detest and try to seize any Arab who might come near. It was a sight to see one, with its masters, passing a group of home-going Arabs. It would become aggressive; bark, growl and slaver, up on its back paws, straining at the leash to get at them. On the other side of the road the Arabs would cower, sometimes actually crying out with fear, imploring and cringing in their terror. At night, at irregular hours, the dogs would make rounds of the stacks, and also of the spare tyre and tool store. They had names like Tex and Grab and Punch and Jock.

But these were not enough to keep the top brass at Pal. Base sleeping quietly in their beds at night. We also had a company – about 150 strong – of East African Pioneers, whose job was to stand sentry on the stacks by day and night. They had English officers: a gentle, rather ineffective but pleasant major, very much a civilian in uniform, who once showed me a photograph of a pretty, dark-haired girl whom he said was a prostitute of his acquaintance in Alexandria. If I fancied he would give me her telephone number. Captain Rawlings, their 2 i/c, I came to like well. He was devoted to his men, obviously enjoyed his job and was becoming fluent in Swahili under the tuition of his interpreter, Corporal K'booy. (The black soldiers spoke no English and came from several different tribes, each with its own lingo. Swahili was their *lingua franca*.)

These East Africans, simple, ingenuous people straight from their villages, were mad keen on soldiering. Spit and polish was the breath of life to them; so was drill. They were proud to be serving Kingi Georgie. As you went among the stacks, they would give you a butt salute like a pistol shot, which could be heard four hundred yards away. Their audibility was not confined to butt salutes, either. It was an odd phenomenon. At night, widely dispersed among the solitudes of the stacks, they could converse with one another without raising their voices over considerable distances. Their voices were quiet, unexcited, resonant and very deep, with plenty of vowels, and for some reason carried further than any European's: quite as far as the next sentry. I became used to the sound, low and intermittent; it came to form, for me, an integral part of the plain by night.

Thirdly, there were the Arab labourers. Their job was, quite simply, humping. They humped cans of petrol and diesel and drums of oil. It was astonishing how much humping there was to do, considering that we were not an operative depot committed to 8th Army's desert campaign. There must have been something like six or seven hundred labourers all told, for I know it took me three hours to pay them their poor little weekly pittances; sweltering, with a nasty headache, under the corrugated-iron roof of an open-fronted shack, while they waited outside, squatting in the hot sun.

They were surely among the poorest men in the world. They had bare feet and awful teeth. They wore dirty head-turbans and filthy, ragged garments soaked in petrol, oil and diesel. Diesel is caustic, and I have more than once seen an Arab labourer's back raw with diesel burns. No doubt they had some sort of better clothing at home, but they had no clean water or regular means of washing. They smelt more of diesel and petrol than of their own sweat and dirt. A large number always had suppurating, yellow-oozing eyes; not one of them, under medical inspection, would have been passed fit by European standards. They were not idle, for they worked in gangs of about twenty, each gang under a leader or *rais*, who was responsible for them. (I never learned how an Arab became a *rais*: they were usually men, to all appearances, of slightly better social standing, and cleaner, since they themselves did not labour, but only organized and 'encouraged'.) At the top was the 'boss *rais*', a young Arab of about twenty-five, dressed in clean khaki shirt and shorts and able to speak English pretty fluently. His name was Ahmed Mohammed Mudhorn, but he was universally known as 'Aussie', having once been interpreter to an Australian unit temporarily in the locality. Aussie had a short way with protesters or complainants. He would put his hands on his hips, push his curly head forward and bellow, asking unanswerable questions, calling pejorative names and pouring out invective until the wretched victim, usually old enough to be his father, was dazed into acquiescence.

By gum!, though, those half-starved, poverty-stricken Arabs could work; and, amazingly, with a will. I have never forgotten one evening during the summer of 1943, when there was a train to be loaded which had to go up the desert that night. For sweltering hours they humped and loaded, while the red sun slowly sank towards the unseen Mediterranean and little nocturnal creatures, mice, crickets and the like, emerged, cautiously and at a distance, for the night's activities. Corporal Goldie, a cheerful young Cockney, was in charge, standing tall on a rail truck, pointing here and there and commanding the *raises* in soldiers' Arabic. '*Ta'al hinnah*', (come here) '*ijjri*', (run) '*stannah shwire*' (wait a bit) and so on. At last, in near darkness, the exhausting job was finished and the train driver began to get up steam. Then a funny thing happened. Spontaneously, the Arabs began to dance. Some plucked flowers and put them between their teeth, joining hands, singing and capering. *El zarbed*, the officer (me), was drawn in and found himself hop, skip and jumping, taking each *rais* by the hand and twirling round. (It was not unlike some sort of English country dance, really: take hands, round and back, with everybody clapping and stamping.) The train steamed slowly out to cheering and cries of delight, pelted with flowers. It didn't matter, then, who was the white officer or who was the exhausted, impoverished Arab labourer. We just all knew we'd loaded the damned train and, most movingly, it stirred these simple men to genuine delight and self-congratulation.

They were all thieves, of course. Who'd blame them? But it is odd, and you never quite get used to it, to live in a society where literally everything, however worthless, is liable to be stolen. Once, we made a bit of a rifle range, out on the plain. All it had in the way of artifacts were some rough target-frames (flimsies again) mounted on sticks. They were stolen. For what, I wonder? In my billet, on the shelf, I had a Hohner chromatic mouth-organ in its box. The mouth-organ went, but the box was left as it was, so that I should be less likely to notice the theft at once and start enquiries. Also on that shelf was my army 'emergency ration'. These were standard issue: everyone had one. They consisted of a block of horribly unpalatable chocolate mixed with meat extract, in a tin fastened at the side with a kind of clip. They were deliberately made unpalatable so that no one would want to eat one unless he were *in extremis*. Well, my emergency ration was removed from the tin and the empty tin left unsullied and unblemished: only when (and if) you picked it up did you realize that it was empty. I recall, too, having to sit on a court of enquiry into the theft – the brilliant theft – of a dozen heavy lorry tyres from a windowless, padlocked hut surrounded by a high barbed-wire fence. No one man could have carried one of those tyres alone; that's how heavy they were; and the wire wasn't even cut.

You might have thought that these hungry, diseased, begrimed, unwashed men could hardly be either religious or respectable: you would be wrong. It was impressive to see them turn with dignity towards Mecca and pray, standing upright with folded arms and intermittently prostrating themselves, and then kneeling with foreheads to the ground for a few seconds before rising again. They fasted – fasted! – too, if you can believe it. During Ramadan – a period of a lunar month – they ate and drank nothing from sunrise till sunset, and did a full day's work into the bargain, though plainly the sides of nature could hardly bear it. Incidentally, they also refrained from sex during that whole month. They were, if you like, devout. Talk to one, and you soon found yourself respecting him as man to man. Our soldiers treated them, as a matter of course, with insults and contempt, frequently calling them 'wog bastards' and the like to their faces. I used to do my best to stop this, but the soldiers' dislike, contempt and lack of any least desire to understand Arabs made it impossible.

The camp was always open to raids by pie-ards, the feral dogs of the plain. (No Arab will touch a dog, let alone keep one.) They are 'unclean'; wild scavengers, wily, wary and vigilant. They would come to the swill-bins by night, in packs of as many as ten or twelve. They could knock a bin over and get the lid off, no matter what we had done to make it impossible. My mental picture of a pie-ard, though they came all sorts, is of a big, white, fluffy animal rather like a chow. By day they usually came singly, day being much more dangerous for them. I took to shooting them with an ordinary Lee-Enfield rifle loaded with .303: I kept it in my office. Sooner or later an Arab would come dashing in with a cry of '*Fe kelp, sidi, fe kelp!*' ('There's a dog, sir!') and I would grab the rifle and sally forth. All too often the cunning dog would make off in time, slinking quickly round a Nissen hut or sagaciously putting some human beings between me and itself. But I wasn't a bad shot and I got quite a few. I aimed at the head, because if you hit it that killed them dead. You couldn't do anything with them, of course. You left them for the kites, which soon closed in. Pie-ards, however, continued to be a great nuisance in the camp on the unfenceable plain, upsetting swill-bins and even stealing the Arabs' sorry little mid-day bites from wherever they had left them.

The insects were, as they say, something else. There were malarial mosquitoes, as there were everywhere in the Middle East. We all slept under mosquito nets and took mepacrine daily. But much more frightening were the scorpions. I understand now that no species of scorpion is actually lethal, but nevertheless the sting is dreadful. These particular scorpions were not very big, some two-and-a-half inches long, and coloured grey-yellow like the sand. The great fear was that you might inadvertently put your hand or foot on one while, for example, rummaging along a shelf or getting into bed. They liked a cranny among books or papers, and they liked blankets. All beds' legs stood in individual pots of paraffin (made out of flimsies). Nevertheless, one night when getting into bed Driver Hills, a decent lad from Harpenden, felt a scorpion move near his foot. He whipped his leg out on the instant and it struck him only glancingly. He was in hospital for a week.

The akrebah were almost worse. They are the local centipedes. In colour they are dark red, sort of maroon. They are long – fully six inches – and, with the legs, nearly an inch broad. They have a forked tail which is a sting. Moreover, each foot (and there are many) is a sting in itself. If you find one on you and strike at it or brush it, it immediately drives each foot into you. They have to be cut out in hospital, and you are ill. They, like the scorpions, also dislike cleanliness and paraffin. All the floors were cleaned often with solutions of paraffin: to me the smell is the smell not only of Horris Wood but also of No. 2 Petrol Depot. What akrebah do is get up into the roof. All the roofs of the Nissen huts were of pitched corrugated iron. During the wet season the rain pounded and drummed on them all day and night. Every now and then an akrebah, making its way upside-down across the smooth corrugated iron, would lose its footing and fall. They could easily fall on a human beneath, and would then immediately dig in with their feet. I never saw it happen, but I've seen some near misses; frightening. They were very hard to kill. I once stamped one flat and threw it out of the door of my billet. In the morning it was still wriggling. After that I always used to cut them into pieces with a pair of scissors.

The flies were indistinguishable in appearance from our houseflies in England: but they bit. They would alight on your stockinged leg (we all wore shorts, of course) and you couldn't feel them. A moment or two later you felt the 'bite', which was a little like that of an English horsefly, and went on irritating in a similar manner.

The hornets were magnificent creatures, like huge wasps. One morning I was riding back from Gaza on a motor-cycle when I suddenly felt a terrific sting at the interior top of my right thigh. I swerved but didn't stop. I had got back to camp and was having a drink in the mess, sitting in a chair, when the hornet came crawling out of my shorts onto my knee: having stung once, however, it didn't sting again. Perhaps it wasn't used to the victim not dying.

The praying mantises still please me in memory. They were big – about four inches long – and green or brown in colour. I believe they could change colour to fit their surroundings. They couldn't hurt you, and they weren't afraid of you. If you sat one on the table it would remain still: but then, if you moved your finger from side to side in front of it, it would turn its head back and forth, watching it with its big eyes. They preyed all right: they preyed on moths. The moths were big, too, but I don't know what kind. Along the front of the verandah of the officers' mess Nissen hut was a trellis, up which grew flourishing, thick ipomea (morning glory). The mantises used to crouch just under the bell-flowers. When a moth, at evening, came to a flower, the mantis would grab it with its two forelegs, holding onto the foliage with its four others. The moth would flutter and struggle. I have seen yards of the creeper shaking in commotion as a battle was fought out. Sometimes the moth got away, but not as a rule.

One thing I have not forgotten is the orange grove near my billet. There are – or used to be – a great many of these groves in southern Palestine, the hinterland of Jaffa (Joppa), Tel-Aviv. In plan they were square, the plain offering no features in its flat expanse to dictate otherwise; and I suppose two acres or so in extent. Orange trees are very beautiful. They are about as big as small apple trees – or these ones were, anyway – and symmetrical, with glossy, dark-green foliage, very thick. They all seemed exactly the same size and shape, so that the grove had a formal, slightly unreal quality, as though some giant's child had set out rows of beautiful toys from a box. In May, when they bloomed – greenish-white, waxy and multitudinous – the scent was more poignant and beautiful than words can describe. It was heavy and sweet, yet at the same time as fresh as running water. You never became tired of it. It is the most beautiful smell I know; more beautiful than frangipani, even. All the way down to Gaza stood these groves, and the spring air was laden with scent. I wonder, are they still there, nearly fifty years later? They must have known many vicissitudes during that time.

In Gaza one day, needing a leather belt, I bought a very ordinary, broad one, with a plain brass buckle, in an open-fronted, penthouse-flapped Arab shop. I hadn't time to bargain.

'*K'dish?*' I asked the elderly Arab squatting on the stone floor.

I can see him now, looking up at me with a beady eye, not unfriendly; but here was a white *zarbed*, and they didn't happen along every day.

'*Sabatash,*' (seventeen), he said softly, drawing out the syllables.

I gave it to him. Seventeen piastres were the equivalent of 3s. 6½d. in those days. (That would convert at 17p.) I still have the belt, so it hasn't proved bad value.

During the summer there were almost daily trips for the soldiers to swim in the sea, about two miles away. The beach and the sea were as featureless as the plain, the level sand shelving evenly down into the shallow water for as far as could be seen in each direction.

There was a fair roll of surf, though, with quite an undertow as it slid back: you were helpless in it for the few seconds during which it dragged you. As a fairly experienced swimmer, knowing what I was doing, I used to enjoy this; but there was always the possibility of someone drawing in a lungful. The rule was that every swimming party had to be in the charge of an officer, and take with them a rope and a whistle. One afternoon our party had stopped off en route to pick up some other ranks from a neighbouring unit. I was sitting in the cab with the driver. They came out and jumped into the back of the lorry, and the following dialogue took place between their senior N.C.O. and ours.

'All set, then, Bill? Got the rope, 'ave yer?'

'Yeah.'

'Got the whistle?'

'Yeah.'

'Got the f—g officer?'

'Yeah, 'e's in the front.'

'O.K., let's go.'

While we were coming back from this trip, an unusual and rather bizarre little incident took place. We were coming through Majdal, the local village, when our lorry was brought to a halt by a commotion in the road in front. A male donkey, led on a rope by its Arab owner, had come to a halt more or less opposite a female being led the other way by an old, black-clad woman. The donkey refused to budge for any amount of beating. While Driver Porritt blew his horn and revved his engine impatiently, it became – and this was remarkable – a dangerous, savage animal in heat. It actually seemed to grow in size, frothing at the mouth and lashing out with its hooves. It shed its burden, kicked its owner into the ditch, stick and all, and rushed across the road, barging the shrieking old woman out of the way. The soldiers began cheering and giving a running commentary. The female was acquiescent, merely breathing heavily, hung-down muzzle drooling into the dust. With bared teeth, raging and frenzied, the donkey did what it wanted, taking not the least notice of the blows raining on it from the old woman's stick as well as its owner's. It didn't take very long. When it had finished, it shrank and turned back into an ordinary, patient, ill-used little Arab donkey standing resignedly on the sand, while its owner whacked it a bit more for good measure.

Yet I thought, as we drove on, that I detected a certain look of 'Well, try and take that away, blast you!'

Most nights the sodden, be-winged major O.C. (for he had been in the Royal Flying Corps in the First World War) and the other officers would set off for the distant open-air cinema, to see Abbott and Costello, or Alice Faye, while I contentedly sat at home as orderly officer. In Tel-Aviv I had been able to obtain all the other Jane Austens (except *Persuasion*). The night was quiet as few nights are today: no traffic, no wirelesses; only the light breeze and occasionally the low voice of an African sentry far out on the stacks.

Sometimes, having told the mess waiter more or less where I would be if anything happened, I would walk through the Nissen-hutted camp and out into the vast, unvarying plain. It was easy to stroll gently onwards, for the ground was as flat as can be imagined; never an undulation, never a bank, not even an occasional hollow. Away and away it stretched, eighty miles to Beer-Sheba, where I had never been. Could it, perhaps – legendary Beer-Sheba – be *three* shit-bins and *two* camels? It was refreshing to be in such solitude, in the scented night; but it was easy to feel homesick, too, alone under that great, unbroken hemisphere of sky. Yet precisely there lay the consolation – the stars. They were, over most of the sky at any rate, the same stars as at home, and I would look for Orion and Sirius, Leo and Gemini, Perseus and what Thomas Hardy calls 'the great, gloomy square of Pegasus'. It reminded me of Robert Graves's poem 'Are you awake, Gemelli?', about the soldier looking at the stars: except that that's so cold, and this was warm enough to make you sweat, even standing still among the dry, crackling haulms (for the plain had little or no grass, only tough, foot-high stalks of flowering scrub).

Now and then I managed to go to Jerusalem, where I had made Arab friends. It was a beautiful city, quiet and jasmine-scented at night; and in the morning you would wake to hear from the street outside the approaching, stylized cry of the news-vendor. 'Fal-as-teen Po-o-ost! Fal-as-teen Po-o-ost!' I had a nice, kind-of girl-friend. I say 'kind-of' because our meetings were inevitably infrequent and nothing ever passed between us but a kiss. Her name was Georgette Khouri ('Khouri', I rather think, means 'tailor' – Taylor) and her father, who was dead, had been a don at Jerusalem

University. I continued writing to her for about four years.

On Christmas Eve, 1942, I went out to Bethlehem, all empty; and it snowed! (I assure you it did.)

During May 1943, a private soldier called Ron Coomber and I made an expedition to Petra by way of Amman and Ma'an. In those days, of course, Petra was far, far away and utterly desolate. We saw what Burckhardt, the 'modern' discoverer, must have seen in 1812 – the silent, shard-strewn valley, the rose-red, maroon and sand-yellow carved façades, the split, pagoda-centred pediments, the flowering oleanders (though poisonous, they made good mattresses), the peacock-blue lizards on the red rock, the few scrawny Bedouin smoking camel-dung all night beside their glowing, camel-dung fire. (They seemed never to sleep.) There is a ruined Crusader castle high up on one of the hills. I wonder how the garrison used to feel in the thirteenth century?

All through this year I kept up my attempts to join Airborne Forces. It was fruitless: nobody wanted to know. I very much doubt whether my applications ever got beyond Pal. Base.

Meanwhile, Muriel Shaw (who, not hearing from me, had written to my father in England for my address) had come up from South Africa to take up a mysterious job in Cairo. We corresponded regularly and once she came to Jerusalem on leave, with her brother, who was also stationed in Egypt – at Heliopolis. So at last I met G. D. Shaw, a real, live, published Faber poet. I remember giving a dinner party, with the Shaws, some Arab friends and what wine the house could manage – several bottles of sparkling red burgundy. The visit was all too short; but it was reassuring, back on duty on the great Gromboolian plain, to know that at any rate as good a friend as Muriel was in Cairo.

All through 1943 the 8th Army continued their victorious advance: through Libya, through Tunisia; into Sicily, into Italy. And now British units were being returned to England for the Second Front. Palestine was emptying. We had a new O.C., a vain, coarse but good-natured fellow called Betton (not his name), who did no harm as long as you flattered him.

We received our orders to leave Al-Jiyah and entrain for Egypt. It so happened that Major Betton had to go into hospital for some sort of treatment; he would be rejoining us before embarkation for England. (The Med. was clear now, of course, and we would be sailing home direct, via Gibraltar.) With typical egocentricity and vulgarity, he devised a formal 'handing over command' parade (there isn't one prescribed) in which he, of course, played the leading rôle. It was embarrassing: Salute: salute. Loud shout: 'Captain MacLeod, I hand over the Unit – to YOU!' Salute: salute. Mac. hadn't been briefed on what he was supposed to do now, so he simply marched the blokes off. I expect it might have been past Betton at the salute, only he hadn't thought of that.

Back on the railway; through Gaza, past Rafah, out of Palestine and into Egypt. My black cat, Ramadan, travelled with us. He was a great favourite with everybody and I was sorry to think that I should have to leave him in Egypt. In the event, Muriel 'placed' him with the Yacht Club at Gezira and I learned later that, as cats do, he had settled in quite happily and forgotten all about No. 2 Petrol Depot.

It was at the Base Depot in Egypt that I at last had some good luck mixed with the bad luck about my Airborne efforts. Army-wise, it makes a rather quaint little story. The Base Depot was under the command of a certain Colonel Sinclair, a white-moustached, Great War-medalled veteran who looked very like C. Aubrey Smith in *The Four Feathers*. You knew exactly where you were with him: he was a soldier (like Marian Hayter's father: all these have I observed from my youth up). I tried my airborne spiel on Colonel Sinclair, stressing the 'young officer fretting for action' stuff. It just so happened that a day or two later, on his rounds of the camp, the Colonel dropped in on an Army Bureau of Current Affairs session (in plain English, a talk with the men about the news), which I was taking. I gave him the old 'Party – party 'shun!' Smart salute. 'No. 2 Petrol Depot, sir. A.B.C.A. session on Japan's rôle in the war!' 'Right; carry on, Mr Adams, please,' replied the Colonel, and stayed for the rest of the period, at the close of which he said a few complimentary words. He was clearly on my side.

The next day I managed to get a recreational day pass into Cairo. Once there, I telephoned Muriel and took her out to lunch. Over the coffee, I told her about Colonel Sinclair and my recent efforts.

Muriel looked very carefully all round and then, in effect, behind the curtains and under the carpet. Then she said 'Richard, are you quite sure about this?' I assured her that I was, and asked her why she asked.

'Because that's what we do.'

'Who? Do what?'

Muriel came clean. Since her arrival in Egypt she had been a member of a high security organization. What they did was to train volunteers for liaison with the Resistance and for sabotage in Yugoslavia, including, of course, parachute training. Then they dropped them and kept in touch with them by radio.

'But where do you come into it?' I asked.

'I do the high-grade cypher: teach it to the trainee agents and then keep in touch with them after they've gone off. Until they no longer come up on the wireless, that is. That's why I asked whether you really wanted to do it.'

'I still want to; although of course I realize that if you're taken prisoner you get shot.'

' 'Bit more to it than that. They – talk to you first.'

I replied that the whole idea was very frightening, but nevertheless I'd still be glad of her help. Actually, this disclosure of Muriel's had taken me unprepared. Hitherto, I had always thought in terms of joining Airborne Forces proper – the red berets. This sabotage cloak-and-dagger stuff I'd never contemplated. Yet here was the opportunity, and I felt I ought not, after all my posturing, to say 'Well, thanks very much, but I don't think I quite meant *that*.'

I walked back with Muriel to her place of work and found myself talking to one Captain Proudfoot. (That was not his name.) I explained my situation.

'It's a pity your unit's on the point of embarkation,' he said at length. 'But never mind: I think I may be able to keep you in the Middle East a little longer. Leave it with me.'

Next morning, back in camp, I received a summons to the adjutant: not our adjutant – the Base Depot adjutant. I went into his office, stood to attention, saluted and remained at attention. At the other end of the room sat Colonel Sinclair, pretending to be absorbed in some papers.

'You went to Cairo yesterday?' began the adjutant.

'Yes, sir. I had a day pass.'

'But while you were there you went to see – well, you saw someone called Captain Proudfoot, didn't you? Who gave you authority to do that?'

I drew breath. Ho hum.

'Well, sir, may I explain the circumstances?'

'Yes, do,' he replied, in the tone of someone who would be glad enough to have them explained.

I told him the tale, conscious of Colonel Sinclair silently emanating 'not-disapproval'.

'Yes, well,' said the adjutant finally, 'that's the worst, of course, of doing things unofficially.'

'I didn't plan it, sir: I simply took the opportunity.'

I can't remember the rest, but apart from anything else, of course, the adjutant was in the position of dealing with someone who was seeking – well, excitement – while he himself was not. (No doubt he had a wife and children: I entirely applaud him.) I emerged with testicles intact.

Later, like Falstaff – or rather, not like Falstaff – I was sent for soon, at night. Colonel Sinclair said he was very sorry that they couldn't help me. They had tried. No way but I must go back with my unit. But he would write a letter for me to take with me.

Such a letter! It was everything that such a letter can be: gentlemanly, respectful (never know who it might get to), 'in my opinion', 'in my experience' (very wide, implied), warm, avuncular: implied reference to the Prime Minister's policy of encouraging people who wanted to pursue the war actively. 'Have observed on duty and talked to this young officer', etc., etc. 'I reckon you've cooked your goose all right,' said Captain MacLeod, with whom I'd always got on well.

The voyage home was uneventful. All I can really remember about it is that over Christmas – for we had Christmas 1943 at sea – I sang tenor in the drummed-up carol choir. To this day I can never hear what Laurie Lee calls 'Wild Shepherds' without remembering that Christmas.

We disembarked in England and were sent to another depot at Bridgend in south Wales. All I can remember about Bridgend is a church with an eighteenth-century memorial stone to a blacksmith, and an epitaph verse (by the then Vicar, perhaps?) which labours the farrier metaphor in memorable style. 'My iron is cold, my bellows is (*sic*) decayed –' Blacksmiths are, somehow or other, endearing people. 'Felix Randal' is one of my favourite poems, and a lot of other people's too, I suspect.

A day or two after we got to Bridgend, Captain MacLeod strolled into my billet. 'There's a posting in for you, to C.R.A.S.C., 1st Airborne Division. You leave us tomorrow, for Lincolnshire.'

XVII

At this point, reader, there should be something in the nature of a caesura: an induction in the text, an arsis in the voice of the narrator. What is that proximate glow in the sky ahead? No, you need not suspend disbelief. We are, in cold truth and with no hyperbole of my making, approaching great excellence and splendour, common as sunrise, greater than Alexander and his hosts, more glorious, tragic and terrible than Troy or Byzantium: the fury and the mire of human veins.

When George Orwell wrote that in America in the mid-nineteenth century human beings were free as they had never been before, he meant precisely that. And I am about to write of the bravest men who ever lived. But at that rate, I suppose, I cannot avoid antagonizing readers who have themselves served with men whom they believe – know – to have been unsurpassed. So I will simply call the British Airborne Forces *as* brave, *as* great-hearted as any men who have ever lived. Some – I suppose – may have been as valiant, but none more so. I never heard them spoken ill of.

I was not one of those valiant: but I was with them in a subordinate capacity; I wore their uniform and – largely because criteria were not exacting in all the exigency, haste and commotion of the war – was never sent packing. My leaky, ill-trimmed little craft fell in with the most heroic and glorious fleet that ever sailed, and for two years it was granted me to limp along with them, at least tolerated and undismissed. You should have known them. I have never felt more proud, fulfilled or happy before or since.

'There's a posting in for you, to C.R.A.S.C., 1st Airborne Division.' When MacLeod said this, my heart turned over in real apprehension. They had taken me at my word! I had for long insisted that I wanted to do it and at last someone had said 'Very well.' This was real. There was no going back on it now. The roller coaster had started and I was on it.

My trembling resolution was saved by two things, both of which I now know to have been illusions. First, at this time in my life, graded physically A.1 as I was, I genuinely believed that what one man could do, another man, given the determination, could also do. Granted the physique, it was all a matter of purpose, will and intent. And I was determined all right.

Secondly, I supposed, with an inward qualm, that the discipline would be a prop and support. Presumably I was now on my way to a division in which firm discipline was the order of the day. I'd been in the Army for three and a half years, but no doubt I'd seen nothing yet.

I couldn't have been more mistaken. There was unbounded group morale but very little formal discipline in Airborne Forces. If they didn't like you, they didn't waste time in discipline: they didn't have to. They just got rid of you. They could pick and choose – officers and N.C.O.s anyway, and all parachutists, for they were volunteers. What I was going to find out was whether they wanted to keep me.

What was my real motivation? I can't, in all honesty, say whether or not it was the same as everybody else's, for truth to tell, one thing I have never heard talked about by parachutists is their motivation. There was a bit more pay but not a lot, and in any case I doubt whether anyone's motivation can ever have been financial.

What had allured me from the start, back in 1942, had been the red berets and the flamboyant blue-and-maroon shoulder flash – Bellerophon riding on Pegasus to kill the Chimaera. These men must be a special band – couldn't not be – for the authorities had conferred upon them a uniform to tell everybody as much. I coveted that uniform, that distinction.

But as 1942 and then 1943 wore on, I came to have another reason. On the whole I didn't like the company I had to keep. Roy, Paddy and Piggy had been, of course, another matter – they were unique – but by-and-large I didn't terribly care about my colleagues and in particular about my commanding officers. Other ranks, of course, differ little from one mob to another. As General Montgomery said, there are no bad soldiers, only bad officers. I'm bound to say, though, that on the whole the N.C.O.s in No. 2 Petrol Depot had been no great shakes. Like Kent, I had seen better faces in my time than any I beheld about me there.

I had come to believe that if only I could get into Airborne Forces, both officers and N.C.O.s would be of an altogether different quality. I proved to be entirely right: they were. But where did that leave me?

It was January and very cold after the Middle East. I made the usual slow, disagreeable rail journey northwards, and at the end of it reported to Divisional Headquarters at Fulbeck, some eleven miles south of Lincoln. With no delay at all I found myself talking to Lt.-Col. Michael Packe, C.R.A.S.C., 1st Airborne Division.

Within a few minutes I felt that I was breathing a new air. I need only say here that I got on very well with Colonel Packe, then and throughout the next eighteen months. After we had chatted for a time, he said he was going to post me to the Light Company – 250th Light Company, R.A.S.C. (Airborne).

At this point I had better explain that, in those days at any rate, an Airborne Division's R.A.S.C. (who were divisional troops) consisted of three companies – two heavy and one light. The two heavy companies (each a major's command) were equipped with 3-ton Bedford lorries and did not differ essentially from any motorized R.A.S.C. company. Their job in action was to follow up an airborne attack together with the relieving ground troops, to bring in the division's heavier equipment and then assist it in its ground rôle.

The light company was different in function and kind. It consisted of three parachute platoons and three platoons of glider-borne jeeps. Each parachute platoon was commanded by a captain, with a subaltern 2 i/c: the N.C.O.s and men were all volunteer parachutists. Their rôle in action was to drop with the division, and thereupon to have the responsibility for collecting and distributing all subsequently dropped supplies; medical, food, ammunition (and conceivably petrol). They might well find themselves required to fight for possession of these supplies: if, for instance, containers happened to be dropped outside the area controlled by the division, or if the enemy attacked the dropping zone. They were equipped and trained accordingly.

The three platoons of glider-borne jeeps were not volunteers, although in 250 Light Company everyone was positively moti-vated. (If not, they were posted.) The rules were that any soldier at all could be ordered to travel in a glider, but only qualified parachutists could be ordered to jump from planes. Each platoon was organized in seven sections of about six or seven men, each under a corporal, and there were two sergeants to each platoon. The rôle of these platoons was to go into action with their jeeps in gliders (two jeeps to each Horsa glider) and then make themselves useful either in co-operation with the parachute platoons or as otherwise required by Divisional H.Q.

As I was to discover, the O.C. of 250 Company preferred all his officers to be parachutists, whether or not they were members of a parachute platoon.

That same evening I was driven to Lincoln and reported to Major John Gifford, commanding 250 Company.

It would be wearisome – and not really helpful – to give a character sketch of each officer in the company. There were about twelve or thirteen altogether, and they comprised a very strong team, much stronger than any I had yet come across. Apart from that, collectively they have importance to this book, since later, from my memory, they provided the idea for Hazel and his rabbits in *Watership Down*. By this I do not mean that each of Hazel's rabbits corresponds to a particular officer in 250 Company. Certainly the idea of the wandering, endangered and interdepen-dent band, individually different yet mutually reliant, came from my experience of the company, but out of all of us, I think, there were only two direct parallels. Hazel is John Gifford and Bigwig is Paddy Kavanagh.

I cannot really avoid a description of John Gifford – although he will hate it and may even be angry with me, though I very much hope not – because he has had as much influence on my life as James Hunt or Richard Hiscocks, if not more. Yet of all things he always hated any kind of flourish, ostentation or – well, bullshit; so I apologize to him.

John Gifford was at this time, I suppose, about thirty-three or four. He had been an architect in civilian life before the war; and he was a bachelor. He was about five feet nine inches tall and had a rather high colour and black hair. He was pleasant-looking without being spectacularly handsome, and he wore glasses. He moved well and had a quiet, clear voice which he never raised, except when giving commands on parade. He seldom exclaimed and he never swore.

Everything about him was quiet, crisp and unassuming. He was the most unassuming man I have ever known. When giving any of his officers an order he usually said 'Please', 'Would you like to –?' or 'Perhaps you'd better –'. He could be extraordinarily cutting; at least one sensed it like that, because a rebuke from him was so quiet and so rare, and because everyone had such a high regard for him that you felt his slightest reproof very keenly.

He was an excellent organizer. One of his strongly held principles was that it was important to get the right person into the right job, and the wrong person out. This went right down to the level of Private. I had never consciously thought about this principle before ('Anybody can do anything'), but I realized it all right after I had been under John Gifford's command for two or three weeks, when he gently pointed out to me that the reason why my platoon administration was in such a mess was that Lance-Corporal Tull was entirely the wrong sort of person to be trying to do what I had told him to. Since then I have needed no further telling.

John Gifford was brave in the most self-effacing way. One morning a few months later, when I had learned my way around in the Company and knew what was what, I missed the O.C. at breakfast and, since no one else happened to be near by, asked the mess waiter, Ringer, if he knew where he was.

'Oh, the Major went out early, sir. He heard last night that some of the gunners were jumping this morning and fixed up to join them.'

No one else knew about this. Jumping is a frightening and unpleasant affair. John Gifford was not in command of a parachute platoon, but he made it his business to do as many jumps as anyone else in the Company and to say nothing about it.

Turn-out was important in the Company, as throughout the whole Division. I recall that once a directive was included in Company Part I Orders that for the future people would not wear airborne smocks (camouflage jackets) off duty and particularly not in pubs. A couple of days later, I was with John Gifford and one or two other officers when we went into a local pub. The first thing we saw was my sergeant, Smith, together with two of my

Richard Hiscocks, circa 1944

James Hunt, circa 1935

Left: Anthony Jacobs, July 1936, from the J. C. R.
photograph of that summer. Anthony was always against
anything pertaining to the establishment, and he is scowling
accordingly

Right: My sister Katharine on the verandah at Oakdene, circa 1934

Myself, aged 16 or 17. ('Can't recall exactly where)

Above: My brother John at the Newbury Corporation swimming bath, circa 1935

Right: The Quad at Worcester, showing the New Building (left) and the Cloisters and Library. These are by Dr. George Clarke and date from about 1720 or thereabouts

Opposite above: The Scholars' Table in Hall at Worcester College. Gentleman finishing up a sconce. This is one of the College's largest sconces, holding seven pints and known as a 'Blue Peter', because anyone awarded a Blue or a Half-Blue customarily stands one. ('Or did so in my day!)

The War Memorial, in Worcester cloisters, to the fallen of the Second World War. The names include those of William Brown, Alasdair Christison, Cullen Powell, George Revnell, Frank Savory, Frank Schumer, Mike Seale, Jim Sharp and Roger Wright (who was also an Old Bradfieldian)

My father, aged 75, in 1945

Myself, thinly disguised as an Airborne Captain, in the same year

These photographs were taken by mutual agreement and we
exchanged them before I left for the Far East

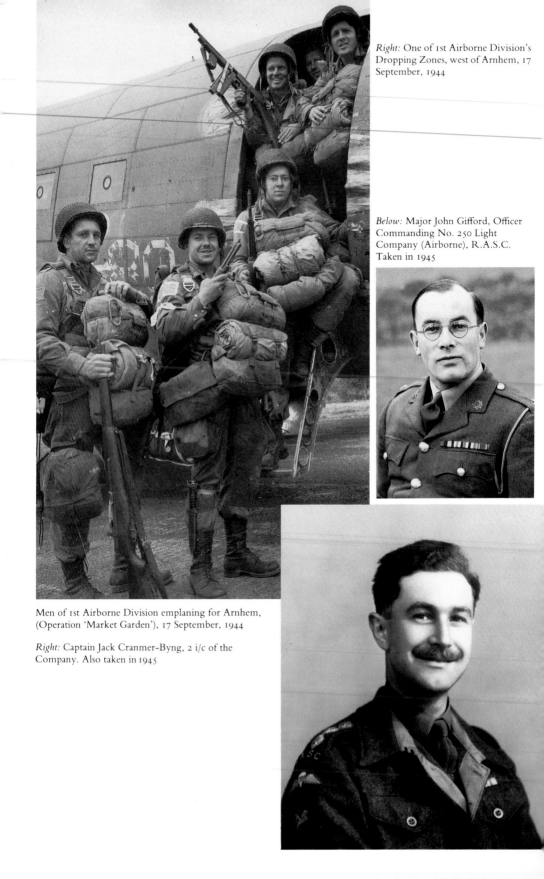

Right: One of 1st Airborne Division's Dropping Zones, west of Arnhem, 17 September, 1944

Below: Major John Gifford, Officer Commanding No. 250 Light Company (Airborne), R.A.S.C. Taken in 1945

Men of 1st Airborne Division emplaning for Arnhem, (Operation 'Market Garden'), 17 September, 1944

Right: Captain Jack Cranmer-Byng, 2 i/c of the Company. Also taken in 1945

The first Allied troops (these happen to be Americans) entering Brussels, 3 September, 1944

Elizabeth Acland, aged 17, summer 1946

corporals, drinking at the bar; all were wearing airborne smocks. Nobody said anything, since the O.C. was the senior officer present and the matter was therefore at his discretion. John Gifford led the way to the further end of the bar and ordered a round. Next day, he happened to be looking informally over my platoon location when we encountered the sergeant, who came to attention and saluted. 'Good morning, Sergeant Smith,' said John pleasantly. 'I hope your beer tasted equally good in airborne smocks?' Nothing ensued. Having dwelt on this, I perceive that it was really a communication from one comrade to another. 'Unfortunately I happen to have the job of commanding you: I'm sorry.' That was how it worked on Sergeant Smith, too: he didn't forget it. He did not.

Everyone in the Company was an individual, known by name and ability to the O.C. I remember now, particularly, the quartermaster sergeant, Greathurst. Greathurst was a personality in the Company, gentlemanly, light-hearted, buoyant and amusing, extremely good at his job, with a wheelbarrow full of surprises (as any good quartermaster should have) and his own little coterie of assistants, including Lance-Corporal Goodfield. Goodfield, amongst other things, was a brilliant pianist and, together with Greathurst, splendid company in a pub. Particularly memorable was their dual rendering, prestissimo, of 'Susie, Susie, sitting in the shoe-shine shop, she sits and shines and shines and sits and sits all over the shop.' (Anyone who got it wrong had to buy a pint.)

Sergeant-Major Gibbs was like a sergeant-major in a music-hall sketch. Almost illiterate himself, he was a veritable scourge on parade and would bawl out his victims mercilessly, until they, standing to attention before him, were deeply relieved to receive at last his customary conclusion: 'Right! On yer way, on yer way! Outa me sight! Yer idle, yer idle.' It once fell to my lot to read the first lesson on church parade, about the oppression of the Israelites in Egypt. This was from Exodus and included Chapter V, verse 13. It was only our respect for the O.C. which enabled most of us to keep straight faces.

I remember John Gifford once telling Sergeant-Major Gibbs that he should communicate something or other in a letter to Div. H.Q. 'Me, sir?' said Gibbs. 'Write a letter, sir? Got 'ighly trained staff do that, sir.'

After Arnhem, it was one Corporal Wiggins, rather than any of the officers, whose death John Gifford seemed to feel most keenly. We were all equal in his sight.

At one time the Company had wished upon it one Lieutenant Cordery, a big, burly man who before the war had been a regular soldier in the ranks. Though not yet qualified as a parachutist, he was appointed as subaltern to Captain Kavanagh's platoon. Cordery soon made himself unpopular. He was forever telling the men (he customarily addressed a man as 'sonny') that *he* was no war-time soldier; that if they thought they were smartly turned out then he, Cordery, could inform them otherwise; that he could show them hills in comparison with which they would call that a valley, etc., etc. 'Oh, they must *love* him!' remarked Kavanagh one day to John Gifford.

However, after a short sojourn, Cordery was no longer to be found among those present. He had been posted. No one said anything at the time, or during ensuing weeks. At least, I heard nothing. Much later that year, when we were in Normandy, his name came up.

'Oh,' said John Gifford, 'there was nothing wrong with Cordery. He was just too good for us, that's all. He was a soldier: we're not soldiers.'

John was always very selective indeed about accepting officers into the Company. Anyone who came was very much on approval. Some time during 1944 we received a young officer called Dale, who was sent to me to see how he made out. Dale was keen as mustard: nothing was too much trouble for him. Perhaps – I think now – he may have been a little *too* eager for approval: I don't know. One thing not his fault nor yet in his favour was that he was physically small – an unusually short man. My stated opinion to the O.C. was that, while Dale lacked charisma and was not likely to make people exclaim 'Gosh! *There's* an Airborne officer if ever I saw one!', he was nevertheless a good little chap who deserved to be taken on. But John Gifford wouldn't have it. 'I don't think we really *want* him, do you?' he said to me in his quiet way. Now Dale, whatever his merits, was not worth contention with so experienced and able a commanding officer. So I knuckled under, and Dale disappeared too. I know he thought I must have reported against him: he was terribly hurt and disappointed. Still, I suppose

John Gifford was right: he nearly always was.

I may have given an impression of a rather serious – even humourless – man. Nothing could be further from the truth. In the mess John was excellent company and most amusing, while always retaining that slight degree of reserve that a commanding officer must. I well remember our drinking parties, at which John often showed a predilection for a particular bawdy song, no doubt still in circulation, about Three Men of Nor-or-folk, Nor-or-or-or-folk, folk, folk. Terrible things happened to this trio. They all fell down a pre-ci-pice (pre-e-e-ci-pice, pice, pice) and had to go to hospitool, but there were no be-eds va-a-cant. John would join in singing this song with a kind of joyous gravity, as at the celebration of a rite. He drank his whack, but I never saw him the worse for drink. He was very fond of contract bridge, and there was nothing he liked better than a four. I was shocking bad – still am – but the M.O., Dr Willard, was good, and so was Phil Bushby, the Workshops officer. Once, at Nijmegen, we played bridge with the odd shell dropping from time to time. No doubt lots of other people have, come to that.

From the top of the Company to the bottom, the men all had the greatest liking and respect for the O.C., and it was only necessary to say to your N.C.O.s 'The Major doesn't like –' or 'The Major thinks we need to –' for his will to be done without the least demur.

Captain Paddy Kavanagh was quite another thing. He was about twenty-nine and before the war had been a journalist. He was, of course, Irish, though he had no brogue. Paddy was a sensationalist; by temperament entirely the public's idea of a parachute officer; good-natured, debonair, generous, always in high spirits (I know John Gifford, despite his liking for him – you couldn't not like Paddy – found him a bit much at times), a deviser of dares, afraid of nothing (including jumping), so it seemed. He once jumped with a kit-bag on *each* leg, to show that it could be done: another time he jumped with a large wireless transmitter. He had a bucko sergeant, McDowell, and the two of them used to get up to some rare old larks. Once, Kavanagh was going to make his platoon crawl under live fire from a Bren gun, and began by setting them an example. After about a quarter of a minute he called to McDowell, on the gun, to aim closer. Afterwards, they found bullet holes in his airborne smock. Another time, when he had his platoon out on the Derbyshire moors on a bitterly cold day in the winter of early 1944, they came upon a steep-sided reservoir. 'Fancy a swim, Sergeant McDowell?' asked Kavanagh. The sergeant looked at him and bit his lip. 'I will if you will, sir.' So the pair stripped off and plunged into the near-freezing water. Paddy was out first, heaving himself up the shelved walling. But Sergeant McDowell was below middle height, and what with the terrible cold, simply could not pull himself out. Instead of helping him, the platoon stood round laughing at him and he very nearly died in the water before someone gave him an arm. Sometimes Kavanagh and McDowell would take the pin out of a live grenade and toss it between them until one of them ('Sissy!') threw it down the pit or over the wall.

John Gifford's quiet certitude, however, was always finally a match for Paddy, as Hazel's was for Bigwig.

I recall one of my own men, Driver Fisher, saying 'I'd like Captain Kavanagh to train me, but I'd hate him to take me into action, because I'm sure he'd kill me.'

The evening I joined the Company, I went out drinking in Lincoln with the O.C., Kavanagh and one or two more. I don't know whether or not I was being looked over, but they couldn't have been nicer: Kavanagh was perfectly charming, as a matter of fact. I remember seeing some Other Ranks near by, with their red berets pulled under their shoulder straps, and that I asked Paddy whether that was the thing to do. 'Well,' he replied, 'we don't *quite* do it.' (Meaning officers.) He could have said 'Good God!' etc., couldn't he? That evening I was treated like a guest and no one asked me anything military at all; but somehow I felt confident. This was the new deal at last.

Next morning John interviewed me formally in the office. 'How do you feel about jumping?' he asked.

'I want to jump, sir.'

'Well,' said John, 'we can see about that. There'll be time. But I think an officer of your experience should have an independent command, rather than being subordinate in a parachute platoon. I'm going to give you C Platoon.' (This was one of the platoons of glider-borne jeeps.)

Oh, C Platoon! Reader, please forgive a brief rhapsody. Was there ever such a platoon – was there? What a plague could I do for C Platoon that they couldn't have done without me? That wasn't *quite* true, actually – there has to *be* an officer, or things start getting wugular – but jolly nearly. Both the N.C.O.s and the men were beyond the wildest dreams of any subaltern. They were not only extremely competent – Sergeant Smith (Gerry) was a great deal more competent than I – but splendidly keen and very diverse. From Corporal Bater (Devonshire) – whom I have personally seen drink sixteen pints in an evening and then drive a jeep (I was in it) – to Corporal Herdman ('Wheel him in, ah ha ha ha!'), a Geordie, there wasn't a dud in the lot. Well, of course, there couldn't have been, not in 250 Company, only I just wasn't used to that sort of style, see? Even the Lance-Corporals (Barnard and Rushforth) would have made damned good corporals anywhere else. And when I start remembering the men individually – Eggleton, Fisher, Williams – well, a reader is bound to feel this tedious; but don't forget that I'm not the first writer to have found commanding a good platoon the most fulfilling and rewarding thing they have ever had to do. Herbert Read, for a start. And Robert Graves and – a whole lot more. I wish I were back there, straight I do.

The first thing C Platoon had on their plate after I'd taken them over was to go to Wellington, in Shropshire, and collect forty jeeps and eighty trailers – to make us effective according to establishment. Now airborne trailers were tricky things. Towing one empty one behind you was dangerous: towing two was even more dangerous. If you went too fast, the empty trailer might well turn over, and if it did, then the open-sided jeep went over with it. I have known at least one man (not mine) killed in this way. With two trailers per jeep, we had to drive back from Wellington to Lincoln at no more than twenty m.p.h. all the way.

The evening we got to Wellington was actually the evening of the day on which I had taken up command of the platoon. I asked the N.C.O.s how they intended to pass the evening and they said they were going out on the beer. I immediately asked whether I could come along, and of course they said Yes: they couldn't say anything else, really, but I saw an apprehensive shadow cross a few faces. They thought I and my pips were likely to be a drag on the evening. I knew that it was vital for the future of our relationship that I should join them and that in the course of the evening they must come to decide that they liked me without, at bottom, losing respect for their new officer. Well, it worked. It was really that they liked themselves and their red berets so much that they were essentially good-natured and well disposed. They liked being who they were, they liked what they were doing and they liked being under the command of John Gifford. They felt no resentment against the army or against the set-up they were in. As the pints took hold and Corporal Rawlings talked to me of how the company had been formed, in 1942, under the command of Major Packe, and of what they had carried out in North Africa, Sicily and Italy, I felt even more fully committed to what we were doing and to trying to be an airborne officer. I had never dreamt that there could be a platoon – or a company – like this. They should have every scrap of me, twenty-four hours a day. I honestly believe that the N.C.O.s went to bed that night feeling that the new officer at least liked his beer, had a sense of humour and might turn out to be not too bad.

As for the men, there was none of the peevishness, shoulder-shrugging or ill-concealed resentment with which I had become all-too-familiar elsewhere. Neither was there any of the kind of spirit expressed in 'We are Fred Karno's army, we are the A.S.C.' They did not regard themselves as Fred Karno's army. They were glider-borne troops of the 1st Airborne Division: Hitler had a nasty shock coming. I don't mean that they had no sense of humour, or that I didn't get my leg pulled in all the minor and time-honoured ways. But none of them ever ran down the Company or the Division. (' 'Wish Ah was out o' this f— lot.' To which the answer would have been 'Well, you can go tomorrow morning – easily. Your passport shall be made and crowns for convoy put into your purse.')

With everyone in this frame of mind, of course, the role of the platoon commander became according. You could treat the men with semi-familiarity. You didn't have to drive them. You didn't blast people, threaten them or put them on charges. (If there was one thing John Gifford hated like poison, it was a charge. 'Couldn't this have been avoided?') On parade I reproved mostly by mock, histrionic severity. ''Orrible man!' became a platoon catchword. Lady Godiva reappeared, and another crack I had acquired from somewhere. 'I *will* not have this place left looking like a Chinese revolving shit-house!' In Tunisia they'd all picked up the Arabic, of course – *Maaleesh, stannah shwire* and so on – which at that time was still a sort of initiates' language. With a platoon like this, all you really had to do was try to work still harder than they did, prevent them from being buggered about by anyone else (outside the company, I mean), appeal to their self-respect when necessary and take every opportunity to set an example: get the first needle-jab, be the first man up in the morning, change a flat tyre with your own hands and generally have a bash at anything that offered. When in doubt, ask yourself what Gifford or Kavanagh would do. Given youth, health, energy and enthusiasm, it was simple.

Anyway, I know it worked (relatively) because since the war I have talked to demobbed people who were on the receiving end and are now free to say what they thought.

An example of what zest and esprit de corps can do to your metabolism was the cross-country. The cross-country was John Gifford's idea. He devised a course of about four miles over the rural western outskirts of Lincoln and gave orders that *everyone* would participate – clerks, medical orderlies, mess waiters – the lot. Now I had never been any good at running. At Bradfield I used to stagger round on appointed afternoon runs with less than no enthusiasm, and had been only too delighted when being a fives colour had got me out of the senior steeplechase. But this was different. I knew there were some very rapid people among both the officers and the other ranks. I suspected that I might well be still on approval. Somehow, I had *got* to do creditably. With an effort that nearly killed me I came in sixteenth. (John Gifford himself was eighth and Paddy fifth.) C.S.M. Gibbs was the only man excused: I think it was thought that it would excite risibility and be bad for discipline if he appeared puffing and blowing with a place in three figures.

As spring drew on and the unknown date of the invasion of Europe (D-Day) came closer, airborne activities began hotting up. I was sent to some local aerodrome or other to get glider experience, and spent a couple of wonderful days flying from somewhere near Lincoln down to the south coast and back, as theoretical co-pilot in a Horsa in tare (empty). The real pilot was a delightful chap and I learned a lot from him about how to be helpful to glider pilots and what not to do in a loaded glider.

Then C Platoon went to Hope, near Edale in the Peak District of Derbyshire. 'Edale' was a particular private wheeze of 1st Airborne R.A.S.C., the invention of Major David Clark, 2 i/c C.R.A.S.C. David was a hell of a goer, one of the most rugged, stalwart officers in the Division. He had been an amateur county cricketer (Kent) and he could cover steep, mountainous ground for hours at almost incredible speed. (Late on, in 1945, when he was among starving prisoners in Germany and being marched backwards and forwards between the collapsing fronts, David was an inspiration and a hero, whose compassion and endurance saved many lives.)

David had devised a week's mountain 'course' at Edale, to toughen the blokes up (and half-kill some of them). All platoons (including those of the heavy companies) were sent on this course in turn. It was a good racket for David, since he lived in two rooms at the New Inn, and administered the course – when himself not out on the tops. Mr Herdman, the landlord, was also a keen walker, beer drinker and singer of songs; he couldn't have had a more congenial guest and companion than David, and of course a steady succession of thirsty airborne soldiers in large numbers was exactly his ticket.

I reported C Platoon to Major Clark at about four o'clock on an early spring afternoon. He was in what I can only call his parlour at the New Inn. 'Hullo, Adams,' he said. 'Do you like Delius?' I said I did. 'Sit down for a bit, then.' It was, as I remember, *A Song of Summer*. It seemed appropriate.

That was a week and a half! The platoon climbed Kinder Downfall (yes, they did), with the help of one or two ropes put up by David; walked miles all over Kinder Scout in battle equipment; did a grisly night exercise in which all N.C.O.s had to use prismatic compasses; and in between whiles drank Mr Herdman's beer in gallons. One night at Edale there was a dance, with the local girls brought in lorries (illegally authorized by David). At about ten o'clock he, Sergeant Smith and I were drinking in the bar when David said that for two pints he would now, personally, go out, climb the top that stands north of Edale (1,937 feet) and be back in fifty minutes. He did so. (He said he'd done it and no one dreamed of doubting him.)

Another day, I had to take the platoon on a fairly wearing walk (it wasn't a march: we went by sections, I think) over the tops. We reached our destination at about half-past two, where we lunched on haversack rations, after which the men were free to laze about until lorries came to take them back.

A Kavanagh-esque idea occurred to me. 'I'm going to *walk* back,' I said to Sergeant Smith and Sergeant Potter. 'Care to come too?' They said they would not. I put it to the platoon as a whole. Only two people felt like coming: Lance-Corporal Rushforth and Driver Williams. So we set out.

Well, it was a sod: I don't say it wasn't. But we did it – just. Williams, a nice lad, was first class: he covered the distance without distress. It was poor old Rushforth who really suffered: I remember we pretty well had to help him down the last stretch, a steep valley known as Golden Clough; but he was game all right.

I left Edale with a very proper sense of my own limitations on Kinder Scout. You see, I had always hitherto had a good notion of my abilities as a walker, based on my childhood on the Downs, my ramblings with Alasdair in the Trossachs and so on. Before going up to Edale I had even felt impatient and begrudging of David Clark's reputation in 1st Airborne R.A.S.C. The outgoing lot before us was one of our own para. platoons, Captain Gell's. I remember saying fatuously to Daniels, their subaltern, 'What's so marvellous about Clark, anyway? Can't any fit bloke walk on the tops?'

Daniels, a big, husky fellow, paused for a few moments. At length he replied 'You seen him go?'

A week or two after we had come back to Lincoln, it became noised abroad that there was to be old utis. General Urquhart, the Divisional Commander, was coming to inspect 250 Company. Apart from being the Divisional Commander, Urquhart as a man enjoyed the sort of esteem you'd expect. An officer of the Highland Light Infantry, he had been on the staff of 51st Highland Division in the Western Desert, and had taken over 1st Airborne after the previous commander, General Hopkinson, had been killed by enemy fire in Italy in 1943. He was known to be completely fearless but to hate gliding, which made him feel sick. As a rule, of course, he concentrated his attention on the six parachute battalions and three glider-borne battalions of infantry which were the fighting guts of the division, but naturally his gunners, sappers, signals, R.A.S.C. and other brigade and divisional troops also needed looking over from time to time.

John Gifford was not the sort of O.C. to be put in a tizzy by inspections from anybody at all, but nevertheless a divisional commander's visit had to be taken seriously. Sergeant-Major Gibbs was given carte blanche, and for days his roars of rage and disapproval could be heard from North Hykeham to Washingborough. C.Q.M.S. Greathurst, an instructed scribe, brought forth out of his treasure things new and old. Chinese revolving shithouses were swept and garnished within an inch of their lives. When the great day came C Platoon, in their rather isolated, Nissenhutted, jeep-ranked location at North Hykeham, were ready for anything: not a boot-eyelet unpolished, not a Pegasus out of alignment.

We had a watcher out at H.Q., of course; it was Corporal Pickering, who came duly zooming back on his motor-bike. The General had arrived, and the O.C. had given him, Pickering, a nod that he meant to bring him up to C Platoon. In our apprehension was mingled real pride. With the whole company to select from, Major Gifford had decided to take the General to C Platoon.

The cortege duly arrived and Urquhart, a dark, big-built, hefty man, got straight out of his car and walked ahead into our location as Corporal Simmons slammed the turned-out guard into the present.

'Where's the platoon commander?' he asked.

I found myself walking with him easily away from the Div. H.Q. retinue. Alone together, and amicably, the General and I strolled round the location. We chatted. I realized he was not looking for faults. This was a different sort of inspection.

'What are your problems?' he asked.

I couldn't even invent one for him. I showed him a few patches of damp, and that was the best I could do. I introduced two or three of the N.C.O.s, who told him they were as happy as larks and ready to take their sections anywhere.

General Urquhart had not come to carp or to pick holes. He had come to inspire trust and win our confidence. He did that all right. He left after about twelve minutes, telling John Gifford that we were first-rate, or words to that effect. It was, as you might say, anti-climactic. Later, in the mess, John remarked quietly 'I'm glad the General seemed pleased.'

. . .

It must have been about a week after General Urquhart's visit that Paddy's platoon, one morning, were jumping at a near-by airfield. Lincolnshire was full of airfields. On the flat land south of Lincoln, east of the Grantham road, they were laid out side by side like Brobdignagian tennis courts. It was from these that the hosts of Lancasters, Stirlings and Flying Fortresses used to set out to bomb Germany. We grew accustomed to seeing hundreds deployed in the sky, manoeuvring into position before their departure.

An airfield, ready-cleared, makes an excellent dropping zone (D.Z.). A morning's activity for a platoon – nothing in it, really, as long as it's not you. Someone had mentioned to me that Paddy and Co. were jumping, but I hadn't given it much attention, being too busy with C Platoon's rifles. We'd just been told that all rifles which weren't accurate in the aim were to be handed in. About mid-day I had come down to Company H.Q. to talk to C.Q.M.S. Greathurst about this matter, when I ran into Sergeant-Major Gibbs.

'You 'eard, sir – we 'ad a man killed this morning? Private Beal.'

The way he said it, it sounded like 'Private Bill'; almost like a joke. It was no joke, however, but, like all fatal accidents, a horrible business.

What had happened was this. There were at this time two methods of jumping; one standing up, from the port rear door of a Dakota (C.47), and the other – the first-devised, original way – sitting down and propelling yourself feet forward through an aperture in the middle of the floor of a Whitley bomber. ('Jumping through the hole', as it was called.) Twenty men could jump from a Dakota, but the complement for a Whitley was only eight.

For a 'stick' of eight men to jump correctly required cool heads and accurate counting off. Sitting sideways on the floor and inching forward, each man in turn had to swing his legs and body through a right angle into the hole, and then push himself off to drop through it. There was a song (to the tune of 'Knees Up, Mother Brown'):

> Jumping through the hole,
> Whatever may befall,
> We'll always keep our trousers clean
> When jumping through the hole.

I have never jumped through the hole, but John Gifford told me once that, in comparison with a Dakota, you got a much more frightening view of the ground rushing past below.

Normally two containers, each with its own parachute and filled with arms, ammunition, etc., were fastened under the body of the plane and released by the pilot to drop in the middle of the stick (to ensure the best possible accessibility on landing). When the green light came on, the whole stick used to shout aloud as they jumped: 'One, two, three, four, container, container, five, six, seven, eight!' With number eight out, the despatcher would shout to the pilot 'Stick gone!' This is why old airborne soldiers still sometimes talk about a 'container-container' when they mean a container (e.g., in Marks and Spencer's or somewhere like that).

A man on a parachute has, as many people today have seen for themselves, a good deal of directional control. Containers, being inanimate, exercise none. What had happened was that poor Beal, jumping number four, had had a container dropped immediately after him (and therefore above him). The container, oscillating on its parachute, had bumped into Beal's canopy and collapsed it, and he had fallen to his death.

The incident cast a gloom over the company for several days. Many, many years later, when I was on the Great Barrier Reef off Australia, I met Arlene Blum, the American girl who led an all-woman expedition to climb Annapurna in 1978. Among other things she said to me was 'What I learned on Annapurna is that you can be well-equipped and well-trained and do everything properly, and you're still in horrible danger.'

XVIII

Now preparations for the invasion were mounting by the day. There were tanks and guns all over the place. Nazi-occupied France was attacked nightly by Mosquitoes – fighter-bombers – with the main object of destroying enemy communications. The railways were bombed to pieces, and I remember hearing that it was intended to leave not a bridge – any bridge – intact north of the Loire. This was actually achieved. (Such was our air supremacy that during the subsequent campaign, which culminated in the German debacle in the so-called 'Falaise box', German troops could not move at all by day, and even by night were severely restricted by the universal devastation.)

The Allies' efforts along these lines were backed up by the French Resistance (or 'Maquis', as they were called: *maquis* means 'undergrowth'). Part of the Allied plan was to keep supplying the Resistance with arms, ammunition, explosives, medical gear and so on. All this stuff used to be dropped, by night and parachute, at pre-arranged places and times. Keeping these appointments was difficult and demanding for our pilots. They flew and navigated, of course, in darkness and could expect only the briefest and least conspicuous of signals from the ground.

The supplies were packed in strapped and lidded laundry baskets, since these were cheap, convenient to handle, drop and open, and could stand a lot of rough treatment. (Even in the event of a 'Roman candle' – a parachute not opening – the contents often turned out to be serviceable.) It was 1st Airborne R.A.S.C.'s job to pack these baskets, fit each with a parachute, load them on the planes, fly with them and push them out when the pilot said. Along the floor inside each plane was fixed a line of metal rollers. On these rollers the baskets were strapped in tandem: when the straps were released, they were free to be shoved down the plane, through a right angle and out of the port rear door. The only possible danger was that a despatcher might somehow or other get his own equipment or belt tangled up with a basket's straps and go out with it. I never heard of it actually happening, but I once or twice knew it almost to happen.

The supplies were kept out of doors, widely dispersed in quite small dumps (smaller than an average drawing-room) in the area north of Fairford in Gloucester – the valleys of the Leach and Coln. It was to this area that C Platoon were sent, southward from Lincoln, to come temporarily under the command of one of the division's heavy R.A.S.C. companies. Naturally, the loading job was principally one for lorries, but the heavy company also needed more sheer manpower than they could muster on their own. We brought our jeeps, of course, and they often came in handy. We were camped in tents in a big field at a village called Southrop, about three miles north-east of Fairford. The dumps were all over the place, along the lanes round villages with beautiful names such as Quenington, Hatherop, Coln St Aldwyn, Eastleach St Martin and Fyfield. The planes usually flew from the airfields at Down Ampney and South Cerney.

I rather missed John Gifford, Paddy Kavanagh and other friends of 250 Company mess: I even quite missed the bawling of Sergeant-Major Gibbs. On the other hand, as everyone knows who has ever been a junior officer, there were great advantages to being on detachment. The heavy company's commanding officer, a Scot called Major Gordon, known as 'The Jontleman' ('Noo, jontlemen, theer's warrk to be done'), was a perfectly reasonable person to deal with, even if he lacked the charisma of John Gifford, and treated his visitors considerately. C Platoon enjoyed a considerable degree of autonomy: I can't recall that Major Gordon ever inspected our camp or ourselves. The men knew we were doing essential and important work and were in good spirits and full of energy. We didn't fly every night, and this meant that there were a few evenings to spend in local pubs. Once, I remember, some of the N.C.O.s and I simpled as far as Bourton-on-the-Water, about twelve miles away, where we had trouble with Yanks. (At this time, the summer of 1944, there were Yanks in the woodwork and under the bed, as Corporal Simmons remarked.) There is a narrow brook – the upper

Windrush, I rather think – running down the street at Bourton-on-the-Water, crossed at intervals by a number of parapet-less foot-bridges. Sergeant Smith, having been much provoked, had a fight with a Yank on one of these bridges and knocked him off it into the water. We left quickly after that, since there were numerous other Yanks around, and in particular I, as the platoon officer, didn't want to be called to account for failing to restrain my men from fighting. Relations with our American allies were always so precarious and the authorities were accordingly so touchy that I might easily have found myself on the mat without a parachute, as the saying went.

My own favourite pub for a quiet evening was a place called the Hill Oak at Ampney St Mary, which no longer exists. Some of the locals sang authentic folk songs and a friend of mine called Pat Jerome and I would find ourselves listening to versions of things like 'John Barleycorn' and 'As I Roved Out One Morning Fair'. This was rural south Gloucestershire in 1944.

I flew over France several times with the laundry baskets, until I became satisfied that there was no real danger and none of the men was likely to say (or think) that I was keeping out. German night fighters seemed non-existent, and although we sometimes encountered a little flak, it was sporadic and short-lived, for we by-passed towns and our dropping zones were always in lonely, rural places. Being inside the aircraft, I never saw a ground-to-air signal, but pilots told me that they were momentary, a mere flash of a torch. The Resistance men could see and recognize the aircraft, of course, and needed to signal only once as it came overhead.

From time to time there was every opportunity to look at the splendid wool churches in this neighbourhood, and I came to know them well – Cirencester itself, Fairford with its marvellous glass, Northleach, Eastleach St Martin and the rest. At least, while you sweated away on the dumps and took convoys to South Cerney, you got plenty of gratuitous and unsurpassable illustrations of what the war was being fought for. If Fairford glass had survived Cromwell, it could surely cope with Hitler. Yet it still chafes me to think that once, before the seventeenth century, there were many, many glassed churches like Fairford.

In the middle of all this April- and Maytime junketing, someone from the past turned up with great impact. I received a letter from

Jennifer. It was not a happy letter. She was still more or less heart-broken over her R.A.F. lover killed in training. But she had further news, fully as bad if not worse. The younger of her two brothers, Roger, had become a wireless operator in the merchant navy. Roger, whom I had met back in 1940, had been a light-hearted, amusing fellow, a great hand at a party or in a pub, with a keen sense of human absurdity. He and Jennifer had been full of their own particular kind of brother-and-sister nonsense games. Her news was that Roger's ship had been torpedoed and that he had died on a raft. Her grief, of course, was consuming. It was lonely, too; denied parental comfort, for at about this time she herself had been called up into the A.T.S. and was stationed as a clerk at the huge Ordnance depot at Bicester; a right dump if ever there was one.

It wasn't far to Bicester, as luck would have it: a little over thirty miles. During these wound-up weeks, with the whole place full of British and American convoys, despatch-riders going every which way and Air Force lorries carrying all manner of odd things to odd destinations, it was unlikely that any military policeman would ask an airborne officer in a jeep to show him his written journey authorization (or 'work ticket', as it was called). Besides, there was the much-emphasized matter of security: it was a case of 'everyone knows where he's going, but nobody else must.'

I handed over to Sergeant Smith and set off for Bicester. The depot did indeed prove a depressing place; miles of asphalt roads and identical Nissen huts – both billets and offices; cook-houses whose environs, as I passed them, made me heave; and uniformed personnel, both men and women, who looked about as demoralized and dispirited as Arab donkeys.

After a search I found Jennifer in a Nissen office with four or five other privates of both sexes. They were the sort of people in uniform whom Evelyn Waugh describes so memorably in *Men at Arms*. They belonged to no particular unit nor felt any loyalty to one; they knew nothing of esprit de corps, never went on parade or got inspected and hardly knew an officer when they saw one. (Another memorable account of the sort of life this was is given by Mary Lee Settle in her war memoir *All the Brave Promises*.)

I drove Jennifer out of the depot and took her off to lunch near-by. She told me again, with bitter tears, what she had said in her letter about Roger. I soon realized that I loved her as deeply as ever I had. Three years is a long time when you're young, and much had happened. Grief had changed her, of course: I felt myself less changed – almost younger, now, than she. I asked her whether there was anything at all that she thought I could do for her. She replied, instantly, get her out of the Bicester depot; anywhere, on any terms. I promised to do what I could, but didn't think it was likely to be much good.

On my next visit from Southrop, I asked for an interview with Jennifer's (very nominal) officer. I thought I'd see what a red beret could do. I went into her office, saluted her and stood to attention. She was a pleasant, nice-looking woman of about thirty-five. I told her I was a friend of the family and had promised Jennifer's mother that I would keep an eye on her in the army jungle. Might there be any chance of a posting to one of the clerical support groups of Airborne Forces? The good lady was kind, polite and sympathetic: but no, she said, to be honest there wasn't a hope. Everybody hated the Bicester depot and everyone wanted to get out of it on any terms. If I knew Mr Churchill, that might possibly help. Otherwise she could offer no ideas.

During those last weeks before the invasion (the date of which, of course, no one knew) I chanced my arm again and again to go and see Jennifer. It was lucky that the Jontleman was a decent old stick who, as long as we did our work properly, left us largely to our own devices in our meadow at Southrop. (If John Gifford had been coming down he would have told me first: he was a jontleman, too.)

It was fine, warm weather. I would drive over to Bicester of an evening, and we would have dinner somewhere and then sleep out of doors in my issue sleeping-bag. So, at last, Jennifer and I became lovers. I remember the owls, and the stars, and the smell of the grass, and the fleets of bombers flying on exercises, towing their gliders precarious in the gentle night. Once Jennifer managed to get away for a long week-end. I can't remember where we went, but I remember her telling me how later, on the evening when she returned to the barrack-room, one of her companions remarked 'Must seem funny in a single bed, Jennifer.' For of course the girls had come to know all too well the sight of me and my Pegasus jeep.

One early morning, returning alone to Southrop, I was hit and damaged by an American left-wheel-drive lorry which never signalled it was turning right. This was awkward, for I could not very well give particulars of my journey or details of my non-existent work ticket. Still, we fudged it up somehow – the Yank wasn't much damaged and Americans were always easy-going. I got the Jontleman's Workshops officer to repair the jeep and no questions asked.

For me it was a new experience in a love-affair to carry responsibility as well as warmth and desire. Jennifer was in a veritable pit of bereavement, loss and grief, and her lover needed to remember this all the time. I like to think – to hope – that I may have made things a bit more bearable for her during those summer months. She certainly made me very happy. Yet it was all snatched: there was so much else to be done which necessarily had to take priority.

On the night of the invasion of Normandy, 5–6 June, none of us had any idea of what was in the wind, and were carrying on our normal routine. We weren't required to fly out to drop supplies that night, but there was nothing unusual in that: we were quite used to being stood down, sometimes for nights in a row. That we were relatively closely involved and yet had no foreknowledge whatever of the date of the invasion shows, I think, how very good Allied security was. In point of fact, as many readers of this book will know, the invasion was originally to have taken place on 5 June, but was postponed for twenty-four hours because of unfavourable weather. We knew nothing about that, either.

As the campaign began, we were simply required to carry on as we had during past weeks. We attended to our dumps and went on dropping stuff to the Maquis. We knew 6th Airborne Division had achieved marvellous things in Normandy, and felt a bit surprised that apparently 1st Division were not as yet being held in instant readiness. If the division had been on alert, C Platoon would, we knew, have been ordered back to 250 Company at Lincoln.

The order wasn't, in fact, all that long in coming. Exact dates escape me now, but I suppose it must have been in early July, perhaps, that C Platoon returned to Lincoln. At that time we were still supposing that 1st Division would be used in the Normandy campaign, and that that was in fact the intention of S.H.A.E.F. (Supreme Headquarters, Allied Expeditionary Force). With two

British and three American airborne divisions, plus an independent Polish parachute brigade and a British air-transportable division, S.H.A.E.F. had at their disposal an airborne army (one sixth of the Allied total fighting strength) – and it was as the Airborne Army that it was referred to by the media. The Germans were popularly represented as living in mortal terror of this army of the sky and never knowing when and where it might strike. The notion was good for public morale, at all events.

Yet in terms of strategy and logistics, things weren't quite so straightforward. Here I would recommend anyone who wants to know more than is really appropriate to a personal memoir like this to consult a book by Colonel Geoffrey Powell, called *The Devil's Birthday*. Geoffrey Powell refers to the Allied airborne forces, after the Normandy landings, as 'coins burning holes in S.H.A.E.F.'s pocket'. To be sure, this splendid strike force should be used – *must* be used – but where, precisely, and when?

The whole idea of airborne forces in an attack was to put them down in strength (not in penny packets as sabotage groups – that notion had been discarded quite early on – as early as 1942), either to destroy something likely to be a nuisance to our advancing forces (such as the German heavy gun emplacements on the Normandy coast on D-Day) or to seize and hold something valuable to us, like a bridge or an area of land covering the flank of a landing beach. What 6th Airborne Division principally achieved on D-Day was to seize and hold a position along the river Orne, thereby preventing the Germans from attacking our landing beaches from the east, and covering the left flank of the Allied forces as they advanced inland. American airborne forces had similarly covered the right flank.

It was always imperative that dropped airborne forces should be joined quickly by relieving ground troops, since they could carry into action only a limited amount of food and ammunition (the latter weighs very heavy) and because they were of necessity relatively lightly armed. They could be supplied by air, of course, but only to the extent of a sort of supplement; and even so it was apt in practice to turn out a bit fortuitous. 6th Airborne Division had been reached by ground troops on the very evening of D-Day. In the Second World War it was axiomatic that infantry always needed the support of tanks and guns. Airborne troops couldn't carry these into action and consequently, after their initial seizure of their objective, were confined to the defensive, and more than usually vulnerable to enemy tanks, guns, heavy mortars, etc., which they could not be expected to resist indefinitely.

However ready the troops, a large-scale airborne attack needs time to plan and prepare. During the Normandy campaign, events kept overtaking the plans. As fast as it was planned to drop 1st Airborne Division at X or Y, our land forces would drive on and take it; or the situation, changing, would render the seizure of X or Y unnecessary. One planned airborne operation in France was code-named 'Seventeen', it being the seventeenth to be planned.

There were other snags, too, connected with the availability of aeroplanes and the efficiency of their pilots. There simply weren't enough aeroplanes to carry the wonderful 'airborne army' into action in one go (or 'lift' as it was called). And of course, with two lifts, the enemy were likely to form a pretty fair idea about the coming second one. As to the accuracy of dropping, the two large-scale airborne operations already mounted by the Allies had demonstrated a thing or two. In the invasion of Sicily in the summer of 1943, 1st Airborne Division had been landed all over the place. The country was covered with lost parachutists trying to find the places to which they were supposed to go, while there was more than a trace of the Marx Brothers about General Hopkinson, the divisional commander, sitting awash on his glider, which had been cast off too soon by its American pilot and left to ditch in the sea off the coast. On 5–6 June 1944, the night of the invasion of Normandy, many parachutists and glider-borne troops found themselves miles away from their appointed dropping and landing zones and often without their officers. Lt.-Col. Otway, commanding 9th Parachute Battalion, attacked and destroyed his objective, the German coastal battery at Merville, with a mere handful of his battalion. The rest were all lost, mis-dropped and wandering about Normandy.

I never heard the R.A.F. blamed for any of this.

250 Company were, inevitably, a little vague about how we were likely to find ourselves split up when the division went into action. At first we supposed that, naturally, all our parachute and glider-borne platoons would be airborne, while the remainder of the company – workshops, Quartermaster Greathurst's team, the orderly room and so on – would follow up with the so-called

'seaborne tail' in a ground role, as would the two heavy R.A.S.C. companies. However, in the event things didn't work out like that. It must have been some time during July that we learned that, although the three parachute platoons would remain in England as part of the striking force of the division, ready to fly from home airfields, the rest of 250 Company, including the glider-borne jeep platoons, were to embark for Normandy. I dare say it was thought that in the event there wouldn't be sufficient gliders or aircraft available for jeep platoons, but things turned out differently, as will be told.

At this point I think I will include – and not omit – a short inconsequential; an incident which I remember. At one time after our return from the south I found myself, for some reason or other, again briefly up at Edale, together with David Clark and the 250 Company second-in-command, a nice chap and a good friend of mine called Jack Cranmer-Byng. One fine summer evening the three of us went out to dinner at a country hotel with a well-kept garden all in bloom. We were playing bowls in the sunset on the lawn when suddenly there appeared, drink in hand and accompanied by a major noticeably older than she or ourselves, a staggeringly beautiful girl. She was raven-haired, lustrous and vibrant with confidence in her own appearance and, one could not help thinking as one gazed at her, her own success and renown. 'Have a good look at me,' her air suggested. 'There aren't many about.' She was plainly a girl whose name must be known, and she seemed vaguely familiar – her face, that is, though not the overwhelming impact which only her actual presence could make. Covertly, we asked the barman who she might be. She was Pat Kirkwood, a very popular actress and singing star of the day. Many of my generation must remember her.

XIX

Given the tremendous circumstances of the time, nothing could have been more quiet and uneventful than the crossing of 1st Airborne's 'seaborne tail' to Normandy and our setting up camp in the bocage a good long way behind the British lines. Not a shell, not a German fighter came our way. In fact, the only incident of our crossing that I now recall is of an undramatic nature. 250 Company, minus its parachute element, was drawn up for embarkation on one of the Portsmouth 'hards', standing easy and rather detachedly watching a young naval officer bringing a destroyer up to the quay. You could see him, looking fidgety and nervous, on the bridge. He brought the destroyer in too fast and at too sharp an angle: the port bow struck the concrete with force. But she was going so fast that she went ahead for several yards, and the young officer had no recourse but to take her round the basin and bring her up to the quay a second time. This time, however, she struck the concrete even more bow on, and fetched up shuddering and stationary. At this moment one of her A.B.s – Sailor Vee, no doubt – somewhere below decks, stuck his head out of a porthole, looked genially round at the world and enquired ' 'Oo's doin' this lot, then: Errol fucking Flynn?'

We pussy-footed our jeeps to the Normandy beach along one of the floating causeways of the impressive 'Mulberry' harbour and soon after found ourselves in camp not far from Bayeux. Although there was as yet not a lot to do and not a lot to see except for the partly-tidied-up wreckage of the early battle-fields, we were all strung up to a pitch of excitement which even the coolness of John Gifford couldn't altogether dispel. The division was going into action at last! We had grown tired of khaki-bereted louts outside pubs at closing time shouting 'Yah! Airborne – stillborn!' and similar witticisms. 6th Division had been the flower of the invasion; we felt sure we were to be the flower of the final victory.

I had quite a bit of swanning around to do – locating supply points and so on. I recall my driver, Farley, soundest and steadiest of Worcestershire swede-bashers, staring rather doubtfully at a crossroads Calvary ('One ever hangs where shelled roads part . . . ') and asking 'That s'posed to be Jesus Christ on the cross?' 'Yes,' I said. 'They have them like that here. We'll be seeing a lot more.' We were on our way to Saint-Lô. When we came in sight of it I felt bewildered and overcome. There was nothing to be seen which could be called a town or even the ruins of a town. There was no longer anything, anywhere, recognizable as a building. Saint-Lô, many, many acres in extent, was nothing but a locality strewn with wreckage and fragments. There were no soldiers there, either. General Patton's tanks were already far to the south, forty miles away near Avranches.

I found time to go and see Bayeux Cathedral – the first European cathedral I had ever seen. After English cathedrals, the first impression it made on me was of being cluttered with paltry Popery props, which got in the way of the architecture and of the honest Protestant visitor. All the same, I admired its splendid thirteenth-century Gothic (wishing Hiscocks were there – 'the real significance, er, Adams –'), the western towers and the apsidal chapels round the choir with its lovely carved stalls.

This was the time during which the Allies were holding the Germans where they were by close engagement south of Caen (Hitler himself was holding them there, too, for their commanders, von Kluge and the others, would have liked to pull them out), while the Americans, under Patton, broke through in the west at Avranches and then turned eastward to encircle them. On 20 July there had taken place the abortive assassinative bomb plot, when von Stauffenberg and others had tried to blow up Hitler at his headquarters in East Germany. As everyone knows, it didn't work. That passed us by, really: since it hadn't worked it didn't matter. Only a few old desert veterans couldn't help feeling ambiguously and paradoxically sorry for Rommel, who had been arrested and compelled to shoot himself. We somehow felt he deserved a better end: he was too good for Hitler, really.

All this time there were continual abortive stand-by orders for

1st Division. The division was going to drop to the south of the Germans, to the east of the Germans – anyway, on top of the Germans – at Argentan, at L'Aigle – God only knew where. But as fast as these various plans were made, the military situation would overtake them. John Gifford and the Jontleman never knew where they were from day to day. The plans came so thick and fast that we couldn't help feeling some of them must be a bit half-baked. We were to find out that they certainly were.

It was mid-August when the German crack-up came in Normandy. Largely owing to Hitler's refusal to let them pull out in time, hundreds of thousands of German soldiers, together with their guns, tanks and lorries, were trapped along the line of the Falaise-Argentan road and its environs. The magnificent Polish armoured division had made a dash and sealed off the eastern way out at Chambois and the upper valley of the Dives. Some broken German units had managed to escape, and they were going hell for leather all the way back to Holland. And still 1st Airborne had had no part to play, waiting near their airfields in England to strike the blow which would finish the war.

It so happened that about the end of August Farley and I, on some mission or other, had to drive down the Falaise-Argentan road: some fifteen miles. It was very bad indeed – too bad to attempt to describe. William Golding, author of *Lord of the Flies*, *The Inheritors* and the others, shows a preoccupation with what happens when a society – or just a man – goes beyond the point of disintegration. He should have seen the Falaise pocket. Auden hadn't yet written his great poem 'The Shield of Achilles':

> Column by column, in a cloud of dust,
> They marched away, enduring a belief,
> Whose logic brought them, somewhere else, to grief.

Well, here was the 'somewhere else', after ten or eleven years of the belief. I've never seen a place after an earthquake, but it might look like that. There was no artifact whatever to be seen, large or small, which was not in fragments. No doubt there were mothers and wives now weeping for these horribly bent, stilled, waxen-faced men, but it wasn't our fault. They had set out to kill us if they could. The smell reached you in intermittent waves, rather like azaleas across a garden.

.   .   .

Well, then it came time to follow up, along with 2nd Army's
pursuit. And, my God, did we move? 1st Airborne might drop at
any time – only the High Command knew when – and its seaborne
tail was required to be in the van, close behind our tanks and
infantry. We crossed the Seine on a Bailey bridge at Vernon, and
after that it was simply a question of keeping going night and day.
Sleep when you can, eat when you can. I got so sick of Spam that
I could be really hungry and still unable to face another plate of it.
The cheering villagers were generous with their apples. I remember
our column halting for a time on a road beside which two elderly
Frenchmen, watched by others, were sitting and playing chess while
observing themselves being liberated. I got out of my jeep and
began watching too.

'*Voulez-vous jouer, monsieur? Allons, je vous en prie.*'

So I sat down to play. I got White, and opened P-Q4, followed by
P-QB4. There were mutterings.

'*Gambie de la reine!*'

'*Oui, oui; gambie de la reine; il sait bien jouer.*' (Dear me!)

We had to move on, of course, before the game was finished.
But what a pleasant and – er – liberating thing to happen!

Gisors, Beauvais, Breteüil, Amiens, Doullens, Arras, Tournai in
Belgium and still never a German. About 150 miles – no real
distance today, of course, but hard going in the stop-start
conditions of thousands of vehicles on a narrow axis of advance.
The columns threw up such dust as I'd never seen since my infancy
before tarred roads. As you sat waiting, with engine idling, to go
forward, motor-cyclists riding the other way would flash up out of
the dust and be gone three feet from your elbow.

It was one wet nightfall somewhere short of Ath, on 2 September,
when John Gifford told me that the reserves of canned petrol we
were carrying with us had grown very low. The advance had been
so hectic that we had outrun any close source of supply. Every unit
around was short of petrol. The nearest place where Airborne
Forces were holding any quantity was in the neighbourhood of
Doullens. Doullens lies between Arras and Abbeville, about sixty
miles from where we were. John asked me to take C Platoon, go
to Doullens and bring back as much petrol as possible.

We set out, the men driving the jeeps, the N.C.O.s on their motor-bikes. It was pitch-black – no moon – and of course we could use no lights. The wind was blowing hard and the rain was like a monsoon. There were many other groping vehicles on the roads. I was the only person in the platoon who had a map. It was all that could be done to keep our convoy together. At each road junction, either Sergeant Smith or Sergeant Potter would wait to direct the jeeps and count them all past. Every half-hour I halted the column for the section commanders to report to me that all their men and vehicles were in order. If this sounds over-zealous, you might try it one night: forty light vehicles, each with two trailers, no lights and no guide, in rain and darkness along roads you don't know, in a foreign country. I had never before felt so helpless as a platoon commander. You couldn't get to the blokes to talk to them, the N.C.O.s were soaked through and chilled to the bone and you couldn't share it with them because somebody had to drive in front and read the map. It seemed to go on for ever, and the blackness was full of strangers and tumult. We heard rushings to and fro, so that sometimes we thought we should be trodden down like mire in the streets. And coming to a place where we thought we heard a company of fiends coming forward to meet us, we stopped, and began to muse what we had best to do. Well, Christian made it all right, but God alone knows how all those jeeps contrived to suffer not a single accident or breakdown. (If there had been one, of course, we'd have had to leave the driver with his vehicle.)

It took us a little less than three hours to get to Doullens; pretty good, I thought. Then we had to find out where the petrol dump was, for John had been unable to get a map reference. Farley and I were obliged to leave the platoon closed up and halted, and set off to find someone to ask. I wondered bleakly whether I ought, like Theseus, to be trailing a thread behind me. Would we ever be able to get back to them again? After a few minutes, however, we had the luck to spot a Pegasus directional sign beside the road, and not far away was the dump.

The platoon drove onto the heavy wire mesh doing duty for tracks surrounding the dump. Those who weren't wet through already were able to put it right now, for we had to get out and load up. We all had army groundsheets, of course, but anyone who has worn one in a steady downpour knows how little comfort they really were. The blokes loaded, the N.C.O.s loaded, I loaded. We crammed every jeep and every trailer as full as possible with petrol. (By this stage of the war they were British jerricans.) The corporal in charge of the dump asked me into his tent to sign the necessary papers, although he said it didn't matter how much we took. At length we were ready to return.

Going back was much the same, except that everyone was very tired, and hungry as well. We reached the company location – a field much like any other – and the platoon off-loaded the cans while I went to report to John Gifford. I felt we'd done rather well.

'How much did you get altogether?' asked John.

I told him.

'It's not enough.'

'Sir, every jeep and trailer was bung full.'

'Well.' John paused. 'You'd better go back and get some more.'

'Now, sir?'

'Yes, please.'

I went back and gathered the N.C.O.s. They took it very well. They were a fine platoon but, setting that aside, I was beginning to wonder how much more they *could*, physically and mentally, do. Mere endurance was not enough. To drive a jeep and trailer in convoy you had to be reasonably alert, and more than reasonably in these conditions. Well, we would find out. I was clear about two things. To read the map and find the way was my responsibility and I dared not delegate it. It couldn't be done properly on a motor-bike. But, secondly, I didn't think the N.C.O.s could go on safely riding motor-bikes much further. We might perhaps be able to manage with fewer, but some motor-bikes there obviously had to be. How few? Sergeant Smith thought five. I reckoned six. I asked the assembled platoon whether anyone thought he had the know-how to ride a bike in these conditions. One man volunteered. He was very young, a boy named Driver Sutton. I want to put it down here that Driver Sutton did everything a sheep-dog motor-cyclist ought to do throughout the whole of that nasty journey. He was excellent.

That left five other motor-bikes and a total of nine N.C.O.s. Sergeant Smith worked out some sort of turn-and-turn-about system to give everyone a stand-down during the trip, and off we set again.

It would be tedious to prolong this account; but we got there, loaded up and started back without accident. I was beginning to feel a sort of affinity with Captain Cook. That was the whole point – that he *didn't* have an accident – or only one, anyway. He must have had some first-class subordinates, don't you think? I recall two things about our return journey.

During the first run, we had all perceived along one length of the very dark road a vile smell – the smell of corruption. As we were coming back from the petrol dump for the second time, the rain gradually stopped and light came into the sky. We were now able to see what it was that was nauseating us. The adjacent fields were full of dead horses; cart-horses, most of them. Our Typhoons had destroyed all the Germans' motorized transport, and in their retreat they had commandeered horses and carts for their gear. But the Typhoons had got them, too. They looked so pathetic and pitiable, those great, innocent beasts, their legs sticking stiffly up at all unnatural angles and foul white bubbles blown from every orifice of their bodies.

We were just getting over this when suddenly Driver Farley said (just like a policeman) ''Ullo, 'ullo, what's this?' He had seen quicker than I. Three figures in uniform were approaching us down the slope of a field. They were Germans, evidently bent on surrender. We pulled up and I gestured to them to come up to me.

One was Luftwaffe. He looked like a veteran and turned out to be one, for I found in his pocket an iron cross (made of plastic) which bore the date '1939'. He also had a picquet pack which I've still got. The second was an infantry officer in jackboots, a mere child who looked about seventeen. The third was a Kaporal, black-haired and dour. I motioned them into the jeep and, when we came to the next small town, handed them over to the Maquis, in accordance with standing orders. That was the last we saw of them.

When we finally got back, the company had already up and gone. John had left someone behind to tell us where. The going was easier that day, even though we were all so sleepless; there seemed to be less on the roads. We caught up and that morning were among the first Allied troops to enter Brussels.

· · ·

Guards Armoured Division, the spearhead of the Allied pursuit,

reached Brussels on 3 September. Hard on their heels followed the
'seaborne tail' of 1st Airborne Division, ready to go forward as
soon as the airborne attack on Holland should begin.

I have been told that the liberation of Paris had nothing on the
liberation of Brussels, and I can believe it. Every street was
thronged with people, laughing, weeping, cheering, climbing on
our jeeps and lorries, covering us with flowers and paper-chains,
pinning red-black-and-yellow emblems and boutonnieres on our
airborne smocks; girls by the hundred kissing us, men pressing
upon us glasses of everything you can imagine. *('M'sieu voilà, le vrai*
Scotch whisky! *Pour ce jour je l'ai caché quatre ans! Vive*
l'Angleterre!') Everywhere the bells were ringing, bands playing. It
was unreal – dream-like. I found, somehow or other, in my jeep,
a pretty Belgian girl of about my own age – twenty-four. Her name
was Janine Flamand, the daughter of (I think, having visited her
home) a rather wealthy wine merchant. As we rode on, something
amusing occurred which showed up my rotten French. The jeep was
moving jerkily, as best it could, through the clamouring benediction, when Janine suddenly cried *'Oh, j'ai perdue l'equilibre!'* In all
the hubbub I heard it phonetically as *'lait qui libre'*, and wondered
what on earth free milk could have to do with all this. I knew they
were all *'libre'* now, but the *'lait'*? An idiom? Anyway, Janine got
liberated good and proper. During the next ten days – and later –
I had quite a lot to do with the Flamand family and liked them
very much.

John Gifford, while certainly no killjoy, sat a bit loose to all this
wild melarky. It was not only that he had the Company to be
thinking of. It was, rather, that this kind of rapturous frolicking
and emotional carousal with strangers wasn't compatible with his
naturally impassive, self-possessed temperament. I have a memory
of our being together one evening in some sort of club or dance-
hall, with a band. We were continually being importuned to dance,
of course, and John obliged with the best of them; but after a while
the band struck up a conga. The conga of those days was an affair
simple to the point of childishness. Everyone formed a line; you held
the girl in front of you round the waist and the girl behind you held
you round the waist. There might be a hundred or so people thus
engaged. Then the chain cavorted rather ponderously round the
room, flinging out right and left legs alternately as they went. I

recall watching John's back, four places ahead of me. It looked what you'd call unco-operative and long-suffering. Later that night, when we were out of the city and snugly back in our village near Louvain, he pointed to the brightly coloured wooden Belgian emblem pinned on my shoulder and said quietly 'I think we'll take these things off, shall we? We've liberated Belgium now.'

We were comfortable enough in that village, hearing and discounting military rumours; getting the vehicles – and ourselves – to rights after the rigours of the advance from Normandy; the blokes going into Brussels in relays for rest and recreation – rather more of the latter – and at last receiving letters from home. I found I could generally communicate what I wanted to in French, but understanding it was more difficult, because the locals spoke so idiomatically and quickly. The officers' billets were in a friendly farmhouse. I remember that one early afternoon it began to rain heavily. After a minute or two Yvette, the grown-up daughter of the house, came running in with her hands and shoes dirty from the garden and poured out to me a torrent of urgent French. *'Lentement, mademoiselle, je vous en prie: plus lentement!'* Yvette, hopping from foot to foot and drawing in her breath with hard-won self-control and patience, said *'Les fenêtres'* – (nod) – *'de votre chambre'* – (nod) – *'sont ouvertes'* – (nod) *'et la pluie –'* The franc dropped, and I was half-way up the stairs.

Phil Bushby, our Workshops officer, was a much better linguist, and in the evenings used to read the local newspaper to get a bit of atmosphere. I recall him, after dinner one evening, reading out from the 'Wanted' column: '*"Bonne sérieuse"*: how would you translate that, John? "Steady girl"?'

It was all too short a rest and refit in the autumn sunshine. John, who was now acting C.R.A.S.C. of the seaborne tail (Colonel Packe being in England with Jack Cranmer-Byng, Paddy Kavanagh and the rest of the airborne element), was often summoned to conferences in Brussels. Returning one afternoon he sent for me.

'Dick, three of your glider-borne jeep sections are to go back to England today, as soon as they can be got ready. Will you see to it now, please?'

'Am I to go too, sir?'

'No.'

'Does it matter which sections go?'

'You can decide that yourself.'

'Is it for –'

John looked at his watch, looked away and then at the papers in his hand. I saluted and set off for C Platoon lines.

There was no section of the seven in the platoon with which one would seize the opportunity to part. Sergeant Smith, Sergeant Potter and I decided to put seven bits of paper into a beret and draw three out. The three names which came out were Corporal Bater, Corporal Pickering and Corporal Hollis. Level-headed and cool, they got their men together and were off within the hour. I was not to see them again until well after the end of the war.

A few days later we found ourselves once more on the road, in and out of the company of Guards Armoured Division, each of whose vehicles bore their cognizance of an open eye. We were getting to know the sight of that eye. Slowly, we moved about forty miles north-eastward, towards the border with Holland. Around and ahead of us were heavy concentrations of troops and armour – that much we could tell. Most of us passed that night dozing in our jeeps, though some were lucky enough to be invited, subject to instant call by their mates, into their homes by the friendly Dutch. We were in Limburg, a little south of what was then called the Escaut Canal, but which I see is now called (in *The Times Atlas*) the Kempisch Canal, and about thirty miles south of Eindhoven in Holland.

The following morning, 17 September 1944, John Gifford told his officers what was going to happen. We were on the threshold of a major operation code-named Market Garden. 'Market' was the airborne part and 'Garden' was the land offensive. The intention was to get the Allied 2nd Army, in one blow, across the Rhine and into northern Holland. This was expected to finish the war before the end of the year. The operation would begin early that same afternoon, soon after one o'clock (1300 hours), when the first lift of parachute and glider-borne troops would arrive from England.

The airborne army, three divisions strong, was due to land in relays during the next forty-eight hours, at different places along the fifty-odd miles between Eindhoven in Brabant and Arnhem in Gelderland. Not far east of its great delta at Dordrecht and Rotterdam, the Rhine divides into two arms – the Waal and the Neder Rijn – each a formidable river in itself. Only a few miles south of the Waal runs the river Maas. The 101st American Airborne Division were going to seize Eindhoven and the road leading northward to Grave. Meanwhile, 82nd American Airborne Division would capture the bridge over the Maas at Grave, and also Nijmegen, with its great bridge (the biggest road bridge in Europe) over the Waal. The star role, however, had been given to 1st British Airborne, who would in a few hours be in possession of the bridge over the Neder Rijn at Arnhem.

2nd Army, of which we were a very humble part – non-combatant, really – would attack that same afternoon, to synchronize with the airborne landings. They would advance on the axis of the Valkenswaard-Eindhoven road, linking up with 101st American Airborne. From there they would go on northward to Grave, cross the Maas bridge held by 82nd American Airborne, reach Nijmegen, cross the Waal and by Tuesday evening 19 September, be at Arnhem. There, then, our lot would meet up with Paddy, Jack Cranmer-Byng and also, no doubt, Corporals Bater, Pickering and Hollis. John said that the planned final objective of the whole operation, once 1st Airborne and the land forces had linked up at Arnhem, was Apeldoorn, about fifteen miles north. After that, the High Command (S.H.A.E.F.) would assess the situation and (as Captain Stanhope in *Journey's End* says to his sergeant-major) advance and win the war.

This was heady stuff. This was what airborne soldiering was all about; a swift, dramatic blow to finish the enemy for good and all. The Allies had total air supremacy – not a Jerry plane in the sky. The Germans had already been smashed to pieces in Normandy and had retreated to Holland without offering further resistance. Their morale was plainly shattered. 1st Airborne was now to play a major part in the Allies' triumph: it would be a *gâteau* promenade of appropriate distinction.

I passed this information on to the four-sevenths of my platoon who were still around. I have never known morale higher. The men were excited and eager to go. About mid-day the company had a hot dinner and then waited about in the fine, slightly hazy autumn weather.

Our gliders and parachute aircraft (though we hadn't actually been told this at the time) were to fly into Holland along two separate routes from south-east England. The northern route lay over Walcheren and thence a little south of 's Hertogenbosch, where they were to diverge to the various dropping zones and landing zones of 1st Airborne and 82nd American. The southern route, 101st American Division's, lay over Ostend and Ghent and then, a little east of Louvain, turned northward for their dropping and landing zones between Eindhoven and Veghel.

It was the fly-in along this latter route that we watched. About one o'clock the planes and gliders came in sight and passed right over us. I don't know the official numbers, but I would guess that we must have seen about a hundred bombers towing Horsa gliders and perhaps five hundred parachute aircraft. No such sight had ever been seen before and probably never will be again. The noise of the engines filled the sky, drowning all other sounds. The ground seemed stilled and the sky moving. The continuous streams of aircraft stretched out of sight, appearing, approaching and passing on overhead. They were quite low and from time to time we could plainly see people at the open doors and wave to them. I didn't hear anyone in the Company utter any comment. We simply looked at each other with a wild surmise. Here, mighty beyond anything we could have imagined, was the war's great climax. Even Driver Rowland, the platoon cynic, was plainly staggered. This lot was certainly not being done by Errol Flynn.

Now I know it tells in the books how General Horrocks, commanding XXX Corps, began his ground offensive as the first airborne troops landed that early afternoon, and how the Guards Armoured Division ran into tough opposition, but by nightfall had covered about nine miles towards Eindhoven. Horrocks has been criticized for not pressing on that night with fresh armoured troops, and for not putting in an infantry battalion to probe forward in the darkness and harass the Germans. I'm not competent to give an opinion. According to the plan as told to us, XXX Corps were supposed to reach Eindhoven that night, Nijmegen the following night and Arnhem on the next (Tuesday) afternoon. As everyone knows, this didn't happen.

However, 250 Company knew nothing of all this, waiting in the fog of war to drive northward up the Eindhoven road. The weather grew worse and by the next morning – Monday morning – it was cloudy and raining; the notorious weather of Arnhem week, which was to be a major factor in preventing our Typhoons from giving

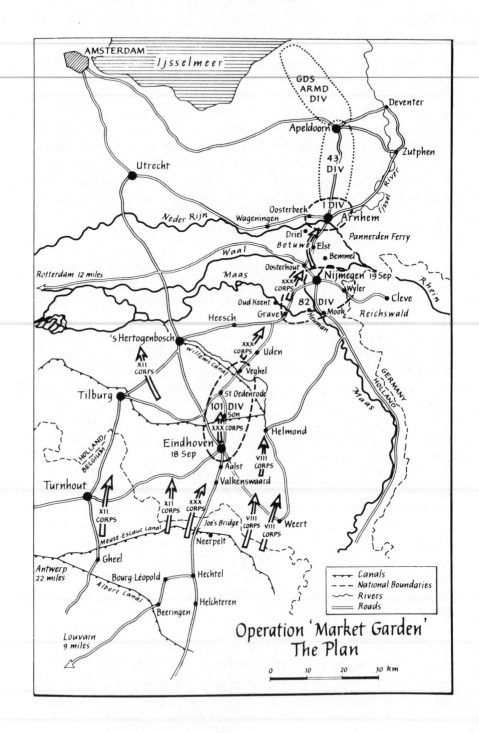

AMSTERDAM
Ijsselmeer

GDS
ARMD
DIV

Deventer

Apeldoorn

Zutphen

Utrecht

43
DIV

Neder Rijn

Oosterbeek
Wageningen
I DIV
Arnhem

Driel
Betuwe
Elst
Pannerden Ferry

Iyssel River

Waal

Bemmel

Maas

Oosterhout
Nijmegen 19 Sep

Rotterdam 12 miles

XXX
CORPS
Wyler

Oud Keent
82 DIV
Cleve

Heesch
Grave
Mook
Reichswald

's Hertogenbosch

XXX
CORPS
Uden

Maas

XII
CORPS

Willems Canal

Veghel

St Oedenrode

GERMANY
HOLLAND

Tilburg

101 DIV
Son

XXX CORPS

Helmond

HOLLAND
BELGIUM

Eindhoven
18 Sep

Aalst
VIII
CORPS

Turnhout

XII
CORPS

XII
CORPS

XXX
CORPS

Valkenswaard

VIII
CORPS
VIII
CORPS
Weert

Meuse-Escaut Canal

Joe's Bridge

Neerpelt

Gheel

Antwerp
22 miles

Bourg-Léopold
Hechtel

Albert Canal

Helchteren

Beeringen

Louvain
9 miles

	Canals
	National Boundaries
	Rivers
	Roads

Operation 'Market Garden'
The Plan

0   10   20   30 km

1st Airborne the vital support they needed.

It was Tuesday afternoon – a nasty, wet day – before we went into what had become known as 'The Corridor'. We had seen great numbers of tanks and lorried infantry go past us, and no end of sappers with loads of bridging materials; and we had watched grubby bands of German prisoners being shepherded to the rear. More gliders and parachute aircraft – the second lift – had flown over us during the previous day. We had no least idea that anything might be wrong. Very likely, we supposed, XXX Corps were even now making whoopee at Arnhem with General Urquhart and the boys. All the time there was gunfire and throughout the nights there had been continuous noise and movement of vehicles. We were all sleepless. Still, that didn't matter: now we were on the way.

I have only vague recollections of our journey up the Corridor to Nijmegen: about sixty to seventy miles. The extraordinary thing is that all the way we never saw a German and never came under fire. It was slow going, as usual. Along the road were signs, put up by the Sappers, warning against leaving the road, the verges not yet having been cleared of mines. We met with groups of American 101st, exhausted but glad to be alive. I recall a huge American signaller, using wire and pliers at the top of a tall telegraph pole and singing at the top of his voice 'This is the G.I. jive – Man alive –'. In the little town of Veghel we waited a long time in the dark and the men quite rightly went to sleep. There were rumours of a German counter-attack and of The Corridor having been cut, but nothing happened. At length we were told to get moving again, and the whole place came to life with a great deal of noise – shouting and movement – in the midst of which an outraged voice yelled 'Here, cut it out, all the damn' row! *We've* got to *stay* here!'

I suppose it must have been very early on Wednesday morning that we crossed the Maas on the captured bridge at Grave. It was all high girders, and stuck between two ribs thereof was an unexploded shell. That shell looked distinctly wobbly. From Grave it was only about seven or eight miles to Nijmegen, where fighting was going on near the bridge and along the south bank of the 400-yard-wide river.

By this time we had all become more or less aware that the original scheme couldn't have gone according to schedule; nevertheless, we were still in no doubt that we would soon get to Arnhem, where the 1st Division would be in possession of the bridge. 250 Company was ordered to camp in a field on the southern outskirts of Nijmegen, right next to two batteries of 25-pounder guns which were firing in support of the troops advancing northwards from Nijmegen. I'd never felt so tired or sleepless in my life. And still it rained and rained.

By that evening we knew – everyone in Nijmegen couldn't but know – that things had gone badly wrong. The plain truth was that it was proving a hard and dreadful business to get over the Nijmegen bridge, to cross the Waal and establish a bridgehead on the northern bank. On either side of and below the embankment carrying the road northward to Arnhem lay the Betuwe polder – low-lying, marshy land, partly flooded. It was impracticable for tanks. German artillery was firing on Nijmegen. German infantry were resisting the Allied efforts to cross the bridge.

Why hadn't the Germans blown the bridges at Arnhem and Nijmegen, reader, you may well ask? The answer is that General-feldmarschall Model had said not. He took the view that the bridges could be successfully defended against the Allied advance, and that they would then be needed for a German counter-attack. Other German generals had doubts about this, but Model's view prevailed.

By the Wednesday afternoon, soon after we had arrived in Nijmegen, the Grenadier Guards and the American 82nd had fought their way to the southern end of the huge bridge, below which the river was running (as Geoffrey Powell tells in *The Devil's Birthday*) at eight knots. The Americans, whose skill and courage throughout this dreadful week were beyond all praise, then crossed about a mile below the bridge in light assault craft. In the face of heavy German fire, only about half of them got across. Many were hit; many drowned. Yet those who got over routed the Germans on the other side, while meantime our troops had driven the enemy out of Nijmegen altogether – back over the bridge.

Four Guards Armoured tanks followed across and still the bridge wasn't blown. Two of those tanks were hit, but the other two demolished the German anti-tank guns. By nightfall the Guards and the Yanks had joined up at a village called Lent, just north of the bridge, and the bridge and the Waal crossing were safely in

Allied hands.

That night, we in 250 Company were all waiting for the order to join the advance to Arnhem and the bridge. As we waited, John Gifford characteristically sat his officers down to a four of bridge. I'm afraid I didn't play very well. 'But, Dick, we could have made four spades.' (Bang!) 'Sorry, sir.' (Bang!)

The order never came. It wasn't until about eleven o'clock on Thursday morning that Guards Armoured got orders to press on up the Arnhem road. During the night the Germans had rallied: they were now ready and waiting. The tanks, of course, couldn't get off the road. As Geoffrey Powell says, they were like shooting-range targets at a fairground. The three leading tanks were knocked out and our infantry, doing everything they could to attack across the wet, flat polder on either side, had a very bad time. In brief, there was no getting on to Arnhem that day.

Meanwhile, what had been happening to Paddy Kavanagh and Sergeant McDowell, to Jack Cranmer-Byng, to Captain Gell (commanding our third parachute platoon), and to my three sections of glider-borne jeeps? By Friday we at least knew how desperate the general situation was, for on the Thursday night two senior officers of 1st Airborne, Lt.-Col. MacKenzie and Lt.-Col. Myers, acting on General Urquhart's orders, had escaped from north of the Neder Rijn and reported to the headquarters of XXX Corps details of what was happening at Oosterbeek.

Today everybody knows, of course, the essential story: how the division's first lift dropped on that fine Sunday afternoon, 17 September, and set off the eight miles eastward for the bridge: how Colonel John Frost, with a good proportion of 2nd Parachute Battalion, reached it, together with Major Freddie Gough, commanding the Reconnaissance Squadron. With them were a few divisional troops; some Sappers, some Gunners and our Captain Gell's parachute platoon. David Clark was there, too. The rest of the division were prevented by the Germans from getting into Arnhem, and after very heavy losses on the afternoon of Tuesday, 19 September, were forced into a defensive perimeter, about a mile in diameter, most vulnerably based on Divisional Headquarters in the Hartenstein hotel at Oosterbeek, about a mile or so west of Arnhem. The southern end of the perimeter rested on the north bank of the Neder Rijn, and here there was a ferry of sorts. This was why it was considered worth hanging on. As explained, by Wednesday evening the Nijmegen crossing was in Allied hands, and it was still expected that the 2nd Army would reach the south bank of the Neder Rijn in force, take the ferry and relieve 1st Airborne.

During the week the eastern and western sides of the Oosterbeek perimeter were gradually squeezed closer together. By Sunday 24 September, they were only about half a mile apart, and full of holes at that. The Germans were prevented from cutting off the division's precarious hold on some 600 yards of the north bank, to the east by a scratch force under the famous Major Dickie Lonsdale, one of the heroes of Arnhem, and to the west by what was left of the Border Regiment, who suffered badly.

By Thursday morning, 21 September, all resistance at the bridge had ceased. The remnants of 2nd Para., Colonel Frost (badly wounded), Freddie Gough, David Clark, Captain Gell and what was left of his platoon were prisoners in German hands. I want to emphasize that the whole division was only meant to hold the bridge for forty-eight hours. Colonel Frost and his men had held it for about eighty hours, against much heavier German opposition than had been expected, and if XXX Corps had come they could have had the crossing.

Of some 10,000 men of 1st Airborne who landed north of the Neder Rijn at Arnhem, about 1,400 were killed and over 6,000 – about one-third of them wounded – were taken prisoner. By Thursday morning, 3,000 sleepless, starving men were holding the Oosterbeek perimeter. 4th Parachute Brigade had virtually ceased to exist. (In the event, it did cease to exist: the survivors were transferred to 1st Para. Brigade and 4th was never re-formed.)

Corporals Bater, Pickering and Hollis, their blokes and their jeeps all fell into the hands of the Germans. One soldier, a nice chap called Driver Eggleton, a Newbury man, escaped with the help of the Dutch Resistance after the glider he was in had force-landed in Holland short of the true landing zone.

Jack Cranmer-Byng (hit in the hand) and his platoon were among those shut into the Oosterbeek box. So were Paddy Kavanagh and Sergeant McDowell. I will now relate what happened to Paddy.

During the week, despite the adverse weather, planes were flown from England to drop supplies to 1st Airborne. They had a bad time from German flak and many were lost. There was no ground-to-air communication (a bad fault, surely?). On account of this and also because the situation on the ground was so confused and in the rain visibility was so bad, most of the panniers fell outside the Oosterbeek perimeter. Colonel Packe asked Paddy to take his platoon and try to collect what he could of the nearer ones.

Paddy and Sergeant McDowell, their blokes and their jeeps set out from the 1st Airborne lines and drove down a narrow, empty lane bordered by fairly thick woodland. As they were coming over a little hump-backed bridge they were caught in German small-arms fire. Corporal Wiggins and several more died instantly. Several jeeps were smashed up.

Paddy grabbed a Bren gun and leapt into the ditch beside the verge, whence he returned the German fire. Sergeant McDowell joined him.

'Take the blokes, sergeant!' yelled Paddy. 'Get them out of here – back through the woods. I'll cover you.'

'You sure of that, sir?' asked McDowell.

'Yes,' answered Paddy. 'Get out! That's an order!'

Somehow or other Sergeant McDowell got most of the platoon together inside the edge of the wood. Three or four lay writhing and screaming on the road. There was blood everywhere. Paddy, who had several magazines, continued firing. The platoon retreated on foot. After a minute or two they stopped to listen. Sergeant McDowell told me how you could hear the *rrrrip, rrrrip* of the German Schmeissers against the slower rat-tat-tat of the Bren – a dreadful counterpoint. Suddenly there was an explosion, and then nothing more.

Paddy lies among the others in the divisional cemetery at Oosterbeek.

Let other pens dwell on guilt and misery; the misery of that weekend at Nijmegen, anyway. Until the very end we continued to believe – not just to hope, but to feel sure – that we *would* get to the Neder Rijn and reach the division at Oosterbeek. On Thursday evening the Polish Independent Parachute Brigade dropped on the south bank of the Neder Rijn at Driel, more or less opposite the 1st Airborne perimeter, and were joined next day by some of the Household Cavalry from Nijmegen. Only a few of the Poles, however, managed to get across the river in the mere couple of amphibious vehicles (DUKWs) available. The Somerset Light Infantry, the D.C.L.I. (Durhams) and the Worcestershire went forward from Nijmegen. Heavy fighting in the Betuwe – the low-lying area between Nijmegen and Arnhem – went on all Saturday and Sunday. The long and short of it was, however, that the Germans couldn't be entirely driven away and no effective link could be established between 2nd Army at Nijmegen and 1st Airborne in the box.

Throughout all this the 'seaborne tail' of 250 Company had nothing to do but to wait, uselessly, at Nijmegen. We might as well not have been there. It was on Sunday evening, the 24th, that John Gifford said to me 'Apparently, if it's no better by tomorrow night they're going to pull the division out, back over the river.'

'Pull them *out*, sir? You mean, the whole thing's off? We're not going to Arnhem at all?'

'Looks like it.'

And as everyone knows, that is what happened. Of the 10,000 men who had landed at Arnhem, about 2,160 got back during the Monday–Tuesday night, the 25–26 September. Among them was Jack Cranmer-Byng, with a handful of our lot, including Sergeant McDowell. Jack subsequently got the M.C.

It is interesting to record what was going to happen if they hadn't. Generalfeldmarschall Model wasn't going to send in his soldiers – even with armour – finally to reduce the starving Oosterbeek box. He knew what they could expect. 1st Airborne was going to be destroyed by heavy artillery at long range. Very brave and prudent, I'm sure.

At some time in the early evening of Tuesday, the 26th, I was sent down to the centre of Nijmegen to ask the Divisional Camp Commandant, Major Newton-Dunn (generally known in 1st Airborne as Hoo Flung Dung), about certain arrangements made for 250 Company. I asked him whether, as the survivors had come in during the night, he had happened to see Jack Cranmer-Byng. Hoo Flung replied that he hadn't been able to notice any one particular person more than another. Then he said 'And if you like I'll show you why.' He guided me a short distance to a huge building – I think it must have been a gymnasium – with a wooden floor and no tables, chairs or any other furniture in it at all. That's all I can recall about it. It was all in twilight, so you couldn't see much anyway. As we approached the open door, Hoo Flung laid a finger to his lips.

Inside, those who had got back from Oosterbeek were lying on the floor, huddled asleep under grey army blankets. The majority had not slept for a week. At Driel, during the previous night, they had been given a light, hot meal (they had been starving for about five days) and then, having got to Nijmegen, been put in the gym. to sleep.

On account of the dim light in the big building, visibility was limited. The grey rows of unconscious, motionless shapes stretched away until they blurred and you couldn't make out the far end.

As well as Paddy, we had lost two other officers killed: Lt. Daniels, the big chap whose blokes C Platoon had succeeded at Edale: and Thompson, who had been subaltern in one of the other para. platoons.

Later, looking at the lists, I learned that people whom I had known well at Horris Hill and Bradfield were also among those killed: Roddy Gow; David Madden. Their names are on the appropriate war memorials.

XX

'If you did not get *all* the bridges, it was not worth going at all.'
This is the well-known comment of Brigadier Shan Hackett,
commanding 4th Parachute Brigade at Arnhem. Many efforts were
made at the time – by Mr Churchill, by General Montgomery,
General Browning and General Urquhart (who had suffered more
than almost anyone) – to represent Operation Market Garden as a
victory. For the sake of public morale, they had to say something:
so they said it was a triumph for the Allies. It was not. Though
reflecting nothing but enormous credit on the courage and endurance of the British and American combatants, it was nevertheless
a failure. The intention had been to seize the three bridges, to get
them securely into the possession of 2nd Army and thus enable the
Allies to cross the Rhine. This was not achieved, and it was no good
trying to represent what actually happened as 'ninety-per-cent
success' (General Montgomery). You might as well say that the
answer to a sum was ninety-per-cent correct, or that a woman
was ninety-per-cent pregnant.

1st Airborne Division, that unparalleled formation, the like of
which had never been seen, lay shattered literally to fragments. The
two parachute brigades (each consisting originally of some 3,000
men) came back from Arnhem about two companies strong in all:
1st Airlanding Brigade numbered well under 1,000. After Arnhem,
the 1st Division never went into action again. Not only its numbers
but the superb morale with which it had gone to Arnhem had been
lowered. The general feeling was that while the operation had been
a gamble worth trying, the Division had been let down by the
failure of 2nd Army to arrive as planned. The planning, of course,
had been too hasty; yet if it had been deferred, German resistance
would have been still more strongly built up during the time.

There will always be argument. I personally believe that despite the fog of war, the thing could have been done better. The fundamental fault, at Command level, was over-confidence. After the German debacle in Normandy, everyone supposed that now that the war was so obviously lost, the Wehrmacht would have no real heart for further resistance. If we seized the bridges, they wouldn't put up very much of a fight. But they did.

The time-table for the airborne landings, spread over more than twenty-four hours, was sadly amiss. With the 'planes we had, all three divisions could have been landed in twelve hours and should have been.

The dropping zones and landing zones for 1st Airborne were ill-chosen. They were too far away from the Arnhem bridge. The Germans had time to get themselves together while our men were doing their best to cover the eight-mile distance.

1st Airborne's wireless sets didn't work properly in that sort of arboriferous country and over those distances, which meant that there was no proper communication between General Urquhart and his brigadiers and other senior officers. Also, there was no communication from Division back to Corps headquarters.

The weather prevented proper air support being given: that was just one of the bits of bad luck.

With all these things in the scale against them, nevertheless the Division succeeded in carrying out their intention. They had been ordered to hold the bridge until Tuesday afternoon, 19 September. In the event Colonel Frost held it for more than twenty-four hours longer than that.

Why didn't the 2nd Army arrive? Right from the start, at the Escaut Canal, German resistance was stronger than expected. It had not been foreseen that Nijmegen Bridge and the Waal crossing would be so difficult, or that the wet polder land beyond would constitute fatal obstruction.

Geoffrey Powell thinks that General Horrocks and XXX Corps were at fault, that they *might* have got to Arnhem on Tuesday afternoon if they had pressed on harder. He was a combatant of 1st Airborne, and himself suffered terribly at Oosterbeek. As I didn't, I won't intrude a personal view: but I'm not disagreeing with Colonel Powell. XXX Corps didn't do what they'd undertaken to do, anyway. That's beyond argument.

What it came down to was that 1st Airborne Division, the nonpareil, had been lost in a gamble open to criticism which, even if it had succeeded, would not (it is now known) have ended the war by Christmas. I have more than once wept for the division: and in *Traveller* I tried, under a cloak of fantasy, to depict something of what they suffered as they fought on, on their lost wicket. Yet like Traveller, 1st Airborne themselves were not defeated. *They* performed what they had set out to do.

. . .

250 Company, now having once more on its strength Jack Cranmer-Byng and such N.C.O.s and men as had come back from Oosterbeek, returned down the Corridor and so to the Brussels area again. While we were there I went to see the Flamands. I remember knocking on the locked and bolted door at about eight o'clock in the evening. Chez Flamand was like a fortress. Those were the sort of times we were living in.

'Qui est là?' called M. Flamand stoutly, behind the door.

'C'est Lieutenant Adams!'

'Qui?'

'C'est le lieutenant anglais des airportées!'

'Ah! Par exemple!'

It seemed both strange and sad to eat dinner at a table with a cloth and silver: they couldn't have been kinder to me. I struggled as hard as I could to explain that I hadn't been involved in the action, but I don't think they really believed me: they didn't want to, you see.

We were flown back to England and in due course returned to our old location at Lincoln. Here John Gifford told a friend of mine, Peter Allsop, and myself that we were both promoted to Captain.

We still had no reliable news about any of my missing N.C.O.s and men, and one of my first jobs was to write – as best I could – to the next of kin. Thank God all C Platoon's missing eventually turned out to be prisoners.

It transpired that Paddy had no next of kin: no one in the world; or no one known to 250 Company, anyway. So an auction was held of his things. Paddy had a well-known duffle-coat, fawn in colour and fastening at the front with loops of rope. He had often worn it on duty, over his uniform, when strictly speaking he shouldn't have: but John had winked at it. The duffle-coat was part of him, like Mr Churchill and his cigar. I bought it for a memento: I've still got it somewhere.

Suppose the whole Division had gained their objectives in and around Arnhem and held the bridge (living on what?) for a week, would the 2nd Army have come? *Could* they have come, across that flooded land between Nijmegen and the Neder Rijn?

After Arnhem, the attention of S.H.A.E.F. was turned right away from Holland and directed further south. We left the brave Dutch to be famished and tortured by the Nazis right through the winter. The war was to last more than another seven dreary, plodding months, based on Eisenhower's dubious strategy of the Broad Front (clean contrary to everything in Clausewitz). Unless you experienced them, reader, you can't imagine how depressing those months were.

One of Paddy's men was called Charley Lawes. Charley, before the war, had been a professional boxer, and he had become what my mother used to call 'a bit biffy, dear.' Charley was all right as long as he knew exactly what he had to do. Before they dropped, Paddy gave him a P.I.A.T. (Projector Infantry Anti-Tank) and told him that, come what may, he was not to relinquish it. 'Got that, Charley?' 'Yessir, yessir: all right, right, sir.' A P.I.A.T. weighed a great deal more than a rifle. Charley carried that P.I.A.T. from the dropping zone to the Oosterbeek box. He was in the ambush where Paddy was killed and he carried the P.I.A.T. back through the woods. On the night of the evacuation he took it across the Neder Rijn and carried it the eight miles to Nijmegen, where he finally relinquished it. No one had told him to do so before.

. . .

In the event I was to serve another fifteen months in Airborne Forces. I can't say I really enjoyed them, or enjoyed being a captain. I missed C Platoon very much – they never re-formed, anyway – and I shared the general feeling of disappointment and reduced spirits. As far as I was concerned, the odds were gone, and there was nothing left remarkable beneath the visiting moon.

Now, at last, there was time and opportunity to send me on a parachuting course at Ringway. Jumping I found frightening – most people do – but I was fortunate in having a first-class stick commander, John Pengelly of the Devons – the Bloody Eleventh. Our despatcher, Jimmy Blyth, was also first-rate. John Pengelly joked and clowned and set us all an example we couldn't not follow. Jumping is really a matter of group morale. You feel you can't let the others down. How people jump alone I've never understood.

The Ringway training people found me out all right. When I got back to Lincoln, John Gifford – who, like Gallio, cared for none of these things – gave me my confidential report to keep. 'This officer was of a nervous disposition, although he assumed a pose which suggested confidence. He was always bright and cheerful, and kept the spirits of his stick high by being "the life of the party". Rather nervous but jumped without hesitation.'

The course of eight jumps included a night jump. This is supposed to be in darkness, so that you don't know when you're going to hit the ground. Ours took place in brilliant, full moonlight, with snow lying. As I floated down from eight hundred feet, there was a superb view of the shining, niveous landscape stretching away to disappear into the far distance.

There is an old airborne chestnut about the night jump. The last jump of a certain course happened to be the night jump, and it was very dark. In the darkness, a voice was heard descending, shouting 'I've got my wings! I've got my wings!' Then there was a bump, followed by silence. One of the instructors said ''*E's* got 'is wings! Bring 'im over 'ere and I'll give 'im 'is bloody 'alo!'

The completion of our course was delayed by something like three weeks by bad weather, too windy and stormy for jumping. When at last the weather let up, we still had three jumps to go. The authorities wanted our lot out of Ringway: we were gumming up the works, staying there. We did those three jumps in one and the same day. I wonder whether any other course has ever done three jumps in one day? After we dispersed, I lost touch with John Pengelly, as I had lost touch with Roy Emberson. Horses for ever saying good-bye.

· · ·

There was another good-bye at about this time which hit me hard. I lost Jennifer. I'm told that nowadays things have changed and I'm glad to hear it; but in those days, as a rule, if an unmarried girl became the lover of an unmarried man, the relationship didn't remain on an even keel indefinitely. The girl would not allow it to: she would press the man to marry her and if he wouldn't she would break off the relationship. (There was no question of two unmarried people living together openly, you see: they'd have been ostracized, unless perhaps they were very rich or else members of the comparatively enclosed world of the stage. Throughout my entire 'teens and twenties during the 'thirties and 'forties, I personally never knew – or even knew of – a single unmarried couple living together.)

Yet how could I possibly marry Jennifer? I loved her all right, but from my point of view it simply wasn't on. I was twenty-four, stuck in the Army indefinitely – not just till Hitler was finished – when? – but until the Japs were finished, too – and more than likely to be sent on further service overseas, and to the Far East at that. I had no capital – no money apart from my pay – and if and when I did eventually get out of the army, obviously my first priority would be to go back to Oxford and get my degree. And then what? I had no idea. To marry would have been folly, and my circumstances gave me no confidence in the idea. Jennifer, however, brushed all this aside. If I loved her why couldn't I marry her? So we parted, and very sorry I felt about it, too. It wasn't all that long – about four and a half years – since we had climbed the copper beech in Wadham, but a great deal had happened in the time, and we had both grown up.

Having returned from Ringway, with wings if not halo, I was asked by John Gifford to take over command of what was left of Paddy's parachute platoon. I didn't fancy the job; it was like being asked to drive a large, fast car that you know you're not really up to. And anyway, how the hell was I supposed to step into the shoes of Paddy?

The men, like children under a stress they are not altogether conscious of, were more difficult than they knew or intended. I don't blame them, either. Without setting out to be, they were sullen and resentful. What on earth were we all supposed to be doing, anyway? Training? But they were already trained, and who if not they? And in all their minds hung the unspoken question 'Are we going to be sent on something like that again?' (To which the answer was 'Quite probably, yes.') And were they, who had been at Arnhem, supposed to have the faith in me that they had had in Paddy?

The long and short of it was that I couldn't really succeed in getting that job off the ground; and frankly, I'd like to have seen the man who could (though I suppose somebody must have, eventually). John – 'the right man in the right job' – could see how things were going, but there wasn't another appointment for a captain in the company. And at this very time the appointment fell vacant for a Brigade R.A.S.C. Officer (they called it 'Brasco') at 1st Parachute Brigade headquarters. A Brasco's job was liaison between the divisional R.A.S.C. and the units of the brigade – getting them what they wanted or, alternatively, telling them that they couldn't have it; and in general, ironing out problems between the battalions on the one side and Colonel Packe and his people on the other.

It was hard to leave 250 Company and John Gifford, after what had turned out the most eventful year of my life. John and I parted in his usual way: he said he thought I'd done very well with C Platoon (I hadn't been one of those who'd quietly disappeared, anyway) and wished me luck for the future. I thanked him very sincerely 'for everything', saluted and went away. I was also, of course, re-wound and pointed in my new direction by Colonel Packe.

I remained a little over five months at 1st para. Brigade H.Q. I wish I could say I enjoyed it. I've already explained the principal reason why not. The truth is that we were all of us not really on top form – and can you wonder? – from the Brigadier downwards; or so it struck me.

Brigadier Gerald Lathbury was one hell of a man – one of the most heroic and notable people in the Division. Physically, he was immense, overwhelming; the tallest and biggest man I have ever known, I think. He had very little warmth of manner and a customary facial expression which always seemed to me haughty and detached. He didn't talk much in the mess. I'm sure he wasn't cold to everyone, but that was the way he struck relatively junior officers. I was in awe of him, and felt constrained.

His record was impressive by any standards. He was a regular soldier, and as a Lt.-Col. had been in on Airborne Forces from the start, having taken command of 3rd Parachute Battalion in autumn 1941, when 1st Parachute Brigade was originally formed. From there he had gone for a time to the War Office, but had re-joined his battalion in Tunisia – where they saw much action – in

1942; and while there had taken over command of 1st Brigade. He led the airborne attack on Sicily in 1943. At Arnhem he was Urquhart's senior brigadier, but never got into the action, as he was among those badly wounded on the second day, paralysed and unable to walk. With Dutch help he escaped from the German-controlled hospital and was brought to a private house in Ede. I was told that the Brigadier finally got back with eighteen splinters of shrapnel in his body, and I believe it. He was a man I enormously admired, although quite honestly he never did much, as far as I personally was concerned, to make me take kindly to him – as General Urquhart had. I think I was beneath his notice, really. But he was cheesed off: we all were.

I did make one very good friend at Brigade H.Q. – Captain John Smith, the Signals officer. John had been at Arnhem all right. The Signals had had almost the worst time of anyone. He was a very gentle, kindly person – 'wouldn't hurt a fly', as they say. Yet of all the hundreds of parachutists I used to know, I think he and Paddy were the only two whom I honestly believed weren't afraid of jumping. Even the Brigadier didn't like jumping: he was much too big, for a start. It must have been a job for him to get out of the door at all.

In the event, John Smith and I were to remain mates through the liberation of Copenhagen; our subsequent transfer, via Bulford, to 5th Parachute Brigade; through that brigade's journey to India and thence to the Malayan coast and the liberation of Singapore.

John, of course, could read Morse as easily as he could read English. I remember, the first night when we were in liberated Singapore, our leaning over the ship's rail and chatting; enjoying the scene, the whole harbour and the city beyond ablaze with lights. Suddenly, John broke off what he was saying and exclaimed 'Good Lord!'

'What is it?' I asked rather apprehensively.

'D'you see that flashing light?' replied John. 'It's sending "Singapore" in clear. And that is literally the only time, Dick, that I've seen a light sending anything in clear since I joined up five and a half years ago.'

Peace had broken out.

To return to 1st Brigade H.Q.: we were stationed at Syston Old Hall, a beautiful house at a village a little way out of Grantham.

People at H.Q. were given to practical jokes, which at least helped to raise the spirits a bit during that dismal winter. For example, someone would unobtrusively put a blank round on the hob and then slip back to his desk. After a bit the round would go off: the thing was not to jump – not to bat an eyelid.

One of the commodities I had to deal in as part of my Brasco's stock-in-trade was canisters of coloured smoke – red, blue, green, yellow. They were used for marking dropping zones and rendezvous points – different colours for the various battalions. The canisters were flat, and about twice the size of an ordinary tin of boot polish. You set them off with a striker like a big match. The smoke was copious, brilliantly coloured, very thick and went on a long time. It was, after all, meant to.

One dull afternoon, while the Brigadier was out for a run with one or two other officers, I put a canister of blue smoke well up one of the chimneys and lit it. I had never imagined what it would be like in that confined space. It was choking thick and seemed to go on for ever. Aghast, I went outside. It looked even worse, and nothing could stop it.

Brigadier Lathbury, a mile away in his running shorts, suddenly saw a whelming plume of peacock-hued smoke ascending to the sky. I learned of his reaction from one of the officers who was with him: but I never heard any more about it.

XXI

Although 1st Airborne Division was too much depleted to take part in the crossing of the Rhine, which began on 24 March, nevertheless it did come within half a plank of once more going into action against the Germans. As the ultimate catastrophe fell upon the Third Reich and the Russians poured across Poland and into Prussia, the German armies, forced almost literally back to back, retained one last aim; to hold the line of the Elbe facing east, in order to enable the streams of west-bound refugees to cross it and thus to come under British and American rather than Russian domination. Far more than any other enemy, the Germans feared the Russians. This was why they fought on for eight days after the death of Hitler on 30 April 1945.

During March and April a certain anxiety was felt among the Allies that some of the hard-core Nazi forces might make a kind of fortress out of Denmark and, as part of the process, set up a defence line along the Kiel Canal. 1st Airborne were at one time put into preparation to fly from England and drop to prevent this. None of the men was told: they could hardly have been expected to take to the idea, just as the war was ending. I myself never learned any details – they were too secret to get down as far as a mere Brasco – but I do very well recall waiting among others on the tarmac at Barkston Heath airfield, parachutes on, all ready to emplane. As a stick commander I had been given an envelope of sealed orders 'not to be opened until airborne'. (We had been told that it was 'an airborne exercise'.) In the event these sealed orders were re-collected by Captain 'Shirley' Temple, our G.3 Ops., before take-off. Whatever grisly task they had enjoined (for all I know, it may have been nothing to do with the Kiel Canal at all) there was now no more need for it. Nazi Denmark, like everywhere else in Europe, had capitulated. Copenhagen, therefore, needed to be occupied forthwith.

Since 1st Parachute Brigade were now all set for take-off, they were obviously the most convenient lot to send. We flew in to Kastrop airport and landed among scenes of rejoicing no less wild than those which had taken place in Brussels eight months earlier. This time, however, the triumph and jubilation were, if anything, even nearer to Cloud Nine, since this was – for the Danish people at all events – the end of the entire war. And there were, perhaps, two or three subsidiary reasons. First, during the Nazi occupation the Danes had suffered relatively little in the way of shortages. In fact, they themselves told us that the only thing they had really missed had been chocolate. So there were plenty of bottles of Schnapps, plenty of caviare, beef steaks and smoked salmon for the brave English (who had done nothing to save Denmark except to fly from England). Secondly, the Danes have a close ethnic affinity with English people. About fifty per cent of us *are* Danish, by descent: it wasn't hard to make sincere friends. Thirdly, however, most Danes are, by contrast with the English, light-hearted and pleasure-loving, good at merriment and without the self-consciousness and rather chilly disposition of so many English people. To most of British Airborne, this encounter with Copenhagen was the most delightful surprise of their lives. I have myself remained in love with the place ever since, and go there often.

One marked aspect of the surprise was the drinking capacity of the Danish girls. They didn't at first glance strike one as seasoned drinkers. Danish girls are most of them very pretty, and the ubiquity of bicycles and long, woolly socks (no petrol, see) enhanced not only their charm but also the engaging impression of adolescence. My general experience of British soldiers during the war was that for all their talk of what they would do once they got to Belfast/Tel Aviv/Brussels et al., when it actually came down to brass tacks, a pint or two was usually enough to throw them off balance. Here and there you came across a Corporal Bater, but not very often. The Danish girls, even those no more than nineteen or twenty years old, were quite accustomed to 'one lager, one schnapps; one lager, one schnapps' in almost indefinite succession. This rattled our men, who found they simply could not do it. All the same, the girls were co-operative, sympathetic and understanding: indeed, they were all those things.

Another surprise I recall was the Wonder Bar. Brigade Head-quarters was set up in the Dagmarhoos, one of the big public buildings in the centre of Copenhagen, situated on a square. Not far away, on the other side of the square, was a well-known fun haunt – to whit, the Wonder Bar. In appearance and décor the Wonder Bar was similar to many such places all over the Euro-American world. It was luxuriously appointed, thick-carpeted, white-coat-attendanted, discreetly piano-ghosted. In the centre was a free-standing, oval bar, perhaps thirty-five to forty feet long, surrounded by high stools. Upon these stools, if you dropped in of an evening, would be sitting unaccompanied girls. These girls were young and nearly all strikingly pretty. They were stylishly and quietly dressed, beautifully behaved and spoke fluent English (German, too, I dare say). They knew how to converse and were not ill-educated. You could, without the least embarrassment, have taken any one of them home to meet your mother. They were courtesans. We had never before encountered ladies of the town in the least resembling these. They were not ill-regarded or treated contemptuously, like their counterparts in England: and neither was the Wonder Bar regarded as anything but a sort of joke. 'You don't take your wife there,' one of my Resistance friends said with a chuckle, 'in case all the bad girls say "Hullo! Hullo!"'

I never, I may say, patronized any of these ladies. In liberated Copenhagen it was not merely unnecessary: if you were a British soldier you had virtually to ward off the girls with both hands. Otherwise it was hard to get any work done.

The reaction of the Danes to the departing Germans was noteworthy. The Germans had been ordered to lay down their arms, surrender their transport and then to proceed home on foot. As they marched along the streets, the Danes on the pavements stood still, fell silent, turned towards them and stared. Mile by mile, as they went on, the silence continued. The buses and taxis switched off their engines, the cyclists dismounted and stood waiting while they passed. This the Germans found demoralizing. Here and there a group might try to sing, but it soon petered out and all that could be heard was the clump of boots – those boots which had stamped all over the faces of Europe. I hope they wore out well before the German frontier.

Lilac time along the western shore of Øresund, the blue sea stretching away to Sweden. Not too much work to do and friends everywhere. For the first time for more than five years, there was no need to take thought for the enemy. Walking on the battlements at Helsingør (Elsinore); looking across to Helsingborg and watching, midway, the German ships at their appointed task of clearing the narrow strait of mines. Every now and then would come a satisfying explosion, suggesting that a mine had gone up before being swept.

At the Royal Opera House there was a production of *Porgy and Bess*, and most of us went to see it. It was, of course, unavoidably under-rehearsed, but since it was so opportune – an opera by a Jew about negroes – nobody was concerned to find fault. Indeed, no one was concerned to find fault with anything much.

One night, coming out of a theatre, I found myself dancing arm-in-arm with a tubby, middle-aged Danish gentleman in a straw boater. Round and round: we grew very merry. I took off his hat, wrote 'FRIJ DANMARK' all round it and put it on. We attracted quite a little crowd. In the end I became a shade nervous in case some senior officer might pass by (we had all been adjured to maintain soldierly behaviour and remain correctly dressed at all times) so I bowed out, shaking his hand; but not before he had given me the hat. I'm afraid I didn't offer him my red beret in exchange, though. It was much too precious to me: and of that more anon.

Despite the jollification we all knew very well – all save the older veterans – that for us this was nothing but a respite, a breathing-space. Hitler had ceased from troubling, Europe lay in ruins and someone was no doubt going to be detailed to pick them up. It wouldn't be us, though. Far away, east of India, stood the still-unconquered Mikado. He might be groggy, he might be on the ropes, but he was still undefeated and he had an appalling reputation for fighting to the last man and taking no prisoners if he could possibly help it. The Americans, as well as our own poor men in Burma, had suffered untold horrors at the hands of the Japanese. And this enemy still remained against us in the field. If the experience of the Australians in New Guinea and of the Americans in Okinawa and Iwojima was anything to go by, there seemed likely to be a very bad time ahead.

The Japanese had no airborne forces. We had been told that they had said that they did not recognize airborne troops as soldiers and that their stated policy was to kill all whom they might encounter. I myself felt deeply, horribly afraid of the coming campaign and it was only pressure of group morale which prevented me from showing it.

I already knew that I didn't qualify for demobilization. The criteria were simple and fair. Only two things counted; your age and the length of time you had been in the service. These, coinciding on a sliding scale, produced your 'demob' number. The lower it was, the quicker you were due for release. Mine turned out to be 32. To be demobbed forthwith, I would have to have rated a number of 26 or lower: I'd only done five years.

So in due course I found myself again on Kastrop airfield, technically in command of 'a hundred men' – some due for demobilization, some in the same boat as myself. We were just a scratch lot: most were strangers to me. When we reached England an amusing incident occurred. The R.A.F. immigration control officer, armed in the usual way with a load of papers, came up to me where I stood at the head of my 'hundred men' and said 'These chaps of yours aren't carrying any goods liable to import duty, *are* they?' 'Well,' I replied, slow in the uptake as usual, 'I really don't know: you see, I was only put in charge of them –' 'But they're *not* carrying any imported tobacco, spirits, dutiable porcelain goods, jewels or similar precious articles' – he thrust the papers, on a clip-board, under my nose – '*are* they, *are* they? You sign here, by the way. *There!*' It said 'Captain Adams and a hundred men.'

I signed, and the hundred men, staggering slightly under the contraband loads, hoisted their bulging kit-bags, right-turned and marched into the adjacent hangar for a cup of tea.

I had a fortnight's leave before reporting to – yes – to Bulford. I spent it at home, fishing on the Kennet, for it was the mayfly season. I fished wherever I would, for the riparian owners were mostly themselves away at the war, and the keepers, if not also away, were either in the local or readily amenable to a five-pound note. I kept thinking 'What does it matter, anyway? I doubt whether all that many of us will be coming back.' The state of mind of most people during the months between the defeat of Germany and the capitulation of Japan must, for those who did not experience it, be hard to imagine. The whole country was sick, sick to death of the war. Apart from our casualties and our orphaned children, our cities were all dismally dilapidated. There were shortages of everything – meat, eggs, milk, coal, clothes, sweets, petrol, even bread. Apart from these deprivations, everywhere marriages lay in ruins; and friends, sweethearts, sons, daughters, business partners – all those archetypal companions who make life worth living – were separated far, far apart. For most people, life had grown increasingly wearisome and had few or no pleasures. And this state of affairs was believed likely to continue, possibly even to get worse; no one knew for how long. In the Far East, thousands of our soldiers were dying of starvation and ill-treatment at the hands of a cruel enemy who did not recognize the Red Cross and who allowed his prisoners no medicines and no letters to or from home. Many of us were convinced that these evil men would probably take a long time to defeat, for each one of them was readier to die than to surrender. For example, when forced by the Australians to retreat to the northern beaches of New Guinea, they had constructed defence trench walls from the rotting bodies of their own dead before being literally driven into the water. Their air force had no lack of volunteer kamikaze pilots, and these, we reckoned, could not but cost us very dear.

One fine evening in mid-June I caught, downstream of the little plank bridge which crosses the Kennet at Halfway, the best trout I had ever yet taken from that happy river. I had no business there, of course: that made it all the more delightful. It was early dusk: I was using a Coachman and was standing on the gravel in the water and my gumboots. I had let my fly drift down to right angles of me, under the overhanging boughs of, I think, a weeping willow, though it may have been a horse chestnut, and was about to recover it when the trout rose. He ran upstream like blazes. When he leapt I did not for a few moments realize that it was my fish, for he seemed so far away. When I did realize it, I became excited by the size. He leapt two or three times, falling back each time into a bed of reeds. I fully expected to lose him, but at length he came out. Then he ran downstream, gaining any amount of slack line which I couldn't take in fast enough and finally swimming between the legs of my boots before turning upstream yet again. I pulled one boot off, put my foot back in the water and freed my leader. The trout was still there and a minute or two later I had him on the bank. I remember thinking that while this would probably be the last trout I'd ever be likely to catch, nevertheless that evening couldn't, now, be taken away. Like all the best things – the begonias, for example, or Jennifer – the adventure was illicit; but it couldn't very well catch up with me. I was bound for the Far East. This was the best parenthesis I have ever known.

Then off to Bulford. So I've soldiered at Aldershot and at Bulford, though never at Catterick. John Smith and I reported together to H.Q. 5th Independent Parachute Brigade; he still Brigade Signals officer, I still a Brasco.

5th Para. Brigade, paradoxically, turned out to be a lot more enjoyable than 1st. This, to me, was unexpected, for the brigade were part of 6th Airborne Division and veterans of Normandy and the Rhine crossing (where they had had a lot of casualties). Yet no one treated us as anything but friends. The brigadier was Nigel Poett (now General Sir Nigel). Poett was, of course, a regular, and had commanded the newly formed 5th Brigade in the Normandy landings. He was a very courageous commander, who liked to show a lot of dash and personal example. For instance, he had been firm that on the night of 5–6 June 1944 he himself was going to be the first member of his brigade to land on Norman soil. During the brigade's subsequent action east of the Orne, he had shown most gallant leadership; and had done so again in the so-called 'Operation Varsity' – the Rhine crossing operation – which began on 24 March 1945. (The casualties there were awful.) He was now taking 5th Brigade to India as the spearhead of the larger airborne force which was to follow. We were going to attack the Japanese as part of an amphibious invasion of the Malay peninsula.

Poett and I were, of course, not at all compatible types. (Later, after I'd been demobilized from the brigade, I learned from my friend Denis Rendell that one day Poett had recollected me, in the mess, as 'that quite awful ass'.) Yet you couldn't dislike him. He was polite to you. He wasn't frigid, like Lathbury. Nor was his entourage made up of people from the *Tatler*. He may not have liked me personally, but he was always friendly, pleasant and what Roy Emberson used to call 'genuine'. When I was in hospital in Poona, having had a minor operation, he came to see me. I didn't forget that. I found his mess much jollier and fuller of likeable people than 1st Brigade's: but then, of course, they weren't brooding on the after-effects of Arnhem.

Names mean little or nothing except to the memoirist himself: but all the same I'd like to put down a few. Jim Webber, M.C., commanding the H.Q. Defence Platoon; an exceptionally kindly, gentle man; Denis Rendell, his second-in-command, one of Colonel Frost's original officers in Tunisia. Denis, a true Mercutio, came of a military family. He had been awarded the M.C. after having escaped in Italy and proceeded to organize and maintain an Allied escape route through the Italian lines. He told me that he had stayed to do this on account of an Italian girl whom he didn't want to part from. His M.C. cut little ice at home, for his father was a V.C. and his brother a D.S.O. John Reidy, Denis's subaltern, was perhaps the most amusing person I have ever known; he made you howl and roll about. ('Twarn't what he said, 'twas the way that he said it.) Tommy Farr, the G.3 Ops., (who had been wounded in Normandy), became a good friend; an even closer friend was Tommy Hanley, the Brigade H.Q. medical officer, with whom I was to share a billet in Singapore. I also, of course, made various friends among the officers (my 'customers') in the battalions, and of these I recall with particular warmth a certain John Awdry. Thirty years later I put him into *The Plague Dogs* as the parachute officer who refuses to shoot Snitter and Rowf on the orders of the time-serving Secretary of State. We met again recently and he was much the same.

The Brigade flew out to Karachi via Corsica and Alam Halfa: and it was at Alam Halfa that an incident occurred which still hurts in memory after more than forty years. The plane had landed at mid-day and I was one of a group of officers invited to lunch in the R.A.F. officers' mess. Of course, like all 'ports of passage' messes, it was accustomed to entertaining heterogeneous bunches of people – anything from royalty to civilian journalists.

Naturally, I had become very fond of my red beret. It was the one which I had been dished out with on my first night with 250 Company at Lincoln; the one Paddy Kavanagh had told me that we 'didn't quite' tuck under our shoulder epaulettes. By now it and I had seen a lot together, and I had done it proud. There was a place in London where you could buy hand-embroidered regimental cap badges and have them stitched on. They cost a bit, of course, but they were worth it. John Gifford had encouraged his officers to wear them. Nearly all of us did, including myself. I had hung that beret up in innumerable messes, pubs, estaminets and hospitable homes in France, Belgium, Holland and Denmark. It had never occurred to me that it might be stolen. Before going in to lunch at Alam Halfa, I left it on a table in the ante-room in the usual way. When I came out it had been stolen. It was irreplaceable, of course: no embroidered cap badges in India. For my remaining six months in the Army I wore a plain brass cap badge, and felt the loss every day. I feel it still.

At Bahrein it was so hot that you couldn't sleep and had no need to dry yourself when you stepped out of the shower. European camp personnel rose at first light, worked until about eight or nine a.m. and then went under cover. Work resumed at about five p.m. and continued until early dark. Only the natives could bear middle-of-the-day conditions. I have to say that from what I saw they seemed to work well enough.

Having reached Karachi from England in three days, we then took a week to travel by train to Bombay via Delhi. It was during this journey that Tommy Hanley taught me to play 'Five Letter Words', while I taught him to play piquet. These pastimes whiled away many wearisome, clanking hours.

It was during this trip that an incident took place which I wish with all my heart that I could lose from mind. In those days the railway carriages in India were huge and solid and stood very high off the ground. (For all I know they still do.) In my recollection, the distance from the sill of a carriage door down to the ground was a good seven feet. On this account, during halts, when doors were opened, iron ladders used to be placed against the doorway openings into the train's corridors. They were not steep, and most people – most Europeans, anyway – used to descend facing forwards. This was mainly because one usually found oneself descending into a jabbering crowd of beggars, hawkers, porters and the like. If you had your back to them, your pocket could be picked before you knew what had happened. Coming down face forwards, you had to shove your way to the ground, firmly refusing to dispense alms and cigarettes or to buy fruit, eggs, chapatis and the like.

One evening during our week-long journey, we had stopped at some station or other between Karachi and Delhi, and I had decided to stretch my legs on the platform for five or ten minutes. As I was descending the ladder, a boy aged about twelve or fourteen, with an open cotton bag slung round his neck, pushed his way through the throng on the ground, made his way a rung or two upwards and flung his two arms up into my face. He had no hands. What he thrust into my face were the stumps of his wrists.

I recoiled in sickened shock and went back into the corridor. Some little way along it I met our Indian liaison officer, Captain Gokral. I asked him what possible explanation there could be of this horrible experience. 'The boy's too young to have been a soldier and too young, I'd have thought, to have been involved in any sort of industrial accident or –'

'Oh, Captain Adams,' he interjected, 'when you've been in this country a little longer you'll come to realize the kind of things that happen here. The boy will have been deliberately mutilated to excite pity. Somewhere in the town there will be a man like Mr Fagin making use of ten or more such boys. If they don't bring back enough money each evening, they don't eat.'

Does God know about this? I thought. During the last forty and more years it has never taken much to recall it to my mind. Captain Gokral was right: on that day I learnt a heavy matter about the world.

Arrived at Bombay, we went into camp at Kalyan, as very many have done before us. So it was here that we experienced our first monsoon. The monsoon was actually coming towards its end when we moved into Kalyan camp, but what we had of it was quite enough. And there was little or nothing to do, except to wonder what form our attack on the Malay peninsula was likely to take. I whiled away some of the time by going into hospital at Poona with an abscess of the nipple. When I came round from the anaesthetic, the Indian surgeon who had done the job was sitting beside my bed. 'Well,' he said genially, ''didn't know much about *that*, did you?' I never learned his name, but I've always remembered what a nice chap he was, and how solicitous and kind. That was the time when Brigadier Poett took the trouble to come and see me.

Back in camp, one evening in early August, I was having a casual drink with Tommy Farr when I happened to say something about the Mikado and our forthcoming activities.

''Doesn't look as though we'll be making his acquaintance now, after all, does it?' said Tommy.

'However d'you mean?' I asked.

'Well, haven't you heard about this new bomb they've dropped?'

I hadn't. Tommy told me. He himself felt sure that it could only push Japan into surrender. Myself, I didn't know what to think. During the next two or three days we were told very little, but sitting in our muddy, sodden camp, we wondered and speculated. On 9 August the Allies dropped the second atomic bomb, on Nagasaki. The war was over. We weren't going to have to fight the Japanese now. How could any reasonable person in our position not feel glad and thankful for the bomb?

Quite soon afterwards the brigade boarded a ship called the *Chitral* and sailed for Malaya. It had been decided that, since the Allied attack had already been worked out and organized, the simplest way to carry out the reoccupation of Malaya would be for all units to do what they would have been going to do anyway, but without, of course, any contribution from the Japanese.

5th Brigade duly landed on the shores of the Malay peninsula, and I recall how, while clambering down from the *Chitral*, I hurt my left thumb rather painfully on the metal gunwale of the landing craft. (The landing craft was bouncing up and down in a choppy sea and the gunwale came up and hit my open hand, hard.) We marched about ten miles inland and passed the night in torrential rain and a rubber plantation. No one slept: you couldn't. I came to realize that prolonged exposure to this sort of rain would be bound to make anyone, however fit, unserviceable. Jungle warfare was something to feel grateful to have been spared. No wonder 14th Army veterans tended to be touchy on the subject.

Next morning we found ourselves the centre of a crisis. We were *white*! It was imperative, for political reasons, that the first Allied troops to enter Singapore should be white and not Indian. Apparently this vital matter had hitherto been overlooked. We, at the moment, were the nearest white troops to Singapore; so we must re-embark and sail there forthwith.

And so we did; and a foul march back to the ship it was, on foot, through the sweltering humidity and the rubber groves. The salt tablets with which we had been issued were palatable and refreshing, but even so a lot of people dropped out along the roadside. We simply weren't used to these conditions, we husky

European parachutists.

I rather think it was on 3 September that we landed at Singapore. We weren't the only white troops to arrive. There were other units – as many as could be rushed in at short notice – veterans of the Burmese war. Initially, these didn't take too kindly to 5th Parachute Brigade, who had only been in the Far East for about five minutes. Such feelings, however, were soon swallowed up in the general reaction to what we found on entering the city – incidentally, the third capital in which I had happened to have been with the first relieving troops.

We were not, of course, expecting acclamation, as in Brussels or Copenhagen. This was not a European capital. However, from my own direct, first-hand experience I can assure the reader of one thing. The inhabitants of Singapore were beyond all argument glad to be rid of the Japanese. They had had three-and-a-half years of the Dai Nippon Asiatic Co-Prosperity Sphere, and as far as they were concerned you could keep it. There had been precious little prosperity, and no prospect of any.

Most of us were already mentally inured to the poverty, squalor, disease and beggary common to Oriental cities. I had myself experienced not only Karachi and Bombay, but also Cairo and Alexandria, Jerusalem, Amman, Ma'an and, of course, in weekly doses for a year, Gaza, that celebrated couple of shit-bins and a camel. Yet all these places had been, in their own ways, going concerns, and were inhabited by people pursuing traditional styles of life which collectively they more or less accepted. You knew where you were and felt that at least there was a certain stability about local ways and daily life, even if those ways were not ours.

By contrast, you felt at once that throughout Singapore there was something badly wrong; a dislocation which seemed to permeate everything. The place might be compared to a run-down engine which was being mishandled and likely at any moment to seize up for lack of oil or water or because of flat batteries. It was like a city in a fantasy film, a city run by some sort of intelligent apes with just about enough know-how to keep things going at the roughest level. To start with, inflation was over the moon, but although that was one of the basic factors it wasn't, of course, among the visible, tactile first impressions which struck us at the outset. Everything was worn-out or broken: nothing worked properly and no Japanese seemed particularly aware of it. John Smith (who was, you will recall, Brigade Signals officer) told me that the whole telephone exchange was in the most awful state. I myself, as Brasco, couldn't find a single refrigerator on the island in working condition: the Japs just weren't interested in refrigerators, let alone in air conditioning. (The island, by the way, is about the same size and shape as the Isle of Wight.) Other specialists – Sappers, R.E.M.E. and so on – reported similar states of affairs on their respective fronts.

The brigade's first task, of course, was to get the Allied prisoners out of Changi jail. As the world has learned, their condition was very bad indeed: too bad to try to describe. They were divisible into the dying, those who would soon die, and those whose lives would be shortened on account of what they had suffered.

Indifference, callousness and cruelty are three different things. Most of the horrible suffering we saw was really due, I think, to indifference: that same indifference which had left the refrigerators and the sewage works to break down. The Japanese were indifferent to mortal illness. You can see the like any day in the treatment of animals by deprived or backward people all over the world. These prisoners were not animals, however, but human beings. It was hard to believe, except that it was there before your eyes, that one group – any group – of human beings could be indifferent to another group to a degree which had brought about such suffering as this.

So much for the Japanese collectively. Those who actually had the task of guarding and dealing with the prisoners, however, needed, to achieve this result, to be more than indifferent. They needed to be callous – to administer the suffering day by day and not to care about it. Finally, a third category had to be actually cruel – that is, to inflict torment and suffering, over and above that brought about by starvation, squalor and neglect, and – yes, I'm afraid – to enjoy it.

Of course we were angry. Wouldn't you have been? I have avoided dealings with the Japanese ever since: the only dignified way, really, of keeping in check the feelings aroused by that terrible business. Though if a Japanese asks me sincerely for forgiveness, I will forgive; as I know certain other people have. And before you laugh, reader, at the absurdity of the very idea, let me tell you that

I *have* been asked for forgiveness, with sincerity, by Germans; more than a few. One lot were Christian pilgrims to Coventry: they were carrying a brick, which they showed me, from Dachau, to be built into the new cathedral.

I am not going to try to describe what it was like dealing with the released prisoners, or organizing such immediate relief as we were able to administer before the specialists took over. The Brigade as a whole had other necessary things to be seeing to – so many that you wondered whether they'd ever be done – but until further notice all medical officers and medical staff on Brigade strength remained on duty at the jail and the hospitals.

As I have said, one of my closest friends at this time was the Brigade H.Q. medical officer, Tommy Hanley (who was only about my own age, twenty-five). That evening, in his continued absence at the jail, I grabbed a billet for us and got his gear more or less laid out along with my own.

Tom himself came in about midnight, exhausted. There was no electric light (you have to realize that at the outset there were no services at all in Singapore, even the water not being reliably potable until treated), but my batman, Tommy Hearn, had managed to scrounge a Tilley lamp and some paraffin, and we conversed while Tom did his best to relax and finish his unpacking. The humidity was appalling and we were both sweating to an extent which made an ordeal of any activity whatever.

'Do you know, Dick,' said Tom, 'if I had my medical books here – the ones I left in London – I could write an article which would burn the covers off *The Lancet*? Medically speaking, it's almost unbelievable. There are diseases down there which no European has contracted in living memory and hardly any living European can ever have seen at all.'

'How do you diagnose them, then?' I asked.

'Oh, it's not hard to diagnose,' replied Tom. 'Not hard at all. The symptoms – once I'd told you what they were you could pretty well do the diagnoses yourself. They – well, they thrust themselves upon your attention, so to speak.' I could see that he was trying not to cry. 'Of course,' he went on at length, 'I'd foreseen for a while back that it was going to be very bad, but not like this.'

'Is it – well, copable with?' I asked.

'They're flying in antiseptics and all the other stuff they can from

Ceylon, round the clock,' answered Tom. 'And flying patients out, too, of course: all the ones they reckon can stand to be flown. Medically speaking, this is something that'll probably never be seen again. Anyway, let's finish up that rum and get to sleep.'

The following morning Brigadier Poett sent for me personally, thereby cutting through at least two 'usual channels'. As I've said, he was well-known as a getter-onner when he wanted something done.

'You're the Brasco,' he began.

'Sir.'

'There isn't a 'fridge on the Island that works.'

'Sir.'

'But there *are* any number of 'fridges, I'm told.'

'Sir.'

'From now until it's complete, your job is to get a working 'fridge into every officers' mess in the brigade.'

'Sir.'

'Any questions?'

'Yes, sir. Do I get any technical help?'

'You can commandeer anyone or anything you think you need, on my authority. As for *what* you do, that's up to you. Now get on with it.'

I got. I had my jeep, my Brasco's corporal (a rather colourless individual) and Tommy Hearn, a batman/driver who certainly wouldn't have disgraced C Platoon. It seemed to me that the first thing we needed was someone who knew why the 'fridges didn't work, and what was required to make them work.

So began the most unorthodox and extraordinary job of my whole time in the Army. We had always been taught that R.A.S.C. officers had to be highly flexible and capable of turning their hand to whatever might arise. Well, here was a real ingenuity test. Poett was not a man likely to be patient with slow results, either.

After a bit I found a Chinese civilian called Mr Kwek Choon Chuan, who confessed to having been a refrigerator engineer before the fall of Singapore. He explained to me that the 'fridges all ran on some fluid called 'Free-own'. But there wasn't any Free-own: not anywhere in the Dai Nippon Co-Prosperity Sphere. There wouldn't be any nearer than Ceylon. If only he had some, he could set about the job of tackling each 'fridge individually and making it work.

Without Free-own, the job couldn't even be attempted.

Mr Kwek, like everyone else, needed money, for at a stroke all Japanese currency had been declared invalid, possessing no exchange value. He had struck me right away as a nice chap and we got on well. I at once obtained authority to have him paid a reasonable wage. However, this still left two problems: how to procure the Free-own from Ceylon and where to find the manpower and transport I would need to get the 'fridges to Mr Kwek (or him to them) and then distribute them to the various officers' messes.

Those who know the Army will appreciate the impracticability, at such a time, of indenting in writing to Ceylon for urgently needed Free-own. We were in a city where we had arrived to find nothing working – no repaired roads, no gas, no electric light, no refrigeration, no air conditioning (Singapore is spot-on the Equator), no telephones, nothing potable out of a tap – you name it, we hadn't got it. From Singapore to Ceylon is something like 1,500 miles. (No jets in those days.) The foremost out-going priority was for sick and/or dying men. I could never have got a place on a plane for Ceylon. I doubt whether the Brigadier himself could have got one. Of the inward priorities I have no idea: they must have been worked out daily, I imagine, at a far higher level than mine. Mr Kwek's English was good, but not up to explaining to me in detail exactly what sort of a fluid Free-own was, how it worked, how it was packed, how it behaved at equatorial temperature, whether it evaporated, how it ought to be stored, how long it lasted and how much we were going to need. How much space would it take up on an incoming plane? Apart from all this, I didn't even know whether there *was* any Free-own (or any to spare) in Ceylon; and if there was, who was in charge of it, where to look for it or whom to ask for it. I didn't know the answers to any of these questions, and I was going to see my first Heffalump, in the form of Brigadier Poett, quite shortly.

It was at this point in the story that the grey-eyed goddess Pallas Athene appeared. As the reader will recall, she often used to appear in the likeness of somebody or other. This time it was Frank Espley, no less.

Walking along the street with Mr Kwek, I became aware of a soldier wearing a shoulder-flash which I had never seen before. It was quite big – almost as big as a Pegasus flash – and depicted, if

I remember rightly, a yellow aeroplane on a blue ground. The regimental flash above it was 'R.A.S.C.' I stopped the man and asked him what his unit was. He told me that they were something very new in the R.A.S.C., namely, an air supply company; he wasn't sure how big, but it was a major's command. I told him to take us to his leader forthwith. Into his jeep we piled and off we set for the outskirts of Singapore.

The major turned out to be Frank Espley! A field officer at twenty-five. This wasn't so very surprising. Frank had always stuck out a mile – a born officer. He had been promoted Captain at twenty-one and given a virtually independent command; R.A.S.C. transport officer in a medical field ambulance unit. Well, here he was in Singapore, with the command of a completely new kind of R.A.S.C. unit, whose work involved daily co-operation with the R.A.F. (and with the Yanks, too, I gathered, if the situation should require).

We fell on each other's necks and talked long and happily of old days (three-and-a-half-years ago!) in Northern Ireland. Of course there was no kind of lifemanship between Frank and myself, but all the same I felt easier because if he had a crown, I at least had wings. It amused and delighted me to hear his men speak of 'Major Espley this' and 'Major Espley that'. As far as I could make out he'd become a sort of John Gifford. They obviously thought the world of him. Did he send chaps to Doullens twice by night? I wondered. He was proud of his company. They could do anything, he said – and had already proved it in many a tight supply corner.

In this way, quite naturally, came up the matter of the Free-own. Frank listened carefully and asked for all the necessary information – most of which, as I've explained, I hadn't got. Finally he said 'Right, Jeep' (it was splendid to be called 'Jeep' again): 'I can't go to Ceylon myself, obviously, but I've got a first-rate chap who goes regularly and he's top-hole in emergencies like this.'

Frank thereupon sent for his trusty subaltern (whose name I can't remember) and told him, in effect, not to bother to come back from Ceylon next time unless he brought untold floods of Free-own with him. In less than three days I had it in my possession and at my disposal.

I knew where all the 'fridges were and so did Mr Kwek. We had the power to commandeer them. What we now needed, however, was manpower, transport, floor space and people who were ready to do what Mr Kwek told them. (In those days Europeans didn't usually like working to the instructions of non-Europeans.) Frank's lot were far too busy to help and anyway, 5th Para. Brigade's 'fridges were none of their business.

It was here that desperation brought forth ingenuity. To explain, I must digress.

Each of the two British airborne divisions included, as divisional troops, an Independent Parachute Company. Their special job, in an airborne operation, was to jump first, to secure the dropping zone, mark it out with coloured smoke and fluorescent panels and then do whatever might be necessary to hold it for the in-coming troops. After the drop, they came under the direct control of the Divisional Commander as a tactical reserve. During the Arnhem operation, 21st Independent Parachute Company, under their famous commanding officer, 'Boy' Wilson, had played a vital part, first in holding the dropping zone and then in the defence of the Oosterbeek pocket. With 22nd Independent, their counterpart in 6th Division, I had not had a great deal to do until 5th Brigade actually reached Singapore. However, I had certainly got to know them then, as we went about our task of patching and mending the bled-white city.

As you might suppose, the people in the Independent companies tended – some of them, anyway – to be highly individual, not to say well-nigh idiosyncratic, in character. They were entertaining. Not only was the relationship between officers and men more personal and rather less formal than in the infantry battalions, but the sort of people you were likely to come across – at any level – were in some cases distinctly out of the ordinary. Apart, of course, from physical fitness and a high standard of self-reliance, what the Independent companies really valued was motivation. As long as a man possessed that in a high degree, they seemed positively to welcome unconventionality. You were quite likely to find yourself dealing with a former lecturer from Warsaw university, a couple of George Orwell's old comrades from Spain, an ex-Dutch Resistance man, or indeed anybody at all whose one overwhelming desire was to get at the enemy. They cared little for any officers but their own, and the quality of those officers was high.

22nd Independent had a very nice, comfortable little mess, in a relatively high-up and airy location on the outskirts of Singapore. Compared with other units, there were relatively few officers and, as in 250 Company, there was a pleasantly friendly, informal atmosphere. The commanding officer, Major Lane, was a quiet, down-to-earth, direct man who seemed to take everyone as he found them (he probably needed to, in his job). He had a marvellous line in rude stories, but he didn't compromise his position as C.O. by telling them very often. If ever an officer's authority rested on individual personality, it was Major Lane's.

22nd Independent – like every other unit in the Brigade in those early, exiguous days in Singapore – often found that they could do with the services of the Brasco. I took good care to cultivate them, their informal readiness to oblige you without military formality (and their relative carelessness about rank) being a great help to myself, who often had problems that needed a hand or two, and no soldiers of my own to draw upon. I took good care that 22nd Company got their fair share – their distinctly fair share – of whisky, cigarettes, chocolate and whatever else was going in the way of amenities.

They liked Mr Kwek and treated him as they treated people of all nationalities who were on our side. There was no awkwardness for him in their mess.

It was in these circumstances that there grew up a friendship between myself and Independent's second-in-command, Captain Doug Campbell. Doug , although very different from Paddy Kavanagh, also (I should imagine) must have struck a lot of people as the very acme of a parachute officer. He was a big, broad-shouldered man, whose sheer physical appearance was impressive. Instead of the bravado and sometimes rather exhibitionist dash of Paddy, he had an air of smooth, easy-going optimism and unshakeable reliability. In story-book terms, you could picture Doug putting his shoulder to a heavy, barred door while the others stood back, and the door collapsing inwards, Doug thereupon remarking 'Well, I reckon that ought to be all right now.' His quiet good nature and self-confidence – the self-confidence of a titan – must have made a very firm fulcrum for that disparate bunch of unorthodox heroes.

It wasn't long before Doug and I discovered that something we had in common was a passion for swimming. By this time the

Brigade had managed to get one of the swimming pools in Singapore into working order, but it was usually as full as you'd expect and anyway what Doug and I fancied – if we could get it – was something to extend us a little more. This was how we came to invent point-to-point swimming.

There are two huge reservoirs – great, inland lakes, each about two miles long and half a mile broad – on the island of Singapore, known as the Peirce and the MacRitchie. At this time neither of these was under any supervision whatever. They were remote and lonely. The Peirce, actually, was too remote for our purpose, for it lay in rather dense jungle in the very centre of the island; the access roads were in bad repair and the overgrown shore seemed a likely place for snakes. The MacRitchie, however, was exactly what we wanted. The open, sandy foreshores were accessible and there was no one about at all. The temperature of the water, of course, was well up in the eighties or even a little more.

The MacRitchie is irregular in shape, with points and inlets all round the circumference. Doug and I – it gives me a pang now to think how very fit and energetic we were – used to take a jeep out to some convenient place and stroll down through the trees to the shore. Then we would select some bay or point to swim to on the far side of the reservoir – anything from half to three-quarters of a mile away. It was splendid to find yourself far out in open water, making leisurely for the other shore. Having got there, we would lie around in the sun, relax and talk about nothing until we felt ready to go on. Then we would select another place to make for, this time usually somewhere further along the same shore, perhaps across an inlet or round a point. In this way we might quite often, I suppose, have swum two or three miles in an afternoon, before drifting lazily back to the mess for whatever there might be in the way of a drink and a meal. Looking back on it, I can't remember many things I have ever done which were more enjoyable than this.

My own anxiety was for my batman, Tommy Hearn. Tommy couldn't swim a stroke, but he didn't want to be left out of the fun to pass the afternoon idling by the jeep. So he used to thrash across the reservoir on an inflated inner tube. The trouble was that he wouldn't keep inshore: he was determined to follow us across. We left him to his own devices, for we had come to extend ourselves and settle into the satisfying rhythm of fairly long-distance swimming. When you were at last lazing on the warm sand of the destination beach, however, it didn't exactly add to your peace of mind to see Tommy flailing along, more than four hundred yards out.

'What on earth is he going to do if the valve blows?' I asked Doug. 'Or if something punctures the tube, come to that?'

'P'raps it won't,' replied Doug, sleepily. He was a man who positively seemed to create calm and security. In his ambience, things didn't go wrong much. Anyway, he was relaxing after what must have been a very bad, stressful year: I don't know – I never asked. I expect he'd have manhandled Hearn out somehow or other; if not, well, many airborne soldiers were silly, reckless sods, anyway, and it was my batman, not his.

From all this the reader will no doubt have grasped that, although I had no soldiers under my own command – apart from my administrative corporal – I was nevertheless able to find a few spare people to give Mr Kwek a hand with the refrigerators. We got the job done, every mess in the Brigade duly received its working model and I reported as much to the Brigadier. However, he was now somewhat preoccupied with other matters.

Singapore was by this time getting back on its feet and the place was daily becoming more normal. So was the military set-up. Several fresh units were arriving. A regiment of Ghurkas came into camp next to us. It was the first time that I had had any experience of these renowned soldiers, and I was as deeply impressed as everyone else who has had to do with them. Not only was Lord Mountbatten in Singapore (he had presided at the formal surrender of the Japanese on 12 September) but also General Slim, the commander of the 14th Army, which had first retreated through and then re-conquered Burma.

As I got to know a fair number of people who had served in the Far Eastern campaigns, I realized – we all did – that most of them felt a certain sense of grievance and resentment against people coming out from the United Kingdom. They thought not only that they themselves had had a very bad time, fighting the worst and most merciless of all enemies under horrible conditions, but also that the Allied European armies had been given priority over them and that they had been left at the bottom of the list for equipment and reinforcements. The press called them 'the forgotten army' and

I personally came to be convinced that there was a good deal of truth in it. They had first defended India and then re-conquered Burma on a shoestring, and they reckoned little to people newly out from England who had not been through what they had. It was widely believed that General Slim himself shared his soldiers' views. He had commanded them through some horrible actions – Kohima, Imphal and Myitkina must have been as bad as anything that took place during the whole war – and it would have been surprising if he had not thought as they did, especially as it was he himself who must have felt more frustrated than anyone else by the shortage of supplies.

Brigadier Poett was keen for General Slim to dine in 5th Brigade's mess, and in due course he came. I got the impression – I think all the junior officers did – that he actually meant to show how little he cared for red berets and for whatever reputation they might have brought with them from Europe. This – if it is true – was perhaps a bit unfair, for Brigadier Poett had shown himself, in two airborne operations, to be a most heroic and competent commander. He had, however, always been well supplied and he hadn't been in the Burmese jungle.

General Slim turned up late for dinner, without (unless I'm much mistaken) having changed out of the day's working clothes. He wasn't complimentary about anything and he wasn't conversational or warm to the junior officers (as General Dempsey, commanding 2nd Army in Europe, had been on an earlier occasion at which I was present). In fact, not to mince words, he seemed off-hand, grumpy and not particularly concerned to conceal it. I had – and still have – nothing against Brigadier Poett, and the professional ambitions and aspirations of regular Army officers meant nothing to me; but I think that if I had been Evelyn Waugh I might have felt sardonically amused by the Brigadier's compunction to show respect and to try to please the General, and the General's corresponding implication that he cared for none of it. It was a distinctly sticky evening: there wasn't much conversation, and it was embarrassing to hear the Brigadier's courteous remarks dropping like lead pellets between the General's corroborative nods and shakes of the head.

It was at about this time – as a lot of the fun went out of Singapore, the notorious 13th Para. Battalion mutiny took place, and there began, coincidentally, to be talk of the Brigade moving on to cope with the troubles in Java (which it eventually did) – that I became a great deal more conscious of something of the greatest importance to me. I qualified, and was due, for what was known as 'Class B' release. This was demob queue-jumping. The Government – it was Attlee's Socialist Government now, of course, Mr Churchill having been heavily defeated in the 'khaki election' earlier in 1945 – had decided that with the war won, it would be in the public interest for certain categories of people to be demobbed and back in their civilian occupations as soon as possible. One of these categories was that of undergraduates whose academic courses had been interrupted by the war. I was officially told that I qualified and so was a friend of mine at H.Q., Rob Stevenson. Naturally, we became expectant.

However, weeks slid by and nothing happened. At length, having talked it over with the Brigade Major and one or two other senior brigade H.Q. officers, I decided to ask the Brigadier if he could help. I requested a personal interview and got it.

The Brigadier's greeting, after I had saluted and been told to stand easy, was not particularly cordial. In reply to his asking what I wanted, I said 'Well, sir, as far as I can see I'm being mucked about for my Class B release.'

I guess it wasn't very tactfully put. People aged twenty-five aren't always terribly diplomatic. Perhaps it seemed to imply inappropriate criticism of authority: I don't know. Anyway, the Brigadier replied 'It annoys me when you say that. Class B release is a *privilege*, for which anyone who gets it ought to feel thankful. It's not something to *demand*.'

It was on the tip of my tongue to reply that surely the position was that the Government had decided that it would be best for the country if certain categories of people – but you don't say that sort of thing to brigadiers. I apologized and said I didn't want to press the matter against his wishes.

However, the Brigadier, as was often his way, having said a piece to make it clear who was the boss, then showed himself ready to be reasonably helpful. As though grudgingly and against his will, he said 'Well, if I send a telegram about it, stating the details – which you can give to someone in the office – will that satisfy you?' I said it would, thanked him very much and got out.

My release duly came through, but not Stevenson's: a pity, as I'd hoped we might have been able to travel home together. But now another obstacle appeared. I – and others – were supposed to be sailing home on the S.S. *Orontes*. She was known to be somewhere between Hong Kong and Singapore, but that was all that was known. As she became more and more overdue we grew worried, for in those days you could never be sure of anything and for all we knew she might well have been diverted elsewhere. At length the delay became quite the talk of Singapore. I used to go down every day to the docks to have a look. So did many others. When at last she arrived, a large blackboard was put up at the berth, saying 'Believe it or not, the *Orontes*!'

I realized, now, that I was glad to be getting out of the lashing, three-times-a-day rain of Singapore, and out of the humidity and damp. When I came to pack I found a lot of things ruined either by rust or by mildew.

The prospect of actual release from the Army had given matters a different aspect altogether. It took six weeks to sail home but, naturally, it was a happy voyage for everyone on board. From Biscay onwards we were in the heart of winter, and after the Equator it struck cold indeed.

At the demobilization centre everything went smoothly. Indeed, they seemed to me anxious to rush us through as quickly as they could. For the final formalities, I found myself in the office of a fairly young, rather abrupt major, who told me to 'sign here, and here' and gave me my Class B release papers (which I still have).

'That's all,' he said at length, as I stood waiting.

'Thank you, sir,' I replied. 'I wonder, could I ask you to be so kind as to look into the case of a friend of mine, a Captain Stevenson, a fellow officer due for Class B, whom I left in Singapore? I've got his details written down on this bit of paper –'

'Why don't you get out?' he said. 'You've got your release: I don't know what more you want.'

It seemed a fitting conclusion to the Army. Quite as good, in its way, as the Aldershot bus conductor's ''Ow the 'ell d'you expect me to know?'

XXII

I arrived home to find my father very weak and confined to bed. He was nearly seventy-six. I could tell, from the way my mother looked and spoke, that she did not expect him to survive the winter. I sat beside his bed and we talked – as best he could – about all that had happened. To anyone at all who lived through it, in whatever capacity, the Second World War was an enormous, shattering experience. It was – and I say this in all seriousness – difficult to believe that it was really over; one could not remember what things had been like before. Anyway, that no longer mattered much: they weren't ever going to be the same again.

'I think Daddy was just waiting, dear,' said my mother, 'until everyone was safely home.' My brother, of course, had been demobbed months before, having joined the Army at the outbreak of the war. Ironically, my sister, in her reserved occupation as a teacher, had been the only one of us actually to come under enemy fire. She had been blown across the room and nearly killed by a V.2 in Tottenham – one of the last, perhaps, that the Germans had been able to fire before the launching sites were overwhelmed.

I went over to Oxford from Newbury, saw the Provost, the Bursar and my tutor, and without difficulty made the necessary arrangements to return for the Hilary term of 1946, due to begin in a few days' time. Digs were a trouble to find, for the whole university was crowded with ex-services people returned to get their degrees. It was with the help of one of my old friends from The Jolly Farmers, the kindly landlady, Hilda Brown, that I was lucky enough to get rooms with a good soul in Walton Street, almost opposite the College.

Having got things fixed up, I naturally dropped in to the College buttery and was soon chatting over a pint to my scout of pre-war days, Bill Money, and to the manciple, Henry Mallett. They had a lot to say, of course, about the changes brought about by the war, about short staff, rationing, food restrictions and so on.

'I suppose there'll be a lot of ex-services people coming back this term,' I said. 'The place'll be absolutely full up. By the way, do you happen to know whether Mr Christison's back yet? Or Mr Schumer?'

Henry Mallett looked down at the floor and paused. After a few moments he replied 'Well, sir, I think if you care to go across to the Bursary, they'll be able to give you details about the gentlemen you remember from before the war.'

His manner seized upon me with a sudden misgiving. I finished my pint, said I'd look forward to seeing them later, and went across the quad to the Bursar's office.

It is hard to find any appropriate way in which to write about this experience: the worst experience of my life, and one which has altered my outlook of the world from that time to this. It will be best simply to write down what I learned that morning.

Alasdair was dead. I remembered that he had been called up, in 1940, into the Oxford and Bucks. Light Infantry, and that he had expressed his determination to transfer, when he got a commission, into one of the renowned Scottish regiments. The Bursary people were able to pass on to me a good deal about Alasdair, since his parents had sent the College a copy of his company commander's letter.

He had got what he wanted, being commissioned into the 7th Battalion of the Black Watch – part of 51st Highland Division – and had fought as a platoon commander at Alamein. The letter went on to tell how he had received the personal thanks of the brigade commander for playing a leading part in guiding a tricky night march – whether of the battalion or of the whole brigade I am not clear – to a place in the desert called Mersa Brega. This had been Rommel's first halt after Alamein, and Montgomery had attacked him there on 13 December 1942 with the Highland and New Zealand divisions and 7th Armoured.

The details of the Alamein to Tunis campaign are so well-known and have been written about so extensively that I need not say more about them here. The part played by the Black Watch is fully set out in the regimental history. After entering Tripoli on 23 January, the 8th Army pressed on westward, broke the Mareth Line and entered Tunisia.

They then faced one of their most difficult tasks, namely, to force the Germans and Italians out of the position known as the Wadi Akarit. This could not be outflanked for, as a glance at the map will show, the sea lay to the east and, not far inland on the west, the extensive salt marshes known as Shott El Jerid. There was no alternative to a direct frontal assault, and this was made by three infantry divisions, 4th Indian, 50th and 51st Highland. Alasdair, leading his platoon, was killed by Italian shell fire on 6 April 1943. He is buried in the military cemetery at Sfax.

I have often meditated on the discomfort, exhaustion, stress, anxiety and fear which Alasdair must have endured for more than five months during that campaign. The writer of the letter, a certain Major Ian Buchanan, described his platoon's devotion to Alasdair and their grief. He was his parents' only child. 6,000 men altogether died in that campaign.

Few days – if any – have passed during the intervening years when I have not thought of the death of Alasdair and missed him. I have never had another friendship like his.

Frank Schumer was dead. Having been in the University Air Squadron as an undergraduate he was, naturally, called up into the R.A.F. As far as I could learn, his death came about on a ferrying flight, when his plane's engine failed over the North Sea.

William Brown was dead. I think he must have been the first of our little group to be killed. As I was told, it came about in a motor-cycle accident relatively early in the war; I think, some time during 1941.

Mike Seale was dead. I forget whether I was told much detail, but I have always retained the idea that he was serving in the Far East. It was probably in Burma.

'Robey' Revnell was dead. He had been for quite a long time an instructing officer in an infantry training battalion, but during the final months of the war had been posted to a battalion of 2nd Army serving in Europe. He was killed in February 1945, in the bitter fighting to clear the Germans from the area between the Meuse and the Rhine.

Other friends had been killed, also. Both Cullen Powell and Jim Sharp had died in the R.A.F., and Frank Savory (the musician) at

Salerno. I could mention others, but will not, since their names have not previously come into this memoir. The total number, however, was grievous indeed.

The shock took time to enter me deeply, but of course it has remained of permanent effect. You don't feel lucky, really: you feel guilty to be alive: and always full of bitter regret. About once or twice a year (more or less) I dream that Alasdair is alive. If he were to return now, of course, he would be a boy considerably younger than my own daughters. He was twenty-three. They were all about that age, or less. The passage of years has made no difference.

The huge, inestimable wrong – the deprivation and grief – the unhealed wound to the world caused by the two wars of the first half of the twentieth century – will their effects ever cease entirely to be felt? They are very hard, if not impossible, to accept or to make part of any reasonable view of life. Either you are lucky enough not to have to think about it, or else it is something – the hundreds, the thousands, the millions of young men and others killed – that can't really leave your thoughts for long. I suppose that paradoxically, to think about it in general terms is less depressing than to remember individual people. Many say 'The only thing is to forget it', but for people of my generation this is not really possible. Once you know from personal experience that human beings kill each other and that the killed include your closest friends you cannot forget it – ever. It remains a preoccupation.

> Have you forgotten yet?
> Look down, and swear by the slain
> > of the War that you'll never forget.
> > > [Siegfried Sassoon]

The principal effect on me was not, perhaps, to destroy but seriously to weaken my motivation. I didn't feel much interest in getting on and there was nothing that I could feel to be worth doing. I was upset, also, by two minor, concomitant features of the bereavement. The first was that the permanent members and functionaries of the College, from dons to scouts, seemed so little affected. If you tried to talk to the porters or the scouts, their regret seemed perfunctory. Perhaps that was understandable, all things considered. (The son of my own scout, Money, had been among the last killed, in spring 1945, in an armoured car east of the Rhine.) But when I tried to talk to my tutor, reminding him of the names of the many dead – several of them his former pupils – all he replied was 'Hadn't you any friends in other colleges?'

The second was the daily pang of seeing new, unknown undergraduates occupying my former friends' rooms, sitting in their places in hall and so on. They were, of course, nice fellows, and friendly; most of them ex-servicemen, some with distinguished records; but all I could feel, from their reminiscences and conversation, was that they were intruding strangers, almost literally wearing my friends' shoes.

I know only too well that I was difficult company during that term. I was gruff, overbearing, dismissive and all too ready to snap. I didn't really want to be friendly to anyone; although there were those, such as Iain Glidewell and Douglas Johnson, who were understanding and patient, and who in time grew to be friends. I took refuge in academic work, and won unsought tutorial approval with long and carefully researched essays. I tried to think of the College as a different place altogether. This was easier than you might suppose, for post-war shortages, over-crowding and the relative maturity and unfrivolous ways of the undergraduates (most of whom, at twenty-five or more, simply wanted to get on with their degrees and get out) made for an entirely different atmosphere from that of 1938 to 1940.

Another, and by no means minor weight to bear was the sudden ripping away of group morale. For two years I had worn a red beret and Airborne Forces had been my life and my raison d'être . I had had friends of distinction – far above my own worth and status, I who had never even fired a gun at any enemy – among whom it was fulfilment and an honour to live. Esprit de corps, where it is really felt, is an all-embracing thing. (When you actually prefer to wear uniform on leave, you're obviously far gone.) Now, in a moment, all this had been whisked away. I had never expected to feel demobilization as a loss, but I did so now all right. Night after night I would sit alone in my room, remembering C Platoon or the swimming with Doug Campbell in Singapore, and feel sick at heart with the loss of companionship and of all that the Airborne Forces had conferred. One night in a pub, when I had mildly ventured some minor criticism, the barmaid replied 'We make the rules here, not you.' (In those difficult times people were often short-tempered.) I thought, I bet you wouldn't have said that to an airborne soldier.

During January and February my poor father lingered on. He was plainly dying, for he grew weaker day by day. One feature of his illness I found particularly distressing: his legs itched unbearably and he could not control himself from scratching and tearing at them until they were lacerated and bleeding. Sometimes he knew who we were and could talk a little, but he had almost no energy and spent more and more time in a kind of half-sleeping coma.

It was on 18 March that my sister, who was at home with my mother, telephoned me at Oxford and said 'Richard, I think you'd better come home: tonight.' It's not far from Oxford to Newbury. I arrived during the evening. My mother, kind and self-possessed as always, was in complete command of herself but plainly very tired. So was my sister. I knelt by my father's bed, so as to get my head close to his, and said 'Daddy, it's Richard: Richard's here.' He opened his eyes and gave the ghost of a smile and a nod. I like to think he knew who it was, but quite possibly he didn't.

I sat up with him that night, while the others got some sort of rest in their beds. During the small hours his breathing became – or seemed to me to become – intermittent. My feeling was that this could not continue long, but still I was reluctant to disturb my mother and sister for fear I might be mistaken. At quarter past five, however, I called them and they came into the room. My father died a little before quarter to six. He simply ceased to breathe.

My mother, the trained nurse who had first met Doctor Jarge in Edwardian Somerset, did all that was necessary with composure. I was troubled by the sightless gaze of my father's fixed, open eyes. I remember there came into my head a line from *Macbeth*: 'Thou hast no speculation in those eyes.' My mother closed them with pieces of moistened cotton-wool. Seeing that I couldn't be of much use, I walked out into the early morning garden, where from a silver birch the thrush was singing 'Marguerite!' Marguerite!'

. . .

This was a very bad, empty time; as bad as I can remember, lonely and with little comfort. Small things – deprivations of the ordinary material of daily life – affect us, or most of us, I suppose, more than we care to admit: things like the gas pressure being too low to be of any real use; power cuts; the impossibility of getting a pair of shoes of the right size. ('Don't know when we'll be getting any more in, sir.') Having to make do with things that don't match, or having to mend something with the wrong-coloured wool. We ought not to allow discomforts and frustrations like these to affect our frame of mind: but they do. They make a bad accompaniment to consuming, underlying grief.

It was against this background that I lived at home during that vacation, doing what I could to comfort my mother and continuing to read for the History Schools; there was nothing else to do – anyway, we had very little money – and there seemed to be nothing worth doing. The death of my father, my life-long companion and the spiritual duct through which the whole nature and quality of my personal, individual life had come to me, had left me darkling. It should have been a time to turn to friends; but where were they?

I had no idea what sort of a life I wanted to make for myself and whenever I tried to think about it nothing occurred to me. All that came into my mind were matters of the past – a past that could yield no comfort, since its power had depended, really, on time – the age I had been and the people, my father and others, who had been round me – rather than on the places and events themselves. For example, the Bluebell Wood was still there, a few hundred yards away, and the bluebells, primroses and dog's mercury were shooting and would soon be in bloom, but they seemed to have little to give me now; rather, they merely turned my head over my shoulder, to remind me of all that was lost – not only a parent and friends, but a whole course of life.

Early of an evening, I used to drop in at the pub, The Bell at Wash Common, a few hundred yards up the road. In those days it was just a plain village beer house, with a few regulars and a landlord, Jim Spencer, who was a well-known popular local character. The people I had always known – among whom I had grown up – and the down-to-earth, diurnal talk ('Goin' t'ave a drop o' rain, then?'), like bird-song, were palliative. By reciprocating conversation about nothing, your emotions could be lost, diluted, in the common pool of humanity. I remember how, much later, when the Nuremberg trials were drawing to a close, Jim Spencer, with every confidence, bet me two pints that General Goering would not be hanged. 'They'll ~~*never* 'ang 'e,'~~ he announced to the ~~tap-room~~ with the greatest assurance. After Goering had been sentenced, I suggested to Jim that he might now pay up, but he remained firm. 'They won't never 'ang 'e!' And, as we know, they didn't: I lost my two pints. Jim's uncanny prescience was quite the talk of the village. ('Reckon it must 'a bin old Jim sent 'im that lot, then.')

One evening that April, a little before the summer term at Oxford was due to begin, I strolled back home from The Bell to find my mother preparing our meagre, rationed supper.

'Oh, Dicky,' she said. 'Mrs Acland came round a little while ago.'

Mr and Mrs Acland lived next door. Although I had seen almost nothing of them since coming home, they were, I had learned, good neighbours. I remembered them vaguely from before the war. At the time when I was called up they had had two little girls, Elizabeth and Penelope, aged about eleven and nine, and my mother had told me that a third girl, Judith, had been born in the middle of the war. Mr Acland had not long been demobilized from the R.A.F. During my embarkation leave the year before, my father had told me – and such spontaneous praise on his part was unusual – that Mrs Acland was an unusually nice, kind-hearted woman. 'She drops round: she always has some little excuse or other, but it's really to keep an eye on Mother and to see whether we're all right. We're lucky she's there.'

'Oh, did she look in?' I replied to my mother. 'Anything special?'

'Apparently Elizabeth's doing some extra Latin for university entrance,' said my mother. 'Mrs Acland thought perhaps John might be able to give her a bit of help. I explained that John wasn't at home, but I thought your Latin was good enough for you to give her a hand. I said I'd tell you when you came in.'

'All right,' I answered. 'I'll pop over for a minute and see what I can do.'

In the course of the war, my mother and Mrs Acland had worn a little path through their respective gardens between each other's back doors, dropping in with the sort of gifts that people in the days of rationing were only too glad to receive – an egg or two, a few spoonsful of coffee, a morsel of cheese, half a bread-and-butter pudding 'which really needed finishing up'. They would read to each other from their family letters, too; stuff for conversation about husband or children away in the services. I took this path now, through the gap in the hedge, past the wooden summer-house and so to Mrs Acland's back door. It opened directly on the kitchen and she, like my mother, was busy preparing supper. I explained that I had come instead of John.

'Oh, that's kind of you, Richard. Well, Elizabeth's in the dining-room if you'd like to go and see her.'

I went across the passage and through the dining-room door, which was ajar.

Sitting at the table, with two or three books spread out in front of her, was a girl who looked perhaps sixteen or seventeen, somewhere between a grown child and a young woman. She looked up at me with a warm smile and no least trace of self-consciousness.

It was I who felt self-conscious, for she was very beautiful indeed. Her beauty struck me all the more powerfully because I could not have expected it. She had brown hair, perfect, regular features and a firm young figure. But informing these physical qualities was something more difficult to describe. I can only call it the grace of innocence. It was plain that she herself had no least idea how outstandingly beautiful she was, or what power this beauty conferred. Seeing her for the first time against the background of that commonplace room, I had for a moment the fancy that her face possessed a gently luminescent quality, like that of a wave in the tropical oceans. I stood silent, gazing at her in astonishment, and it was she who spoke first.

'Hallo!' she said, 'You're Richard, aren't you? Mother said it might be you coming over, because your brother's away.'

Her beauty disconcerted and constrained me. I know now that this is common enough: young men thus confronted often feel this kind of self-consciousness. The poet Walter de la Mare once said to Sir Russell Braine of a lady whom he had met, 'She was so beautiful that it was embarrassing to look at her. Isn't that strange?'

This same embarrassment was a little heightened now on account of Elizabeth's youthful inexperience. Not that she was gauche – indeed, she already possessed, as it seemed, a distinct style of her own – but she had had little practice in talking to young men and wasn't altogether sure how to deal with them. She had no need to worry. Her mere appearance set her apart from and beyond convention. She looked as though she had come to transcend the workaday world and set it right once and for all, she who knew nothing of grief, or of loss or regret.

'They said you were having a spot of trouble with your Latin,' I answered. 'I thought I'd come and see whether I could help.'

'It's the ablative absolutes,' she said, laughing a little by way of suggesting her own stupidity. 'I think if I could just get the hang of it – you know, how it's supposed to work –'

'Oh, well, that shouldn't be difficult. Would you like me to sit down here?'

'Oh, sorry, I ought to have thought. Yes, do.'

I drew a chair up to hers. She smelt of youth and freshness. Sitting side-by-side with her, I felt tense and excited. It is easy, with hindsight, to attribute marvels, yet in all seriousness I believe I had the inkling, even then, that a great blessing – a promise – was being extended to me; and that this was to prove no single or casual encounter.

'Well,' I said, pulling the open exercise book across between us, 'let's start by making one up and I'll try to explain. "All these things having been narrated, Caesar decided nevertheless to press on." That's the sort of stuff you're apt to get. Now, "Omnibus narratis", you see, is what's called a subordinate clause –'

Index

A NOTE ON THE TYPE

The text of this book was set in Bembo, the well-known
monotype face. The original cutting of Bembo was made
by Francesco Griffo of Bologna only a few years after
Columbus discovered America. It was named after Pietro
Bembo, the celebrated Renaissance writer and humanist
scholar who was made a cardinal and served as secretary
to Pope Leo X. Sturdy, well-balanced, and finely propor-
tioned, Bembo is a face of rare beauty. It is, at the same
time, extremely legible in all of its sizes.

Composed in Great Britain
Printed and bound by Arcata Graphics/Fairfield,
Fairfield, Pennsylvania